No England

Chris Craggs

A rock climbing guidebook
to selected routes on the
gritstone and sandstone edges of
Yorkshire and Northumberland

Text and photography by Chris Craggs
Additional text and diagrams by Alan James
Original ROCKFAX design Mick Ryan and Alan James
Printed by Clearpoint Colourprint, Nottingham
Distributed by Cordee (www.cordee.co.uk)

All maps by ROCKFAX
Some maps based on source maps kindly supplied
by Collins Maps (www.collins.co.uk)

Published by ROCKFAX Ltd. February 2008 © ROCKFAX Ltd. 2008
A CIP catalogue record is available from the British Library

ISBN-13   978 1 873341 71 1

www.rockfax.com

Cover: Adrian Berry on *Western Front* (E3 5c) - *page 105* - at Almscliff. Photo: Duncan Skelton

This page: Colin Binks on *Eastern Arete* (S 4a) - *page 351* - at Berryhill. Photo: Chris Craggs

This book belongs to:

All Rockfax books are printed in the UK.
We only use paper made from wood fibre from
sustainable forests and produced according
to ISO 14001 environmental standard

real climbing...

...indoors!

Hawthorn Avenue,
Hull, HU3 5JX.
01482 223030
www.rockcity.co.uk
info@rockcity.co.uk

ROCKCITY

Laurent DARLOT onsights 'the thin crack', Rockcity - Photo Stephan DELY

Contents

Crag Lough rising above the reed beds and lake that provides its name. Photo Chris Craggs

Ali Kennedy on Western Front (E3 5c) - *page 105* - one of Almscliff's finest offerings. Photo: Jamie Moss

This guidebook covers a huge swathe of Northern England and its high quality outcrop climbing. Some of the venues such as Almscliff and Bowden Doors are well known, though between these are many smaller gems that see few visitors other than knowledgable locals.

Our journey starts near the Yorkshire-Lancashire border with many of the varied venues that make fine gritstone cliffs of West Yorkshire. These crags give a climbing experience similar to their counterparts to the south in the Peak, only perhaps a little less accommodating - sometimes remote, sometimes savage, sometimes wild, but almost always rewarding.
The next stop is the North York Moors where we find a different kind of cliff. The sandstone here offers more short outcrop-style climbing, but there are fewer familiar names and none of the celebrity ticks. That doesn't mean it isn't worth visiting though, and most who make the effort will be pleasantly surprised with what they find.
The final destination is the rolling hills of Northumberland - the Country's best kept secret. There is none of the hectic atmosphere of the Lake and Peak Districts here, just empty hills, beautiful crags and some fine climbing to keep you busy.

The rock types vary from the coarsest gritstone around, to black columns of iron-hard dolorite and onto filigrees and flutings of superb sandstone. The cliffs range in size from some that are little more than overgrown boulders, to buttresses up to more than 20m tall. Whilst the areas don't have the extensive edges of the Peak, or the soaring crags of Wales and the Lakes, they do have variety and quality by the shed-load.

This guidebook draws together this fine array of climbs and crags from right across the three areas. It offers an introduction to these fascinating climbs - explore, enjoy and respect them - there are many great days of climbing between these covers.

Alan James at the top of the classic *Callerhues Crack* (HVS 5a) - *page 265* - at Callerhues Crag. Photo Chris Craggs

The Book

The term 'Northern England' can mean very different things to different people, usually depending where they live in the country. For the purposes of this book we use the word 'Northern' to refer to the gritstone of West Yorkshire, the sandstone of the North York Moors and the dolorite and sandstone of Northumberland. The book doesn't cover the limestone of West Yorkshire, or any of the Lake District, both of which could justifiably claim to be 'northern'. The coverage is aimed more north eastwards focusing particularly on the two rock types of gritstone and sandstone.

The book uses the same presentation style and degree of coverage that was started so successfully with Peak Grit East in 2001, and continued through all our other books since including Western Grit (2003), Northern Limestone (2004) and the follow-up to PGE, Eastern Grit (2006). This level of coverage means that we have probably only managed to document around 20% of the routes in the three areas. Obviously the content focuses on the prime spots and the best routes but I would still be surprised if there aren't at least five crags in this book that you have never heard of let alone visited.

Alan James researching the complex pinnacles at Brimham. Photo: Chris Craggs

Even on the crags that you have heard of you are most likely to find classic routes that didn't attract a second glance before. Use the book to explore a bit, and if you like the areas then the list of other guides on page 14 should give some useful further reading.

Web Site - **www.rockfax.com**

This book is supported by the online Rockfax Route Database which contains a listing of every route in this book (and all our other books) with the opportunity for you to lodge comments and vote on grades and star ratings. This feedback is essential to help us ensure complete and up-to-date coverage for all the climbs since opinions and circumstances around the routes are continually changing. It can also be a useful place for you to seek out others' opinions on a certain route before you climb it, or check out what other people think about the grade.

In addition to the Route Database, the web site has Area Guides to Yorkshire, North York Moors and Northumberland which contain slightly more information than on the introduction and logistics pages of this guide.

Feedback - If you find anything in this guide that you disagree with - a hard grade, and dubious star-rating, a misleading route description or a blatant error - then please let us know.
Email - feedback@rockfax.com

Matt Kilner on the superb crack of *Thin Red Line* (E1 5b) - *page 54* - Heptonstall Quarry in Yorkshire. Photo: Jamie Moss

Most of the crags in this guidebook have no major access problems and all that is required to ensure continued freedom of access is a responsible approach otherwise the freedoms already won could be so easily lost. The most common access conflicts are not caused by the climbing of routes, but the parking of cars, the walk to the crag, the dropping of litter and people who insist on letting their dogs run wild. These are all things that are well within our control as visitors. Please read the specific access information in the crag introductions to check on any parking suggestions and crag restrictions that may be in place. Infrequently new access restrictions do occur mainly due either to nesting birds, or because of potential fire hazards - signs will normally be posted. If you need up-to-date information about access to a certain crag then check the BMC Access database - **www.thebmc.co.uk** - or post a question on UKClimbing - **www.ukclimbing.com**. If you do encounter access problems, contact the BMC via the web site (see advert opposite).

Environmental Considerations

Every time we climb a route our hands and feet, and rope and runners, erode the rock slightly. Our chalk dust, our food waste, our foot prints and our cars all have an impact on the crag environment. These facts are undeniable and something all climbers need to come to terms with as our number increases. Although we can't stop our impact completely, we can do many things which significantly reduce it.
Here are some suggestions:

Rock Damage - Much of the modern damage to rock has occurred when climbers have attempted to retrieve stuck gear. Equipment that gets stuck is invariably gear that is badly placed, so think before you place it. If it does get well and truly jammed it may be better leaving it for someone who can get it out without wrecking the rock. Another way which holds get damaged is when people climb routes without cleaning their boots properly. Remember, clean boots means less eroded footholds and significantly better friction! Brushing on the harder routes needs to be done with great care as even iron-hard gritstone can be damaged by over-zealous cleaning. Finally, there is no reason for attempting to improve holds on any of the routes in this guide and if you think otherwise then you are wrong.

Bouldering Pads - If you own a bouldering pad then use it, not just when bouldering but also when trad climbing. Place it on the grass under the routes when you gear up, place it under the route when you do the first move, sit on it when belaying. By doing this you will help reduce the erosion of grass and vegetation at the base of the crags, as well as maybe saving yourself from a nasty twisted ankle if you slip off before placing a runner.

Chalk - The use of chalk has become almost universal yet it is an unsightly addition to the rock and, being alkaline, is alien to the acid moorlands which many of these crags are on. The pale streaks below well used holds show where the dark lichen that gives the rock its colour is being killed off. Try and use less chalk, use a chalk ball, dip less frequently and zip-up your chalk bag before you reach the top of the route where the wind can invert it.

Top-roping - The action of a rope sliding over the rock on the top edge of a crag can act like a saw, particularly on soft rock like sandstone. Before you top-rope a route, consider leading it. If you really do want to top-rope it then please read carefully the sections on 'Top-roping and Soft Rock' in the North York Moors (page 194) and Northumberland (page 238) introductions which describe the best way to set up a top-rope to minimise damage.

CLIMB IT, WALK IT, PROTECT IT!

THE BMC **CRAG CODE**

Access	Check the Regional Access Database (RAD) on www.thebmc.co.uk for the latest access information
Parking	Park carefully – avoid gateways and driveways
Footpaths	Keep to established paths – leave gates as you find them
Risk	Climbing can be dangerous – accept the risks and be aware of other people around you
Respect	Groups and individuals – respect the rock, local climbing ethics and other people
Wildlife	Do not disturb livestock, wildlife or cliff vegetation; respect seasonal bird nesting restrictions
Dogs	Keep dogs under control at all times; don't let your dog chase sheep or disturb wildlife
Litter	'Leave no trace' – take all litter home with you
Toilets	Don't make a mess – bury your waste
Economy	Do everything you can to support the rural economy – shop locally

BMC Participation Statement — Climbing, hill walking and mountaineering are activities with a danger of personal injury or death. Participants in these activities should be aware of and accept these risks and be responsible for their own actions and involvement.

guide there is no fixed gear so everything you need will have to be carried up the crag. Starting with the correct equipment is essential so it is worth taking a few moments to try and envisage all the runner placements that might be available. It may seem obvious but wide cracks take wide runners so starting up an off-width with a bunch of small wires doesn't make much sense. Taking extra gear 'for the belay' is okay if you are comfortable at the grade but if you are really pushing yourself, then lighten the load a little and wander back down to get the belay gear while basking in the glory of your ascent. No-one ever got any extra points for arriving at the top of a 10m route with most of their gear still on their harness.

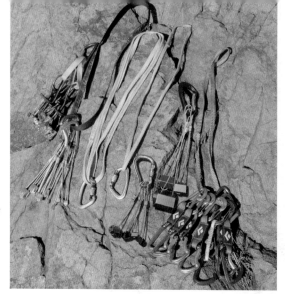

Runners

Many old routes which were bold and unprotected leads in their day are now relatively safe with modern protection. The wide breaks and cracks make gritstone and sandstone ideal places for camming devices, often in positions where nothing else would hold. Hexes can be useful in wider parallel cracks and wires are essential for the narrower cracks. For harder routes micro-wires and more advanced camming devices may be found essential, plus some duplication of wires and camming devices in the useful ranges.

Ropes

Most outcrop routes are short enough to be climbed on a single 10mm or 11mm rope. There are lighter 9mm single ropes available but the abrasive nature of the rock means that you are better advised to go for something thicker and more durable. The only exception to this are routes which wander around in which case you may need 2 x 9mm half-ropes or use one rope doubled.

A Versatile Gritstone Rack

The list below is suggested for taking to the crag but not necessarily for carrying up every route. Use your judgement before setting off to tailor your rack to the route.

- **Full set of wires** across the range racked on separate krabs - one for the small wires, one for the larger ones. Two sets of wires are useful for many routes.

- **Full set of camming devices** if you can afford them. If not then get a few well spaced sizes first and supplement with some Hexes.

- **6 to 8 extenders**.

- **2 or 3 slings** with screwgates.

Other Gear

Beyond these essentials you may find useful; a poker for persuading recalcitrant gear; tape

The British Trad grade is probably never more appropriately used than it is on outcrop routes. Here the subtleties and versatility of the Trad Grade can be appreciated to their maximum.

Bold Routes - Some gritstone and sandstone routes have limited protection and you can easily find yourself in very serious situations, especially on the harder climbs. This possibility should be clear from the route descriptions but please make sure you use your own skill and judgment as to whether you will be able to safely complete a chosen climb. A bold E2 may only feel like an indoor grade 6a on a top-rope but it is a very different proposition as a lead or solo.

British Trad Grade

1) Adjectival grade (Diff, VDiff, Severe, Hard Severe (HS), Very Severe (VS), Hard Very Severe (HVS), E1, E2, E3, E4 and upwards).
An overall picture of the route including how well protected it is, how sustained and a general indication of the level of difficulty of the whole route.

2) Technical grade (4a, 4b, 4c, 5a, ...).
The difficulty of the hardest single move, or short section.

Colour Coding

The routes and boulder problems are all given a colour-coded dot corresponding to a grade band and approximate difficulty level. This colour code is designed to indicate routes and problems that a particular climber might be happy attempting. Since most people are happier bouldering at a harder level than they lead, the boulder problems tend to have harder individual moves on them for the same colour-code.

Green Routes - Severe and under and V0 and under. Good for beginners and those looking for an easy life.

Orange Routes - Hard Severe to HVS and V0+ to V2. General ticking routes for those with more experience including a lot of excellent routes and problems.

Red Routes - E1 to E3 and V3 to V6. Routes and problems for the experienced and keen climber including many of the three areas' great classics.

Black Routes - E4 and V7 and above. A grade band for the talented.

ROUTE GRADES

BRITISH TRAD GRADE (See note on bold routes)

British Trad Grade	Sport Grade	UIAA	USA
Mod (Moderate)	1	I	5.1
Diff (Difficult)	2	II	5.2
VDiff (Very Difficult)	2+	III	5.3
HVD (Hard Very Difficult)	3-	III+	5.4
Sev (Severe)	3	IV	5.4
HS (Hard Severe) BOLD 3c / 4b SAFE	3	IV+	5.5
VS (Very Severe) BOLD 4a / 5a SAFE	3+	V-	5.6
	4	V	5.7
HVS (Hard Very Severe) BOLD 4b / 5b SAFE	4+	V+	5.8
E1 BOLD 5a / 5c SAFE	5	VI-	5.9
E2 BOLD 5a / 6a SAFE	5+	VI	5.10a
E3 BOLD 5b / 6a SAFE	6a	VI+	5.10b
	6a+	VII-	5.10c
E4 BOLD 5c / 6b SAFE	6b	VII	5.10d
E5 BOLD 6a / 6c SAFE	6b+	VII+	5.11a
E6 BOLD 6b / 7a SAFE	6c	VIII-	5.11b
	6c+	VIII-	5.11c
E7 BOLD 6c / 7a SAFE	7a	VIII	5.11d
E8 BOLD 6c / 7b SAFE	7a+	VIII+	5.12a
	7b	IX-	5.12b
E9 BOLD 7a / 7b SAFE	7b+	IX-	5.12c
	7c	IX	5.12d
E10 BOLD 7a / 7b SAFE	7c+	IX+	5.13a
	8a	X-	5.13b
	8a+	X	5.13c
	8b	X	5.13d
	8b+	X+	5.14a
	8c	XI-	5.14b
	8c+	XI	5.14c
	9a	XI	5.14d
	9a+	XI+	5.15a

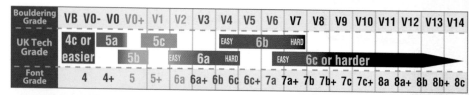

Bouldering Grade	VB	V0-	V0	V0+	V1	V2	V3	V4	V5	V6	V7	V8	V9	V10	V11	V12	V13	V14
UK Tech Grade	4c or easier		5a		5c			EASY	6b		HARD							
		easier		5b		EASY	6a	HARD		EASY	6c or harder							
Font Grade	4		4+	5	5+	6a	6a+	6b	6c	6c+	7a	7a+	7b	7b+	7c	7c+	8a	8a+ 8b 8b+ 8c

Practice makes good.
Practice plus coaching makes perfect.

There's no doubt that if you climb a lot you will improve. You'll learn from your own mistakes and triumphs and progress at your own pace. But you're sure to experience plateaus in your development. Stages where you just can't seem to advance, improve or grasp a new technique.

That's where our climbing coaches can help, getting you back on track. Fast.

What's more, time spent with them will give you added inspiration and confidence, fuelling your development for a long time to come as well as ironing out your 'bad habits'.

Our coaches are amongst the most experienced, highly qualified and enthusiastic in the country. Not only are they excellent climbers, they're expert coaches too. They know exactly how to help you achieve your potential as a climber and they're totally committed to doing it. We firmly believe their unique blend of experience, talent, commitment and enthusiasm makes Plas y Brenin the number one destination for rock climbing development.

So if you want to improve your climbing, come to Plas y Brenin - you'll find it's the perfect choice.

For a free 56-page colour brochure call 01690 720214 or e-mail brochure@pyb.co.uk or visit www.pyb.co.uk

MOUNTAIN

GORE-TEX Guaranteed To Keep You Dry

PLAS Y BRENIN

www.pyb.co.uk

Plas y Brenin Capel Curig, Conwy LL24 0ET Tel: 01690 720214 Fax: 01690 720394 www.pyb.co.uk Email: info@pyb.co.uk

Yorkshire is also well known for its great limestone climbing which is mostly located in the Yorkshire Dales National Park, just to the north west of Rylstone, Crookrise and the Barden Moor crags covered in this book.

Northern Limestone (Rockfax 2004)
This book covers the Yorkshire big three limestone crags of Malham, Kilnsey and Gordale as well as plenty of other smaller venues. As a bonus you also get all the Peak Limestone and the South Lakes Limestone.

For more gritstone coverage take a look at **Eastern Grit (Rockfax 2006)** and **Western Grit (Rockfax 2003)** which cover the main grit crags of the Peak District and surrounding area.

For information on all Rockfax publications - **www.rockfax.com**

Other Publishers
There are several other guides by different publishers which compliment the coverage in this book well with more detailed information on the respective areas.

Yorkshire Gritstone (YMC 1998)
This large book contains many more smaller crags than this book, spread from Heptonstall in the south to Eavestone Crag in the north. All crags have complete route listings and there is some bouldering although only the major problems.

Yorkshire Gritstone Bouldering - Volume 1 (Total Climbing 2008)
A dedicated bouldering guide for the main crags in the Yorkshire area. Another volume is planned for the more esoteric Yorkshire bouldering areas also due to be published in 2008.

Climbing in North East England (SBP/CMC 2003)
An extensive book with an amazing 44 crags listed across the North York Moors, Eastern Pennines, Swaledale and Tyne and Wear areas, of which only 9 make this book. Many are only small but there is certainly plenty more to discover for those who want to explore a bit more.

Northumberland Climbing Guide (NMC 2004)
All the crags in the area traditionally called the 'County'. In addition to the crags listed in this book there are plenty more smaller venues in the area north of Newcastle and south of the border. Some bouldering information.

Northumberland Bouldering (NMC 2000)
The first attempt at covering the fine bouldering in the Northumberland area. Due for a new edition sometime in 2008 or 2009.

Rockfax acknowledge the huge effort in documenting the route and crag information over the years carried out by volunteers and members of the Yorkshire Mountaineering Club, Cleveland Mountaineering Club and Northumberland Mountaineering Club in particular.

This graded list was compiled by pooling my 40+ years of experience of climbing over the whole area, with Dave Musgrove's intimate knowledge of Yorkshire Gritstone, to give the most accurate assessment of these widespread climbs as possible. Tony Marr has helped with his encyclopedic knowledge of the North York Moors. As ever, the upper end of the list is more open to conjecture though we have sought a consensus wherever possible. The secretive world of Northumbrian sandstone has proved more difficult. We have used a mixture of feedback from the Rockfax databases, personal experience and some pointers from interested locals. If you think there are errors in the list, you may be mistaken or it may be an honest mistake; either way, let us know via the Route Database on the web site - **www.rockfax.com**

Bolt-on holds

Training boards

Bouldering Walls

Leading Walls

Mobile Towers

Ice Walls

Artificial caves

Photo: Craggy Island

Entre-Prises (UK) Ltd
T: 01282 444800   F: 01282 444801
info@ep-uk.com   www.ep-uk.com

BMC Partner & British Competition Climbing Team Sponsor

E3

			Page
***		Australia Crack	345
***		The Manta	314
***		The Gypsy	100
***		Eavestone Wall	163
**		The Big Greeny	104
**		Sour Grapes	67
**		Dangler	248
***		Over the Edge	297
***		Blind Valley	80
***		The Sandrider	287
***		High T	338
***		The Wall of Horrors	104
***		West Sphinx Direct	217
***		I'll Bet She Does	136
**		Outward Bound	331
**		Stargazer	228
***		Western Front	105
**		Rotifer	145
***		Candle in the Wind	290
***		The Naked Edge	136
***		Honeymoon Crack	289
***		The Trial	314

E2

***		Ali Baba	219
***		Forked Lightning Crack	55
***		Northumberland Wall	272
***		Sandy Crack	281
**		Crescendo	50
**		Godspell	42
***		The Overhanging Crack	321
**		Charming Crack	142
***		Earl Buttress	66
**		Picnic	156
***		Black Wall Eliminate	110
***		Ranadon	306
***		The Alamo	160
***		Black Chipper	145
**		Smarty Pants	288
**		Ceiling Crack	59
**		Weeping Fingers	264
***		Gronff	84
***		A Question of Balance	135

***		Pillar Front	114
***		Fever Pitch	225
***		The Shelf	120
***		The Witch	328
***		Crazy Diamond	129
***		The Trouser Legs	287

E1

***		Roof Route	331
**		Tufted Crack	73
***		Rock Island Line	258
**		Thunder Crack	300
**		Ridsdale Wall	276
**		Magic Flute	329
***		North West Girdle	104
**		Rake's Crack	273
***		Thin Red Line	54
**		The Pulpit	206
***		Satchmo	222
**		Stretcher Wall	322
**		Woodburn Wall	276
**		Gymkhana	136
**		The Prow (Scugdale)	204
***		Monument Crack	131
***		The Sorcerer	328
**		Delilah	42
**		Thin Hand Special	335
**		North Route	215
***		Ricochet Wall	51
**		Hovis	118
**		Wombat	228
**		No Prisoners	84
***		Scarecrow Crack	228
***		The Waster	85
***		The Gauntlet	338
***		Noonday Ridge	94
**		Tom's Peeping	264
**		Sword Dance	131
***		Birdlime Traverse	110
**		Queer Street	228
***		Z Climb Eliminate	103
***		Frensis Direct	156
***		The Arches	326
**		Duke of York	330
**		Tiger Feet	308

Ali Kennedy soloing *The Sorcerer* (E1 5c) - *page 328* at Back Bowden. Photo: Jamie Moss

Climbing Walls

Steve Smith enjoying a quick solo of *Tippling Wall* (HVS 5a) - *page 206* - at Scugdale. Photo: Jamie Moss

HVS

The **best** in professional instruction
www.ami.org.uk

LEARN
FROM
EXPERIENCE

VS

Bruce Perry on *Allan's Crack* (VS 4c) - *page 140* - on the Main Edge at Brimham Rocks. Photo: Chris Craggs

HS

S

HVD

VDiff

Diff

The remote Rylstone, home to many great routes including a trio of easier classics. Photo: Chris Craggs

The big fella' scoping out Eavestones.
Photo: Sherri Davy

When I first got the climbing bug (obsession) my long suffering parents were tasked with shipping me to such destinations as Brimham, Almscliff, Scugdale, the Wainstones and Slipstones. So started a lifelong interest with these 'little green cliffs' - thanks for the support (and the lifts).

In the very early days I climbed with Adrian Bridge and Alaisdair Amato - we had an epic bivi at Scugdale. Then Pete Ackroyd and Colin Binks helped me spread my wings wider (they both had cars!) before I moved to Sheffield to climb with Steve Warwick, Nigel Baker, Rich Watkinson, Dave Spencer and later Graham Parkes. A couple of years spent living in Scotland and Willie Jeffrey joined me on many visits to the Northumberland cliffs. Another year in York I lodged with John Addey and he became a regular partner on Yorkshire Grit and the North York Moors.
The usual suspects have supported me when visiting and photographing these cliffs for the book: Dave Spencer, Brian Rossiter, Dave Gregory, Colin Binks (as ever) with his sidekicks Mark Binney and Bruce Perry. Colin in particular has been irrepressible - always there when needed, always happy to stop and pose in the most ridiculous positions and never a single complaint!

A special thank you is due to Jamie Moss who allowed us access to his superb set of shots covering all three areas. Other photographers who have helped lift this celebration of the areas are Duncan Skelton, Nick Smith, Simon Jaques, James Rowe, Rob Askew, Dave Musgrove, Mark Glaister and Mike Took.

The text has been looked over by folks who know these areas very well, especially Tony Marr (North York Moors), Dave Musgrove (Yorkshire Grit), Ian Jackson (North York Moors), Jack Geldard (Earl Crag). The document has been expertly proofed by Graham Hoey, Simon Jaques and Simon Caldwell, who managed to pull out many errors - those that remain are mine, often added at the last minute!

Then of course there are the two people without whom there would have been no book at all; Sherri Davy, who has supported me from first to last despite being dragged all over the North of England; and Alan James, who finally caved in after four year's of badgering and agreed that this guide would be a good idea after all - he worked his magic on my raw text and topos; thank you both.

Chris Craggs, January 2008

Guiding Services

AMI Guides - Page 21 - www.ami.org.uk

Inglebrough Hall - Page 35 - www.ingleboro.co.uk
Outdoor Education Centre, Clapham.   Tel: 015242 51265

Gear Shops

Track 'n' Terrain - Page 11 - www.tracknterrain.com
21a Elvet Bridge, Durham City.   Tel: 0191 3843758

Ultimate Outdoors - Inside front cover - www.ultimateoutdoors.co.uk
Keswick, Lancaster, Betws-y-Coed, Skipton.   Tel: 0845 362 4250

Climbing Walls

Awesome Walls - Page 15 - www.awesomewalls.co.uk
The Engine House, Stockport, SK6 2BP. Tel: 0161 494 9949

Entre-Prise - Page 17 - www.ep-uk.com
Kelbrook. Tel: 01282 444800

Manchester Climbing Centre - Page 33
www.manchesterclimbingcentre.com
St. Benedict's Church, Manchester.   Tel: 0161 230 7006

Rock City - Page 2 - www.rockcity.co.uk
Hawthorne Avenue, Hull.   Tel: 01482 223030

Rockworks - Page 19 - www.rockworks.co.uk
Stanley, Co. Durham.   Tel: 01207 281 777

Sunderland Wall - Page 243 - www.sunderlandwall.co.uk
Doxford Works, Sunderland.   Tel: 0191 514 4234

The Leeds Wall - Page 35 - www.theleedswall.co.uk
Gelderd Road, Leeds.   Tel: 0113 234 1554

The Newcastle Climbing Centre - Page 243
285 Shields Road, Newcastle.   Tel: 0191 265 6060

Other Advertisers

Berghaus - Inside back cover - www.berghaus.com
Extreme Centre, Sunderland.   Tel: 0191 516 5700

Black Diamond - Outside back cover
www.blackdiamondequipment.com
Tel: 0162 958 0484

Plas y Brenin - Page 13 - www.pyb.co.uk
Capel Curig, North Wales.   Tel: 01690 720214

Nigel Baker on the *Beeline* (HVS 5b) - *page 77* - on the remote Rocky Valley at Ilkley. Photo: Chris Craggs

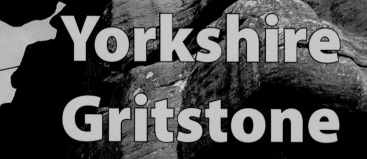

Yorkshire Gritstone

Matt Kilner on *Great Western* (HVS 5a) - *page 105*
- at Almscliff. Photo: Jamie Moss

Yorkshire Gritstone - short, green and severely graded routes by some accounts, or hidden gems on deserted crags in magnificent scenery by others.

It has to be said that some of my early encounters were sobering experiences; like doing battle with the rounded horror of Almscliff's *Goblin's Eyes* (graded VDiff at the time) which felt like the hardest route in the World; or my first VS, *Birch Tree Wall* at Brimham - a classic (though unintentional) sangbag - my partners told me it was VDiff, which they genuinely believed it to be. I wobbled up the final scoop in protectionless terror, my tatty plimsolls offering little in the way of friction or support.

The years rolled by and it got better as I explored the scattered archipelago of gritstone islands that protrude from Yorkshire's green and pleasant lands and worked my way through the many stiffly-graded classics that the area abounds with. A year spent in York meant that Almscliff became my local crag. *Western Front* with two runners was one favourite party trick - a romp up an imposing line of jugs and jams, gritstone glory at its best. I graduated to lead routes I had always considered the preserve of true experts - *Forked Lighting Crack* at Heptonstall and *Wall of Horrors* at Almscliff probably being the most notable, though there were many more. Visits to Rylstone, Caley, Earl Crag and Eastby amongst others proved there are plenty of great routes on these little cliffs.

The truth about Yorkshire is that crags and routes are as good as anything anywhere on Grit. The area may not have the concentration of crags found in the Peak but it lacks nothing in quality and nowadays the sobering experience of the infamous 'Yorkshire VS' is a thing of the past. The following chapters should hopefully inspire those who have laboured under the 'short, green and severely graded' misapprehension to take another look, and maybe encourage those already in the know to explore further and re-visit some old favourite locations.

Chris Craggs climbing the superb *Monument Crack* (E1 5b) - *page 131* - on the isolated Rylstone. Photo: Craggs Collection

Ethics and Style

As a genre, gritstone climbing has always been at the forefront of forming ethics and general practice within the UK. Virtually all climbers spend time on the crags of Yorkshire and the Peak and many of the leading lights of British climbing have left their mark in the history books by making major ascents on these great gritstone outcrops. The general practice of ground-up, leader-placed protection remains as applicable as ever and this is the preferred style for routes in the Yorkshire Grit area and the routes are graded accordingly. In recent years many of the top standard routes are pre-practiced before an ascent, often due to the fact that they have little or no protection available anyway. Top-roping prior to an attempt isn't generally done for routes of E5 and below although obviously the style of any ascent is up to the individual climber. Certain protectionless routes nowadays tend to be climbed above a stack of mats. Once again, this can have a significant effect on the grade of a climb. The thing that matters most is that you enjoy your climbing and that you are happy with what you have done, how you have done it and what you have left behind.

Ali Kennedy getting increasingly less benefit from a few mats and spotters on *Psycho* (E5 6b) - *page 90* - at Caley. Photo: Jamie Moss

Access

Yorkshire Gritstone access issues have been a variable problem over the years but due to continued negotiations and adherence to the various agreements by climbers, the vast majority of venues have good access at present. Clashes over birds, flora, historical sites, parking and dogs have all been causes for access disagreement in the past. The major crags of the Barden Moor Estate used to have stringent access restrictions, though the introduction of CRoW has eased the situation here, a NO DOGS rule still applies though. Car parking problems have caused difficulties at Almscliff and the re-sighting of the parking has helped. Individual crag access is covered in each of the crags section, please read this information carefully and adhere to restrictions. Nesting birds, grouse shooting and fire hazards are the most likely reasons for closure and signs should be posted to indicate the activities and the time-scales involved. If in any doubt contact the BMC (page 9) or check the Regional Access Database (RAD) section of the BMC website **www.thebmc.co.uk**.

Parking - It is all a matter of common courtesy, don't block access, get right off the road if possible and, if the parking is full, try to find somewhere else.

Litter/Fires/Dogs - It should be obvious.

Pate Hill · Shooters · Heptonstall · Widdop · Earl Crag · Ilkley · The Chevin · Caley · Almscliff · Eastby · Crookrise · Rylstone · Simon's Seat · Brimham · Eavestones · Slipstones · Crag Willas · Guisecliff

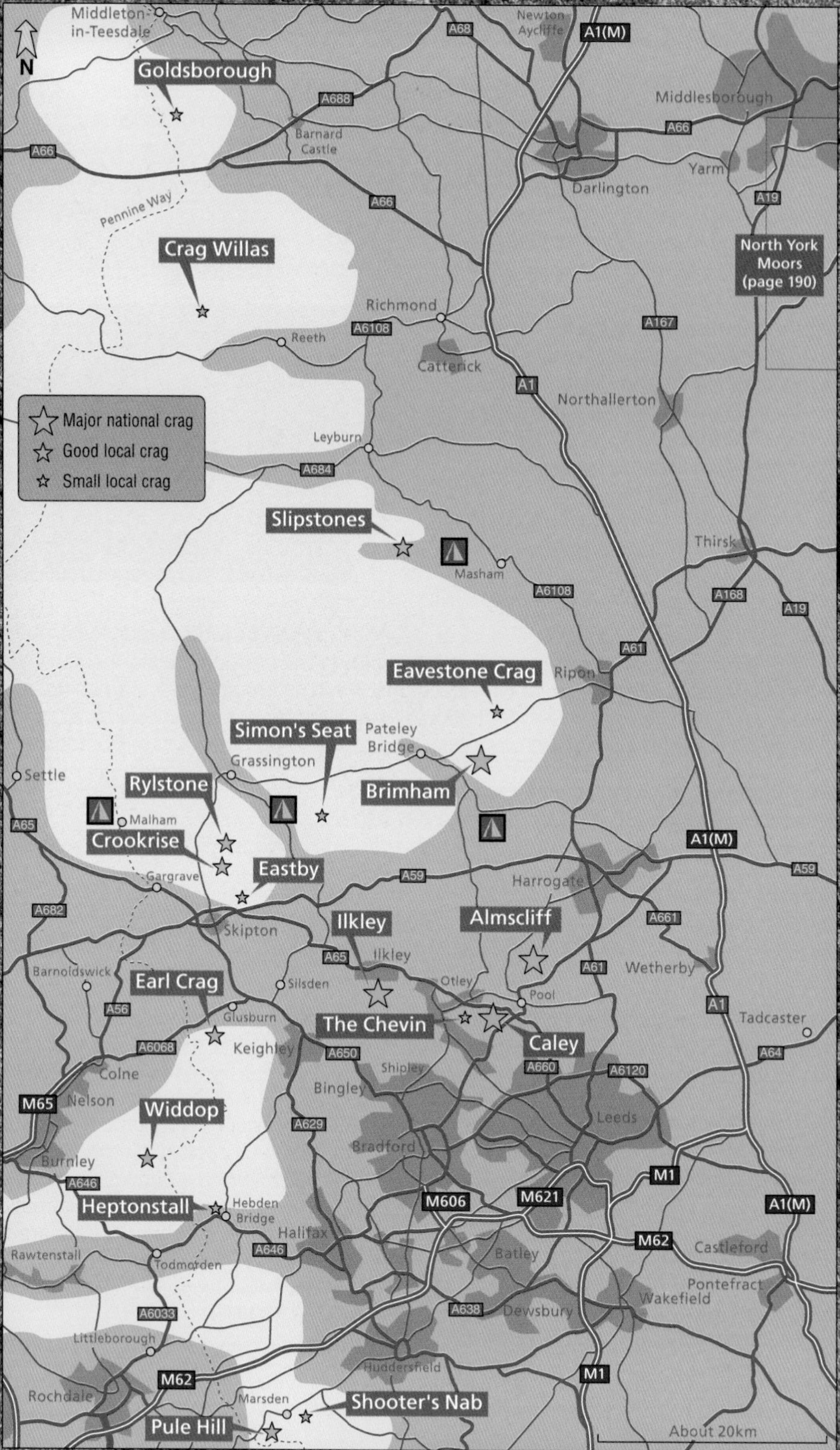

N

Middleton-in-Teesdale

Goldsborough

A688

Barnard Castle

A66

Pennine Way

Crag Willas

A66

Richmond

Reeth

A6108

Catterick

A1

Northallerton

Newton Aycliffe

A1(M)

Middlesborough

A66

Yarm

Darlington

A19

A167

North York Moors (page 190)

Leyburn

A684

☆ Major national crag
☆ Good local crag
☆ Small local crag

Slipstones

Masham

A6108

Thirsk

A168

A19

Eavestone Crag

Ripon

A61

Simon's Seat

Grassington

Pateley Bridge

Brimham

Rylstone

Malham

Settle

A65

Crookrise

Gargrave

Eastby

Skipton

A59

Harrogate

A1(M)

A59

A661

Wetherby

A61

A682

Barnoldswick

A56

Earl Crag

Glusburn

Keighley

Silsden

Ilkley

Ilkley

A65

Otley

Pool

A1

Tadcaster

A64

The Chevin

Almscliff

A650

Shipley

Caley

A660

A6120

Colne

M65

Nelson

Widdop

A6068

Bingley

Bradford

A629

Leeds

M1

Burnley

Heptonstall

Hebden Bridge

Halifax

A646

M606

M621

M62

Castleford

Rawtenstall

Todmorden

A646

Batley

Pontefract

Wakefield

A638

Dewsbury

A6033

Littleborough

Huddersfield

M1

Rochdale

M62

Marsden

Shooter's Nab

Pule Hill

About 20km

Mountain Rescue
In the event of an accident requiring the assistance of Mountain Rescue:

Dial 999 and ask for 'POLICE - MOUNTAIN RESCUE'

All mountain rescue incidents in Yorkshire fall under the responsibility of Yorkshire Constabulary. If in any doubt request Yorkshire Police Operations Room.

Tourist Information Offices

If you need ideas for wet day activities or need some accommodation, take a look at the Yorkshire Dales website **www.yorkshiredales.org**. There are 30 Tourist Information Offices scattered throughout the Dales of which the most useful are:

Skipton   01756 792809
Settle   01729 825 192
Pateley Bridge   01423 711147

The symbol of the National Park - the Swaledale ram

Camping

The Yorkshire Grit area extends over a lot of urban landscape between Manchester and Leeds and, although there are campsites, most climbers will prefer to locate themselves further north, in the actual Yorkshire Dales National Park. There are many campsites in the Park but those listed below are the most popular with climbers. Their approximate locations are marked on the map on the previous page, and on close-up maps where appropriate.

Masons Campsite, Appletreewick (see map on page 132)
Appletreewick, Skipton, BD23 6DD.   Tel: 01756 720275
Popular family site central for the Skipton area crags and close to the limestone as well.

Town Head Farm, Malham
Town Head Farm, Cove Road, Malham, BD23 4DE,   Tel: 01729 830287
A popular base for climbers on the limestone but close enough for the grit as well. Great pubs near by. Can get busy (and noisy) at weekends.

Manor House Farm Caravan Park, Summerbridge (see map on page 138)
Summerbridge, Harrogate, HG3 4JS.   Tel: 01423 780322
Extensive site south of Summerbridge, 15 minutes walk to a pub, close to Brimham Rocks.

Black Swan Holiday Park, Masham (see map on page 164)
Fearby, Masham, HG4 4NF.   Tel: 01765 689477
Well placed site for Slipstones.   **www.blackswanholiday.co.uk**

Not Camping

The National Park is littered with cottages for hire and, if you are in a group, this can be a very cost-effective and pleasant way of staying in the area. A good way to start is putting "Yorkshire Cottages" into Google. Some good sites are **www.yorkshire-cottages.info**, **www.sykescottages.com**, **www.iknow-yorkshire.co.uk**

Youth Hostels - There are hostels at Mankinholes (Todmorden), Haworth, Earby, Slaidburn, Malham, Ingleton and at Kettlewell. Many make ideal bases for exploring the gritstone cliffs. Check - **www.yha.org.uk**.

Pule Hill | Shooter's | Heptonstall | Widdop | Earl Crag | Ilkley | The Chevin | Caley | Almscliff | Eastby | Crookrise | Kyrstone | Simon's Seat | Brimham | Eavestones | Slipstones | Crag Willas | Goldsbrgh

The North West's
Premier
Climbing Venue

75 lines and dedicated
bouldering area
Courses for all ages and abilities
Cafe and Cotswold Rock Shop
Discounts for students, 60+, unemployed
ABC member and AALA

Manchester Climbing Centre, St Benedict's Church,

Bennett Street, West Gorton, Manchester M12 5ND

0161 2307006
www.manchesterclimbingcentre.com

Getting Around

All the crags in this section are all easily reached by car and the approach descriptions are written assuming you have access to a car. If you are trying to get to the crags by public transport here is a list of useful contacts which may help.

Buses - The Tourist Information Centres are the preferred method of obtaining timetables and local knowledge, but the website **www.showbus.co.uk/timetables** lists the various operators in the area and where to obtain timetable information.

Trains - The towns and villages of Keighley, Skipton, Ilkley and Harrogate can all be reached by train. For timetable information go to **www.arrivatrainsnorthern.co.uk**

Climbing Shops

Nevisport - 26-28 Woodhouse Lane. Tel: 0113 2444715   **www.nevisport.co.uk**
Inglesport - 11 The Square, Ingleton. Tel: 015242 41146   **www.inglesport.co.uk**
Cave and Crag - Market Place, Settle. Tel: 01729 823877   **www.cave-crag.co.uk**
Base Camp - 13 Leeds Road, Ilkley. Tel: 01943 816011
Ultimate Outdoors - 1 Coach Street, Skipton. Tel: 01756 794305   **www.ultimateoutdoors.co.uk**

Cafes

Settle - Ye Olde Naked Man Cafe in the centre of Settle. Excellent.
Grassington - Picnics Cafe. Just off the main square.
Malham - Old Barn Cafe. On the left when entering the village.
Clapham - Croft Cafe. In the village centre.

Pubs

There are many pubs in the areas covered by this book, some of the most popular are listed below. More pubs listed at **www.pub-explorer.com**
The Devonshire Hotel - Grassington. Good food with some offers during the week.
Kings Arms - in Kettlewell. Located round the back near the church.
The Marton Arms - near Ingleton. Good food and wide choice of beers.
The Square and Compass - North Rigton, a bit posh but convenient for apres-Almscliff. Has good food and Timothy Taylor's Landlord.
Hunter's Inn - Leathley (near Almscliff) has a good range of guest ales.
Half Moon Inn - Pool-in-Wharfedale. CAMRA pub with good beer.
Dave Musgrove who knows the area better then most (cliffs and pubs) recommends: Almscliff - **The Hunters**; Ilkley - **The Hermit**; Caley - **The Rose and Crown** in Otley; Rylstone - **The Craven Hiefer**; Crookrise and Eastby - **The Elm Tree**; Brimham - T**he Flying Dutchman**.

Climbing Walls

Awesome Walls (page 15) - Old factory conversion, 23.5m lead walls and extensive bouldering. The Engine House, Stockport, SK6 2BP.   Tel: 0161 494 9949   **www.awesomewalls.co.uk**

Boulder UK - Dedicated and extensive bouldering wall.
10a Heaton Street, Blackburn, BB2 2BF.   Tel 01254 693056   **www.boulderuk.info**

Climb Rochdale - Dedicated centre with both bouldering and leading walls.
31 School Lane, Rochdale, OL16 1QP.   Tel 01706 524450   **www.climbukltd.com**

Manchester Wall (page 33) - Modern church conversion, 20m lead walls and extensive bouldering. St Benedict's Church, Manchester, M12 5ND.   Tel: 0161 2307006   **www.manchesterclimbingcentre.com**

Inglesport Wall - Dedicated centre with both leading (up to 13m) and bouldering areas.
The Square, Ingleton, LA6 3EB.   Tel: 015242 41146   **www.inglesport.co.uk**

The Leeds Wall (opposite) - 15m lead wall plus two bouldering areas.
100a Gelderd Road, Leeds, LS12 6BY.   Tel: 0113 2341554   **www.theleedswall.co.uk**

the LEEDS wall

Open 7 days a week
200+ routes, grades 3 - 8a
leading, top roping &
bouldering V0 - V8+
Courses for all
ages & abilities
Families
welcome

Outdoor clothing & equipment shop
Cafe and Vending
www.theleedswall.co.uk
100A Gelderd Road, Leeds LS12 6BY
Tel/Fax 0113 2341554

CAVING COURSES

in the Yorkshire Dales

BCA LCMLA / CIC Training
and Assessment

Guided SRT trips
in the Yorkshire Classics

Technical training & advice

On-site SRT training facilities

Beginners trips for groups,
families and individuals

INGLEBOROUGH HALL
Clapham, North Yorkshire LA2 8EF

Telephone: 015242 51265
E-mail: cave@ingleboro.co.uk
www.ingleboro.co.uk

Routes		up to Sev	HS to HVS	E1 to E3	E4 and up
Pule Hill	76	27 ✓✓	41 ✓✓	8 ✓	- ✗
Shooter's Nab	25	2 ✓	15 ✓✓	7 ✓✓	1 ✗
Heptonstall Quarry	20	- ✗	9 ✓✓	4 ✓✓	7 ✓✓
Widdop	40	9 ✓✓	13 ✓✓	9 ✓	9 ✓✓✓
Earl Crag	62	9 ✓	21 ✓✓	16 ✓✓	16 ✓✓
Ilkley	147	29 ✓✓✓	59 ✓✓✓	31 ✓✓✓	28 ✓✓✓
The Chevin	16	1 ✓	8 ✓✓	4 ✓	3 ✓
Caley	91	8 ✓	33 ✓✓	18 ✓✓	31 ✓✓✓
Almscliff	115	17 ✓✓	41 ✓✓✓	33 ✓✓✓	24 ✓✓
Eastby	16	5 ✓	8 ✓✓	2 ✓	1 ✗
Crookrise	61	14 ✓	26 ✓✓	16 ✓✓	5 ✓
Rylstone	63	17 ✓✓	24 ✓✓	15 ✓✓	7 ✓
Simon's Seat	32	10 ✓	11 ✓✓	10 ✓✓	1 ✗
Brimham Rocks	169	31 ✓✓	76 ✓✓✓	41 ✓✓	21 ✓✓
Eavestone Crag	28	6 ✓	8 ✓	11 ✓	3 ✓
Slipstones	164	43 ✓✓	65 ✓✓✓	44 ✓✓	12 ✓✓
Crag Willas	53	17 ✓✓	15 ✓✓	8 ✓	3 ✓
Goldsborough Carr	44	10 ✓	8 ✓	18 ✓✓	8 ✓

Quality and range of routes in different grade bands: ✓✓✓ - Excellent   ✓✓ - Good   ✓ - Okay   ✗ - Not worth a visit

Approach	Sun	Dry	Green	Shelter	Windy	Summary	Page	Crag
10 min	Afternoon				Windy	A west-facing cliff and natural edge looking out over wild moors. The quarry is rather esoteric but the natural edge is well worth a visit.	38	Pule Hill
30 min	Evening		Green		Windy	An extensive north-facing quarry with a small selection of climbs. The gun-club in front of the quarry complicates the access somewhat.	48	Shooter's
10 min	Afternoon		Green	Sheltered		An impressive quarry in a secluded and sheltered setting. Although not very extensive, it is tall and the set of routes includes some major classics.	52	Heptonstall
10 to 18 min	Not much sun		Green		Windy	A fine remote crag, with some great climbs on an imposing set of buttresses in a wild setting. Sadly it is green for much of the year.	56	Widdop
5 to 10 min	Not much sun		Green		Windy	A fine and extensive edge with a good collection of climbs and a lot of bouldering. Green for much of the year and best on warm summer evenings.	62	Earl Crag
2 to 10 min	Sun and shade		Green		Windy	The Cow and Calf contrast with the more remote climbs in Rocky Valley. Often a bit of a cool spot but with loads to go at across the grades.	68	Ilkley
5 min	Not much sun		Green			A tall buttress with a small selection of quality shady routes. There are a few extra climbs in the nearby quarry too.	82	The Chevin
3 to 10 min	Not much sun		Green			A regular quick-hit venue for Leeds-based climbers, the boulders being especially popular. The Main Edge also has some great climbs.	86	Caley
5 min	Sun and shade				Windy	The archetypal grit crag. First-timers often find the steep and rounded rock off-putting though most learn to love the place.	98	Almscliff
5 min	Lots of sun					A slabby venue with some surprisingly tall climbs on excellent rock and in a sunny setting. Pity it isn't a bit more extensive.	112	Eastby
20 min	Afternoon				Windy	A great crag, a bit of a hike from the road, but that doesn't put the locals off. It is a good evening venue in the summer.	116	Crookrise
35 min	Afternoon				Windy	Rylstone is a bit of a hike from the road, but a superb set of climbs makes it well worth the effort, as long as you pick a suitable day.	124	Rylstone
30 to 40 min	Sun and shade		Green		Windy	A very remote cliff with the main buttresses facing north, it is primarily a high summer venue. The south side offers some short sunnier stuff.	132	Simon's Seat
2 to 15 min	Sun and shade		Green			A fine destination, which takes some time to get to know. The northern classics are often green but there is plenty of other stuff to do.	138	Brimham
3 to 6 min	Sun and shade		Green	Sheltered		Yorkshire's lost world crag, very sheltered though the vegetation is gradually taking over the valley. Worth a visit for something different.	158	Eavestones
15 min	Lots of sun				Windy	Only a short crag, but quite extensive, and very popular with boulderers, mainly because of its sunny outlook and fine rock.	164	Slipstones
30 min	Lots of sun				Windy	A remote crag of high quality gritstone, worth a visit if you want to get away from the crowds. A few good routes and plenty of easy bouldering.	178	Crag Willas
10 min	Lots of sun				Windy	Another remote crag, but with easy access and a sunny setting. Some great bouldering over the steep undercut starts.	184	Guldsb'gh

	No star	⭐	⭐⭐	⭐⭐⭐
Mod to S	16	8	3	-
HS to HVS	26	11	4	-
E1 to E3	3	3	2	-
E4 and up	-	-	-	-

A cliff with two contrasting sets of climbs. In the centre are the extensive and impressive old quarry workings, which offer some hard climbs on rock that is not always above suspicion. To left and right are the natural outcrops that offer more good routes, many in the friendlier lower grades.

The cliff is not hugely popular, a sad accident of geography; if it was sat on the edge of the Burbage Valley it would see ten times the user visits. As it is, Pule Hill is a good choice (on the right day) for somewhere a little different.

Conditions

The crag faces west and is at its best on late summer afternoons and evenings. The whole crag can be windy and is inclined to be green in the winter.

Approach

There is a long lay-by on the uphill side of the A62 between Marsden and Oldham, directly under the quarry and the chimneys that vent the railway tunnel and canal buried deep in the hillside. The crag is reached in a steep ten minute grind via the old quarry inclines.

Colin Binks on *Hangover Edge* (HS 4c) - *page 46* - typical of the climbing on the natural outcrop at Pule Hill. Photo: Chris Craggs

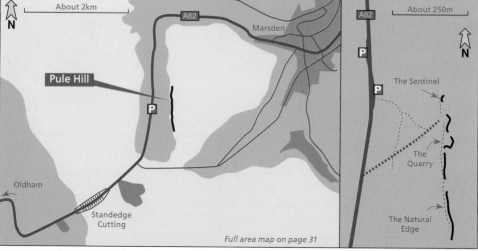

About 2km

N

A62

Marsden

Pule Hill

P

Oldham

Standedge Cutting

About 250m

A62

P

N

P

The Sentinel

The Quarry

The Natural Edge

Full area map on page 31

Pule Hill · Shooter's · Heptonstall · Widdop · Earl Crag · Ilkley · The Chevin · Caley · Almscliff · Eastby · Crookrise · Rylstone · Simon's Seat · Brimham · Eavestones · Slipstones · Crag Willas · Goldsborough

Dave Spencer on the final wall of *The Great Scoop* (VS 5a) - *page 42*
a fine climb on the quarried section of Pule Hill. Photo: Chris Craggs

The Sentinel
A fine steep buttress to the left of the quarried sections of the cliff. The routes are short but action packed and their position above the steep bank adds atmosphere.

❶ The Peeler . . . . 🎲 **S 4b**
6m. The short steep and strenuous crack on the left.
FA. Rimmon Mountaineering Club members early 1960s

❷ Overlapping Wall . . . . . 🪨🧗 **E1 6a**
6m. A taxing line through the centre of the mid-height overlap.
FA. Tony Nichols 1966

❸ No Traverse . . . . 🎲 **VS 4c**
6m. Steep and tricky moves lead up the rib and through the overhang using awkward holds.
FA. Rimmon Mountaineering Club members early 1960s

❹ Tony's Traverse . . . . 🧗 **HS 4b**
18m. A mini-expedition, pumpy, though on good holds. The finish up the side wall is tricky.
FA. Tony Howard and Rimmon Mountaineering Club members early 1960s

❺ No Exit . . . . 🎲🧗 **VS 4c**
8m. The prominent thin-hand crack leads to juggy bulges.

❻ Traverse Not . . . . . 🎲🪨🧗 **VS 5a**
8m. A taxing layback start up the blind groove gains jug-pulling above and then an awkward exit.
FA. Rimmon Mountaineering Club members early 1960s

❼ Bed End . . . . 🎲🧗 **HVD**
10m. Short but steep and exhilarating. Start just right of the arete and climb the crack before looping out left and back right to reach the throne. Exit steeply to the left.
FA. Rimmon Mountaineering Club members early 1960s

❽ Sentinel Wall . . . . 🧗 **HS 4b**
8m. The side wall has taxing moves to pass the overlap.
FA. Rimmon Mountaineering Club members early 1960s

❾ Sentinel Chimney . . . . **Mod**
8m. A constricted rift which is easier if you stay on the outside.

The Quarry

❿ Schmarren . . . . 🧗 **VS 4c**
10m. Climb past the orifice to the wide break then up the short steep wall above to finish.
FA. Mark Kemball 1982

⓫ Staub . . . . 🧗 **HVS 4c**
10m. The right-hand side of wall is a bit dusty and leads to a pull right onto the upper wall.
FA. Mark Kemball 1982

⓬ Skull Climb . . . . 🎲🧗 **VDiff**
10m. Unique. Follow the flake to the left edge of the wall then trend right to the top. The direct exit is loose - best to escape left. A more direct finish offers better climbing but less novelty.
FA. Rimmon Mountaineering Club members early 1960s

Pule Hill
Shooter's
Heptonstall
Widdop
Earl Crag
Ilkley
The Chevin
Caley
Almscliff
Eastby
Crookrise
Rylstone
Simon's Seat
Brimham
Eavestones
Slipstones
Crag Willas
Jgt of

⑬ Skull Climb Right-hand . . . . 🧗 ▢ **S 4a**
10m. A steep right-hand start leads to the parent route.
FA. Steve Clark 2005

⑭ The Iliad . . . . 🧗🧗 ▢ **VS 5a**
10m. Fingery moves up the centre of the cracked wall.
FA. Brian Cropper 1977

The impressive face of The Great Scoop has a big roof and a distinct scalloped cave on its left-hand side. To the left of this are a few minor routes.

⑮ Retreat . . . . 🧗 ▢ **Mod**
8m. Trend right to the groove and exit left from it. No belay.
FA. Rimmon Mountaineering Club members early 1960s

⑯ Midas . . . . ▢ **VS 4c**
8m. Follow the edge of the slab to a slanting groove. Climb up this and the short but exposed arete.

⑰ Midas Direct . . . . ▢ **HVS 5a**
8m. Follow the previous route but head up into the scoop above with some trepidation. Finish direct.
FA. Paul Cropper 1981

⑱ Lethal Lemon . . . . 🐏 ▢ **E1 5a**
8m. The blunt rib is bold and delicate.
FA. Gary Gibson 1981

⑲ Geoff's Groove . . . . 🧗 ▢ **Diff**
8m. Pull into the deep groove and follow it. Exit with care.
FA. Rimmon Mountaineering Club members early 1960s

The Quarry

Much of the rock in the old quarries is poor but there are some worthwhile climbs scattered along the cliff. Belays above many routes are difficult to arrange; there are widely spaced stakes hidden in the grass, though on some routes it is better to belay at the cliff edge - care is needed. The first routes described are on the short wall on the left, characterised by a blocky dry-stone wall filling a cave near the cliff top. The rock is not the best, though it is the sunniest wall in the quarry and therefore just about worth describing.

Descent

First Triple Wall - 50m

The Great Scoop

The (second) most impressive rock feature at Pule Hill is the huge scooped face with a large roof above known as The Scoop. There are several worthwhile climbs here though they don't see much activity.

1 The Great Scoop **VS 5a**
18m. Well worth calling in for if you are passing this way. Traverse the slab to its apex and make an awkward move to access the ledge and a possible stance. Move right for a nicely exposed finish. *Photo on page 39.*
FA. Malc Baxter 1962

2 Godspell 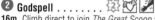 **E2 5b**
16m. Climb direct to join *The Great Scoop* at its awkward move. Move left then pull up to the roof and make dramatic moves left to eventually gain the hanging rib. Finish direct with some relief.
FA. Jim Cambell 1977

3 Sandy Hole **HVS 5b**
10m. Short but witheringly steep climbing up the cracks past the hole and a big jammed block. Finish up the next route.

4 Annual Route **HS 4b**
10m. Climb into the groove which gives steep moves to a ledge. Move awkwardly out left past the bulges to an easier finish.
FA. Rimmon Mountaineering Club members early 1960s

5 The Bulger **VS 5b**
10m. Technical moves on great rock lead to the ledges. Move right around the arete to a finish up a groove.
FA. John Smith 1977

6 Dedfer **HS 4c**
10m. Gain the groove of *The Bulger* directly, or via the pleasant left arete.
FA. Rimmon Mountaineering Club members early 1960s

The First Triple Wall

7 Fusion Chimney **HVS 4c**
14m. The long chimney on the left is a bit harrowing.

8 Necronomicon **E3 5c** (1pt)
16m. From the chimney move right and follow the thin crack up and to the sandy cave. Reach over the left side of the roof and use the old bolt (**A0**) to access the wall above. Finish direct.
FA. Paul Cropper 1980. The upper wall was originally part of Odyssey, an aid route up the centre of the face. FA. Bill Birch, Tony Howard 1969

9 Odyssey Variant **E3 5c** (1pt)
18m. Monkey up the nose on the right (useful drill-hole) then climb the crack to its end. Move left to the sandy cave and finish as for *Necronomicon* - (**A0**). The original direct start over the bulges in the centre of the wall still requires the use of a couple of aid points.
FA. Nick Colton 1979

10 Delilah **E1 5b**
18m. A fine climb, though with an exhausting start. Swim up the narrowing cleft until the ledge on the left can be gained for a breather. Move right and follow the groove to the roof, then move right again and finish up the short wall.
FA. Brian Woods 1960

Pule Hill · Shooters · Heptonstall · Widdop · Earl Crag · Ilkley · The Chevin · Caley · Almscliff · Eastby · Crookrise · Rylstone · Simon's Seat · Brimham · Eavestones · Slipstones · Crag Willas · Gordale · Gouthwaite

Leprosy Wall
(not described)

Descent - scramble
and down-climb

8

7

9

10

11

12

First Triple Wall

---

11 Gold Rush **E2 6a**
16m. The flat face of the buttress is climbed to gain a ledge with difficulty (peg). Trend right up the face (harder than it looks) to an easier finish up the final arete.
FA. Brian Cropper 1974

12 Sampson . . . . **HVS 5b**
12m. From the right arete, move up and left to reach the hanging crack and power up this. The iron foothold is taboo.

The Second Triple Wall
This is the short clean face up and right, in the back of the bay. It is passed on the way down and has three quick ticks.

13 The Ratcher . . . . **VS 5a**
8m. Trend up right to a tricky mantelshelf.
FA. Malc Baxter 1962

14 The Ratch . . . . **V2 (5c)**
8m. The direct start gives a nice boulder problem.

15 The 8-foot Kid . . . . **VS 5b**
8m. The counter diagonal is harder.

The Third Triple Wall is at right angles to the routes already described. It is home to three routes that see little attention, being loose and usually green. The path climbs out of the quarry and heads rightwards for 70m to find the delights of the natural edge.

Triple Walls
The right-hand side of the quarry has three areas of rock that have been climbed on, known logically as the Triple Walls. The first of these is impressive and has some fine routes, the second is short and sweet, whereas the third one is rather poor. They are all inclined to be green especially in the winter.

Second Triple Wall

13

14

15

Natural Edge - 70m

The Natural Edge - Left

Running southwards from the quarry workings are a nice set of small buttresses with an interesting set of climbs, best enjoyed on warm summer afternoons.

1 Crude Crack . . . . **VDiff**
8m. An indifferent offering up the short bulging crack and the crusty crack in the left wall.
FA. Rimmon Mountaineering Club members early 1960s

2 Tarrif Wall . . . . **HVS 5b**
10m. Climb into the shallow cave, exit left to finish on the arete.
FA. Paul Cropper early 1980s

3 The Token **E1 5b**
8m. Powerful moves lead through the roof of the cave.
FA. Paul Cropper early 1980s

4 Godsend . . . . **HS 4b**
10m. Exit rightwards from the cave - lower is easier - to a bit of a stretch for jugs. A well positioned micro route.
FA. Rimmon Mountaineering Club members early 1960

5 Dusky Doddle . . . . **HVD 4a**
10m. Broken climbing up the tiered buttress above a tricky start.
FA. Rimmon Mountaineering Club members early 1960s

6 Atlas . . . . **VDiff**
10m. From the block, stride the gap then climb the steep face.
FA. Paul Cropper early 1980s

7 Whacker's Wall . . . . **Diff**
8m. Meander leftwards following the best holds.
FA. Tony Howard early 1970s

8 Amen . . . . **VDiff**
10m. The left-facing corner leads to a steep exhilarating finale.
FA. Rimmon Mountaineering Club members early 1960s

9 Sobeit . . . . **VS 4c**
10m. The face just right of the arete is a touch harrowing.
FA. Brian Cropper or Mark Kemball 1982

10 Wrinkled Wall . . . . **HS 4c**
10m. Trend right up the face - awkward but with good rests.
FA. Rimmon Mountaineering Club members early 1960s

Across the gully to the right is the curiosity that is the Flying Buttress, a tower with a tunnel clean through it. There are some fine climbs here.

11 Minotaur . . . . **HVS 5a**
8m. Bridge up across the through-tunnel until a bit of a wild swing rightwards enable the front face to be reached.
FA. Rimmon Mountaineering Club members early 1960s

12 Flying Buttress . . . . **HS 4b**
12m. A mini-classic. Climb to, and up, the thin crack in the face then exit up and right awkwardly. Move up left of the arete for a steep finish. It is also possible to make a long traverse out to the left arete for an airy variation. *Photo opposite.*
FA. Rimmon Mountaineering Club members early 1960s

13 Flying Arete . . . . **HS 4b**
12m. The arete on the right of the buttress is easier on its right-hand side apart from the finish which is easier on the left. Swapping these around makes it nearer **VS 4c**.
FA. Brian Cropper early 1980s

14 Pilot Crack . . . . **S 4a**
12m. Follow the ledgy groove up to the back door of the arch then access the hanging corner above with difficulty/hilarity in appropriate measure.
FA. Rimmon Mountaineering Club members early 1960s

Brian Rossiter on *Flying Buttress* (HS 4b) - *opposite* - perhaps the best of the micro routes on natural outcrop at Pule Hill. Photo: Chris Craggs

The Tomb

Descent

Descent

4

10 11 12 13

Overhanging Arete

1 2

3 5

6 7 8 9

Windy Wall

Coffin Corner

Apse Wall - 30m

Natural Edge - Right
The final scattering of buttresses have some short but worthwhile routes and they tend to be a little quieter than the stuff further to the left.

1 Hangover Edge . . . . 🔲 HS 4c
8m. The left arete is short but pumpy and has a tricky start.
Photo on page 38.
FA. Rimmon Mountaineering Club members early 1960s

2 Windy Wall . . . . 🔲 HS 4b
8m. The centre of the wall is marginally easier.
FA. Rimmon Mountaineering Club members early 1960s

3 The Swinger . . . . 🔲 HS 4a
10m. Pass the first roof then swing boldy out to the left arete.
FA. Rimmon Mountaineering Club members early 1960s

4 Celtic . . . . 🔲 HVS 5a
10m. A short and sharp finish over the roof.
FA. Brian Cropper 1983

5 Kletterschuhe . . . . . 🔲 S 4a
10m. The steep flaky wall leads to a rest on the left. Move out right past the large jammed block to a reachy finish. More direct versions are harder and pumpier.
FA. Rimmon Mountaineering Club members early 1960s

6 Coffin Corner . . . . 🔲 VDiff
10m. Enter the coffin slot then exit steeply up the right wall.
FA. Rimmon Mountaineering Club members early 1960s

7 Route One . . . . 🔲 HVS 4c
10m. Pumpy climbing leads rapidly to easier ground.
FA. Con Carey 1983

8 Route Two . . . . 🔲 VS 4c
10m. The centre of the face.
FA. Con Carey 1983

9 Blind Buttress . . . . 🔲 HS 4b
8m. The right-hand side of the face past a couple of 'orbits'.
FA. Rimmon Mountaineering Club members early 1960s

10 Furly 'ard . . . . 🔲 S 4a
8m. Up the side wall of the buttress.
FA. Rimmon Mountaineering Club members early 1960s

11 Overhanging Arete . . . . 🔲 HVD 4a
8m. Steep and juggy fun.
FA. Rimmon Mountaineering Club members early 1960s

12 Left Route . . . . 🔲 HS 4b
8m. Sprint up the wall just left of centre.
FA. Rimmon Mountaineering Club members early 1960s

13 Right Route . . . . 🔲 HS 4b
8m. The wall just right of centre.
FA. Rimmon Mountaineering Club members early 1960s

30m to the right is another buttress.

14 Apse Arete Indirect . . . . 🔲 S 4a
8m. Traverse the shelf out to the arete and balance up it.
FA. Rimmon Mountaineering Club members early 1960s

15 Apse Crack . . . . 🔲 S 4b
8m. The steep crack rising from the right edge of the Apse cave.
FA. Rimmon Mountaineering Club members early 1960s

16 Apse Wall . . . . 🔲 HVD 4a
8m. Balance up the arete then continue up the narrow wall.
FA. Rimmon Mountaineering Club members early 1960s

17 Eel . . . . 🔲 VDiff
8m. From a block swing right to the front face and finish direct.
FA. Rimmon Mountaineering Club members early 1960s

Apse Wall

Descent

14 15 16 17 18 19

18 S.H.M. .... HVD
8m. Gain the arete from the left then, from its top, move left into a hanging groove until a move right can made. Finish direct.
FA. Rimmon Mountaineering Club members early 1960s

19 Has Been .... VDiff
8m. The right-hand face of the buttress direct is worthwhile.
FA. Rimmon Mountaineering Club members early 1960s

20 Ladder Gully .... Mod
6m. Bridge the easy cleft.

21 Ladder Ridge .... VDiff
6m. The awkward stepped buttress in the back of the gully.
FA. Rimmon Mountaineering Club members early 1960s

22 Deceit .... Diff
8m. The chockstoned right-hand crack to a ledge. Finish easily or, better, move right to an exposed finish on the arete (**S 4a**).
FA. Rimmon Mountaineering Club members early 1960s

23 Flack E1 5b
8m. Climb the left-hand side of the main arete. The stretch for a chipped hold is at an uncomfortable height.

24 Scoop Wall .... VS 5a
8m. Climb up to, and then through, the centre of the hanging scoop. A tasty little teaser.
FA. Rimmon Mountaineering Club members early 1960s

25 Cloister Wall .... S 4a
8m. Mantel on to the large ledge then climb the short arete to the hole (sit-down-rest) of the Cloister. Finish left or right.
FA. Rimmon Mountaineering Club members early 1960s

26 Suspension .... HS 5a
8m. Enter the severely overhanging groove with great difficulty.
FA. Rimmon Mountaineering Club members early 1960s

27 Cracked Ridge .... S 4a
8m. Up a rib then enter a hanging scoop on the right with difficulty.
FA. Rimmon Mountaineering Club members early 1960s

55m to the right is the appropriately-named Square Buttress, the last significant piece of rock on the cliff.

28 Squaring the Circle .... HVS 5a
8m. The centre of the left-hand wall of the buttress.
FA. Con Carey 1983

29 Bung .... HVS 5b
8m. The arete of the buttress is started on its left-hand side by a problematical couple of moves.
FA. Brian Cropper 1975

30 Square Buttress ... VS 5a
8m. The front face is climbed right to left - standing in the wide mouth-like slot is tricky. Finish straight over the bulges.
FA. Rimmon Mountaineering Club members early 1960s

	No star	 ☆	☆☆	☆☆☆
Mod to S	1	1	-	-
HS to HVS	9	5	1	-
E1 to E3	1	4	1	1
E4 and up	-	1	-	-

A long abandoned quarry overlooking the town of Marsden, to the south west of Huddersfield. The quarry is very extensive and would make one of the most impressive venues hereabouts if is wasn't for the fact that it is north-facing, there is some loose rock around and there are access issues.

Access

The land in front of the quarry has long been used as a rifle range and the quarry wall forms a distant backdrop to some of the target areas. Over the years access has generally been allowed when the range is not being used, in fact parking used to be allowed at the shooting lodge which eased the approach to the crag considerably. Sadly an incident in 2006 jeopardised this and currently the shooting club do not want people on their land. Negotiations are ongoing so check the BMC RAD for up-to-date information - www.thebmc.co.uk

Conditions

The crag faces almost due north and is at its best on warm summer evenings or as an escape from the heat of summer. A few of the buttresses protrude far enough to catch the afternoon sun and one wall of The Rostrum is the most notable of these. The crag is green and unattractive in the winter and is best avoided.

Approach

There is parking by the south east corner of the dam - the signs indicate that the road is private (water board) but the local dog walkers and bird watchers certainly use it. The old quarry tracks lead into the left-hand end of the workings. Parking further down the road, by the no access sign adds about 10 minutes to the approach. Alternatively, park on the side of the B6107 Meltham Road, just east of Marsden and follow the public Right of Way that runs up the old quarry road across the moor all the way to the quarry. From the dam the approach takes 20 minutes, from the other two parking spots, 30 minutes.

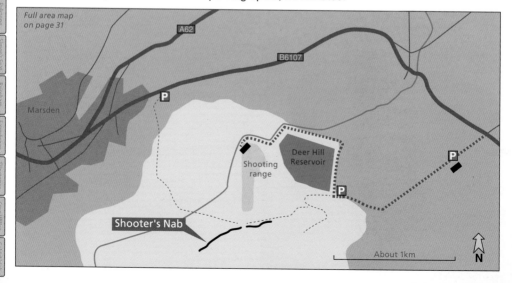

Full area map on page 31

Matthew Thompson on the superb *Ricochet Wall* (E1 5b) - *page 51* - at Shooter's Nab. Photo: James Rowe

The Rostrum

Descent

The Rostrum

The finest feature of the quarry is the great jutting prow of The Rostrum - this is home to several fine climbs. Although the quarry faces pretty much due north, The Rostrum sticks out far enough to have a west-facing wall which catches the afternoon sun.

① Panic Knott . . . . **S 4a**
14m. The right-trending groove left of The Rostrum.
FA. Bryn Higgins 1958

② Wanderlust . . . . **VS 4c**
24m. A well named trip that skirts the left-hand side of the quarry's biggest buttress. Layback the groove to the roof then move out left to a grassy ledge (possible belay). Gain the left arete from round the corner, then move out right for an exposed finish up the hanging wall.
FA. Tony Howard 1963

③ Eric the Cosmic Fiend . . . . . **HVS 5b**
20m. Avoid the loop out left on *Wanderlust* by making powerful moves up into the thin hanging crack above the stance.
FA. John Hart 1971

④ Crescendo **E2 5c**
24m. A fine climb with a harrowing finale. Start below the huge roof and climb the wall deviously to a small ledge below the old bolt ladder. Head up the face, just right of the old bolts, to reach a break under the roof, then swing wildly left to a rest on the arete. Finish direct.
FA. John Stanger 1970. The bolts were placed a short time earlier as he aided the big roof in a thunderstorm as Thunderball, A2.

⑤ Sweatyman . . . . **HVS 5a**
22m. A devious classic with a weird finish. Pull rightwards onto the wall from a recess then climb cracks to a small but good ledge below the upper face (belay recommended here). Pull up to the break then move left to the arete. Move up and left again then crawl through the horizontal slot to an exposed exit on the front face. Told you it was weird.
FA. Graham West 1957

⑥ Cool Man's Wall . . . **VS 5a**
20m. A direct finish to *Sweatyman* up the wall, past the deep break, and up the precarious scoop.
FA. Paul Cropper 1981

⑦ Rifleman's Chimney . . . . **HS 4b**
20m. The big groove on the right of The Rostrum contains twin cracks and is a bit of a misnomer.
FA. Graham West 1957

⑧ Slip Arete **E2 5c**
18m. Balance up the bold arete to the roof, then jig right into Magpie before stepping back out left for the upper arete. Oddly reminiscent of its Chatsworth namesake.
FA. Paul Cropper 1981

⑨ Elbow Jump . . . . **VS 4c**
20m. Another oddity. Climb the groove to the roof then escape awkwardly right to a rest. Move up and left to finish.
FA. Graham West 1957

⑩ Magpie . . . . **HVS 5a**
20m. Climb the slabby face leftwards to enter the groove of *Elbow Jump* then finish up the steep gritty crack above.
FA. Barry Kershaw 1959

The Rostrum

Ricochet Wall

Descent

Ricochet Wall

Beyond the prow of The Rostrum is a wide green wall then further on, a well-cracked face which faces just a little more to the west. It is vaguely reminiscent of Yarncliffe's Zapple wall.

19 Light Fantastic . . . . □ **HVS 5a**
16m. Climb the wall right of the wide crack centrally to the upper break. Move right then graze a way to the top.
FA. Paul Cropper 1981

The Walk Off

To the right is some more broken ground then a final clean wall split by a large ledge sloping down to the right. This is only short but it does have a small collection of interesting climbs. It is named after the convenient escape ledge.

11 Bull's Eye Crack . . . . □ **VDiff**
20m. The straight crack (big gear) leads to a turfy exit.
FA. Graham West 1957

12 Redeemer's Wall . . . . . □ **HS 4b**
20m. The wide crack has the odd loose block and leads to a tricky grassy exit - at least at the moment it does.
FA. Graham West 1957

13 The Cuspidor . . . . □ **VS 4b**
20m. Climb the flake left of the arete.
FA. Tony Howard early 1960

14 Tind . . . . □ **HVS 5a**
20m. Edge up the diagonal undercut crack to reach the blunt arete, then climb this more boldly to finish up a short crack.
FA. Graham West 1957

15 Born at a Price . . . . □ **E4 6b**
20m. Climb past a hole to reach the highest break. Fill this with gear then climb the centre of the upper wall via a blunt rib, using some poor pockets, until things ease.
FA. Chris Booth 1986

16 Ricochet Wall. . . . . □ **E1 5b**
20m. Classic. The cracks splitting the centre of the wall are reached up a shallow groove, with runners to the left. At its top, step left and blast the fine jamming cracks. *Photo on page 49.*
FA. John Stanger 1970

17 Scot's Wall . . . . □ **E1 5c**
20m. Not as fine as *Ricochet* but still worth doing. Climb the slanting cracks rightwards to the break, move right again to the wide finale.
FA. Bob Whittaker 1976

18 The Light. . . . . □ **VS 4c**
20m. The wide crack that bounds the right-hand side of the wall is awkward to get established in.
FA. Graham West 1957

20 Ball Bearings . . . . □ **HVS 5a**
12m. Climb through the bulge at some spidery cracks, then head right up the slab above.
FA. Probably John Stanger early 1970s

21 Surprise . . . . □ **E2 5c**
12m. The right-hand side of the rib leads to hard moves to enter the large scoop feature on the arete. Finish leftwards.
FA. Paul Cropper 1982

22 Barney Rubble . . . . □ **VS 4c**
10m. The grubby and awkward corner, to a rightward exit below the 'hanging death'.
FA. Harold Heald 1963

23 Stimrol . . . . □ **E2 5b**
12m. The fine square-cut arete gives good climbing, with runners in the big break, before the bold final section.
FA. Harold Heald 1963

24 The Long Reach . . . . . □ **E3 6b**
12m. Follow the crack right of the arete to the ledge then harder continuation above. The name is a giveaway.
FA. Brian Cropper 1971

25 Chimp Crack . . . . □ **VS 5a**
10m. Zig-zag up the crack to the ledge then tackle the thinner right-trending crack in the wall behind.
FA. Barry Kershaw 1959

	No star	☼	☼☼	☼☼☼
Mod to S	-	-	-	-
HS to HVS	2	3	3	1
E1 to E3	1	1	-	2
E4 and up	-	6	1	-

A secluded but imposing quarry, cut into the hillside, below the charming 'village that time forgot' of the same name. It has a fine set of climbs that are bigger than is usual for grit, following powerful lines on good rock. Most of the better routes follow crack-lines and corners with good gear and solid jams being the order of the day. The steep angle and long pitches will take its toll on your forearms though so make sure you are ready for a battle. The harder routes tend to follow the walls between the cracks giving tenuous and technical climbing but mostly with good gear in the near-by cracks.

Conditions

The crag faces south west and is both sheltered and rapid drying. Although it offers protection from the wind, the surrounding trees make it midgy in humid weather.

Approach

The quaint village of Heptonstall is reached by a narrow road that rises steeply from the A646. There is no access to this when west bound so continue for a few hundred metres until a signed turning circle on the left is reached. On entering the village, follow signs to the extensive car park by the Working Men's Club. Walk up the track to the left of the houses for 200m then turn left down a walled track. This soon leads to the rim of the valley where a set of substantial gritstone steps wind down into the quarry, which is located just round to the left, an easy 10 minutes from the car.

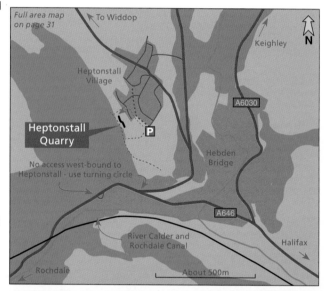

Full area map on page 31

To Widdop

Heptonstall Village

Keighley

N

A6030

Heptonstall Quarry

P

Hebden Bridge

No access west-bound to Heptonstall - use turning circle

A646

Halifax

River Calder and Rochdale Canal

Rochdale

About 500m

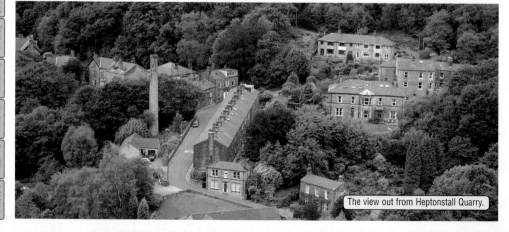

The view out from Heptonstall Quarry.

① **Curving Crack** . . . . . VS 4c
16m. The pumpy crack in the right-facing side wall.
FA. Don Whillans 1961

② **Vertical Speed** . E7 6c
18m. Climb the corner then launch out onto the wall. Climb past two pegs to a juggy lump, then gain *Hard Line* with difficulty.
FA. Matt Troilett 1997

③ **Thin Red Line** E1 5b
20m. One of the best routes in the quarry, steep and pumpy but with good runners to catch you if/when you finally run out of steam. Follow the crack to the break then step right and make long moves to reach the continuation. Sprint up the flake to a breather in the easy chimney before topping out. A solid E1.
Photo on page 7.
FA. Mike Quinn (1 nut for aid) 1967. FFA. Barry Rawlinson 1972

④ **Hard Line** E5 6b
20m. Start up the crack of *Thin Red Line*. Where that route heads right, tackle the withering continuation crack above and left. Finish rightwards through the overhang with a flourish.
FA. Pete Livesey 1974

⑤ **Anticyclone** E5 6b
20m. The arduous link-up of *Thin Red Line* and *Hard Line*.
FA. Dougie Hall 1985

⑥ **Demerara** E4 6a
20m. A fine direct line, up the central crack system, which is best taken at a gallop. Once *Thin Red Line* is joined, things ease.
FA. Ron Fawcett 1975

⑦ **Brown Sugar** E2 5c
20m. This long crack can be climbed direct, or via a diversion out to the right (where the holds go), either way, the roof proves tricky for most. Above this things gradually ease as long as you have a little puff left.
FA. John Harley 1957. FFA. John Syrett 1973

⑧ **Pulpit Route** . . . . HVS 5a
26m. Climb the ledgy groove left of the arete to reach the end of a ramp running across the face below the steeper rock. Follow this - scary and delicate - until the final couple of moves of *Demerara* lead into the easy upper chimney.
FA. John Hartley 1961

Above the ledge used by Pulpit Route for its sideways shenanigans are a couple of desperate outings.

⑨ **A Step in the Light Green** E6 6b
24m. From the ledge, climb the leaning wall (peg) to reach the curving overlap. Up this powerfully then back left up a short steep ramp to easy ground.
FA. Mark Radtke 1987

⑩ **Orange Crush** E6 6b
24m. From the ledge, climb the right-hand side of the wall (pegs) then move out onto the exposed leaning arete. This gives hard and harrowing climbing until better holds signal the end of the significant difficulties.
FA. Mark Radtke 1990

⑪ **Cream** E4 6a
24m. The long angular arete separating the Red and Yellow Walls gives a good pitch, though protection is sparse.
FA. Barry Rawlinson 1972

Afternoon | 10 min | Green | Sheltered

⑫ Fairy Steps Direct . . . . ☆2 ⬜ **VS 4c**
24m. A fine climb up the corner that falls from the left edge of the long roof capping the wall. Follow the corner direct (good gear) passing the jutting nose with difficulty. From a small ledge, move out onto the airy arete for a fine finish.
FA. Bob Whittaker 1967

⑬ Trepidation . . . . ☆1 ⬜ **VS 4c**
24m. Start up *Fairy Steps Direct* but move onto the left wall and climb a flake-crack until a mantel reaches the finale of *Fairy Steps*.
FA. M.Day 1962

⑭ Fairy Steps . . . . ⌐Top⌐ 50 ⬜ **HS 4b**
24m. A lower grade quarry classic. Follow ramps and ledges leftwards to a niche (possible belay) then move left and climb the groove to a ledge (possible belay). Move left onto the highly exposed arete for a memorable finish.
FA. John Hartley 1958

⑮ Strange Brew . . . . ⬜ **E2 5c**
30m. ... and a strange line too, though it manages to reach parts of the crag that are rarely travelled. Start up *Fairy Steps* but follow the main corner up to the big roof. Traverse the break rightwards, past *Forked Lightning*, to finish steeply up the next roof-crack.
FA. Barry Rawlinson 1972

⑯ Forked Lightning Crack . ⌐Top⌐ 50 ⬜ **E2 5c**
24m. The striking zig-zag crack is the best known route in the quarry and remains one of Grit's 'big-ticks'. Climb easily to the base of the crack, stuff in some gear and go. Although mighty intimidating, the climbing is a little easier than it appears from below and much of the crack is a useful width. The short horizontal sections offer runners and holds.
FA. Don Whillans 1961

⑰ Bull's Crack . . . . ☆3 ⬜ **HVS 5a**
24m. A fine climb up a great line; the soaring corner bounding Yellow Wall. Layback and jam the corner passing the jutting nose with difficulty. The shelf of Rabbit Ledge offers a lie-down rest (and a possible belay). Once recovered, step left into the continuation chimney and wriggle up this to the top. *Photo on page 53.*
FA. Derek Bull 1959

⑱ Senility . . . . ☆1 ⬜ **HVS 5b**
14m. Pumpy climbing up the leaning wall right of the corner. Generally the holds are good, but they are well spaced and the angle dictates that a forceful approach is needed.
FA. Pete Grindley (1 peg) 1961

⑲ Grindley's Grunt . . . . ⬜ **HVS 5b**
14m. Climb the wall right of the arete to the niche in the roof and cross this by a pig of a move - get grunting! Originally started from the col to the right.
FA. Pete Grindley (1 peg) 1961. FFA. Bob Whittaker 1965

⑳ Monkey Puzzle . . . . ⬜ **HVS 5a**
14m. A worthwhile extension to either of the two previous climbs. From Rabbit Ledge, follow the horizontal break out right past the arete to an easier finish.
FA. John Barron 1965

Forked Lightning Crack
The are few more recognisable or compelling lines anywhere on grit. Don Whillans' ascent in 1961 was memorable - he had top-roped it previously, sucked on two calming 'fags' then led it with a single runner - a peg bashed into a wooden wedge. When I first visited the quarry ten years later, ascents were still being counted on the fingers of one hand according to the rumours.

	No star	⚁	⚂	⚃
Mod to S	4	4	1	-
HS to HVS	6	3	3	1
E1 to E3	2	6	1	-
E4 and up	-	4	2	3

A fine set of rounded buttresses looking out over the Widdop Reservoir and the high and wild moors of the bandit country on the Yorkshire/Lancashire border. Although Widdop is well known for its bouldering, the routes tend to be off the regular circuit, but call in on a fine warm afternoon and a good time is pretty much assured with quality routes from VDiff to E9.

Conditions

The crag faces due north and, set at an altitude of 350m, it is best enjoyed as a high summer venue. Sadly the crag is often a lurid green colour even in the summer so visits are best made after a good dry spell. Fortunately the rock is often in rather better condition than its appearance might suggest so it is always worth a closer look. It will catch any wind that is going, especially a cold one from the north.

Approach

There is an extensive car park just below Widdop Reservoir on the minor road that runs from Hebden Bridge to Burnley. Cross the dam and scramble up to the buttress of your choice - the routes are 10 to 20 minutes from the parking.

Paul Clarke looking apprehensive on *Swift and Sure* (E5 6b) - *page 61* - Widdop. Photo: Dave Musgrove

Mystery Buttress

The fine buttress above the dam is home to a good collection of rather devious routes that include some of the longest in the area. Sadly the crag is green for much of the year and many of the holds are very rounded.

1 Ordinary Route . . . . VDiff
30m. An 'ordinary route' but an extraordinary outing that spirals its way up the cliff. The old-timers used to do it in five separate pitches and used peg belays at several of the stances. It covers some interesting ground and includes a dreaded stomach-traverse. Above the stomach-traverse climb past the 'Bull's Horns' and exit rightwards from the highest (4th) ledge.
FA. Herbert Hartley 1929

2 Birtwhistle's Crack . . . . VS 4c
24m. From *Ordinary Route*, continue up the awkward crack, moving left to its continuation. Finish up the easier groove above.
FA. Arthur Birtwhistle 1936

3 Ordinary Route Direct . . . . . VDiff
28m. Climb the disjointed groove to the right joining *Ordinary Route* at the 2nd Ledge.

4 The Three Cs . . . . . VS 4c
30m. A varied outing with stances available along the way, or use double ropes. Climb though bulges to the 2nd Ledge (*Centipede*) then move right under the overhang to a wall which is climbed on small holds (*Cascara* - a laxative) to the 3rd Ledge on the left. Follow the ramp to the jutting lump of *The Corbel* and pass this awkwardly to access the final easy corner.
FA. (The Corbel) Herbert Hartley 1929. FA. (Centipede) Frank Simpson 1939

5 The Flake Direct E1 5b
10m. The direct finish. Reaching the final flake is bold.
FA. Arthur Dolphin 1948

6 Krypton Route . . . . S 4a
30m. Pull over the roof into the right-facing groove, up this then the face to the left to the 3rd Ledge. A short wall leads to the 4th Ledge. The easiest escape from here is to move right to the finish of the *Ordinary Route*.
FA. Herbert Hartley 1929

7 The Flake Finish . . . . . . VS 4b
10m. Move left to access the exposed flake and sprint up it.

8 The Layback Finish . . VS 4c
10m. The short lived crack above the 4th Ledge is hard.
FA. Herbert Hartley 1929

9 The Krypton Eliminate . . E1 5b
20m. The right edge of the main buttress gives a worthwhile pitch - rounded and quite bold, big cams help.
FA. Allan Allsop 1948

'Crag X'
Widdop was one of the last major gritstone cliffs to be developed. When it was discovered by Herbert Hartley and Maurice Linnel in 1928 they decided to keep the place a secret just in case the hotshots of the day (Fred Piggott and Morley Wood in particular) nipped in and grabbed all the glory. To this end they duly named the biggest piece of rock Mystery Buttress - some things never change.

⑩ The Gully . . . . [ ] **Diff**
18m. The gully that bounds the right-hand side of the cliff gives an easy climb, or an awkward way down.

⑪ Wrinkly Arete . . . . 🔲 🔲 [ ] **HVS 5a**
14m. The right arete of the gully is perhaps a good choice for the older climber.
FA. Derek Hargreaves 1986

⑫ Wrinkled Wall Direct . . . 🔲 🔲 [ ] **VS 4b**
14m. Climb the face to a ledge then balance right to a small groove to finish.

⑬ Wrinkled Wall . . . . 🔲 🔲 [ ] **HVD**
14m. Climb the crack then, from the ledge on the right, trend left to the centre of the face and finish direct.
FA. Allan Allsop 1936

Overhang Buttress
70m across the hillside is Overhang Buttress with its impressive set of roofs.

⑭ Hammertime . . . . . 🔲 🔲 🔲 [ ] **E6 6b**
6m. A bold micro route up the bulging rib at the left edge. It is often done as a highball boulder problem - **V6**.
FA. Roy Healey 1999

⑮ Canine Fruitbat . . . . 🔲 🔲 🔲 [ ] **E5 6b**
14m. Imposing climbing up the left-hand side of the main buttress. Climb the juggy wall to a rest on the left then make hard moves up and right to reach a pocket then a poor break. One more hard move remains.
FA. Mark Radtke 1996

⑯ Felicity . . . . 🔲 [ ] **HVS 5a**
10m. The wide leaning crack feels like a refugee from Ramshaw.
FA. J.Greaves 1947

⑰ Ceiling Crack . . . . 🔲 🔲 🔲 🔲 [ ] **E2 5c**
14m. Swing right along the crusty flakes to reach solid jams in the upper crack, finish with aplomb. A memorable experience, though less so than when it was VS!
FA. Don Whillans 1955

Overhang Buttress
The central section of rock at Widdop takes the form a series of imposing overhangs. In general the routes are either hard overhangs or awkward green cracks.

⑱ Thirty Seconds Over Winterland
. . . . 🔲 🔲 🔲 [ ] **E5 6b**
14m. The right-hand crack is approached from below with great difficulty to reach (marginally) easier jamming. Originally it was started from the right - worthwhile at **E4 6a** (once graded HVS!).
FA. Mike Hammill 1974. FA. (Direct Start) Jerry Peel 1996

⑲ Slime Chimney . . . . [ ] **VDiff**
14m. The green groove and chimney that skirts the right side of the biggest overhangs.
FA. Allan Allsop 1936

⑳ Slime Chimney Direct . . . . . 🔲 [ ] **HVS 5b**
12m. Power up the nose on the right then step into the chimney.

㉑ VDiff Crack . . . . 🔲 [ ] **HVD**
14m. The wide crack is an awkward customer.

㉒ Easy Chimney . . . . [ ] **Mod**
14m. The easy chimney!

㉓ Gallon Drunk . . . . 🔲 🔲 [ ] **HVS 5b**
10m. Stagger up the side wall of the buttress, trending right.
FA. Derek Hargreaves 1998

㉔ Stage Fright . . . . . . 🔲 🔲 🔲 [ ] **E3 6a**
12m. Climb the bulge above the slabby groove, then move left and balance up the rounded arete. Bold and worthwhile.
FA. Roy Healy 1986

㉕ Celebrity Buttress . . . . 🔲 [ ] **VS 5a**
12m. Climb the awkward left-slanting crack to a ledge then finish up the fine jamming crack. A more elegant start is possible up the ramp on the left.
FA. Arthur Birtwhistle 1936

㉖ Libel . . . . [ ] **VS 5a**
14m. Use any start to reach the base of the crack then traverse round right to a groove in the side wall.
FA. David Jackson 1939

Pule Hill · Shooter's · Heptonstall · Widdop · Earl Crag · Ilkley · The Chevin · Caley · Almscliff · Eastby · Crookrise · Rylstone · Simon's Seat · Brimham · Eavestones · Slipstones · Crag Willas · Giddeigh

Piton Crack

Not much sun | 18 min | Green | Windy

Pete Robins finds the last of the chipped holds that allow the topping out on the cliff's strangest outing *Artificial Route* (VS 4c) *opposite.* Photo: Chris Craggs

Piton Crack

High up on the hillside is the main bulk of Purgatory Buttress. To the left, the diminutive green face of Piton Crack has a few tiny but technical outings.

1 Scuppered . . . . **HVS 5c**
6m. The left-slanting groove was pegged less often than its near neighbour to the right.
FA. Derek Hargreaves 1998

2 Forty Calorie Cocoa. . . . **E3 6a**
6m. Trend right to access the shallow scoop then up this warily.
FA. Derek Hargreaves 1998

3 Piton Crack **E1 5b**
8m. The left-slanting and once-pegged crack is tenuous and protection is indifferent.
FA. Jerry Peel 1977

4 Mantel Madness. **E3 6a**
8m. Trend right to a shallow groove, climb this and finish direct with difficulty, or cop out rightwards.

Purgatory Buttress

To the right is the main Purgatory Buttress with its magnificent blank front face.

5 Argon/The Final Step. . . . **E3 6a**
30m. A girdle of this fine buttress. Start round the arete and traverse out right across the slab and round onto *Artificial Route (Argon).* Follow this to the roof then traverse the break all the way out to the right arete and a finish (*The Final Step*).
FA. (Argon) Alan Austin 1974. FA. (The Final Step) Don Eastham 1985

6 Pulp Friction **E3 6a**
20m. The scary left arete of the buttress until relief arrives in the form of *Artificial Route* and its chipped holds.
FA. P.Dudgeon 1995

The Widdop Boulders

If you arrive at the crag and the routes do look cold and uninviting, the seven big boulders sat below the right-hand end of the crag will generally be found to be clean and dry and may even be sitting in sunshine. They contain dozens of excellent problems and micro routes. Full details in *YMC Yorkshire Gritstone* (1998) or the *Yorkshire Gritstone Bouldering - Vol. 1* (2008).

Pule Hill • Shooters • Heptonstall • Widdop • Earl Crag • Ilkley • The Chevin • Caley • Almscliff • Eastby • Crookrise • Rylstone • Simon's Seat • Brimham • Eavestones • Slipstones • Crag Willas • Guisecliff

The Guinea Pig

Descent

Piton Crack - 10m

Pule Hill
Shooter's
Hepton Tor
Widdop
Earl Crag
Ilkley
The Chevin
Caley
Almscliff
Eastby
Crookrise
Rylstone
Simon's Seat
Brimham
Ravenstones
Slipstones
Crag Willas
Guisecliff

7 Sisyphus . . . . 1 ☒ **E5 6a**
20m. Climb direct to the runners on *Artificial Route* then step right and climb the scoop to the triangular roof. Pass this to reach the top break and then finish direct.
FA. Paul Wheeler 2002

8 Afternoon Delight . . . . . 1 ☒ **E4 6a**
24m. Follow *Sisyphus* to the junction with *Artificial Route* then step right and balance across the line that runs across the wall, passing pockets and a couple of old bolts, until an escape into the chimney is possible.
FA. Jerry Peel 1977

9 Swift and Sure . ☒☒☒☒ **E5 6b**
20m. One of the best hard routes on Yorkshire Grit offering superb but harrowing climbing crossing *Artificial Route* at its runner. Above this move out right then climb boldly to a short crack (more runners) then exit left with difficulty. *Photo on page 57.*
FA. Jerry Peel 1984

10 Artificial Route . . . . . . ☒☒ **VS 4c**
22m. Bizarre in the extreme but oddly enjoyable too. Follow the chipped ladder to the top left edge of the face then exit round to the left via the well hidden final chipped holds. *Photo opposite.*
FA. Jack Umpleby late 1940s. There are reports that suggest it may have been someone else who climbed this first.

11 Purgatory Problem . ☒☒☒ **E6 6b**
18m. Follow the old bolt holes to a pair of ancient bolts then move right to the arete. Either escape into the chimney or, much better, climb the bold arete above. A fine route that has stopped a few notables.
FA. Martin Atkinson 1983. FA. (Direct Finish) Dougie Hall 1988

Purgatory Buttress
Originally known as Guinea Pig Buttress (look at the boulder on its crest) this is arguably the finest piece of rock at Widdop - pity that most of the routes are so damn hard. Lower grade climbers can call in for the tough rift of *Purgatory Chimney* (it's all in the name) or the weird chipped line of holds that is *Artificial Route*. All of the rest of the routes are the preserve of the talented and bold. *Reservoir Dogs* and *Widdop Wall* in particular offer magnificent challenges that see few ascents.

12 Purgatory Chimney . . . . . . 1 **VDiff**
16m. The rift is awkward, especially for those of a fuller figure who may dispute the grade of the initial fissure.
FA. Maurice Linnel (of Stanage's Manchester Buttress fame) late 1920s

13 Reservoir Dogs . . . . Top 50 ☒☒ **E8 7a**
14m. The magnificent arete tapering to a shark's fin hanging in space is a stern test of any cragsman's ability. As appears to be so often the case with classic grit aretes, there are runners available in the half-height pockets. The loss of pebbles after the third ascent has made it harder - it may be unrepeated in this state.
FA. Robin Barker (southern raider) 1995

14 Widdop Wall . . . . . ☒☒☒ **E9 7a**
14m. The imposing impending wall has runners at half-height again but not much in the way of grips. The finish is especially taxing.
FA. John Dunne 1998. He had done the upper part the year before starting to the left - this was called Savage Earth.

	No star	⚘	⚘⚘	⚘⚘⚘
Mod to S	7	2	-	-
HS to HVS	5	10	4	2
E1 to E3	5	5	5	1
E4 and up	2	7	5	2

One of Yorkshire's finest gritstone cliffs, though its rather remote setting, coupled to its altitude and aspect, means the place doesn't always see the traffic it really deserves. Earl Crag takes the form of a series of interesting buttresses that look northwards, below the twin monuments of Lund's Tower and Wainman's Pinnacle, out towards the upper Aire valley and on to Skipton.

Conditions

The crag faces due north and, set at an altitude of 350m, it is not a great venue when the weather is out of sorts. It is at its very best after a good dry spell, with fine summer evenings being the prime time. Despite this it can offer some shelter from strong south westerlies and it dries out quicker than might be expected. The place is worth a look after any decent spell of weather whatever the time of year.

Approach

A minor road (Dick Lane) runs from Cowling, passing the left edge of the cliff, and on across the moors to Oakworth. Just before the crest of the moor, there is limited parking by the small quarry at the left (eastern) end of the cliff - please park considerately, especially if the weather is good. A track leads through the quarry workings and onto the moor; smaller paths run along the base of the cliff. Alternatively, continue up the hill and take the first right turn into Buckstone Lane then follow this to reach a small car park on the right, level with Wainman's Pinnacle. A path leads from here to the monument.

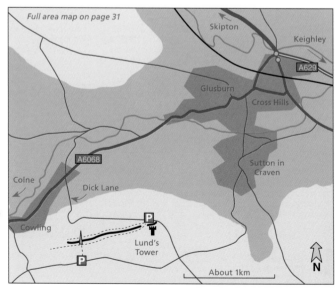

Full area map on page 31

Colin Binks in a superb position on *Tiger Wall* (VS 4c) - *page 67* the classic route of its grade at Earl Crag. Photo: Chris Craggs

Erasor Slab

The first section of rock encountered is home to a few problems. Further right is an area consisting of two steep walls, the right-hand one has a short slumped slab in front of it. The *Erasor* routes are the most popular here but the whole area sees a fair amount of action.

❶ Mind Bomb . . . . . . 🏔️🧗☁️ ⬜ **E7 6c**
8m. The open groove in the undercut arete is hard and serious.
FA. Dave Pegg 1989

❷ Early Riser . . . . . . 🏔️☁️📖 ⬜ **E5 6a**
8m. The narrow ramp cutting rightwards up the centre of the face is a classic. Balancy and unprotected - scary stuff.
FA. Al Manson 1974

❸ Hatchet Crack . . . . 🧗 ⬜ **E3 5c**
10m. A grubby off-width in the back of the bay is a character building exercise.
FA. Ken Wood 1971

❹ The Kipper . . . . 🏔️☁️📙 ⬜ **E4 6b**
18m. Boulder out the bulges to reach the ledge (**V4 6b**) then continue up the fine arete on its right-hand side. Bold.
FA. Ron Fawcett 1976

❺ Erasor Slab . . . . . . 🏔️🧗📖 ⬜ **HVS 5b**
10m. Climb the slab to the break, fidget left then stretch for the ledge. Walk off or, much better, do *Fishladder*.
FA. Dennis Gray 1952

❻ Erasor Slab Direct . . . . . 🧗📖 ⬜ **V3 (6a)**
Head straight up the steepening slab. Only really one move but its a sweet little rockover.
FA. John Syrett 1972

The rest of the climbs take the rock above the halfway ledge, and the short wall to its right. They can be most easily reached by scrambling round to the right.

❼ Fishladder . . . . 🏔️☁️ ⬜ **E1 5b**
8m. From the ledge, climb onto the arete and balance awkwardly round the corner to access the straightforward ramp. Often dirty.
FA. Alan Austin 1960

❽ Edge of Darkness 🏔️🧗☁️🧗 ⬜ **E5 6c**
6m. The thin seam in the centre of the wall is desperate.
FA. Jerry Peel 1976

❾ Problem Rib . . . . . 🏔️🧗☁️ ⬜ **V1 (5b)**
The rib is problematical and superb. Escape right along the break into the gully for the problem. If leading, then a runner in the high break is useful for the **E1** version. Originally given VS!
FA. John Syrett 1971

❿ Grey Wall . . . . 🏔️🧗📙 ⬜ **HS 5a**
8m. A tricky start reaches better holds. Move right along the break to exit. A direct finish is **E1 5b**. The arete to the left is **V2**.

⓫ Mantelshelf Slab . . 🏔️🧗📙 ⬜ **HS 4b**
8m. The pocketed slab (just off the topo) gives a pleasant pitch finishing with the expected move.

Little Greeny

50m across the slope to the right, past a shorter wall is a recess under a green wall and above a pedestal.

⓬ Pedestal Wall . . . . 🧗 ⬜ **E3 6a**
6m. From the top of the pedestal, trend left up the wall to gain and climb the shallow groove, with a bit of a pop for the top.
FA. Jerry Peel 1988

⓭ Pedestal Rib . . . . 🏔️☁️ ⬜ **HVS 4c**
6m. From the pedestal, climb the wall then move right around the arete to finish. Finishing direct to the left is **E2 6a**.
FA. Allan Austin 1958

⓮ Pedestal Rib Direct . . . . 📙🧗 ⬜ **V3 (6a)**
Dyno to the hole. Either jump off or continue up to gain the original.

⓯ Overhanging Wall . . . . 🏔️ ⬜ **HS 4b**
8m. Climb the rib to a ledge then move left to finish.
FA. Neville Drasdo late 1950s

⓰ Overhanging Wall Direct Finish
. . . . 🧗📙 ⬜ **E4 6a**
8m. Cross the roof above the start with faith.
FA. Derek Hargreaves 1981. Given HVS for years!

⓱ Awkward Crack . . . . ⬜ **S 4b**
8m. The well named crack in the angle is often dirty too.
FA. Allan Austin 1958

Little Greeny

A long jumbled section of short walls, jutting buttresses and steep cracks. There are several worthwhile routes and classy boulder problems here though it is seldom busy.

18 Cave Traverse . . . . HVS 5a
12m. Climb the tricky groove to the break then follow this rightwards to a nice finish on the arete.
FA. Ken Wood 1973

19 Cave Wall . . . . VS 4b
10m. A counter diagonal to the last route, sadly the finish is often too grubby to be worthwhile.
FA. Allan Austin 1958

20 Deep Chimney . . . . Diff
10m. The profound rift.

21 Little Greeny E2 5c
10m. The centre of the narrow face to the right.
FA. John Syrett 1973. The same year he did Big Greeny at Almscliff.

22 Duke of Earl E4 6b
8m. The blunt rib has a hard move at the top.
FA. Steve Coates 1997

23 Flake Crack . . . . VS 5a
10m. A good jamming problem up the hanging crack.
FA. Allan Austin 1958

24 Indicator Crack . . . . S 4a
10m. The steep right-hand crack can be started direct or by a traverse from the right. Either way, finish past the jutting 'indicator'.
FA. Allan Allsopp late 1940s

25 Time to Go . . . . HVS 5a
10m. The leaning face gives a worthwhile pitch.

26 Slab Corner . . . . VDiff
8m. Follow the scratched holds up the right edge of the slab.

There is some good bouldering on the blocks above Little Greeny.

27 Hanging Crack V5 (6b)
The crack on the left-hand side wall is desperate.

28 Sloping Beauty V8
The right-hand side wall using a sloper to gain the top.

29 Trick Arete V4 (6b)
A good little arete problem.

Butterfly Crack

About 100m further to the right are a diagonal track and wall, just beyond these is a buttress with a prominent central groove with a shot-holed wall to its right.

30 Green Rib V3 (6a)
The rib is climbed on its right-hand side.
FA. Ken Wood 1971

31 Green Rib Right-hand V5 (6b)
Use pockets and edges to gain the arete.

32 Slim Shady V11
The thin wall to a break. Jump off.

33 Butterfly Crack . . . . . . VS 4c
8m. The tough crack in the angle. Despite the name, front crawl is an altogether better technique.
FA. Allan Austin 1958

34 Superfly V8
The arete and shot-holes are often dirty. The wall to the left is the neglected **Butterfly Wall** which is around **V7** when clean.

35 Shothole Ridge . . . . VS 4c
8m. Gain it with difficulty then follow the slab leftwards - a bit bold - to a finish up the left-hand arete. Variations are numerous.
FA. Allan Austin 1958

Butterfly Crack

Descent

Tiger Wall - adjacent

Earl Buttress

Arguably the best bit of rock on the crag with a small but excellent set of climbs covering the grade spectrum. Sadly the buttress is often a bit green, though it comes into its own on hot summer days after a decent dry spell.

1 Abstract Attitude E5 6b
20m. The taxing shallow groove in the wall to the left of the arete is gained from the left. The upper wall is easier.
FA. Martin Wood 1991

2 Desert Island Arete . E6 6c
20m. The soaring left arete of the buttress has a highly technical start and a memorable finish, with tough moves to reach the final break, miles above the gear. Continuing straight up the arete is **Last Blasphemy, E7 6c**.
FA. (DIA) Jerry Peel 1986 (soloed!)

3 DIA Start V7
The start is a classic problem in its own right. Start on the right and improvise around to the left-hand side.

4 Dougie Lampkin ... E6 6c
20m. An imposing wall which is started by traversing in from *Viscount's Route*. Climb the wall to a ledge then climb a short crack to the final break, finishing up the arete just to the right.
FA. Ben Bransby 2001

5 Viscount's Route ...... HVS 5a
20m. Gain the hanging crack from the right by a swift hand-traverse (or direct at **5b**) and jam it to a possible stance on the big ledge. Finish up the groove to a tricky exit.
FA. Tom Cranfield 1949

6 Perch Wall .... HVS 5b
22m. Start as for *Viscount's Route* then follow the break out towards the arete before climbing to the mid-height ledge. Finish up the broad rib above.
FA. Tom Cranfield 1950

7 Earl Crack .... VS 4c
20m. The wide corner-crack is a must-do line, giving laybacking bridging and jamming, generally with good gear.
FA. Arthur Dolphin 1949

8 Earl Buttress E2 5c
20m. Fine climbing up the face to the right of the crack. Approach from the right and climb the face then layback powerfully up the thin crack to reach juggy romping on the upper wall.
FA. John Syrett 1971

9 Evasion E1 5b
12m. Layback through the bulging start to gain the arete and continue with care. Easier for the lanky.
FA. Ken Wood 1975

10 Trite Rib E3 5c
12m. The right arete of the buttress is gained from the right. Move onto the front face and balance up the scoop. A **Direct Start** up the arete is **V8**.
FA. Ken Wood 1975

11 Chockstone Crack .... S 4a
8m. The wide crack in the angle.

Tiger Wall

Across the grassy gully is the fine jutting prow of the well positioned classic of Tiger Wall and several other worthwhile routes, a few in the lower grades.

12 Prow Chimney .... Diff
8m. The deep rift on the left side of the prow.

13 Prow Buttress .... HVD 3c
14m. Climb the centre of the face until it is possible to traverse out to the left arete. Up this for a couple of moves then finish up the groove on the right.

Tiger Wall   Sour Grapes

Descent

The Monument - 5 mins

Pule Hill · Shooter's · Heptonstall · Widdop · **Earl Crag** · Ilkley · The Chevin · Caley · Almscliff · Eastby · Crookrise · Rylstone · Simon's Seat · Brimham · Earestones · Slipstones · Crag Willas · Goldsbrugh

⑭ Jock Jones . . . . VS 4c
10m. A worthwhile line up the centre of the face.
FA. Neil Herbert 1993

⑮ Tiger Wall . . . . Top 50 VS 4c
14m. Superbly positioned climbing up the centre of the face then out to the dramatic, hanging right-hand arete. *Photo on page 63.*
FA. Arthur Dolphin 1949

⑯ Tiger Traverse . . . . . . VS 4c
14m. The horizontal break high on the right-hand side of the face gives a good exposed pitch. Hand traversing the lower break is a pumpy **HVS 5a**.
FA. possibly Arthur Dolphin 1943. He called it Demon Traverse.

⑰ The Extinguisher. . . . . Diff
8m. The awkward narrowing chimney on the right. A through-route is available for slim caving types.

⑱ Bring Your Own Bombs . . . . HVS 5b
8m. The brushed rib on the left side of *Mousehole Slab*, is tackled direct to reach a hole then the top.
FA. Paul Wheeler 2005

⑲ Mousehole Slab . . . VS 4b
8m. A mini *Three Pebble Slab* maybe. Head out right onto a ledge then balance up the slab passing the useful orifice (runner OR foothold) that gives the route its name.
FA. Arthur Dolphin 1958

⑳ Rat Juggling E1 5a
8m. The rib on the right is bold and precarious.
FA. Al Manson 1975

㉑ Rat au Vin V3 (6a)
Layback the technically tasty arete.
FA. Mike Hammill 1975

Tiger Wall
The prominent jutting snout is home to a classic VS and a couple of marginally less worthy offerings. The short walls to the right have some taxing but short lived test-pieces and a couple of classic problems.

㉒ Sweet Apples E4 6b
8m. Pull over the undercut base to access the scary arete.
FA. Jerry Peel 1984

㉓ Sour Grapes E3 6a
8m. Gain the niche and ensuing crack with difficulty, then finish up the wall. If you can't do the start, don't worry, the rest is crap.
FA. Mike Hammill 1975

㉔ Boundary Wall . . . . HVS 5b
6m. Climb the face above the restored wall, using it with care.
FA. Alan Austin 1958

㉕ Grape Nut V8
A fine problem up the arete. Jumping from the block onto the good hold drops the grade to **V6**.
FA. Derek Hargreaves 1984

㉖ Wall Chimney. . . . . Diff
6m. The rift is the last feature of any consequence.

㉗ Krafty V10
The undercut arete gives a very hard problem.

Further to the right is the other man-made tower; Wainman's Pinnacle. The rocks around its base have long been a popular bouldering venue. Check Yorkshire Gritstone Bouldering - Vol. 1 (2008) for full details.

	No star	{1}	{2}	{3}
Mod to S	10	14	4	2
HS to HVS	17	23	14	4
E1 to E3	6	19	5	1
E4 and up	3	12	8	5

Ilkley has been a popular destination for generations of climbers. Sitting proudly above the town of the same name, the crag almost seems to have adopted the character of a dour Yorkshire man - the Quarry can be dark cold and oppressive, especially in high winds; the Cow and Calf are sturdy and uncompromising; and the remote edge of Rocky Valley is understated and steeped in history. As with Yorkshire men, be patient and tackle them on your terms and you could well be rewarded.

The most famous routes are on the Cow with *Milky Way* and *New Statesmen* being great test-pieces of their eras. The Cow's smaller sidekick has some popular bouldering and micro-routes. Probably the least attractive of Ilkley's venues is the Quarry which manages to feel cold and desolate even on summer days. Bits of the Quarry have collapsed over the years and the council's removal of the rock above *Wellington Crack* has added to the general air of neglect. Despite this, there are some excellent climbs and a day spent here should be rewarded with a healthy set of ticks. Rocky Valley just over the hill adds some more remote feeling climbs to the mix.

The accessibility of Ilkley means that it has long been a forcing ground and the first ascent names and dates of some of the climbs make impressive reading. Just remember that hat.

Conditions
The crag faces north east and doesn't get a great deal of sun, though the right-hand side wall of the quarry is the exception to this, hence its popularity.

Approach
There a large car park (tea waggon normally in-situ) opposite the Cow and Calf pub, a short walk from the entrance to the quarry, the big buttress of the Cow and the huge boulder of the Calf. Rocky Valley lies hidden over the ridge and is reached in 10 minutes from the parking by tracks that pass either side of the quarry entrance, then head across the moor.

Side tabs: Pule Hill, Shooter's, Heptonstall, Widdop, Earl Crag, Ilkley, The Chevin, Caley, Almscliff, Eastby, Crookrise, Rylstone, Simon's Seat, Brimham, Eavestone, Slipstones, Crag Willas, Goldsbrgh

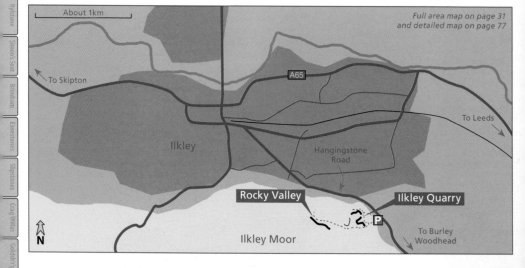

Full area map on page 31 and detailed map on page 77

About 1km

To Skipton

A65

To Leeds

Ilkley

Hangingstone Road

Rocky Valley   Ilkley Quarry

P

To Burley Woodhead

Ilkley Moor

N

Heading across the traverse on *Walewska* (VS 4c) - *page 73* - in the Quarry at Ilkley. Photo: Dave Musgrove

Doris's Route

To the left of the entrance to the Quarry there are a couple of faces with an interesting selection of climbs. The routes often look greener than they actually are.

1 Sinister Cracks . . . . VDiff
12m. Move right from the large block to a ledge on the arete. Follow the crack above then the slab just to the right.

2 Bald Pate E1 5a
18m. Start as for *Sinister Cracks* but follow the break that bisects the slab away towards the right arete.
FA. John Ball early 1940s. A peg belay was used part way along the traverse and there was no chipped escape route back then.

3 Doris's Route . . . . . S 3c
18m. Mild but bold and well chipped. Start under *Sinister Cracks* and gain the arete on the right then continue following the chipped holds out to the centre of the face. Finish direct with care. **The Direct Start, V9**, is a fearsome boulder problem.
FA. Probably Dave Gibbons (the Ilkley Chiseller) mid 1950s
FA. (Direct Start) John Dunne 1997

4 Sinister Rib E3 5b
14m. Gain the hanging rib direct (chipped holds) and climb to the break. The upper arete feels bold, especially as the top approaches and the runners recede. Not bad for its day.
FA. George Steele 1959

5 Black Ball E3 5c
14m. Start up *Sinister Rib* but shuffle right then pad up the bald, bold slab. A bit blinkered but very engrossing.
FA. Chris Bray 1978

6 Bald Pate Superdirect E6 6c
12m. The hanging right arete of the block is climbed on its front face and has a highball finish.
FA. Andy Brown 1980

7 Bald Pate Direct E2 5b
12m. Fine climbing. From the ledge on the right, traverse the wall to the arete then step boldly up and round to join *Bald Pate*.
FA. Neville Drasdo 1957

8 Deathwatch E7 6b
10m. Tackle the side wall as directly as the line of holds allows.
FA. John Dunne 1986. It has been soloed by James Pearson using a head torch (for aid?).

To the right the gully that separates the two walls provides a way down with a bit of scrambling.

9 Grand as Owt E3 6a
10m. The arete on its right-hand side past indifferent runners.
FA. Adi Gill 1997

10 Serendipity E2 5b
10m. From blocks, climb to and up the crack. Might need de-grassing early in the season.
FA. Iain Edwards 1974

11 Piton Wall . . . . HVS 5a
12m. Sprint up the ramp (scary) to jugs, balance up using a second ramp and finish direct.
FFA. Allan Austin (two pegs runners - the old aid pegs) 1956

12 Transparent Wall . . . . . HVS 5a
12m. Climb the once-pegged crack then trend left past a second crack and a useful pocket. Finish more easily. Sadly, the route is often green, so if you find it clean, get it done.
FA. Brian Evans 1957

13 Sticky Fingers E2 5c
12m. The right-hand crack is followed with a short loop out left in its central section. The direct version is **6a**.
FA. Iain Edwards 1975

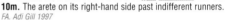

Pule Hill · Shooter's · Heptonstall · Widdop · Earl Crag · Ilkley · The Chevin · Caley · Almscliff · Eastby · Crookrise · Rylstone · Simon's Seat · Brimham · Eavestones · Slipstones · Crag Willas · Goldsbro'gh

Not much sun | 3 min | Green | Windy

① Highfield Corner . . . . . . HVS 5a
14m. Follow the wide slanting crack, or the start of *Nailbite*, until a ledge on the left can be gained. Move back right and continue precariously to a tricky shelving exit.
FA. John Ball 1941

② Nailbite . . . . VDiff
14m. Climb the widening vertical rift then stay with the right-slanting crack and finish up its wide upper section.

③ Central Wall E1 5b
14m. Climb the crack that splits the bulge (or boulder up the wall to the right) then the steep and bold arete on the right.
FA. Arthur Dolphin 1946

④ Sand Chimney . . . . VDiff
14m. The left-hand curving cleft is awkward, especially the start. Its alternative name of *Fat Man's Misery* gives the clue as to why. A 'classic of its genre' and we all know what that means!

⑤ Demolition Derby . . HS 4a
14m. The right-hand cleft was a semi-classic Diff (*Wellington Chimney*) that was severely affected by the council's 'stabilisation work'. Climb the ridge then the wide crack left of the huge block to a leftwards exit.
FA. Craig Watson 2000

⑥ Wellington Crack E4 5c
16m. The stunning crack is a classic product of the 70s. The crack is relentless, but the gear is good throughout, stopping to place it is the only problem. If successful, it is time to head south for a crack at *London Wall*, which many think is about the same.
FA. Arthur Dolphin 1948. FFA. Pete Livesey 1973 (initially with 1 rest, then a little later, all free).

⑦ Loaded E8 7a
18m. Climb *Wellington Crack* to just above mid-height, load the crack with all the gear you have (you won't need it above) then head out right to the arete and a desperate finish.
FA. John Dunne 1997

⑧ Snap Decision . E7 6c
16m. The sinuous and committing line up the wall, passing two old peg runners, to a taxing exit.
FA. John Dunne 1986

Wellington Crack
The left wall of the quarry has one outstanding feature - the searing thin crack that was the crag's most popular aid route for 25 years. The buttress used to be capped by a large overhang which was removed by the local council in 2000 due to it being perceived a danger.

⑨ Curving Cracks . . . . VS 5a
18m. Climb the awkward curving crack, complete with jammed blocks, to ledges and a potential stance. Finish up the thinner crack in the upper wall to the right of the corner.
FA. Arthur Dolphin 1947

⑩ Gibbon's Wall . . . . HS 4c
8m. A short line of chipped holds.

⑪ Letterbox Crack . . . . HS 4b
8m. The tricky wide crack in the right-hand side of the wall, passing a useful letterbox just below the top.

⑫ Peg Wall V4 (6b)
A boulder problem up the wall. The letterbox on the previous route is used near the top, without, it is a good **V6** eliminate.
FA. Ron Fawcett 1976

⑬ Peg Crack . . . . HVS 5a
8m. A short worthwhile problem up the thin crack. Worth **V0**.
FA. Alan Swithenbank 1962

The two routes above the ledge are gained by one of the lower routes, or the easy crack/ramp on the left.

⑭ High Street E3 5c
10m. Move out left to access a ramp. Follow this leftwards into increasingly serious territory until it is possible to reach up and right for jugs. Step left to finish.
FA. Allan Austin 1956

⑮ Curving Corner . . . . HVS 5b
8m. The short rib above the centre of the ledge. Steep and safe.
FA. Arthur Dolphin 1947

Pole Hill · Shooters · Heptonstall · Widdop · Earl Crag · **Ilkley** · The Chevin · Caley · Almscliff · Eastby · Crookrise · Rylstone · Simon's Seat · Brimham · Eavestones · Slipstones · Crag Willas · Goldsb'r'gh

Guillotine

Descent

S Crack

Not much sun | 3 min | Green | Windy

Guillotine
At the back of the quarry is a small buttress featuring the sharp arete of *Guillotine* and a few other hard routes.

1 Quatre Bras **E1 5b**
6m. A short but exciting traverse of the break high on the left.
FA. John Hunt 2006

2 Guillotine **E6 6b**
12m. The unprotected axe-edge arete in the back of the quarry is climbed first left, then right. An old-style 'chop route'.
FA. Pete Livesey 1975

3 Big Buels **E6 6c**
12m. The right-hand side wall climbed leftwards, past a poor peg runner, then finished direct with haste.
FA. Dave Kells 1997

4 The Maid of Wakefield . **E4 6b**
9m. An exacting traverse. Start up the off-width corner, then traverse the thin horizontal crack all the way to *Guillotine*.
FA. John Hunt 2006

Josephine Area
To the right is a rockfall area that took a selection of routes with it when it headed towards the pub.

5 Propeller Wall **E4 5c**
14m. Starting behind the rockfall, climb the two part arete, passing the grubby break, to escalating difficulties on the upper wall.
FA. John Syrett 1972. He gave it VS!

6 Old Crack . . . . **VS 4b**
14m. The first crack in the wall gives a good strenuous pitch.

7 S Crack . . . . **VS 4c**
14m. A venerable and varied classic. The wide start is tricky, the rest is sustained and interesting.
FA. Allan Allsop 1939

8 Fairy Wall **E2 5c**
14m. The wall has a hard mantel move to reach the break (cam runner) and a sustained upper section.
FA. Iain Edwards 1979

9 Fairy Steps . . . . **HVD**
14m. Climb the ledgy rib (polished) to a position below the left-trending ramp. Gain this direct or, easier, by moving right first. Finish up the ramp.
FA. Charlie Salisbury 1935

10 V Chimney . . . . **VS 5a**
14m. The cleft between the two smoother walls has a torrid exit.

11 Josephine Super Direct . **VS 4b**
14m. Climb the twin cracks (awkward to start) then continue to the bird-limed cave. Finish up the bulging groove directly above.
FA. Arthur Dolphin 1941

12 Cherry Valley Rib . . . . . **HVS 5a**
14m. Follow the twinned cracks until the narrow buttress on the left can be gained, just above the jutting beak. Finish boldly up the rib.
FA. John Ball 1944

13 Josephine Direct . . . . **HS 4b**
16m. Follow the *Super Direct* to the poo, then make a tricky move right to another ledge and climb into the sentry box before finishing out left.
FA. Winston Farrer 1931

14 Little John **E1 5b**
14m. Balance across the tip of the slab to the rib, then move up and left to join *Josephine Direct*.
FA. Peter Tuke 1951

15 Little John Direct . . . . . **V5 (6b)**
A worthwhile problem up the rib.

Josephine

Descent

Josephine
The right-hand wall of the quarry has a great selection of routes with many of them in the ever-popular orange zone. There is a couple of days climbing here for most.

16 Short Circuit E2 5c
14m. The centre of the wall is tricky **(V2)** to start and bold to finish. From the ledges, finish up *Josephine Direct*.
FA. Peter Greenwood (1 peg runner) 1952

17 Josephine . . . . HS 4b
18m. Climb the left-trending cracks to reach ledges (possible stance for those practising multi-pitch). Continue left, passing the bulges precariously, to reach a recessed ledge and a leftward exit.
FA. Winston Farrer 1931. The route that started the Napoleon tradition.

18 Napoleon . . . . VS 4c
14m. Start as for *Josephine* but continue direct up the jamming cracks above the mid-route ledge.
FA. Charlie Salisbury 1938

19 Blucher . . . . VS 4c
14m. The right-hand crack and groove directly above the start of *Josephine* provide a worthwhile alternative finish.
FA. Charlie Salisbury 1938

20 Tufted Crack E1 5c
14m. The right-hand crack in the headwall looks innocuous enough but proves to be a struggle. Too fat for fingers and too thin for hands, you could always try and layback it.
FA. George Walker 1954. FFA. Allan Austin 1970

21 Spider Wall V2 (6a)
The right-hand side of the wall on slippery and unhelpful holds.

22 Earwig Rib V3 (6b)
The arete on the right is harder again.

23 Walewska . . . . Top 50 VS 4c
16m. Arguably the best VS in the quarry. Take a good supply of big stuff. Climb steeply to the first ledge then step right and climb to a spike at the start of a hand-traverse. Follow this left to gain the exit cracks. A more direct start up the steep crack just right is a strenuous **5a**. *Photo on page 69.*
FA. Charlie Salisbury 1938

24 Botterill's Crack . . . . . . HVS 5a
12m. The wide crack right of the quarry entrance is a struggle.
FA. Possibly Matthew Botterill (Fred's brother) early 1920s

25 Flake Crack . . . . HS 4a
10m. The short flake-crack on the far right to a rightward exit. The crack swallows gear and doesn't always give it back.

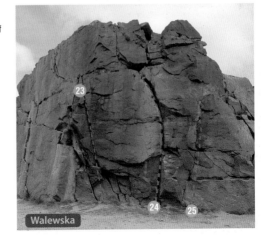

Walewska

Pule Hill · Shooter's · Heptonstall · Widdop · Earl Crag · Ilkley · The Chevin · Caley · Almscliff · Eastby · Crookrise · Rylstone · Simon's Seat · Brimham · Eavestones · Slipstones · Crag Willas · Goldsborough

Descent

Not much sun | 2 min | Green | Windy

The Cow

A huge and imposing block of gritstone, home to some of the hardest routes anywhere. Amongst the desperate deeds are a few easier climbs, so mere mortals can also enjoy this fine buttress.

❶ Old Spice . . . . ⬜ E2 5b
6m. The slabby side of the blunt arete. **V1** with enough mats.
FA. Charlie Salisbury 1962

❷ Baby Spice . . . . ⬜ V7
6m. The steep side of the arete is altogether more taxing.
FA. John Dunne 1997

❸ Ladybird . . . . ⬜ HVD
14m. Climb the slab left of the tree and its continuation - choice of routes, most in keeping with the grade is on the left - to the final ledge. Finish up the arete or the crack to its right.

❹ Cold Chisel . . . . ⬜ HS 4b
8m. The left edge of the slab on chipped holds.

❺ Chiseller . . . . ⬜ S 4a
10m. The centre of the chipped slab is popular.

❻ Gaz . . . . ⬜ S 4b
6m. A worthwhile extension to the last couple of climbs is the crack above and left of the slab.

❼ 'A' Climb . . . . ⬜ S 4b
24m. An excellent mini-expedition. Stances can be taken along the way. Climb *Chiseller* to its top then move round the arete and climb a groove. Cross the flake to a small ledge and then finish up the crucial crack above.
FA. Unknown but around 1900 and Ilkley's first recorded climb.

The next three climbs are on the short south east-facing wall of the Cow and are most easily reached up *Chiseller*.

❽ Cow Crack . . . . ⬜ VDiff
6m. The short hanging crack in the centre of the face is reached from a boulder.

❾ Cow Flap . . . . ⬜ VS 5a
6m. From the boulder, climb the face passing a tiny groove.
FA. David Williams 1992

❿ Cow Rib . . . . ⬜ HVS 5a
8m. The scary hanging arete is normally accessed via the lowest horizontal. A traditional Yorkshire VS and a good continuation to *Cow Udder*. Useful to see how good the old guys were.
FA. John Ball 1941

⓫ Ferdinand . . . . ⬜ HS 4a
16m. A more exciting finish to *'A' Climb*, traversing along the foot of the hanging slab (exposed) to a finish up the chipped slab on the far right.
FA. Allan Allsop 1939

⓬ Desperate Dan . . . . ⬜ E6 6b
10m. The arching left face of The Cow is accessed from a useful boulder. It gives tenuous laybacking above an extremely unfriendly landing. The given grade stands even with the use of the substantial padding that is normal nowadays.
FA. Ron Fawcett 1979

⓭ Cow Udder . . . . ⬜ E1 5a
10m. Spaced and small chipped holds up the shallow groove give a worrying pitch. Another VS from way back when.

The centre of the huge wall to the right is one of Grit's last great 'last great problems'.

14 New Statesman — E8 7a
18m. The soaring right arete of The Cow is magnificent and still sees few suitors 20 years on. Typically, the only gear available is above all the difficulties.
FA. John Dunne 1987

15 Milky Way — E6 6b
20m. A mega-classic, and pumpier than life itself, though at least this one has plenty of runners once you reach the start of the crack proper. Climb to the thin crack using pockets and follow it with great difficulty to the pigeon poo and collection of tat under the roof. All that remains between you and glory is the E5 roof-crack. Mega.
FA. Brian Evans 1956. FFA. Ron (too pumped to untie) Fawcett 1978

16 The Marine Who Slept In — E5 6a
16m. From the gully, trend left to gain a shallow groove. Climb the wall above (bold) to another groove under the roof, reach the sanctuary of the horizontal break and escape out right (the reverse of the start of *Hand Jive*).
FA. Jerry Peel 1987

17 Fast Forward — E6 6c
18m. Follow *The Marine...* until he slopes off right then attack the bulges above to a horrific sloping finish.
FA. John Dunne 1998

18 Hand Jive — E2 5c
16m. A pumpy and exposed trip along the horizontal break high on the right-hand side of the cliff.
FA. Ron Fawcett 1974

The Calf

The huge boulder that lies down the hill from the Cow has been used as a training ground for generations. It is home to much quality bouldering, particularly on the valley face. Although some of the problems listed below are high enough to get significant E-grades, they have all been given bouldering grades since most ascents now are made above a stack of mats and a rope is rarely seen. There are many more problems on the block which are covered in *Yorkshire Gritstone Bouldering - Vol. 1* (2008).

1 Pebble Groove .... ▨ ▨ ▨ ▭ **V1 (5b)**
The slabby groove on the left, hand traverse or walk up it.
FA. (walking way) John Cook 1943. FA. (hand-traverse) Dennis Gray 1956

2 Pebble Dash .. ▨ ▨ ▨ ▨ ▭ **V11**
The desperate slab by linking tiny and spaced pebbles. Highball and probably worth around **E7** or **E8**!
FA. Nigel Poustie 2007

3 Late Fever .... ▨ ▨ ▭ **V8**
From the big sausage-shaped pocket continue warily up the steep blank slab until holds arrive. Also given **E5 6c**.
FA. John Dunne 1986

4 Early Starter .... ▨ ▨ ▭ **V4 (6a)**
Start up the previous route but use a fortuitous pocket to exit rightwards into the easy upper section of *The Ring*.

5 Ringpiece .... ▨ ▮ ◧ ▭ **V9**
A sit-down start to the next route.

6 The Ring .... ▨ ▭ **V2 (5c)**
Using the prominent thread, access the easy groove.

7 Under the Stairs .... ▭ **V1 (5b)**
Right of the arete, pull over the bulge and saunter up the steps.

8 The Chipped Steps .... ▨ ▭ **Easy**
10m. The easiest route in the book.

9 Facet Wall .... ▨ ▭ **V5 (6b)**
The trio of pockets just right of the arete.
FA. Mike Hammill 1974. Given Mild Severe!

10 Super Set .... ▨ ▭ **V10**
The desperate and useless crack and poor pockets.
FA. John Dunne 1987

11 Car Park Crack .... ▨ ▭ **V2 (5c)**
Up the bum-shaped crack facing the car park.

12 Bonnington's Book Problem ▨ ▭ **V1 (5b)**
Wrestle with the big pockets in the arete.

13 Classic Dyno .... ▨ ▭ **V1 (5b)**
Leap from 2 small holds to the big pocket up and left.

14 Three More Reps ..... ▨ ▨ ▭ **V8**
The old peg crack leads right to holds and a gripping exit. Worth **E5**.
FA. John Dunne 1987

15 Bernie the Bolt .... ▨ ▨ ▭ **V9**
Start up the centre of the wall but trend left. Worth **E5**.
FA. Rob Gawthorpe 1985

16 Cindy Crawford ...... ▨ ▨ ▭ **V9**
A direct ascent of the overhanging valley face. Worth **E7**!
FA. John Dunne 2000

17 Gnome .... ▨ ▨ ▭ **V4 (6a)**
Tackle the pumpy leaning groove just left of the arete.
FA. Peter Greenwood 1952

Rocky Valley

Tucked away behind the busy Ilkley Quarry and its associated walls is a much quieter venue. Once very popular, these days more than likely, you will have the buttresses to yourself. Rocky Valley has a very different atmosphere from the Quarry and Cow and Calf, it might even be described as feeling remote. The best of the climbs here are good and if you haven't been already, it is well worth calling in.

Conditions - The crag faces north and so doesn't see much sunshine. It makes a good retreat on hot days, but can be cold and green if the weather's been poor.

Approach - Walk up to the left of the Quarry and skirt round its rim. A good path crosses a stream and leads to the edge of the upper moor, at which point Rocky Valley appears.

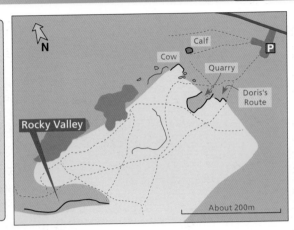

Buttress One

Buttress One is the first reached on the approach from the Quarry and is easily recognised by the fine finger-crack of *Beeline* splitting its left-hand side.

❶ Cooper's Slab . . . . VDiff
8m. The hanging slab is accessed from the left and climbed centrally, or near the arete. Mild but poorly protected and often green.
FA. Reg Cooper 1931

❷ Beeline . . . . HVS 5b
12m. The beckoning hanging thin-hand crack - tricky to reach and pumpy to climb. A little cracker. *Photo page 25.*
FA. Arthur Dolphin 1948

❸ Beyond the Fringe . . E5 6a
12m. The steep side wall has low runners and a hard move high up.
FA. Pete Livesey (side-runner) 1975

❹ Little 'A' Climb . . . . S 4a
10m. The disjointed cracks are pleasant enough, though not a patch on big brother over on the Cow.
FA. Probably Walter Greenwood pre-1911

❺ Dot's Crack . . . . HS 4b
8m. The groove and crack on the right. It improves with height.

Not much sun | 10 min | Green | Windy

Descent

Buttress Two

Across the slope from Buttress One are the twin pillars that make up Buttress Two (looks like two buttresses really) set above a steep bank. The most prominent feature is the wide rift of the old classic of *Stiction Chimney*. It tends to be green after wet weather, though the positions are rather grand.

1 Stiction . . . . VS 4c
9m. The pillar on the left was popular in antiquity.
FA. Probably Walter Greenwood pre-1911

2 Stiction Chimney . . . . . VDiff
9m. The widening rift is great fun, or a nightmare.
FA. Probably Walter Greenwood pre-1911

3 Nordwand E2 5b
10m. Climb the wall and rib to the break then pull onto the hanging arete above, and go.
FFA. Brian Evans 1957

4 Scoop and Hole . . . . . . HVS 5a
10m. Follow *Nordwand* but head right along the break to a jug at the base of a scoop/ramp. Heave aboard and wobble up the scoop.

5 Superb, Too Right . . E6 6c
10m. Access and climb the superb hanging flake in the middle of the blank wall. Finish direct.
FA. John Dunne 1986

6 Berserker. E2 5b
14m. Climb the arete above the blocks with a harder move to reach the break and runners. Follow the break leftwards and finish up the well positioned left arete.
FA. Mike Hammill 1975

7 The Strid . . . . HS 4b
10m. Up the slabby groove until the crack in the left wall can be reached (direct is a grade harder). Climb the crack to a ledge then finish up the slab above, or escape up the wide crack just left.
FA. Probably Walter Greenwood pre-1911

8 Flypaper . . . . VB (4c)
The pleasant slabby face on well marked holds.

9 V Groove . . . . VO+ (5b)
The awkward groove.

10 Ivor the Engine . . . . HVS 5c
8m. A hard start leads to more enjoyable moves up the face/arete above.

Buttress Three

Across the slope to the right are the twinned pair of Buttress Three and Four, split by a steep grassy gully that offers an easy, though often greasy, descent. The routes are most easily reached from directly below.

11 Black Chimney . . . . VDiff
8m. The short rift on the left has a tricky finish.
FA. Probably Walter Greenwood pre-1911

12 Three Slabs Route . . . . S 4a
12m. Pleasant balance climbing up the stacked slab.
FA. Probably Walter Greenwood pre-1911

13 Sod it V1 (5c)
The blunt arete is a nice problem.

14 Bogey Wall . . . . VO (5a)
Polished holds on the green wall lead to the ledge.

15 Hades . . . . HVS 5b
10m. The blunt arete above the two problems eases with height.
FA. Ron Hirst 1949

16 The Flake Climb . . . . S 4a
14m. A mini-classic with an exciting finish. Climb the easy groove leftwards to a cave recess. Exit left from this to reach a small ledge then use the perched flake to access the final rib.
FA. Probably Walter Greenwood pre-1911

17 Oak Tree Slab. . . . . S 4b
10m. Climb the slab (polished chips) to a roof which is passed left or right. Easy climbing remains.
FA. Probably Walter Greenwood pre-1911

18 Oak Tree Crack . . . . S 4a
10m. Layback the thin flake to the fat tree. A short chimney leads to easy ground on the previous climb.

Buttress Four

19 Sentry Box Direct . . . . HS 4b
10m. Climb the clean crack into the sentry box then continue direct - honest hard work. The original is started up the groove to the left and finished back into the left-hand groove - **S 4a**.
FA. Winston Farrer 1931. The original start was done 20 years earlier.

20 Kestrel . . . . VS 4c
10m. The wide left-leaning crack gives a more arduous approach to the niche. 'Old School' climbing at its best.
FA. Winston Farrer 1931. It had been reported as top-roped back in 1911!

21 Shock Horror . . E6 6b
12m. The blunt rib is approached from the left and climbed on a series of small and widely spaced pockets - don't fall! The start is a bit shoddy but it is the finish that really counts.
FA. Ron Fawcett 1977

22 Slide Zone E4 6a
12m. The side wall contains a shallow groove, this is hard as far as a good flake then easier but bolder above.
FA. Ron Fawcett 1977

23 Throstle's Nest Climb . . . . . HS 4b
10m. The main angle is awkward and can be dirty.
FA. early 1900s

24 Twin Cracks . . . . HS 4b
10m. The combined cracks. The right-hand one is most useful.
FA. Probably Walter Greenwood pre-1911

Buttress Three and Buttress Four
The most attractive and popular buttresses in the valley have a good selection of climbs across the grades. They tend to be cleaner than other bits of rock hereabouts.

25 Somersault . . . . VS 4c
10m. The single crack splitting the left-hand arete of the chimney. Lovely jamming and good protection.
FA. Probably Walter Greenwood pre-1911

26 Long Chimney . . . . Diff
12m. Scramble up the grass ledge below and left of the chimney. Stride round right into the chimney then follow it on good holds.
FA. Probably Walter Greenwood pre-1911

27 Long Chimney Direct . . . HVD
14m. Start right under the chimney and climb into a recess. Use the thin cracks in the roof to get out right, then trend up and left to gain the base of the main rift. Finish up this.
FA. Probably Walter Greenwood pre-1911

28 Walker's Hangover . . . . HVS 5a
14m. A fine long pitch. Start up *Long Chimney Direct* but continue up the slab and steepening crack to a ledge and rest. Step out left onto the exposed arete for a good finish.
FA. Ron Hirst 1952

29 Sound Box . . . . VS 4b
14m. Scramble up to an overhanging recess and exit from this awkwardly (big gear). Finish up the crack at the back of the ledge.
FA. Charlie Salisbury 1936

30 Tombstone Crack . . . . VS 4b
14m. The right-hand groove in the wall leads to a ledge. Step right and finish up the blocky arete.
FA. Charlie Salisbury 1954s

Descent

Change in viewing angle

Buttress Five

Buttress Five
A small buttress with collection of routes that will happily fill an hour, if you are up to them. The wall gets the evening sun and is reasonably clean.

1 Blasphemy Crack . . . . . HS 4b
8m. The boot-width crack is a right bugger. Big gear is essential, mountain boots and profanity might help.
FA. early 1900s. Original called Crooked Crack.

2 The Chute . . . . S 4b
8m. The inset slab leads to easier ground. The start is polished.
FA. Probably Walter Greenwood pre-1911

3 Gym Crack . . . . HVS 5b
8m. The left-hand crack in the front face goes from fingers to hands and a finish up the wall. It is harder and more strenuous than it looks.
FA. Allan Austin 1956

4 Sylvia E3 5c
8m. The old peg-crack and wall above on flat holds. Pumpy.
FA. Pete Kitson 1973

5 Sylveste E2 5b
10m. A gem. Start with a tricky mantel to the break then traverse smartly left to exit via the upper wall of *Sylvia*.
FA. Ron Hirst 1950. FFA. Brian Evans 1956

6 Veste E1 5b
8m. The reachy direct finish to *Sylveste*.
FA. Pete Kitson 1972

Buttress Six
The final buttress is hidden away round to the right and is most easily reached from the main path running through Rocky Valley.

7 Catapult Crack . . . . HVS 4c
9m. A compelling wide and narrowing crack. It is hard to enter and hard to make progress on. Great practice for those Yosemite off-widths. A good old 'Yorkshire VS'.
FA. Arthur Dolphin 1950

8 Blue Meanies Tea Party E3 5c
10m. Start up *Catapult Crack* but at 3m balance out to the arete and climb this with a little trepidation.
FA. Roger Lambert 1984

9 Sunburst Finish . . . E5 6a
8m. The right-hand side of the arete is accessed by a flying leap, step left to a ledge then continue carefully.
FA. Ron Fawcett 1976

10 Ruby Parrot E3 5c
8m. The shallow groove in the left wall of the recess is reached from the right and gives good climbing.
FA. Al Manson 1977

11 Gutsie . . . . VS 4c
8m. The wide crack in the corner is another classic thrutch.
FA. Probably Walter Greenwood pre-1911

12 Stump Chimney . . . . VS 4b
8m. Climb the right-hand corner which develops into a chimney.
FA. Probably Walter Greenwood pre-1911

13 Diamond Dogs E3 5c
8m. The right wall of the recess is climbed until it is possible to access the arete on the right. Finish up this.
FA. Ron Fawcwtt 1976

14 Blind Valley E3 5c
12m. An arduous but excellent crack system that splits the nose of the buttress. Reach the crack through the overhangs and follow it direct (good gear) to a tricky finish up the right-trending groove.
FFA. Pete Livesey (solo!) 1973. Originally an aid route called Thor's Wall.

15 Countdown to Disaster . . E8 6b
12m. The proud arete is approached from a ledge on the right and followed with great trepidation - technical and sustained. The name is especially apt and mats won't help much on this one.
FA. John Dunne 1986

Pdie Hill | Shooter's | Heptonstall | Widdop | Earl Crag | Ilkley | The Chevin | Caley | Almscliff | Eastby | Crookrise | Brimham | Slipstones | Crag Willas | Guisecliff

Buttress Six

Pule Hill · Shooters · Heptonstall · Widdop · Earl Crag · **Ilkley** · The Chevin · Caley · Almscliff · Eastby · Crookrise · Rylstone · Simon's Seat · Brimham · Eavestones · Slipstones · Crag Willas · Woodedge

Buttress Six

The final buttress in Rocky Valley is the most extensive and the least visited bit of rock here. Apart from being the furthest from the car park, it also is often green and gets little sunshine, hence the amount of grass on the cliff. Also, the best of the rock rises above an unattractive band of grotty grassy ledges which gives the routes an unexpected feeling of exposure. Despite the setting there are some worthwhile climbs following good lines, and the chances are you will probably be alone.

Approach - Continue down the track past the other buttresses and round the corner, the cliff is located up and left and is reached by a short scramble.

㉑ Matchbox . . . . 　　　　 **HS 4b**
14m. The green groove is approached via grassy ledges. It used to be a popular outing.

㉒ Overhanging Chockstone Crack. 　　　 **Diff**
8m. Used in the past as a way down.

㉓ Double Chockstone Crack . . . . . 　　　 **S 4a**
8m. The crack in the corner has it moments.

㉔ Holly Tree Route . . . . 　　　 **Diff**
14m. A beginners' route for those who like the feeling of exploration. Follow grassy ledges to a better finish up the groove.

㉕ Illegitimate Crack . . 　　　　　　 **VS 4c**
14m. A fine varied climb up the long crack on the right - the best VS in the Valley. Any further description would be superfluous.
FA. Winston Farrar mid 1930s

㉖ Spreadeagle . . . . 　　　　 **HS 4b**
14m. Climb the flake then head left, hand traversing a block, to reach a ledge at the base of a groove. Finish up this.

㉗ Bald Eagle . . . . . . 　　　　　　 **E3 5c**
14m. The bold arete above the block via a useful pocket.
FA. Pete Livesey 1974

⑯ Brush Crack . . . . 　　　 **S 4a**
10m. The main angle is pleasant enough though the approach is a bit agricultural.

⑰ Arrowhead . . . . 　　　 **S 4a**
10m. The right-trending crack past the arrowhead.
FA. Probably Walter Greenwood pre-1911

⑱ Taj Mahal . . . . 　　　 **VDiff**
10m. The left-hand of two cracks. A lower part is best avoided.
FA. Charlie Salisbury 1950s

⑲ Windy Buttress . . . . . . 　　　　　 **VS 5a**
16m. From a lower level, climb to and through a niche to reach ledges. Finish up the right-hand crack.

⑳ The Ogre . . . . 　　　　　　 **VS 4c**
14m. Grotty terrain leads to the imposing left-trending crack-line. Gain and follow this with difficulty.

Not much sun · 10 min · Green · Windy

Buttress Six

	No star	⚝	⚝⚝	⚝⚝⚝
Mod to S	-	-	1	-
HS to HVS	-	6	1	1
E1 to E3	-	1	1	2
E4 and up	-	3	-	-

The Chevin overlooks the lower reaches of the Wharfe Valley to the east of Otley. The main crag here is a fine natural buttress which offers a small selection of good climbs if the conditions are right - it is north-facing so pick a good day. There is also a quarried section which has a few reasonable routes up clean crack-lines and smooth grooves. There is a good spread of grades on generally excellent rock and the pitches are quite long, which is a nice change for gritstone.

Conditions

The crag faces pretty much north and is green for much of the year. It is at its best on warm summer evenings, or as a welcome retreat on hot summer days. The quarry routes can be damp but the main buttress takes little drainage and dries rapidly.

Approach

There is an extensive parking at East Chevin Quarry car park, to the right (a little tricky to spot when driving uphill) just off the minor road (East Chevin Road) that runs between Otley and Guiseley. LEAVE NOTHING IN THE CAR. From the car park, follow the track up the hill to where it flattens out and the surprise view to the north appears (benches for the knackered). The quarries are to the left at this point, quite well hidden by the vegetation - various narrow tracks lead through the trees to the base of the rock. Continuing just over the brow the main buttress soon appears ahead and to the left - five minutes from the car.

David Sutcliffe on the first ascent of *Primate* (E6 6b) - *page 84* - at Chevin Quarry. Photo: John Bannister

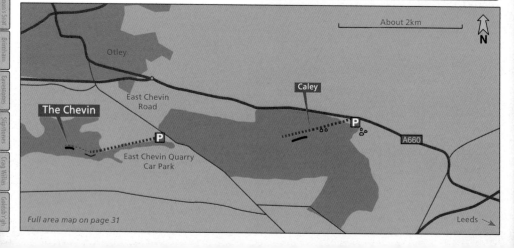

About 2km

N

Otley

Caley

East Chevin Road

The Chevin

P

P

A660

East Chevin Quarry Car Park

Full area map on page 31

Leeds

Side margin tabs (top to bottom): Pule Hill | Shooter's | Hartonstall | Widdop | East Crag | Ilkley | The Chevin | Caley | Almscliff | Eastby | Guiseley | Brimham | Simon's Seat | Brimham | Eavestones | Slipstones | Crag Willas | Goldsborough

Andy Benson stretching for the magnificent flutings at the top of
Chevin Buttress (VS 4c) - *page 84*. Photo: Dave Musgrove

Freestyle

10m gap

Descent

6

3

4

5

Weasel

Chevin Quarries

Not the most sparkling destination, and north-facing to boot. Despite this, the best routes are of reasonable qualit, and, if you are visiting the natural edge, you will be walking past the place.

❶ Freestyle . . . . HVS 5a
20m. The long crack up the left-hand edge of the tallest wall gives a worthwhile pitch. Protection is good but the whole thing is quite uphill. The upper part is easier.
FA. Tim Wilkinson 1977

❷ Jenny Tulls . . . E5 6b
20m. The central line on the wall is hard, sustained and poorly protected in places. The lower roof is hard, once established things gradually ease.
FA. Don Barr 1983

The next four routes are in the more friendly right-hand quarry

❸ Primate E6 6b
15m. Follow an arching line of side-pulls and undercuts leftwards into the corner on the left (**Ladder Climb HS** - not described) then climb the left side of the arete above. *Photo on page 82.*
FA. David Sutcliffe 2003

❹ Weasel . . . . HVS 5b
14m. The blank groove in the centre of the right-hand quarry gives good bridging with reasonable protection.
FA. John Ramsden mid 1950s

❺ Rampant Hippo . . . . VS 4c
14m. The yellow cracks splitting the arete are worth doing but feel a bit soft to the touch - as opposed to a bit of a soft touch.
FA. Dave Musgrove (one sling to surmount the earth cornice) 1971
FFA. Frank Wilkinson 1971

❻ No Prisoners E1 5b
14m. Start up *Rampant Hippo* but jig right to the finger-crack right of the arete and follow this with sustained interest.
FA. Alec Burns 1978

Chevin Buttress

The rest of the routes described are on the fine Chevin Buttress which is a couple of minutes walk north west of the quarries, just over the brow of the hill.

❼ Leech's Wall . . . . VS 4c
8m. The shallow scoop in the left-hand side of the east-facing wall has a tricky bulge (delicate) and not much in the way of gear.
FA. Rod Leech late 1950s

❽ Chevin Buttress . . . . VS 4c
16m. A fine climb with great positions and low in the grade. Follow the cracks in the right-hand side of the side wall until they end then move out right onto the arete for a classic finish. The **Direct Finish** is just a little harder. *Photo on page 83.*
FA. Brian Evans 1957

❾ Gronff Left-hand . . . E4 6b
16m. Start up the overhanging crack and use the layaway/rib to make a long stretch for a distant break. The upper section is easier. The hard moves can be avoided by a (rather pointless) loop out to the right.
FA. Mike Hammill 1975

❿ Gronff E2 5c
16m. A great climb, direct sustained and interesting. Climb onto the ramp then undercut and stretch up and left for distant holds. Continue in a direct line.
FA. Ken Wood 1973

Descent

Chevin Buttress

There is only a small selection of climbs available here, but on a fine tall buttress. The buttress is north-facing and inclined to be green so is best after a dry spell, on summer evenings or as an escape from the heat.

⑫ Vampire's Ledge . . . . . VS 5a

18m. Wandering but worthwhile and doesn't have the teeth you might expect. Climb round the flake and follow the cracks right-wards into the groove of *Central Route*. Up this, then follow the ledge back left and finish delicately up the slab (tiny wires).
FA. Johnny Lees 1950s

⑬ Central Route . . . . S 4a

16m. The central line on the buttress gives a pleasant climb. Trend left up the groove to pass the bulges then finish direct over a small overhang.
FA. Johnny Lees 1950s

⑭ Central Route Direct . . . . . VS 4b

16m. Start up *Central Route* but step right and pull through the bigger bulge on perfect jams. Follow the groove above to the top.
FA. Dennis Gray 1957

⑮ Slide Back . . . . HVS 5b

14m. Climb a left-facing groove to its top then move left and climb through the bulge with difficulty to reach the easier upper wall.

⑯ The Backslider E2 5c

14m. Start up *Slide Back* but at the level of the bulges move right into a slim groove and climb this with difficulty to reach the easier upper face.
FA. John Syrett 1971

⑪ The Waster E1 5b

16m. Another fine climb, this one following a strong natural line. The groove and continuation crack are awkward and sustained. A finish up the short slab adds a little spice.
FA. (solo and exiting left) Alan Austin 1965. FA. (direct) Al Manson 1970s

Descent

Central Route

	No star	☆	☆☆	☆☆☆
Mod to S	5	6	1	-
HS to HVS	3	16	8	2
E1 to E3	7	7	2	1
E4 and up	2	17	4	9

Almost an urban cliff, Caley is the quick-hit of choice for Leeds-based climbers being only a short car/bike/bus ride from the north west suburbs of the city. Many a fine evening's entertainment has been had by climbers over the years sampling the delights of the extensive boulder fields, or venturing up to the crag to tackle one of the superb routes up there.

Since bouldering is very important at Caley, we have gone into more detail than at some other crags in the book, focusing particularly on the significant problems on the boulders around the Great Flake Boulder and under the Main Crag. There is more bouldering available - check out the *Yorkshire Gritstone Bouldering - Vol. 1* (2008).

If it is routes you are after then head up to the Main Crag - there is plenty to go at there although the better ones are probably in the higher grades. Check the conditions carefully since crag is best used as a summer retreat venue.

Conditions
The crag faces north west and so is green for much of the year; it is at its best on warm summer evenings, though the boulderers prefer the cooler conditions of spring and autumn. As in so many areas of the UK, the trees are growing closer and closer to the cliff encouraging greenness on the rocks and reducing airflow so things stay green for longer. Despite this (and gladly) midges don't appear to be quite the problem you might expect. The boulders are on an open hillside, they get more sunshine and are in condition more often.

Approach
There is a long (narrow) lay-by on the uphill side of the A660, close to the Caley Gate, which gives access to both the boulders and the cliff. **WARNING** - this is a very fast piece of road, great care is required when parking and moving around the vehicle.
For the Roadside Boulders, turn left through the gate and scramble across a well trodden path to them - 2 mins. For the Main Crag, follow the track up through the trees until the cliff appears - 10 mins.

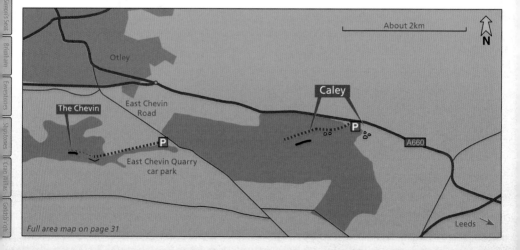

Full area map on page 31

Upper Roadside Boulders

The huge Great Flake Boulder stands proud above the lower set of blocks and dominates the upper slope. This has a few routes on its tallest face. Further left (looking in) there are a few hard test-pieces tucked away, plus some tall walls tackled by the odd highball. There are plenty of other problems in amongst the blocks here and even more further east under the electricity wires in an area known as the Stile Boulders. Check *Yorkshire Gritstone Bouldering - Vol. 1* (2008) for more details.

❶ Blockbuster V9
Powerful moves up the thin holds on the steep wall.

❷ Northern Soul V10
The sit-down start from the left knocks the grade up a notch.

❸ Zoo York V11
An impressive line up the 'ship's prow' arete.

Up and slightly right is a wall that sometimes suffers from a drainage streak.

❹ Ripper Arete V8
Climb the left-hand arete. It doesn't have that many moves but still feels a little high.

❺ Ron's Reach/Ripper Traverse
. . . . V4 (6a)
Follow the thin break rightwards across the wall to a tiny groove. Now go for the top. The direct start is **Wainright's Wobble**, **V9**

❻ Ben's Groove V8
The central groove has a poor set of holds.

❼ The Secret Seventh V9
Climb the right-hand arete of the wall.

Below the Blockbuster boulder is a slabby wall.

❽ Thin Groove . . . . VB (4b)
The curving groove is pleasant.

❾ Thin Slab V2 (5c)
Climb the slab just left of the arete.

❿ Thin Crack V4 (6a)
The thin crack in the side wall.

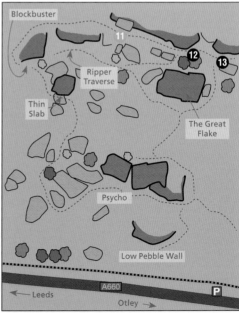

The edge which protrudes at the top of the slope has a few tall walls. There are a number of highball problems here - just the best three are mentioned.

⑪ **The Rocking Stone Roof** . . . . . ☐ **V0+ (5b)**
Climb the wall below and then over the big (rocking) block.

⑫ **Terry** . . . . ☐ **V9**
A big bald wall with a few edges. Probably worth around **E6**.

⑬ **Pebble Wall** . . . . . ☐ **V8**
A very thin slab.

The main attraction in this area is the huge Great Flake Boulder.

⑭ **Andy's Route** . . . . ☐ **V7**
The line through the overhang on the left.
FA. Andy Brown around 1979

⑮ **The Great Flake** . . . ☐ **E6 6b**
8m. The superb flake has a solitary, and well-hidden, runner.
FA. Craig Smith 1984

⑯ **High Fidelity** . . ☐ **V13**
The highly technical blunt arete to the right of *Great Flake*.
FA. Steve Dunning 2003

⑰ **Nothing's Safe** . . . . ☐ **V9**
The right arete of the block past the useful break.
FA. John Dunne 1988

⑱ **Bob's Bastard 2** . . . . . . ☐ **V2 (5c)**
Hang the lip and shuffle left before manteling into the runnels.

⑲ **Bob's Bastard 1** . . . . . . ☐ **V2 (5c)**
Mantel direct using a small pocket.

Pebble Wall

Not much sun | 5 min | Green

⑬

Bob's Bastard

⑱ ⑲

⑰

The Great Flake

Not much sun | 5 min | Green

14

15

16

17

Descent

Rabbit's Paw Wall

Psycho

Psycho and Rabbit's Paw Wall

A couple of huge boulders that lean against each other and present an impressive pair of faces towards the valley. The routes are short in stature but large in impact, runners are in short supply and most of the routes are soloed by the suitably talented. Further right are some more walls and slabs. These offer a mixture of bouldering and routes.

❶ Psycho . . . . Top 50　　　　　　　**E5 6b**
8m. Step onto the face and teeter right to the line of lumps and bumps running up the face. Follow these with trepidation.
Photo on page 30.
FA. Ron Fawcett 1977

❷ Psycho Direct . . . . .　　　　　　　　　**E5 6c**
10m. The true start is a tease.
FA. John Dunne 1988

❸ Adrenaline Rush . . .　　　　　　　　　**E5 6b**
10m. The shallow crack fizzles out short of the top, but not before all the hard climbing is finished. The runners are positioned just below mid-height.
FA. Al Manson 1977

❹ Marrow Bone Jelly .　　　　　　　　　**E7 6c**
10m. The right arete of the block is sustained, technical and unprotected. Start on the left or right.
FA. Al Manson 1984

❺ Little Cenotaph . . . .　　　　　　**VS 5a**
8m. The gloomy groove is worthwhile, a bit of a struggle but worthwhile nonetheless.
FA. Arthur Dolphin 1950. He called it Inverted Crack.

❻ Unfinished Crack . . . .　　　　**VS 4c**
8m. The crack in the right wall fizzles out, then pockets allow the top to be reached.
FA. Alfie Beanland 1953

❼ Ephedrine . . . .　　　　**E4 6a**
8m. The bold wall between the crack and arete.
FA. Tim Clifford 1977

❽ Permutation Rib . . . . . .　　　　　　**E1 5c**
8m. Teeter out right then sprint up the easier rib; short but airy. Traditionally a tricky HVS.
FA. Terry Burnell 1964

❾ Waite/ Welsh Rarebit 　　　　　　　**V9**
The shallow groove is near-impossible to access, fortunately it then eases.
FA. Andy Swan or Christian Durkin 1995. They don't know who did it first.

❿ Rabbit's Paw Wall . . . .　　　　　　**HVS 5b**
8m. The 'paw prints' are gained from the right by crossing the bulge with difficulty. Continue more easily. One of Yorkshire's shorter three star routes, but it is well worth them.
FA. Arthur Dolphin 1950. He called it Overhanging Wall.

⓫ Hanging Groove . . . . . .　　　　　　**E2 5b**
6m. The eponymous feature is tiny but terrifying, the potential fall is double the length of the route and not to be contemplated.
FA. Allan Austin 1958

⓬ Chips . . . .　　　　**V0- (4b)**
The polished chipped 'olds in the right-hand face of the block.

⓭ Otley Wall . . . .　　　　**V2 (6a)**
From the start of *Chips* move out right to gain the hanging slot.
FA. Dave Musgrove 1975

⓮ Morris Minor . . . .　**VB (4a)**
The chipped holds up the slab.

⓯ Morris Crack . . . .　　　　　**HS 4b**
6m. The compelling crack-line is an awkward customer.

⓰ Morris Dance . . . .　　　　　**V0+ (5b)**
The face just right of the crack to a highball finish.
FA. Al Manson 1975

Not much sun | 3 min | Green

Pule Hill | Shooter's | Heptonstall | Widdop | Earl Crag | Ilkley | The Chevin | Caley | Almscliff | Eastby | Crookrise | Rylstone | Simon's Seat | Brimham | Eavestones | Slipstones | Stanages | Crag Willas | Gelderd ran

Plenty of easy bouldering in the sunny 'Playground' behind.

Descent

13

12

4

9

11

10

Rabbit's Paw Wall

Not much sun | 3 min | Green

14

15 16

⑰ **Maurice Chevalier** . 🌟🐾🦎 [ ] **V2 (5c)**
The arete on its right-hand side is a good high problem.

⑱ **Lightning Crack** . . . . 🌟 [ ] **V4 (6a)**
The striking seam in the right-hand face of the boulder.

⑲ **No Pebble Arete** . . . . . 🌟🐾 [ ] **V9**
The left-hand side of the slab. Use the arete after the start.

⑳ **Low Pebble Wall** . . . . 🌟 [ ] **V2 (6a)**
The chips in the centre of the slab.

㉑ **The Cruel Crack** . . . . [ ] [ ] **V1 (5c)**
Well named. Struggle up the short curving crack.

㉒ **New Jerusalem** . . . 🌟🐾🦎 [ ] **V7**
A classic problem up the short red wall.

Afternoon

17

18

Maurice Chevalier

Psycho

Not much sun | 3 min | Green

Low Pebble Wall

The lowest wall in this section has a small set of hard boulder problems. It can be easily reached by descending down the grass slope under *Maurice Chevalier*.

19

20

21

22

Low Pebble Wall

Main Edge Boulders

Walking up the path towards the Main Edge an array of boulders soon appears through the trees. Three of these are large enough to offer both routes and bouldering.

Sucker's Wall

On the left and next to the path is a square boulder peppered with chipped holds.

❶ Twin Pockets .... ☆ [ ] **V1 (5c)**
Around the arete, step off a boulder and move right to gain a hole.

❷ Scary Canary ..... ☆ 🏃 🗺 [ ] **V8**
The line just right of the blunt arete becomes more harrowing with height, hence the name.

❸ Sucker's Rib .... ☆ 🗡 [ ] **V0 (5a)**
The blunt rib is **V0+** without the chipped holds.

❹ Sucker's Wall .... [ ] **VB (4c)**
The line of chips to the left of the arete are very polished.

❺ The Pinch .... ☆ 🗡 [ ] **V5 (6b)**
The right-hand side wall via a tiny ledge and the eponymous hold. Missing the pinch hold by a long dyno is worth **V8**.

Boot Crack

The next boulder has the characteristic boot-width fissure of Boot Crack in its north face.

❻ Pocket Rock .... ☆ 🏃 [ ] **V4 (6b)**
The back arete climbed on its left-hand side.

❼ Rick's Rock .... 🗺 [ ] **E4 6b**
8m. Thin climbing up the wall using some chipped holds.

❽ Black Jumper .... ☆ 🗺 [ ] **E1 5b**
8m. Stretch or leap from the block to reach the first decent hold on the arete and then continue up it. The landing is grim.
FA. Greg Tough 1972

Descent - scramble off the back

Sun and shade | 10 min

Boot Crack

❾ Black Jumper Indirect ☆ 🏃 🗡 [ ] **V8**
Thin moves up the wall leftwards to the arete. Jump off.
FA. Neil Carson 1991

❿ Boot Crack .... ☆ |🏋| [ ] **VS 4b**
8m. The wide fissure.
FA. Denys Fisher late 1930s

⓫ Shoe Shine .... ☆ 🗡 [ ] **VS 4b**
8m. The bold feeling right-hand arete following the almost inevitable line of chipped holds.

Descent run (or slide) down the slab

The Sugarloaf

Sun and shade 10 min

The Sugarloaf
On the other side of the path is the tall pointed block of the Sugarloaf, home to a good selection of fine climbs on its three steeper facets.

12 Angel's Wall . . . . 🖟🖾 **V1 (5b)**
Swing right then climb the centre of the narrow wall to an exciting finish over the bulge that caps it.
FA. Arthur Dolphin early 1950s

13 Angel's Wing . . . . 🖾 **V3 (5c)**
Steep climbing that parallels the right edge of the wall without actually using it, to the final bulge of *Angel's Wall*.
FA. Dave Musgrove (probably, he certainly named it) late 1970s

14 Plantation Ridge . . . . . . 🖟🖿 **VS 4c**
8m. The left arete of the north face is accessed from round to the left and gives pleasant moves.
FA. Nancy Heron 1944

15 Plantation Wall . . . . . . 🖟🖿 **HVS 5a**
8m. Pad up the face and over the bulges a short distance right of the arete (use of which is taboo) to finish up the slab.
FA. Dave Musgrove (probably, another first named by him) 1970

16 The Can . . . . 🖟🖾🖿 **E2 5c**
8m. The centre of the face has tricky and bold feeling moves passing the mid-height bulges rightwards.
FA. Mike Hammill 1976

17 Central Route . . . . . 🖟🖿🖾 **VS 5a**
8m. Follow the cracks to their end, balance left into the thinner continuation then finish to the right, where this ends.

18 The Cavity . . . . 🖾 **V3 (6a)**
Steep pulls left of the arete gain *Sweet Tooth*.
FA. Al Manson c1980

19 Sweet Tooth . . . . 🖟 **HVS 5a**
8m. The arete. Start from a block on the right and climb to the break where the slabby face can be accessed. From the break (runners) gain the upper slab with difficulty and finish direct.

20 Route 3 . . . . 🖟 **VB (4b)**
The left-hand side of the south west face is juggy to the last move where an elusive pocket round the arete aids the finish.

21 Route 2 . . . . 🖟 **VB (4c)**
The centre of the face on a fine array of holds.

22 Route 1 . . . . 🖟 **V0- (5a)**
Sprint up the awkward right-leaning crack to the arete.

There is plenty more bouldering scattered amongst the trees below the crag - check Yorkshire Gritstone Bouldering - Vol. 1 (2008) for full details.

Descent

12

4

6

3

7

8   9   10

5

11

4

1

2   in crevasse between the
boulder and the face

Pedestal Wall - around
the corner

13

Noonday Ridge

The Main Edge at Caley is not very extensive, despite this it is home to a very worthwhile set of climbs. It faces north and so it is inclined to be green for much of the year. Best conditions occur in the spring and autumn, after a dry spell. The encroaching trees tend to slow the drying of the cliff and encourage midges, though these are not as bad as you might expect.

1 Fingerknacker Crack ...   **E2 6a**
8m. The thin leaning crack is a tease, though less so than when it was graded HVS.
FA. D.Cronan 1964. FFA. Ken Wood 1972

2 The Sentry Box ....   **HVS 5b**
8m. Entering and exiting the sentry box are both fun.

3 Holly Tree Scoop ....   **Diff**
10m. Climb past the burgeoning tree to access the scoop.

4 Gary Cooper ....   **E4? 6a**
16m. Climb the bulging face to reach the rest on *Noonday Ridge*. Move round the arete and trend right across the wall to the final moves on *Lad's Corner*.
FA. Steve Bancroft 1976. Originally protected by an old bolt and given E3. The bolt was removed in 2007.

5 Noonday Ridge ....   Top 50   **E1 5b**
14m. A Yorkshire classic. Climb right of the arete until it is possible to move awkwardly left - runners can be poked in before you commit, though they are tricky to place. Once established, the slabby groove gives fine climbing to an exit on the right. This upper section is often wet in the winter.
FA. Allan Austin 1964

6 High Noon ....   Top 50   **E4 6a**
14m. The jutting axe-edged arete gives a great climb, bold and committing. From the good runners on *Noonday Ridge* move back right and, heart in mouth, layback and balance up the arete until jugs (or the air) offer some relief. High in the grade.
Photo on page 87.
FA. Al Manson 1975

7 Fred Zinnerman ...   **E6 6b**
14m. Climb direct to pocket where a skyhook can be placed. Move up to the old bolt scar then step left to finish direct. Probably a grade easier, but no less scary, for the tall.
FA. Al Manson 1977. FA. (Without the bolt) Ben Bransby 1999

8 Welcome to the Neighbourhood   **E1 5c**
14m. The face just left of the big groove has its moments. Finish up the groove, and avoid side-runners for the full effect.
FA. Nigel Baker 1996

Pule Hill
Shooter's
Heptonstall
Widdop
Earl Crag
Ilkley
The Chevin
Caley
Almscliff
Eastby
Crookrise
Rylstone
Simon's Seat
Brimham
Eavestones
Slipstones
Crag Willas
Goldsborough

⑨ Lad's Corner . . . . 🔲 📋 ⬜ **VS 4c**
14m. The big corner is a character building trip, though it can be gritty after wet weather.
FA. Arthur Dolphin 1952

⑩ Block Chimney . . . . . . 🔲 📋 ⬜ **VS 4c**
14m. The tilted rift to the right of the corner is another must-do graunch, great if you enjoy the genre.
FA. Johnny Lees around.1950

⑪ Compulsion Crack . . . . . 🔲 📋 ⬜ **VS 5a**
14m. The right-hand crack is compelling - well it would be!
FA. Peter Greenwood 1952

⑫ Compulsive Viewing . . . . . . 🔲 ⬜ **HVS 5a**
16m. Follow *Compulsion Crack* until the ramp on the left can be reached, up this to the horizontal break, then move left to a good exposed finish up the thin crack.
FA. Nigel Baker 1998 (may be Compulsion Crack Variation, John Syrett 1973)

⑬ Forecourt Crawler . . 🔲 🧗 🕮 ⬜ **E4 6b**
16m. The stubborn crack leads to the roof, pass this and climb the short wall to a final desperate move.
FA. John Allen 1975. FA. (Direct Finish - as described) Ron Fawcett 1975

⑭ Pedestal Wall. . . . . 🔲 ⬜ **S 4a**
18m. Climb the front of the fallen slab to a ledge, then tackle the short awkward chimney-crack behind the pedestal until it is possible to move out left for a well positioned finish.
FA. Allan Allsop late 1930s

Pedestal Wall

Tucked around the corner from *Noonday Ridge* is a slumped slab that gives the edge's best easier route, *Pedestal Wall*, and to its right another of those steep awkward chimney-cracks that the cliff appears to have more than its fair share of.

⑮ Triple 'A' . . . . 🕮 ⬜ **E1 5c**
18m. An interesting variation on *Pedestal Wall*. Climb the right edge of the slab then the front face of the pedestal to its crest. Stride onto the face and finish direct up the slab.
FA. Dave Musgrove 1997

⑯ Cave and Slab . . . . 📋 🕮 ⬜ **VS 4b**
14m. Climb the arete right of the tunnel to a chimney which leads to the top slab. Head up this, keeping left of the line of chipped holds.

⑰ Rib and Slab . . . . 🔲 ⬜ **VS 4c**
14m. The right-hand arete leads to a ledge, the upper slab has a line of chipped slots.

⑱ Square Chimney . . . . . . 🔲 📋 ⬜ **HVD**
14m. Classic chimney work leads to a ledge from where a short awkward layback gains the top.

⑲ Tippling Crack . . . . ⬜ **E1 5b**
12m. The crack in the right wall of the recess to a wide finish.
FA. Allan Austin 1958

⑳ Dypso . . . . 🗲 ⬜ **E2 5c**
12m. Up *Tippling Crack* then right along the break to a tough pull up the wall just short of the arete.
FA. John Syrett 1973

There are three routes just around the corner from Pedestal Wall.

1 Tipster . . . . . ☆1 ◫ HVS 5a
10m. Hop onto the slab then trend left to the block in the break. Finish up the cracked arete.
FA. John Syrett 1971

2 Tip Off . . . . . ☆1 ◫ E2 5b
12m. From the same start as *Tipster*, climb direct to the break then head up the bold wall on pockets to gain the easier rib.
FA. Mike Hammill 1977

3 Flue Crack . . . . ◫ VDiff
8m. The wide crack gives an easier climb - easy but awkward.

Quark
A smooth face with an exceptionally fierce trio of climbs up its left-hand side and a couple of much easier offerings that skirt its right-hand edge.

4 Quark . . . ☆3 ◫ E5 6a
14m. The searing crack just right of the arete gives a fierce pitch - protection is available but it is hard won. At the top of the crack use holds on both sides of the arete. Above the break climb the wall on the right.
The final arete direct is **Quark Quark, E7 6c**.
FA. Mike Hammill 1977. FA. (Quark, Quark) Ben Bransby 1999

5 Charm ☆ ◫ E8 6c
14m. The vague ramp feature in the centre of the face provides the challenge, a side-runner in the previous route lowers the grade to **E6**.
FA. (with side-runner) Graham Desroy 1988
FA. (without) Ben Tetler 1999

6 Strangeness
. . . . ☆ ◫ E7 6c
14m. The right-hand side of the face on poor holds. A marginal RP and poor skyhook provide token runners. *Photo opposite.*
FA. Steve Rhodes 1988

7 The Scoop ☆ ◫ VS 4c
14m. Climb the groove to ledges then a crack trending right and back left to a higher ledge with a sapling. Balance up the scoop warily to finish.
FA. Arthur Dolphin late 1940s. Then 'the hardest climb in Wharfedale'.

8 Zig-zag . . . . ☆1 S 4a
14m. Follow *The Scoop* to the base of the scoop but head right up the jamming crack to finish.

Tipster

Pedestal Wall around the corner

Quark 10m

Quark

Ben Bransby placing the marginal gear on *Strangeness* (E7 6c) - *opposite* - on the Main Edge at Caley. Photo: Dave Musgrove

	No star	☆	☆☆	☆☆☆
Mod to S	1	11	4	1
HS to HVS	2	22	10	7
E1 to E3	3	14	5	11
E4 and up	1	10	11	2

Yorkshire's finest and no arguments are allowed. A warty lump of premier quality gritstone that is perched on the windy hillside between Leeds and Harrogate, looking out over rolling farmland.

Almscliff is a venue best suited to honing gritstone technique rather then learning it, though lessons learnt here will serve you well and take you far. The rock is hard and coarse, flared breaks and rounded holds are the order of the day. The crag has been climbed on for over 100 years and many of climbing's greats have left their mark here - welcome to the Academy.

Conditions

The crag faces all points of the compass. It takes no drainage and dries soon after the rain stops, though its lofty position means it can be cold and windy up here - there is little shelter to be found. The farmer chooses to graze his cattle around the crag, the pats are not a problem but the slurry that develops in wet weather is less pleasant.

Approach

There is roadside parking by the bend on the minor road that runs past the north west face of the crag. The parking is most easily reached from the A658 Pool to Harrogate road by driving through Huby or North Rigton.

The old approach was by the track opposite Crag Farm, though problems occurred with cars blocking access to the fields. The approach described above is now the only one to be used.

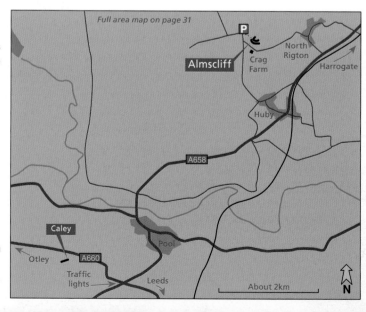

Full area map on page 31

Side column tabs: Pate Hill, Shooter's, Heptonstall, Widdop, Earl Crag, Ilkley, The Chevin, Caley, Almscliff, Eastby, Greakrise, Rylstone, Simon's Seat, Brimham, Eavestones, Slipstones, Crag Willas, Goldsbygrh

Morrel's Wall and B2

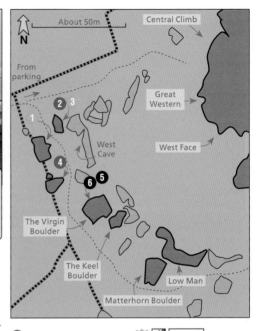

The Virgin Boulder

The Boulders

Below the main edge of Almscliff are a collection of huge blocks that have some great bouldering on them. There are countless problems for those who want to explore - see *Yorkshire Bouldering Guide - Vol. 1 (2008)* - only the most popular problems and routes are listed here.

1 Morrell's Wall . . . . 🔢 🔧 [___] **V2 (5c)**
A popular problem up the shady leaning wall. Big holds lead to a steep pull on fingery holds. Eliminates abound.

2 Overhanging Rib . . . . . . 🔢 ✊ [___] **V3 (6a)**
The steep rib, using the block for your feet. Without the block is **V5**.

3 B2 Eliminates . . . . 🔢 ✊ [___] **V1 (5b)**
Climb the steep face from the flake. As the name suggests, there are loads of eliminates possible.

Opposite Morrell's Wall and Boulder 2 is the West Cave Area - a little high for bouldering although there is a small eliminates section at its right-hand end. The next boulders are the Everest Man Boulder (highballs) and the Flying Arete.

4 Flying Arete . . . . 🔢 [___] **V4 (6a)**
Start off a small boulder and climb the right-hand side of the arete.

The Virgin Boulder

The largest of the boulders is the Virgin Boulder - a huge tilted block, the size of a small planet and home to a small set of routes and some intense bouldering.

The first problems are on the low roof on the steep north face.

5 Stretch Armstrong . . 🔢 ✊ ⬜ [___] **V9**
Make a huge reach from a low hold under the roof.

6 Canine . . . . . . 🔢 ⬜ 🦎 ✊ [___] **V11**
The central line is very hard.
The right-hand side of the roof, followed by a hand-traverse leftwards on the pockets, is **Sewer Rat Connection, V9**.

The routes on the west face look like extended boulder problems but they feel like routes when you are trying to access the block's shelving summit.

7 The Lady . . . . 🔧 [___] **E4 6c**
6m. The left arete of the pathward face to a balding top. Low gear isn't much use when you are trying to top out.
FA. Ron Cowells 1985

8 The Virgin . . . . 🔢 🔧 [___] **E3 6b**
12m. Grovel the deep crack rightwards until a pocket and pinch-grip allow the top to be reached. Large gear protects. The direct start is a desperate **V12** problem.
FA. Pete Kitson 1973. FA. (Direct) John Gaskins 1994

9 Jack on Fire . . . . 🔢 🔧 [___] **E4 6c**
6m. The leaning wall (large cam out right) keeping right of the shallow groove. The exit is very rounded. There are several modern micro variants on this theme.
FA. Al Manson 1988

10 Virgin Traverse . . . 🔢 🔧 🔧 [___] **V4 (6b)**
Start with feet and hands on the block on the left. Traverse the low break around the corner to a niche. The continuation is **V9** on its own, and **V10** when connected.

11 The Gypsy . . . . 🔢 🔧 🔧 🔧 [___] **E3 6a**
10m. Climb the arete left to a break - a popular **V4 (6a)** to this point. Move right then back left above a too-large drop.
FA. Pete Kitson 1973

12 Gypus . . . . 🔧 [___] **E3 6b**
10m. Climb the south face of the boulder dynamically, trending slightly left to join and finish up *The Gypsy*.
FA. Martin Berzins 1982

13 Opus . . . . 🔢 🔧 🔧 [___] **E4 6b**
10m. The centre of the wall is climbed via a set of deep slots to a small overhang and a desperate leftward exit.
FA. Mike Hammill 1975

14 Magnum Opus . . . . 🔢 🔧 🔧 [___] **E5 6b**
12m. Layback up the flake/ramp and a short crack to join *Opus* at its desperate exit. The direct start to the left is **V9**.
FA. Martin Berzins 1988

About 50m · From parking · Central Climb · Great Western · West Cave · West Face · The Virgin Boulder · The Keel Boulder · Low Man · Matterhorn Boulder

The Virgin East Face

Morning

The Keel

Lots of sun | 5 min | Windy

The Virgin

The Keel

Low Man and Matterhorn Boulder

There is plenty more on this boulder including some interesting easier offerings around the back.

⑮ Fisher's Stride . . . . VS 5a

14m. Leap onto the back of the boulder from the nearby slab then trend left to a ledge. Step round the arete and continue in the same line to another ledge. Finish direct from the left edge.
FA. Denys Fisher 1940

⑯ The Virgin Climb . . . . S 4a

8m. A short traverse leads left around the south east arete to a line of polished holds up the slab.

⑰ Chastity V3 (5c)

Climb direct from the start of *Virgin Climb*.

⑱ North Face Arete V0- (4c)

The excellent north east arete on its left-hand side. The right-hand side is **V0 (5a)**.

The Keel is to the south of The Virgin has some of the best hard problems at Almscliff.

⑲ In Limbo V5 (6c)

From a sitting start, pull over the left-hand side of the roof.

⑳ Keel Crack V4 (6b)

The central crack is a great strenuous struggle.

㉑ The Keel/Fin V10

The low arete from a pinch, to a chipped hold on the lip. Loads of variations exist including one eliminating the chipped hold!
FA. John Dunne/Andy Swann 1993. Claimed at roughly the same time.

㉒ Natural Traverse V9

Start on the nose and traverse uphill along the lip on slopers to join and reverse *Sloper Patrol*.

㉓ Sloper Patrol V5 (6b)

Starting at the top of the block, traverse the sloping lip downhill and flop onto the slab at the end. Often done in reverse.

Pate Hill | Shooter's | Hepstonstall | Widdop | Earl Crag | Ilkley | The Chevin | Caley | Almscliff | Eastby | Crookrise | Brimham | Simon's Seat | Brimham | Eavestones | Slipstones | Crag Willas | Woldsbrigh

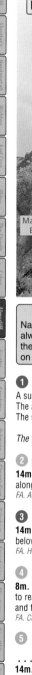

Descent

Matterhorn Boulder

Low Man
Named for it position rather than it height, Low Man is always popular, especially its right-hand side where there is a good collection of lower-grade climbs. Belays on the crag top take a bit of seeking out.

1 Matterhorn Arete . . . . . VO (5a)
A superb boulder problem up the left-hand side of the arete. The arete on its right-hand side is a delightful **VO- (4c)**. The sit-down start is **Baby Jesus, V5 (6b)**

The next two routes are on the left-hand side wall.

2 Pram Pusher's Paradise VS 5a
14m. Starting on the far left, climb to the overhang and exit right along a good break to a finish up the fluted arete.
FA. Al Manson 1972

3 V Chimney and Traverse . . . HVD
14m. Climb the slippery chimney then traverse the slab leftwards below the overhang to a steep finish.
FA. Herbert Ingle early 1890s

4 Pigott's Stride . . . . VS 4c
8m. Climb part way up the Matterhorn Boulder then teeter across to reach the face. Pull across with difficulty then step right to join and finish up *Whisky Crack*.
FA. Claude Frankland 1920s

5 Square Chimney and Whisky Crack
. . . . HS 4b
14m. Back and foot the awkward box-shaped cleft then enter the excellent steep jamming crack above and left.
FA. (SC) Herbert Ingle c1900. FA. (WC) Fred Botterill c1910

6 Whisky Wall E3 5b
12m. Climb the reachy lower wall to the break, then the bold face above to pockets. Swing left to reach the final break then step back right to finish.
FA. John Syrett 1973

7 Fluted Crack. . . . . S 4b
12m. The narrowing chimney-crack that cleaves the centre of the face is worth doing. It has a hard move high up if you manage to stay off the next route.
FA. Herbert Ingle c1900

8 Fluted Columns . . . . . . HVD 3c
12m. The best route on Low Man. Climb the lower face to reach the fluted feature and then the small bulges above.
FA. Herbert Ingle c1900

9 Pinnacle Flake Climb . . . . . S 4a
12m. Start in a niche and follow the steep flakes leftwards to a finish just right of *Fluted Columns*.

10 Low Man Easy Way. . . . . . Diff
12m. After a slippery start the large diagonal flake and short wall above is okay. Don't get your leg stuck in the initial fissure.
FA. Cecil Slingsby c1870

11 Stew Pot . . . . HVD
10m. Start as for *Low Man Easy Way* but step right and climb the wall passing 'the pot' to a finish up a short lived crack.
FA. Herbert Ingle c1900

12 Rough Crack . . . . VDiff
10m. Climb straight up to the crack in the upper section of the wall. It can be reached by a traverse from the gully at **HS 4b**.
FA. Leonard Kiernan 1931

Central Climb

The Gentlemen's side of the cliff - the North West Face - gets the sun in the afternoon and has some great routes. The left-hand side has a set of classy crack and groove climbs. It can be green after wet weather and it manages to catch any wind that is going.

❶ All Our Yesterdays E5 6a
14m. The desperate hanging ramp between the overhangs is traversed from right to left. An old peg provides much needed protection and needs a thin krab to clip, if it is still there.
FA. Al Manson 1982

❷ Finale Slab . . . . HVS 5b
12m. Cross the hanging slab to a tricky exit up a short crack.
FA. Allan Austin 1957

❸ Encore E2 5c
10m. From the flake (wires) traverse boldly left and pass the lip with difficulty and gymnastics.
FA. John Syrett 1973

❹ First Night E2 6a
10m. The nose above the flake gives a short and safe struggle.
FA. John Syrett 1973

❺ Cup and Saucer . . . . VDiff
12m. A polished oddity weaving up the major fault on the left. A mid-height belay is possible. Often used as a descent.
FA. Herbert Ingle c1890

❻ Teaspoon Left-hand V8
Start low and rockover just left of the 'TF' carved in the rock.

❼ Teaspoon Variation V2 (5c)
The polished crack is a classic problem. Eliminating the arete on the right makes it an even better **V3 (6a)**.

❽ Gray's Wall V4 (6a)
A problematic wall.

❾ Z Climb . . . . VS 4c
14m. The steep crack near the left-hand side of the face leads to bulges, zig-zag left then right and finally left again. Amazingly the steep initial crack was first climbed before 1906!
FA. Arthur Dolphin 1940

❿ Z Climb Eliminate E1 5b
14m. A popular eliminate that is a bit of a soft touch, but varied and superb. Climb a thin crack to the end of the initial crack on *Z Climb*, then continue rightwards into *Central Climb*. Follow this until it is possible to pull on to the wall on the right where a shallow flake/groove leads to great finishing holds.
FA. Arthur Dolphin 1946

⓫ Central Climb . . . . VS 4c
14m. The rounded zig-zag cracks that split the centre of the left-hand side of the face are both steeper and harder than they appear from below, though protection is plentiful. Exit leftwards.
Photo on page 107.
FA. Claude Frankland early 1920s

⓬ Overhanging Groove . . . HVS 5a
16m. The shallow overhanging groove in the left wall of *Parsons' Chimney* proves to be quite superb. Layback the lower section and bridge the upper, with an exciting finish on huge jugs. An Almscliff rarity, a route that is low in the grade!
FA. Arthur Dolphin 1941

⓭ Parson's Chimney . . . . . HS 4b
16m. The rift in the centre of the face is a classic two pitch battle. The lower squeeze can be avoided by starting up *Overhanging Groove* - a cop-out - and helmets jam in the final narrow section.
FA. W.Parsons c.1900. Oddly the climb wasn't named because the contortions required are enough to make a parson swear.

Pole Hill | Shooter's | Regional | Widdop | Earl Crag | Ilkley | The Chevin | Caley | **Almscliff** | Eastby | Crookrise | Rylstone | Simon's Seat | Brimham | Eavestones | Slipstones | Crag Wills | Geddelygh

Descent

Great Western

The junction of the North West Face and the West Face presents one of the finest buttresses on Grit with a set of routes to rival anything that the Peak can offer. All the routes tend to be big powerful challenges at their grade and if you can tick the lot in a single day then you can be sure that you are climbing well.

The first route actually starts up Z Climb on the previous page.

❶ North West Girdle..... 🔲🔲 **E1 5b**
65m. A great horizontal outing. Start up *Z Climb* and follow the horizontal line of cracks and breaks. Stances are available in *Parson's Chimney*, on the *Pulpit*, and either in *Long Chimney*, or (uncomfortably) on the pedestal of *Great Western*. Mega-classic!
FA. Arthur Dolphin, John Cook, John Ball 1944

❷ The Big Greeny. 🔲🔲🔲🔲 **E3 5c**
14m. A short fingery wall leads to bulges (large cams) which are tackled leftwards then right using the nostril-like pockets. The right-hand exit is the stretchy **Ginger Whinger, E7 7a**.
FA. John Syrett 1973. FA. (Ginger Whinger) Steve Dunning 2005

❸ Frankland's Green Crack... 🔲Top⌐50 **VS 4c**
18m. A major classic, the luminous crack is usually dryer than it looks - pity about the pigeon poo. The final bulging section often proves more difficult than you might expect, try bridging it.
FA. Claude Frankland 1919

❹ Pulpit Corner........ 🔲🔲 **E1 5b**
18m. Climb the tricky outer arete of the *Pulpit* to its top and a possible stance, then tackle the upper wall left then right.
FA. Claude Frankland (Pitch 1) 1927. FA. (Pitch 2) Alan Austin 1956

❺ Long Chimney....... 🔲🔲 **HVD**
18m. The narrow rift is a well-scoured and impressive. The exposed outside exit is best and may be worth an extra star.
FA. Herbert Ingle 1893. Originally called Great Chimney.

❻ Wall of Horrors Start... 🔲🔲 **V3 (6a)**
Using undercuts, leap for the beckoning horn. The wall just to the left is a good **V8**.

❼ The Wall of Horrors.... 🔲Top⌐50 **E3 6a**
18m. One of gritstone's finest. The leaning start up to the prominent horn proves tricky but the difficult and delicate pull from the mid-height horizontal break tends to stop more attempts (large cams). Zig-zag up the final wall.
FA. Alan Austin (solo!) 1961

❽ All Quiet........ 🔲🔲🔲 **E4 6a**
26m. A superb hulking diagonal, from the jams on *Wall of Horrors* all the way to an exit up *Crack of Doom*. More pumpy than a very pumpy thing that's really pumped.
FA. Pete Livesey 1974

❾ The Niche............. 🔲 **V2 (6a)**
The direct entry all the way in is hard, from the right is easier.

Pule Hill
Shooter's
Heptonstall
Widdop
Earl Crag
Ilkley
The Chevin
Caley
Almscliff
Eastby
Crookrise
Rylstone
Simon's Seat
Brimham
Eavestones
Slipstones
Greg Willas
Woldsbrigh

10 Western Front .... Top 50 ☐ **E3 5c**
18m. A butch outing that is 'only E2' for those who have done it a few times. From the sloping ledge in the corner, pull through the initial bulges (hard for the short) and hand traverse left to the point where strenuous moves up the inverted Y gain the jamming crack; sprint up this to the pedestal. Finish up the short crack above, or more fittingly out right in a glorious position.
Photo on page 4, 99 and the cover.
FA. Alan Austin (solo!) 1958

11 Great Western .... Top 50 ☐ **HVS 5a**
18m. Perhaps Almscliff's most famous classic. The steep corner leads to the roof and a large spike, traverse left into an exposed position and pull into a short crack with difficulty (hidden holds?). From a rest on the uncomfortable pedestal, finish up a short crack or, MUCH better, head right up the jamming crack on *Western Front* - the icing on the cake. Be aware of rope drag problems.
Photo on page 28.
FA. Arthur Dolphin 1943

12 Grand Illusion .... ☐ **E4 5c**
12m. The pocketed roof above *Great Western's* traverse yields most easily to a dynamic approach. Finish up a short crack on perfect jams. Short lived but storming.
FA. Charles Cook 1979

13 Crack of Doom .... ☐ **VS 4c**
12m. Bridge the groove of *Great Western* to the huge roof then escape rapidly out right to jugs and easy ground.
FA. Arthur Dolphin 1941

14 Retribution Rib Direct .. ☐ **E5 5c**
10m. The sharp unprotected and precarious rib is more serious than life itself.
FA. John Hotham 1991

15 West Chimney .... ☐ **Mod**
12m. The easiest route on the cliff and much used as a way down but mildly interesting for all that in a wandering kind of way. Some archaic dry-stone walling is passed en-route.
FA. Cecil Slingsby c1870

16 Jess' Roof .... ☐ **V9**
High up in the gully (reached by *West Chimney*) is a deep cave. This boulder problem crosses the roof to a fingery pull at the lip. The route originally continued over the overhangs above at **E5**.

17 The Nose .... ☐ **VS 4c**
10m. The crack in the roof is a slippery struggle, the wall above is a doddle.

18 The Nose Direct .... ☐ **HVS 5b**
10m. The thinner right-hand crack requires some proficiency in jamming to succeed (and avoid getting lacerated). Above the bulge the rest is easy.

Top of Great Western Buttress

Zig-zag

Descent

West Face
The West Face is the small facet of rock that faces towards the car park. It is rather eclipsed by the routes to either side but has a small selection of well polished pitches, and a couple of much harder offerings that see little action. Around the corner in the dingy gully that divides the cliff in two are a few more routes.

The Nose Direct

❶ **Syrett's Roof** V6 (6b)
The centre of the roof is usually well chalked. A highball.
FA. John Syrett 1972

❷ **Zig-zag** . . . . HS 4c
10m. Climb the slanting groove to the roof then swing left and use a juggy flake in the roof to pull out left onto the final easy slab. Polished.

❸ **Zig-zag Direct** . . . . VS 4c
10m. Take *Zig-zag* to the roof but eschew all zigging and zagging and pull straight over using good holds and solid jams.

❹ **The Goblin** . . . . . . HS 4b
12m. Pass the 'goblin's eyes' with difficulty and no gear, then shuffle left and crawl into the final wide crack - all awkward. For years this was one of the VDiffs that gave the crag its reputation.
FA. Herbert Ingle early 1890s

❺ **Orchrist** E5 6b
12m. The huge nose is crossed on mega-pockets, sadly gaining the wall above the lip is desperate. Runners in the far wall of the gully were used to curtail any tumble on the 1st ascent.
FA. Hank Pasquill 1973

❻ **Si's Arete** V6 (6b)
The tiny arete gives a classic problem. Start from sitting.

In the left wall of the secluded gully are a couple of decent lines.

❼ **Clematis** E2 5c
10m. This is the left-hand one through a series of reachy bulges, finishing leftwards up a shallow groove.
FA. Eric Little 1969

❽ **Oubliette** E2 6a
8m. The right-hand line follows a shallow fingery groove entered from the right and exited (rapidly) rightwards.
FA. Eric Little 1969

❾ **Tight Chimney** . . . . Mod
8m. The gloomy slot tucked away in the left wall of the gully is worth a squirm.
FA. Cecil Slingsby c1870

❿ **Rift Crack** . . . . VS 4c
8m. The right-hand of the two hanging cracks is tricky to access.

Descent

Oubliette

Lots of sun | 5 min | Windy

Descent

7

8 9 10

1

2 3

4 5 6

Bird's Nest Crack

11 12 13 14 15 16

South Face

This face is ever popular with a great selection of short routes that are easier than most offerings on the cliff. There are several worthwhile, if slippery, cracks here and pleasantly technical face climbs in between. There are also two steep and intense bouldering areas with many classic and popular problems.

❶ The Pothole . . . . **VDiff**
12m. The initial difficulties on the direct route can be avoided by a pleasant traverse in from the top of the slabby boulder on the left. Using the upper break is the easiest way of doing it.
FA. Herbert Ingle late 1800s

❷ Jam-pot . . . . **V2 (5c)**
Start low, use small holds to gain a good jam then the pothole.

❸ Pothole Direct . . . . **VS 5b**
10m. The left-most crack in the wall has a butch and brutal overhang to start and then rapidly eases.
FA. Denys Fisher 1938

❹ The Traditional Climb . . **VS 4c**
10m. The steep zig-zagging central crack has plenty of jams and protection but not too many positive holds. The central section is the most difficult.
FA. Herbert Ingle late 1800s

❺ Forgotten Wall **E5 6c**
10m. The narrow wall is climbed left then right with increasing difficulty to the top break at which point things ease a little. Desperate moves, though at least with good protection.
FA. Rob Gawthorpe 1980

❻ Bird's Nest Crack . . . . **HS 4b**
10m. The well polished right-hand crack is the most amenable of the three fissures here and gives a good, perfectly protected introduction to jamming.
FA. Herbert Ingle, late 1890s

❼ High Level Traverse . . . **VS 4c**
16m. Take *BNC* to its final break and follow this to a finish up *The Pothole*. Large cams are helpful. Can be done the other way too.
FA. Alan Austin 1957

❽ Thompson's Traverse . . **HVS 5b**
20m. Climb the thin crack to its end then head left by more strangely satisfying sideways shuffling all the way to *The Pothole*. The hard bit is where the crack ain't.
FA. Sydney Thompson 1935

❾ Bird's Nest Variation . . . **VS 4c**
10m. Good moves lead up the thin crack and the wall above and left, until the protrusion on the original route can be grasped.

❿ Demon Wall . . . . . **HVS 5a**
12m. The thin crack provides an awkward start (primes the pump) then step right to a flake in the bulge. Climb leftwards to a grasping final move. Originally started from the chimney to the right which is easier but less satisfying.
FA. Arthur Dolphin 1940

⓫ Stu's Roof Left-hand . . . **V8**
Gain the two tiny crimps from an undercut on the left.

⓬ Stu's Roof **V10**
A much harder version over the roof using just the two crimps.

⓭ Demon Wall Roof . . **V7**
The centre of the roof is usually well chalked.

⓮ Dolphin Belly Slap . . **V6 (6c)**
The edge of the roof, craft and cunning helps.

⓯ Dolphinian **E1 5b**
10m. The right arete of the wall has a taxing finish with a long stretch for a juggy flute.
FA. Al Manson 1976

Pule Hill | Shooters | Hepenstall | Widdop | Earl Crag | Ilkley | The Chevin | Caley | Almscliff | Eastby | Crookrise | Rylstone | Simon's Seat | Brimham | Farestones | Slipstones | Grey Walls | Goldsb'gh

Descent

Black Wall

Central Crack

18 24 23 20 16 17 19 21 22 25 26 27 28

---

16 Three Chockstones Chimney ⬜ **Mod**
10m. The deep scoured rift is one of the the easiest routes on the cliff. It offers a slippery descent route or a reasonable beginners' climb with an awkward start.
FA. Cecil Slingsby c1870

17 Crack and Wall . . . . ⬜ **HS 4b**
12m. The flake in the right-hand wall of the chimney leads to the overhangs. Shuffle left on flutings around into the chimney then escape out right for the best finish.

18 Acetabulum . . . . ⬜ **E1 5c**
12m. The roof-crack above the final traverse of *Crack and Wall* is hard to enter. The name refers to the hip joint, a clue as how to approach the moves.
FA. Al Manson 1973

19 The Crucifix . . . . ⬜ **V1 (5c)**
The inverted cross-shaped crack in the side wall is a classic boulder problem and is quite tough at the grade unless you are flexible. Countless variations exist.

20 Crucifix Arete . . . . ⬜ **V3 (6a)**
The arete direct.

21 Pebble Wall . . . . . . ⬜ **V5 (6b)**
A classic using tiny pebbles on the face above the roof.

22 Pebble Wall Variation . . ⬜ **V7**
The pebble-less wall just left of the crack requires a long reach.

23 Rectum Rift . . . ⬜ **E3 6b**
10m. Climb *Pebble Wall* to the break and then the hanging 'arse' in the roof by long reaches and rounded pulls. There is gear up there somewhere.
FA. Al Manson 1972

24 Right Cheeky . . ⬜ **E7 6c**
10m. The desperate rounded bulging roof to the right of *Rectum Rift*. Apparently it is "only E6 if you don't fall off"!
FA. Ben Bransby 1999

25 Central Crack . . . . ⬜ **HS 4b**
10m. The well-scoured and kinked crack is an archetypal grit trip - get thrashing.

26 Jacob's Ladder . . . . ⬜ **HVS 5b**
10m. The wall between the two prominent cracks has a slippery start, good runners and a delicate finale. It feels a little artificial but is still worth doing.
FA. Denys Fisher 1943

27 Stomach Traverse . . . . . ⬜ **VS 4c**
10m. The wide crack with a kink at two thirds height is another slippery customer. Originally it started up *Central Crack*, and the linking section can still be stomach traversed by those who want to be historically correct - don't forget the tweeds.
FA. Herbert Ingle late 1890s

28 Fence Buttress . . . . ⬜ **VS 5b**
10m. Carefully use the stone wall to start a tricky sequence first left and then right to reach a flake, then balance up the wall above to easy ground.

Lots of sun | 5 min | Windy

Pule Hill | Shooter's | Heptonstall | Widdop | Earl Crag | Ilkley | The Chevin | Caley | Almscliff | Eastby | Crookrise | Rylstone | Simon's Seat | Brimham | Lawrencines | Slipstones | Crag Willas | Widdot? grit

Black Wall

The section of cliff beyond the stone wall is a favourite sheltering spot for cows. In wet winter weather an unsavoury pool sometimes forms under it, precluding using jumping off as an escape route, in which case you may well really be in the ****!

❶ Dreamland **V7**
Link the two distant breaks in the wall just left of the crack.

❷ South Chimney Layback . . . **S 4c**
12m. Jam the steep narrow crack then layback the flake rightwards to an easy amble up the final section of *South Chimney*.

❸ Shuffle Crack **E1 5c**
12m. From the top of the initial crack of *South Chimney Layback*, continue up the flake then shuffle left along the rounded break with difficulty to reach easy ground. Big gear needed.
FA. Alan Austin 1958

❹ China Syndrome . . . **E5 7a**
10m. The roof above *Shuffle Crack* is climbed (infrequently) using a flake and little else. The route remains amongst the hardest on the crag nearly 30 years on. *Photo opposite.*
FA. Rob Gawthorpe 1980

❺ The Slab . . . . **V2 (5c)**
The polished ramps are a popular and frustrating problem.

❻ The Wall . . . . **V1 (5b)**
The glossy pockets are a touch easier. It is **V5** without the pockets.

❼ South Chimney . . . . **Diff-ish**
10m. The unmistakable rift is constricted and as polished as the other low grade routes hereabouts. The upper section is easier.
FA. Cecil Slingsby c1870

❽ Yellow Wall **E2 5c**
14m. From just below the top of *South Chimney* crawl left along the rounded break (cams in the depths) to escape.
FA. Tony Barley 1966

❾ The Nose . . . . **V3 (6a)**
The short arete to a break. The left-hand side of the arete without the pocket is **V6**. The right-hand side of the arete is also **V6**.
FA. Robin and Tony Barley 1960s

❿ South Wall Traverse . . . . . . **VS 4c**
14m. To the right of the chimney is a narrow ramp on the wall. Climb this and traverse out left onto the arete. Trend right up the slab and step round the corner then climb a short exposed crack through the bulges until a swing right leads to an easy finish.
FA. Claude Frankland early 1920s

⓫ Birdlime Traverse . . **E1 5b**
18m. Follow *South Wall Traverse* to the bulges but step down and traverse awkwardly rightwards below these to reach a poor rest below a thin crack. Up this on pockets then swing right again to a final tricky move. Devious but superb.
FA. Arthur Dolphin 1946

⓬ 'Arries' Ook **E4 6a**
12m. From the ramp used by the previous two climbs, traverse delicately right then climb to the bulges and the first runners. A leap of faith reaches more holds and a much easier finish. The lower wall can be done as a (highball) boulder problem **V5**. The direct start is **V6**.
FA. Pete Livesey 1975

⓭ Black Wall Eliminate **E2 5c**
14m. Start (pond permitting) at a large flake and gain a standing position with difficulty. Pull up the wall then swing left to reach and climb the pocketed crack on *Birdlime Traverse*. At the top of this swing left again to reach a short finishing crack. Slightly butch and totally brilliant.
FA. Tony Barley 1966

⓮ Black Wall . . . . **VS 5a**
10m. Start up blocks to the right of the pool. Pass a bulge and continue until it is possible to move left to an uncomfortable ledge. Finish through a notch with difficulty.
FA. Arthur Dolphin 1941

Pule Hill
Shooter's
Heptonstall
Widdop
Earl Crag
Ilkley
The Chevin
Caley
Almscliff
Eastby
Crookrise
Rylstone
Simon's Seat
Brimham
Eavestone
Slipstones
Crag Willas
Guisecliff

James Ibbertson making a rare attempt on *China Syndrome* (E5 7a) - *opposite*. Photo: Dave Musgrove

	No star	☆	☆☆	☆☆☆
Mod to S	-	3	-	2
HS to HVS	1	4	3	-
E1 to E3	-	1	-	1
E4 and up	-	-	-	1

A great little cliff, slabby and tall, in a sunny position and with the added attraction of only being a few minutes from the road. There are only a few routes here but the star count is high with a number of classics at amenable grades.

Conditions

The crag faces south and is free draining, as such it makes a viable venue for most of the year and can be especially pleasant on clear winter days. The slope below the crag is thick with bracken in high summer.

Approach

The crag is north east of Skipton; from the Skipton by-pass follow signs to Embsay (miniature railway) then Eastby.

As the road starts to climb to the moor beyond the village, the cliff is clearly visible on the left. Park sensibly on the left - room for about five cars. Approach through the gate, just below the parking (with the BMC sign) along a permitted footpath through the field. PLEASE CLOSE ALL GATES. The crag and the moor beyond are on CRoW Access Land.

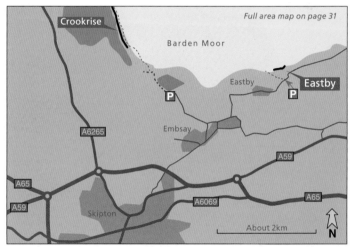

Full area map on page 31

About 2km

Pillar Front — Knuckle Slab — Nose Climb

Descent

Knuckle Slab - 20m

Pile Hill · Shooters · Heptonstall · Widdop · Earl Crag · Ilkley · The Chevin · Caley · Almscliff · Eastby · Crookrise · Rylstone · Simon's Seat · Brimham · Eavestones · Slipstones · Crag Willas · Goldsborgh

Pillar Front

The show-piece of the cliff is the fine slender pillar, home to a great set of climbs from VDiff to E2 and, at 20m, they are longer than is usual for grit.

Descent - Follow the narrow ledge leftwards into an open gully - it can be slippery at times.

❶ Eastby Groove . . . . **S 4a**

20m. The long groove that bounds the left edge of the main buttress is especially worthwhile early in the season, before the ferns get a grip. Start up the left-hand corner, move right then follow it throughout.
FA. Sidney Waterfall 1930s

❷ Heather Flake . . . . **VS 4c**

20m. Climb the short wall to a ledge then continue parallel to *Eastby Groove* to the highest ledge. Move right to a nice finish up the exposed flake in the arete.
FA. John Belbin 1990

❸ Swastika . . . . **HVS 5b**

34m. A bit of a non-line though interesting and popular, with stacks of good climbing. Climb the right-hand groove to a niche, step down and right onto the face and cross to the far arete and a possible stance just around the corner. Continue across the slab via *The Padder* to a well positioned finish up *Whaup Edge*.
FA. Allan Austin 1962

❹ Pillar Front **E2 5b**

20m. A superb and bold outing up the front of the pillar. Climb the tricky but escapable rib to the roof and pull over to reach the left-trending ramp. Up this then trend right (bold) to the upper overhangs. Weave through these then finish direct. Memorable.
FA. Allan Austin 1962

❺ Pillar Rib . . . . **VS 4c**

20m. A great climb. The right arete of the buttress is reached by zig-zagging through the overhangs, followed by well positioned and sustained climbing, until it is possible to move out left to the finish of *Pillar Front*. *Photo on page 113.*
FA. Frank Wilkinson 1965

Descent

13

15

13

11
10 12

14

16

Nose Climb

Knuckle Slab

6 Eastby Buttress. . . . . . . `Top` `50` **VDiff**
20m. The cracks in the right-hand flank of the buttress give one of the best VDiffs on grit. Climb the groove until the cracks can be reached. They are then followed throughout, with good gear and some fine but easy jamming.
FA. Sidney Waterfall 1930s

7 Eastby Buttress Variation **VS 4c**
20m. Continuing up the sustained crack in the side wall gives a worthwhile and neglected variation to *Eastby Buttress.*

8 The Padder **E1 5b**
18m. Good friction climbing. Start up the shrubby groove then shuffle out right to the centre of the hanging slab. Head up this with the final section proving quite testing on rubber and nerve.
FA. Keith Roberts 1965

9 Whaup Edge. . . . . **VS 4b**
18m. A cracking climb, mild but with a bold feel. Gain the hanging rib from the right and balance up it. The lower section is a bit scary but the interest is well maintained.
FA. Allan Austin 1960

Knuckle Slab and Nose Climb

10 Scoop and Crack. . . . . . . **S 4a**
12m. Start up the grassy groove to the roof, then move right and udge up the fine (if a little wide) crack to a belay ledge.
FA. Allan Austin 1960

11 Knuckle Slab Arete . . . . **HVS 5b**
12m. The angular arete gives a short layback pitch on its left-hand side until forced round to the right. Finish up the previous climb, or leftwards as for *Knuckle Slab.*

Knuckle Slab and Nose Climb
To the right the cliff degenerates into a series of blocks buttresses and overhangs scattered along the hillside. A small selection of the best climbs is included here - consult the *YMC Yorkshire Gritstone* (1998) guide for details of the other 50 or so routes available.

12 Index Variation . . . . . . **VS 5a**
10m. An excellent direct line up the centre of the slab.

13 Knuckle Slab . . . . **HVS 5a**
12m. Traverse the break to the arete, layback to the overhang then trend left up the exposed slab or, more logically, finish up the wide crack on the right.
FA. Allan Austin 1960

14 Nose Climb . . . . **S 4a**
14m. A cracker, small but perfectly formed. Traverse the horizontal breaks that cross the face to the right arete. Balance up this then finish up the short lived crack in the top right edge of the buttress. Double ropes are useful.
FA. Sidney Waterfall 1930s

15 Thumper **E4 5c**
14m. From the centre of the traverse of *Nose Climb*, use a couple of pockets to climb up and right, then back left, to pass round the left-hand side of the central nose into a shallow scoop. Finish with trepidation.
FA. John Eastham 1977

16 Nose Climb Original . . . **S 4a**
12m. Climb the right-hand face of the buttress until the ledge on the arete can be reached. Move round onto the front and finish as for the regular route.
FA. Sidney Waterfall 1930s

Pole Hill | Shooter's | Heptonstall | Widdop | Earl Crag | Ilkley | The Chevin | Caley | Almscliff | Eastby | Crookrise | Rylstone | Simon's Seat | Brimham | Eavestones | Slipstones | Crag Willas | Goldsborough

	No star	✧	✧✧	✧✧✧
Mod to S	4	6	4	-
HS to HVS	1	17	6	2
E1 to E3	4	5	6	1
E4 and up	-	3	-	2

One of Yorkshire's premier venues and a long-time evening favourite despite the flog up to the cliff. The cliff consists of some fine steep buttresses separated by more broken areas, so a bit of moving around is needed to get the best out of the place. The path along the base of the cliff is a bit scrambly in places.

There are almost 200 named routes on the main crag and on a complex jumble of huge blocks below the edge. The bouldering is briefly covered here.

Conditions

The crag faces south west and so is in the sun from midday onwards. It is exposed to the vagaries of the weather but dries quickly and suffers little from greenery or drainage. The place is often worth a visit on a sunny winter's afternoon if the wind isn't too strong.

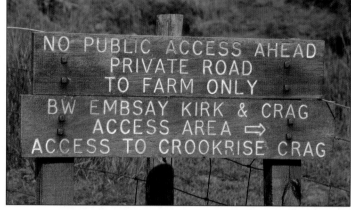

Approach

The crag is located north of the centre of Skipton, and is clearly visible from the Skipton by-pass. From this road, follow signs for Embsay, then in the centre of the village, turn left onto Pasture Road following the narrow lane for 600m before zig-zaging up to the parking place by the reservoir. Continue on foot around the reservoir to where signs point to the moor. Head up the slope, following the best track, to meet the wall and follow this to where it levels out on the crest of the moor. The cliff lies on the other side of the wall and is accessed by one of a pair of stiles - 20 minutes from the car.

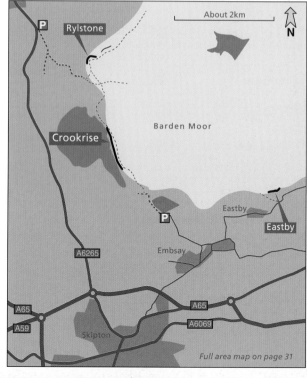

Full area map on page 31

Slingsby's Pinnacle

The wall and tall tower separated from the edge by a small gap is arguably the best buttress at Crookrise, it has an excellent selection of climbs on peerless rock.
Approach - Continue along the cliff-top path to the second stile, the buttress is directly below and most easily reached by scrambling down rightwards (looking out) over and around a series of huge boulders.

1 Streaklet . . . . 🔦 [＿＿＿] **E3 6b**
6m. The centre of the wall has a desperate start to reach the break and a rounded finish.
FA. Graham Desroy 1988

2 Rushlight. . . . . 🔦 [＿＿＿] **S 4a**
8m. The slabby side wall of the left-hand face to a steeper finish.
FA. Norman Elliott 1966

3 Crease . . . . 🔁 [＿＿＿] **VS 5a**
12m. From the blocky rift, gain the face on the right using the pockets then continue up and right to finish.
FA. George Walker 1952

4 Crease Arete . . . . . 🔦🔦🔦 [＿＿＿] **E2 6a**
10m. Starting on the right, gain and follow the arete throughout.
FA. Phillip Osbourne 1997

5 Crease Direct. . . . . 🔁🔦 [＿＿＿] **V3 (6a)**
The technical banana-shaped groove is superb. Escape left.
FA. Allan Austin 1957

6 The Fly . . . . . . 🔁🔦🔦🔦 [＿＿＿] **V8**
A couple of poor pockets point the way up the smooth wall.
FA. Ron Fawcett 1979

7 Slingsby's Chimney. . . . 🔁[👆][＿＿＿] **HVD 4a**
10m. A classic. The start is tricky, then burrow into the cliff to make progress where traditional techniques lead back to daylight.
FA. Cecil Slingsby late 1800s

8 Chimney Buttress . . . . 🔁 [＿＿＿] **HS 4b**
12m. Start up the chimney but move left onto the face, continuing up and left following the line of least resistance.
FA. Possibly Gritstone Club members early 1920s

9 Small Brown . . . . 🔁🔦 [＿＿＿] **E4 6b**
10m. Gain the shallow hanging groove direct or from the left (traditional, though no shenanigans with the rope allowed nowadays) and continue warily until things ease. The **Direct Start** is **V5**.
FA. Joe Brown (with tension) 1958. FFA. Ron Fawcett 1973

10 Massive Attack. . . . 🔁🔦🔦 [＿＿＿] **E5 6b**
10m. Use the direct start to *Small Brown* but continue up the left-hand side of the arete throughout.
FA. Derek Hargreaves 1996

11 Hovis Super Direct . . . . 🔁🔦 [＿＿＿] **V5 (6b)**
Climb direct to reach pockets in the wall left of *Hovis*.
Photo on page 117.

12 Hovis Direct. . . . . . 🔁[👆]🔦 [＿＿＿] **V4 (6a)**
Climb the arete left of the block to a pocket. Escape right or continue up **Wholemeal, E3 6a**, to reach *Flake Wall*.
FA. Mick Johnson 1997. Only the upper section was new.

13 Hovis . . . . 🔁🔦🔦 [＿＿＿] **E1 5c**
10m. From the top of the flake on the right, teeter round the corner and gain the shallow hanging groove with difficulty. Continue up the centre of the buttress taking the easiest line.
FA. Joe Brown 1958

Descent

5m gap

9

15

14

11   12   13

Hovis

Walker's Farewell

16 17   18   19   20

18

Walker's Farewell and Slip 'n' Slide

A pair of attractive steep slabs rising above a narrow bilberry terrace and divided by an area of broken grooves and cracks. There are a number of climbs here on the general theme of 'delicate and bold' though only the original one sees much attention; the rest are generally quite a bit harder and runners are in short supply.

14 Flake Wall . . . . **HS 4b**
10m. Traverse up the flake then step up to the break. Traverse this out to the arete and finish up this.
FA. John Wilson 1951

15 Spellbinder . . . . **HVS 5a**
8m. A direct finish to *Flake Wall* up the face above the centre of the flake.
FA. Richard Davies 1985

Up and right is a high slab above a terrace.

16 Walkover **E3 6a**
10m. Balance along the left-hand rim of the slab. Scary and precarious despite its diminutive size.
FA. Pete Livesey 1977

17 A Lifetime's Dream **E4 6b**
8m. The left-hand side of the slab is tackled direct on a barely adequate line of pockets and a scattering of pebbles.
FA. Derek Hargreaves 1986

18 Walker's Farewell . . . . . **HVS 5b**
18m. The original and best? A ramp on the lower tier leads to a heather cornice and belay on the ledge. Gain the slab with difficulty then pass the big pocket and then the notch in the roof.
FA. George Walker 1952

19 Wonderloaf **E2 5b**
8m. The right-hand side of the slab past a small flake to the tough roof. The name suggests its on the wrong buttress.
FA. Allan Austin 1962

20 Winter Traverse . . . **E1 5a**
10m. Traverse the right-hand side of the slab above the steep gully heading for better holds on the right arete.
FA. Allan Austin 1958

21 Duck 'n' Dive **E5 6b**
8m. The shallow groove. The crack is out of reach.
FA. Jerry Peel 1990

22 Slip 'n' Slide **E6 6a**
8m. The ramp is precarious, unprotected and simply superb. The potential fall is twice the length of the route!
FA. Ron Fawcett 1976

23 Sunstroke Direct . . . . . . **HVS 5b**
8m. Bridge the flared groove to access the hanging crack.
FA. Dave Barry (from the right) 1966

Slip 'n' Slide

21   22   23

Walker's Farewell - 20m

Pule Hill | Shooter's | Hepsonstall | Widdop | Earl Crag | Ilkley | The Chevin | Caley | Almscliff | Eastby | Crookrise | Brimham | Simon's Seat | Brimham | Earl Crag | Slipstones | Crag Willas | Brimstone

The Shelf

A fine tall buttress with several excellent climbs including the cliff's best known mid-extreme *The Shelf* - still a solid E2, originally soloed by Allan Austin way back in 1956 (with Brian Evans dangling a sling over the top). There are other fine offerings including a couple of meaty cracks.

Approach - The buttress is mid-way between the two stiles and difficult to locate from above. The best approach is by dropping down to the crag-base path at the first stile and walking along.

① Chockstone Chimney . . . . . . **VDiff**
12m. The groove is reached via twin cracks.

② Buster Direct . . . . **HVS 5b**
10m. Climb the reachy front of the pillar to gain the slanting crack, then jam this to access the easier arete.
FA. Paul Greenland 1977

③ Buster . . . . **S 4a**
12m. Start up the chimney then shuffle round the first arete and cross the face to the second one. Up this - great positions - to a finish on the right.

④ Open Chimney . . . . **VDiff**
10m. The long rift is an old-style classic, beware the odd loose block. After the second big chockstone, stay close to the outside for the best finish, transferring to the right arete when it finally gets too wide to bridge, or just ramble up the back.
FA. Possibly Yorkshire Ramblers Club 1900s

⑤ The Shelf **E2 5b**
12m. A classic bold outing, now tamed somewhat with modern cunning. Climb the groove to its top and a good pocket. A long stretch reaches The Shelf and a steep and awkward rockover/mantel on this provides a memorable move.
FA. Allan Austin 1956

⑥ The Forager . . . . **VS 4c**
12m. A cop-out from the main challenge but with some good climbing. Up the groove (as for *The Shelf*) but follow the jamming crack leftwards into the chimney and a finish up the right wall, just left of the arete.
FA. Brian Swales 1994

⑦ Long Climb . . . . **HS 4b**
12m. The central rift of the buttress gives a fine outing, steep and quite awkward. A stomach-traverse used to be the way to go, though nowadays there are less extreme ways of getting left to the final short crack.
FA. Possibly Gritstone Club members 1920s

⑧ Lyndhurst **E1 5b**
12m. Makes the most of the rock right of *Long Climb*. An awkward crack (usually avoided) gains the ledge. Climb the wall above via the niche and pull past the overlap to reach the traverse on *Cat's Whiskers*. Move left, sort some decent (extended) gear, then pull through the overhang for a fine finish.
FA. Brian Swales 1994

⑨ Cat's Whiskers . . . . **VS 4c**
14m. Climb the wall to a ledge then make a balancy high step onto the overlap and continue to the roof. A long traverse left completes the climb.
FA. George Walker 1952

Slingsby's Pinnacle — Walker's Farewell — Slip 'n' Slide — The Shelf — Arsenic Slab — The Sole — Tiger Rag — End Slab

Descent

Descent

❶ Arsenic Slab Direct Start ☒ ◄ ▢ **V2 (6a)**
Pull onto the slab with difficulty and finish easily.

❷ Winter Rain . . . . ☒☒ ▢ **E2 5c**
10m. Pull over the roof and plod up the slab. The initial moves are tricky and side-runners are a no-no.
FA. Bob Larkin 1987

❸ Arsenic Slab . . . . ☒▢ **S 4a**
14m. Start up the slippery central crack then foot traverse the slab leftwards then move up to the large perched flake. Climb past this and up the arete above.
FA. Craven Pothole Club members 1950

❹ Old Lace . . . . ☒▢ **HVS 5a**
12m. From halfway along the traverse climb the smooth slab past a useful pocket, easing with height. The route is high in the grade unless a side-runner is employed. Three Pebblesque.
FA. Charlie Salisbury 1952

❺ Diagonal Crack. . . . . . . ☒☒▢ **VDiff**
12m. The slanting rift that bounds the right-hand side of the slab is a bit of a pig to enter, it is easier once established.

Arsenic Slab
A fine clean slab of rock, undercut along most of its length, and not to be confused with End Slab which is the first piece of rock encountered on the normal path.
Approach - The buttress is mid-way between the two stiles and difficult to locate from above. The best approach is by dropping down to the crag-base path at the first stile and walking along.

❻ East of the River . . . . ☒▢ **VS 5a**
12m. Pull onto the slab and continue until it gets scruffy. Move left to finish up the cleaner upper part of *Winter Rain*.
FA. David Williams 1992

❼ Octopus. . . . . ☒▢ **S 4a**
12m. Climb the centre of the slab until forced into *Diagonal Crack* to finish.

❽ Octopus Direct . . . . ☒▢ **VS 4c**
12m. A direct line one metre from the right-hand edge of the slab gives a pleasant pitch.

❾ Face, Arete and Wall Climb ☒▢ **VDiff**
10m. With a name like that, you need a description?

The Sole

A fine jutting square tower with the classic of *The Sole* making its way up the left-hand arete and side wall. There are several other interesting climbs around the bay to the left and the area is usually quiet.

Approach - Drop down to the crag-base path at the first stile and walk along.

① Moulson's Climb. . . . . S 4a
10m. Climb the crack and the large, tilted, jammed block to reach the easy chimney above.

② A Reach too Far E3 6a
10m. Head up the front face, trending rightwards to a hole and a rock horn. A stretch and a pull on a sloper leads to easy ground.
FA. Mick Johnson 1997

③ Longlurch E2 5c
12m. Traverse left from the chimney then climb the face and the small roof via a stretch for an elusive pocket. Escape left.
FA. Long Ron Fawcett 1974. Apparently he did the centre of the upper roof too - this finish may be unrepeated?

④ Griffith's Chimney . . . . . HS 4b
10m. The wide rift in the back of the bay is a graunchy classic, so most folks avoid it.

⑤ Walker's Wall. . . . . HVS 5a
10m. Climb the arete until it is possible to trend right into the centre of the face. Continue up to the roof and pull round it just right of centre.
FA. George Walker 1952

⑥ Craven Crack . . . . VS 4c
10m. The crack is harder than it looks. Follow it to the ledges under the roof then move out right to finish.
FA. Arnold Waterfall 1930

⑦ West Wall Climb . . . . . HS 4b
6m. The blunt rib in the north-facing wall.
FA. Arthur Birtwhistle 1937

⑧ The Sole . . . . HVS 5b
10m. Climb the crack in the arete by a hard layback sequence (it would be 5c if it was 20m up) then follow the easier cracks across the side wall.
FA. Allan Austin 1956

⑨ Family Matters . . . . HVS 5b
8m. Where *The Sole* scoots off left, continue straight up the arete by nice layaway moves.
FA. Paul Greenland 1977

⑩ Mother's Little Helper . . E2 5c
10m. Start up *The Sole*, traverse right between the overhangs (a pig for the long-legged) and pull over its centre to gain the hanging slab. Finish direct up the front of the buttress, and over the roof.
FA. Steve Bancroft 1976. The original name was less tasteful.

⑪ Slab and Nose . . . . S 4b
10m. Climb a groove then follow ledges rightwards up the side wall.

⑫ Slab and Nose Variations. . . HVS 5a
10m. Layback the slabby arete then step left and climb the side wall.
FA. Allan Austin 1956

15 Route 3 .... 🏷️ 🪨 S 4a
8m. Use the break to reach the wide diagonal crack in the slab and finish up this.

16 Route 4 .... 🏷️ 🪨 🧗 HVS 5c
10m. Pull past Long John's chipped initials to reach ledges then move out left. Finish up the slab passing between the eye holes.
FA. Norman Elliot 1966

17 Route 2.5 .... 🏷️ 🪨 ❤️ HVS 5a
8m. A direct line up the left-hand side of the slab aiming for the top of the diagonal crack. Feels bold in the upper part.
FA. Craven Pothole Club members 1949

18 Route 2 .... 🏷️ 🪨 ❤️ VS 5a
8m. Excellent. Climb straight up to the thin crack above the break, pop in a couple of runners, then balance up the final moves.
FA. Arnold Waterfall 1930

19 Route 1 .... ❤️ VDiff
18m. An ancient route (well 1900) that starts up the tricky arete to the mid-height ledge. Traverse this all the way leftwards to the diagonal crack and finish up this. There isn't much gear, but then again, it isn't very hard.

20 Edge .... 🏷️ 🪨 ❤️ VS 5a
8m. Follow the right-hand edge of the slab throughout.

> ### End Slab
> The first piece of rock reached when accessing the crag from the first stile is an attractive slab with a pleasant set of delicate offerings, as might be expected, gear is rather lacking. Don't be put off by the less than inspiring route names.

Halfway between End Slab and The Sole is a small buttress with a tree in front of it. There are two routes on the side wall.

13 Travese and Crack .... 🏷️ 🖌️ VDiff
8m. Cross the steep side wall heading for the beckoning crack

14 Tiger Rag .... 🏷️ 🧗 HS 4c
8m. Gain the ledge on the arete from the blocks in the gully - hard - then continue leftwards up the wall.
FA. John Wilson 1951

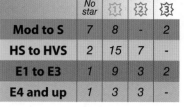

	No star	☆	☆☆	☆☆☆
Mod to S	7	8	-	2
HS to HVS	2	15	7	-
E1 to E3	1	9	3	2
E4 and up	1	3	3	-

A fine crag, one of Yorkshire's best, guarded by a decent walk up which tends to keep the crowds away. The crag consists of a series of buttresses scattered along the crest of the moor and, although a bit of bobbing about is required to get the most out of a day, the effort will be repaid in full. The trio of *Dental Slab*, *President's Slab* and *Monument Crack* are the targets for most visitors but while you are up here it is worth taking a look at some of the other challenges.

For those who like even more solitude, head off to explore the Far Group - the isolated series of towers and pinnacles that run north across the moor towards Cracoe Memorial - see *YMC Yorkshire Gritstone (1998)* for full details.

Conditions

The crag is inclined to be green and gritty after rain and generally visits are best made in the spring and summer, though after any dry spell it can be worth a shout. It faces north west and is at its best on warm summer evenings. On a clear day the views over to the Lake District are superb. The crag is well sheltered from cold Easterlies and fully exposed to roaring Westerlies.

Approach

Just south of the village of Rylstone (5 miles north of Skipton) there is parking on the right for five carefully placed cars, if this is full there is room in the village. Walk down the road (away from the village) for 200m to a track on the left and follow this to a gated track (the second one) on the left with a variety of signs about the Barden Estate. Follow this as it steepens and loops round a wood, through a gate and up towards the crest of the moor. Just beyond a cutting (and uphill of the new fencing) a footpath branches left, under Warm-up Buttress and runs along to the Monument - a steady 30 minutes from the car. The buttresses are most easily reached from above. If heading to the far end of the crag the path on the south side of the wall is better.

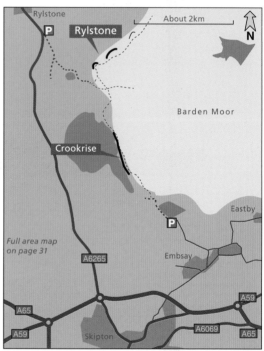

Sherri Davy on the fine *Dental Slab* (S 4a) - *page 129* - at Rylstone. Photo: Chris Craggs

Heart Beat City

At the far left-hand end of the main cliff is this isolated set of slabby faces and flying aretes. It doesn't see much attention because of the combination of a remote setting and mostly hard routes.

Approach - Follow the cliff-top path along the line of the wall (either side), over a rise and down into the dip until the unmistakable buttress appears on the left.

❶ Three Step Buttress. VS 4c
14m. Climb to the bulge, pull over awkwardly and traverse left to a stance round the corner. Pull right onto the arete (feels bold) and sketch up this.

❷ Bare-faced Streak.. E4 6a
12m. Climb the right side of the lower face then from good gear, climb through the overlap and climb sketchily onto a shelf and a breather. Trend left to finish.
FA. Graham Desroy 1989

❸ Halo of Flies .. E6 6b
10m. Up the right arete to the break (large cams) then use a variety of poor holds to scale the upper arete left then right.
FA. Paul Wheeler 1999

❹ Forgotten Friends .... HVS 5a
10m. Climb up to a tricky move up the right-hand arete. Don't forget your Friends!

❺ A Place to Be E7 6b
8m. The slabby arete gives good but mighty bold climbing.
FA. Iain Farrar 1999

❻ Heart Beat City.... E8 6c
8m. The fine jutting fin is started from the right and finished on the left. As ever, there is no gear and the landing is atrocious, the added bonus in this case is that the fall is twice as long as the route.
FA. Dave Pegg 1989

❼ Face Savour............ HVS 5b
12m. Climb the steep rib on its left then head easily to the base of the slab. Step onto it and trend up and left before climbing direct, passing the left edge of the overlap.
FA. Dave Musgrove 1988

❽ Veteran E3 5c
8m. Gain the slab from the right then climb its centre boldly passing the overlap and finishing up the blunt rib. Low in the grade.
FA. Frank Booth 1994

❾ Back Stage Gossip E2 6a
6m. The curved arete on its right-hand side.
FA. Derek Hargreaves 2000

Rylstone Buttress

❿ Up and Over.............. VDiff
10m. The tricky lower crack leads to easier climbing. Finish up the wider crack spitting the final wall.

⓫ Loiner .... VS 4c
12m. Start up the centre of the wall but head left along the break and climb the arete finishing through the bulge.
FA. Dave Berry 1965

⓬ Never Climb with Guidebook Writers
.... E1 5b
12m. A direct ascent of the wall has some very good moves. From the top ledge, finish leftwards up the arete.
FA. Graham Arthur 1988. Seconded by Dave Musgrove, the writer in question. Despite pointing Graham at this fine climb they never climbed together again.

⓭ Bowler's Chimney .... Diff
12m. The green rift is okay when dry and grim when not.
FA. Bill Bowler 1935

Heart Beat City - 100m

Rylstone Buttress

⑭ Wall of the Evening Plight   E1 5c
12m. A worthwhile outing up the pillar to the right of the groove. A long stretch links the upper breaks, then finish steeply via the flake splitting the final wall.
FA. Frank Wilkinson 1988

⑮ Rylstone Crack . . . .   HS 4b
12m. A classic of its kind. Follow the ramp to the base of the flake that forms the left-hand end of the roof. Swarm up the wide crack to a capping block and pass this awkwardly before escaping rightwards into a niche and up a short groove.
FA. Early Gritstone Club members pre-1923

⑯ Rylstone Wall . . . .   VS 4c
14m. Another excellent outing. Start up the green flake/groove to the roof then move up and right to a ledge. Shuffle out right and stretch up the wall to the highest break, then move right to finish up an easy crack.
FA. Barry Cliff 1958

⑰ Karalta E3 6a
12m. Follow *Rylstone Wall* to the roof then stretch up and left to the thin break. A hard pebble-pull reaches the wider break and a bold move gains the finish of *Freebooter*.
FA. Neil Herbert 1999

⑱ Freebooter. . . . .   HVS 5a
14m. A gap-filler but with good positions. Climb rightwards round the lowest roof to join *Rylstone Wall Direct* at its jamming crack and follow this to the point where it heads right. Follow the breaks out to the left and gain the niche via a tricky layaway using a flake in the right wall. Finish more easily.
FA. Tony Barley 1971

⑲ Terror at Five and a Half Feet   E5 6b
12m. Climb the roof above the start of *Freebooter*, then tackle the centre of the wall left of *Rylstone Wall* to the final bulge where an elusive finger pocket gains a rounded finish.
FA. Neil Herbert 1999

⑳ Rylstone Wall Direct   HVS 5a
14m. Yet another good climb. Start on the right and traverse left under the roof to reach a jamming crack. Head straight up the wall until a move right becomes inevitable.
FA. A large YMC party 1965

Rylstone Buttress
A fine buttress, it faces a bit more to the north than the other buttresses here and so is inclined to be somewhat greener. Despite this is has a good collection of old favourites and some modern eliminates.
Approach - Either descend leftwards from Dental Slab, passing Castrol Buttress, or follow the cliff-top path over the first rise after the monument. When it starts to descend the buttress is down and left.

㉑ Beached Whale . . .   E2 5b
12m. Tackle the jutting nose using flake-holds to the right, then access the ledge in the expected fashion. Once regrouped, move out left to a finish up the blunt arete and the nose above
FA. Dave Musgrove 1988

㉒ Balance Crack . . . .   VDiff
10m. The wide crack that bounds the buttress has a tricky start. At the chockstone choose a finish, over or under.

Balance Crack

Rylstone Buttress - 20m

Castrol/G.T.X. Buttress

There is only a small selection of routes on the roofed buttress that lies halfway between Rylstone Buttress and Dental Slab.

Approach - Follow the main cliff-top path past the monument and over a rise into an open hollow. As the path starts to rise again, a minor track branches off to the left passing President's Slab and Dental Slab.

❶ G.T.X. . . . . HVS 5a
20m. A good varied climb up the left-hand side of the buttress. Climb the left-hand side of the wall on surprising holds to a possible stance on a good ledge. Climb up one level then move left to the base of the bulging jamming crack. Finish up this.
FA. Brian Swales 1981

❷ Castrol . . . . VS 5a
28m. An interesting climb, long and devious. Climb to and up the flake in the centre of the wall, to reach a possible stance shared with the previous route. Follow *G.T.X.* but continue the traverse for 4m to a second crack-line. Climb up this to a recess. Access the slab with difficulty (especially tricky when it is dirty) and finish up it, or traverse off right to escape.
FA. (pitch 1) Tom Cranfield 1950. FA. (the rest) Alan Austin 1958

❸ After Eight E4 6a
14m. The beckoning traverse line. Climb the right-hand side of the roof, using a slot and the hanging crack, to reach the break. Pump rapidly leftwards across this (good cams - hard to place) to a position below the crescent-shaped crack. Stretch for this then finish more easily.
FA. Pete Kitson 1973. A bold solo - he graded it HVS!

❹ The Marine Who Had No Friends
. . . . E4 6b
12m. Start as for *After Eight* and follow its traverse for a couple of moves before heading up the face by long reaches, pockets and a tiny groove. Bet the marine struggled.
FA. Greg Rimmer 1986

❺ February Climb. . . . . S 4a
10m. The crack on the right is reached over easy ground and leads to a shelf. Traverse left for 3m, via the slab or the crack, then pull over the capping overlap.
FA. Tony Marr 1998

G.T.X Buttress - across gully

❶ Remembered . . . . ☼ [____] **VDiff**
12m. Climb the crack in the slab on the left and its thinner continuation. A right-hand finish via the flake is **Forgotten, Diff.**
FA. Dave (x2) Musgrove 1988. FA. (Forgotten) Martin Ryder 1980

❷ Laughing Gas . . . . . ☼ 🏔🦎 [____] **HVS 4c**
16m. The left-edge of the slab. Bridge the wide crack to access the slab then follow the edge to a well positioned finish.
FA. Bob Larkin 1979

❸ Dental Slab . . . . [Top 50] 🏔 [____] **S 4a**
20m. The best Severe in Yorkshire and that is quite an accolade! Access the slab from its bottom left corner and traverse up and right into the centre of the face (choice of levels). Continue up the centre of the slab, the easiest line jigs left then right a little, to a fine finish up the middle of the buttress. *Photo on page 124.*
FA. Bill Bowler 1935

❹ Extraction . . . . ☼ 🤚🏔 [____] **HVS 5b**
18m. Fine climbing up the right-hand side of the buttress. Pull through the centre of the bulges - beefy and 5c to impossible for the short. Then move right into the base of the thin seam. Climb this then the blanker slab in the same line by lovely face climbing.
FA. Tony Barley 1971

❺ V Chimney . . . . ☼ 👤 [____] **VDiff**
16m. The rift that bounds the right side of the slab is awkward to start and the exit from the wide middle section is tricky to protect.

❻ False Teeth . . . . ☼ 🏔 [____] **VS 4c**
20m. Fills a gap quite effectively! Gain the bottom right corner of the slab by bridging the gully and hopping on to the slab. Follow the vague line leftwards to the eyes, then step left again and head direct for the top.
FA. Dave Musgrove 1988

❼ Persistence . . . . . . ☼ 🏔 ▯ [____] **VS 4c**
16m. The narrow buttress is split neatly by a crack-line. Pull through the roof to reach it, then follow the crack to its end. Balance up the rounded left arete to finish. If at first.........
FA. Alan Austin 1955

Dental Slab
The most popular buttress at Rylstone and with good reason; a fine seat of climbs across the middle grades, great rock and a stunning setting, if there is anyone else at the cliff, they will probably be here.
Approach - See opposite for Castrol/G.T.X.

❽ Chockstone Chimney . . . ☼ 👤 [____] **VDiff**
14m. The tricky chimney past the spooky swivelling chockstone.
FA. Possibly Cecil Wood early 1920s

❾ Trowel Face . . . . ☼ 🔧 [____] **HS 4b**
14m. The slanting flaky groove is approached strenuously from the right. It is tricky to reach the first of the flakes, then it eases.
FA. Alan Austin 1955

❿ Chimney Slabs Route Two . . ☼ [____] **S 4a**
10m. The centre of the pocketed slab is excellent but rather lacking in gear.

⓫ Lichen Chimney . . . . 👤 [____] **VDiff**
12m. Starting past a big chockstone, climb the chimney and continuation crack. Inclined to be a bit scruffy.
FA. Possibly Cecil Wood early 1920s

⓬ Glass Slipper . . . . . ☼ 🏔🦎 [____] **E2 5b**
12m. Climb the slab to ledges then finish up the unprotected rounded rib behind.
FA. Dave (x2) Musgrove 1991. It was younger Dave's 111th route of the day!

⓭ Lichen Crack . . . . 👤 [____] **Mod**
12m. The next rift is easier and cleaner than its left-hand twin.
FA. Possibly Cecil Wood early 1920s

⓮ Crazy Diamond . . . . ☼ 🏔🦎 [____] **E2 5b**
12m. Fine climbing up the slab and flying arete - it manages to feel bolder than it really is. Pull over the overlap and pad up the slab to ledges. A short crack (last runners) and pocketed face leads to a sprint up the final arete.
FA. John Eastham 1978

Pule Hill · Shooters · Heptonstall · Widdop · Earl Crag · Ilkley · The Chevin · Caley · Almscliff · Eastby · Crookrise · Rylstone · Simon's Seat · Brimham · Eavestone · Slipstones · Crag Willas · Goldsborough

Dental Slab - 20m

President's Slab

Sundowner

President's Slab

A fine slab, not very extensive, but with a nice collection of climbs. Up and right are some interesting shorter climbs which have the added attraction of getting the sun earlier in the day.

Approach - From the Monument Group continue along the cliff-top path for 400m.

1 President's Slab . . . . Top 50   VDiff
18m. The other Rylstone low grade classic. Start at the tip of the slab and trend slightly rightwards to ledges which can be used as a stance if practice is required. Continue up the crack rightwards, then back left.
FA. E.A.Porter (Gritstone Club president) 1922

2 Dead Kennedys . . . . . .   VS 5a
18m. Tasteless name but some nice moves. From the half-height ledges, trend left up a shallow crack to the crest of the wall. A pocket out left will probably be found useful.
FA. Bob Larkin 1979

3 The Hot Line . . . .   HVS 5b
18m. The direct line on the upper slab has a bold move or two and some nice positions. It looks a bit cramped from below but feels independent enough once committed.
FA. Dave Musgrove 1988

4 Misty Moo . . . .   S 4a
18m. Disjointed but with some fine climbing. Take the left edge of the lower slab then cross over to the main slab and trend left then back right to a well positioned finale up the arete.
FA. Peter Keen 1991

The rest of the routes are located up and right and are based on the open green corner with hanging cracks in its left wall.

5 Hanging Cracks . . . . . .   VS 5a
12m. Pull though the roof on good but painful (to those with Fairy Liquid hands) jams, then move left around the arete and finish up its well positioned left-hand side.
FA. Frank Wilkinson 1970

6 Frankie Comes to Rylstone .   E1 5b
10m. Pull through the roof as for *Hanging Crack,* then continue up the face past a useful pocket to a tricky finish.
FA. Frank Wilkinson 1988. Swoops back in for the direct version.

7 Falcon Crack . . . .   VDiff
10m. Pleasant jamming up the central crack-line.
FA. Sidney Waterfall 1935

8 Sundowner. . . . .   HVS 5a
10m. The narrow pillar. A bit of an eliminate (avoid the arete) but with nice moves, and it catches the afternoon sun.
FA. Dave Musgrove 1988

9 Twin Cracks . . . .   S 4a
8m. The main corner is worth a quick visit when dry though it often isn't. The upper section gives nice climbing.

10 Pickpocket . . . .   HVS 5a
8m. The cracked and pocketed wall just right of the corner is better that in looks, as long as it isn't too green.
FA. Bob Larkin 1979

11 Tasslehof Burrfoot. . .   E2 5c
10m. The right-hand side of the wall is climbed to bulges which are tackled leftwards, to access a shelving ledge, with difficulty. Finish straight up the wall.
FA. Dave Musgrove 1988

12 The Artful Dodger E2 5b
10m. Climb the groove and exit right to below the arete. Balance up its right-hand side with trepidation.
FA. Dave Musgrove 1988

Monument Buttress

13 Catwalk . . . .   VS 4c
18m. Start under the roof and cross the slab leftwards where a tricky move gains a ledge running round on the north face where a stance is usual. Climb the delicate left-trending ramp in the middle of the face. Can be a bit green.
FA. (top pitch only) Cecil Wood pre 1923

Monument Buttress
The first of the chief buttresses to be reached and it is a good one, with several fine climbs on great rock and in as lovely a setting as you could wish for.

Descent

President's Slab - 400m across the moors

The original wooden cross was replaced in 1995 with the current concrete one. Pity they couldn't be bothered to carry the old one down - it lies in the gully behind the buttress.

Monument Crack

14 Monument Crack....... E1 5b
16m. A fine climb; THE classic of the crag and not too high in the grade for those who relish jamming, though steep and intimidating for those who don't. Climb to the roof and pull over into the right-slanting crack. Follow this, past one wider section, out onto the open slab and an easier finish.
Photos on page 29 and 125.
FA. Alan Austin 1965

15 Sword Dance........ E1 5b
20m. More quality hand grinding. Get on to a shelf then climb the short crack until it is possible to balance left to reach *Monument Crack*. Move up then follow the descending crack under the roof (big teeth) until it is possible to escape round onto the north face and belay. Climb the wall (bold) to intersect the arete and pull over right using a hidden pocket. Continue over the capping bulge.
FA. Pete Heys 1970

16 Pocket Battleship .. E3 6a
10m. A short tussle with the pocketed wall above the short crack, trending leftwards to a grasping exit.
FA. Dave Musgrove 1988

17 Arm Jam .... HS 4b
14m. Aim rightwards to the crack. (Arm?) jam this then the wider and easier continuation up and left, all the way to the cross.

18 Double Crack .... S 4a
8m. Up the groove to the cracks and take these to a hard finish.
FA. Martin Ryder 1980

19 Beginner's Chimney .... Mod
6m. The rift with a mildly tricky start.
FRA. Dave Musgrove 1988

The final (or first?) routes are on the front of the buttress across the gully from the cross. Scramble round to the south.

20 Highlord .... HS 4b
10m. Follow the bubbly rock leftwards then back right, avoiding the grass, then follow the slanting jamming crack to a tricky finale.
FA. Dave Musgrove 1988

21 England Expects V1 (5c)
The arete is accessed from the right. A **Direct Start** is **V3, 6a**.
FA. Dave Musgrove 1988

22 Terminus .... HVS 5b
8m. Use the slot to climb the wall then escape left or right.
FA. Ken Wood 1972

Terminus

Descent

	No star	⚝	⚝⚝	⚝⚝⚝
Mod to S	5	4	1	-
HS to HVS	2	6	1	2
E1 to E3	2	3	2	3
E4 and up	-	-	1	-

A classic Yorkshire cliff - a true summit, miles from the road and north-facing. It's not all bad news though, there are some very pleasant routes on the sunny South Face and you will probably have the place to yourself. Simon's Seat is a brilliant place to escape the crowds - of climbers at least, I can't vouch for walkers. Beware falling orange peel and banana skins if climbing below the trig point.
The classics of the North Face include some real belters, get the right day and a great time is assured here.

Access
Although the crag is now on Access Land with all the associated conditions, the Devonshire Estate have always intensively managed the moor for grouse breeding and continue to enforce all year-round restrictions regarding dogs. There may be some mid-week closures for shooting in August/September - signs will be posted.

Conditions
The crag is divided into two; a dark and grim North Face, where the best routes are; and a sunny South Face, with some lovely diversions. The North Face is probably the most wintery of all of Yorkshire's seasonal venues - dark, green and cold - you need to choose your day carefully. In contrast the south-facing routes are in condition year-round, it is a pity they are not a bit nearer the road.

Approach
There is parking for about five cars on the right-hand side (Barden Moor signboard) of the private road that runs towards Howgill Farm. This is reached from the B6160 by turning right at Barden Bridge onto the minor road to Appletreewick. The track to the right of the stream climbs (very) rapidly up into the woods and eventually out onto the moor. Bear left and the track rises more gently, paralleling the wall, until the rocky top of the hill appears ahead and is reached by a recently flagged path, arriving at the South Face climbs.
To reach the North Face follow the path round to the right, towards the trig point, then fork left and descend some steep steps until at the bottom of the steepest section. Minor tracks branch rightwards, running round to the base of the cliff, which is hidden until the last minute. 30-40 minutes from the car.

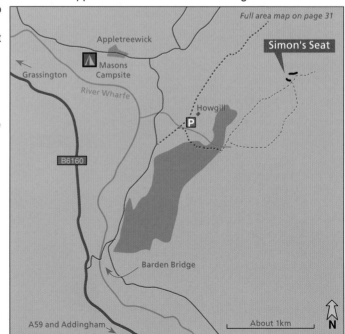

Full area map on page 31

Appletreewick
Masons Campsite
Grassington
River Wharfe
Simon's Seat
Howgill
P
B6160
Barden Bridge
A59 and Addingham
About 1km
N

(Side tabs: Pule Hill, Shooters, Heptonstall, Widdop, Earl Crag, Ilkley, The Chevin, Caley, Almscliff, Eastby, Crookrise, Rylstone, Simon's Seat, Brimham, Eavestones, Slipstones, Crag Willas, Goldsrogh)

Descent

4

8

9

11

10

5 6

7

3

2

1

Turret Crack

Arete Direct

Pate Hill
Shooter's
Heptonstall
Widdop
Earl Crag
Ilkley
The Chevin
Caley
Almscliff
Eastby
Crookrise
Rylstone
Simon's Seat
Brimham
Eavestone's
Slipstones
Crag Willas
Goldsbrgh

The North Face
Gloomy green and gritty for much of the year, BUT when in condition, it offers some fine climbs in a magnificently remote setting.
Approach - Follow the path to the South Face and continue past this. Descend the steps steeply and follow vague paths rightwards to the foot of the face.

❶ Arete Direct . . . . **VS 4c**
20m. A classic, nearly always in good condition and well worth the walk up. Start on the right and traverse out left under the overlap to access the arete itself. Climb this in a grand position and with sustained interest.
FA. Allan Austin 1958

❷ Dog Lead . . . . **HVS 5a**
18m. Start along the traverse of *Arete Direct* but climb through the overhang via the crack. Head up the face slightly rightwards to reach the deep cracks, cross the wall then finish leftwards up a shallower seam.
FA. Johnny Cutliffe 1997

❸ Arete Wall . . . . **S 4a**
16m. Start on the right and climb up and left to reach the prominent cracks that run away leftwards. Follow these out to the arete and a well positioned finale. *Photo on page 133.*
FA. The Waterfall Brothers mid 1930s

❹ Y Front . . . . **S 4a**
12m. Follow *Arete Wall* out into the middle of the face then trend back right finishing up the right-hand fork of the V-shaped cracks.
FA. Brian Evans 1960

❺ Window Chimney . . . . **Diff**
14m. The deep rift that bounds the right-hand side of the wall is entered and climbed in the gloom to an exit via the window. Great fun in heavy snow.

❻ Clappers Crack **E1 5b**
18m. A direct start to the upper section of *Turret Crack* is the character building roof-crack. Best approached at a gallop, you may get a round of applause on completing it. After recovering on the ledge, finish up *Turret Crack*.
FA. Allan Austin 1958

❼ Turret Crack . . . . **HVS 5a**
20m. A fine climb up a compelling line. Climb the green jamming crack to a good ledge and possible stance over to the left. Continue up the easier jamming crack splitting the bulges.
FA. Allan Austin, Frank Spence (alt leads) 1958

❽ Panzer **E3 6a**
16m. The wall directly above the lower half of *Turret Crack* climbed on well spaced pockets and good holds over the bulge.
FA. Nigel Baker 1999

Simple Simon and Gymkhana

Turret Crack

Arete Direct

Descent

8
9

5 6 7

13

10 11

12 14

Turret Crack

Simple Simon - just to the right

9 Outside Finish . . . . HVS 5b

22m. A contrasting finish to *Turret Crack*, it can be done in one pitch, though watch the rope-drag. Harder and bolder than the original. Climb the crack to the ledge then traverse the break rightwards to the arete. Climb its right-hand side a short way then traverse back left to reach the crack that splits the upper bulges. Finish up this.
FA. Allan Austin 1960

10 Finesse E4 6a

16m. The hanging arete of strange blocky rock gives a good and pumpy pitch that requires a forceful approach.
FA. Derek Hargreaves 1988

11 Pothole Chimney . . . . VDiff

20m. A subterranean outing that burrows under the great block and emerges in another dimension.

12 Chockstone Chimney . . . VS 4c

20. The long groove-line to the left of the clean slabs gives a varied pitch. Climb the initial crack and access a grassy niche with difficulty. Extemporise a way up the steeper final section.
FA. The Waterfall brothers mid 1930s

13 Shush Popeye E3 5c

18m. Balance up the rounded left arete of the slab leaving runners and hope far below.
FA. Derek Hargreaves 1998

14 A Question of Balance

. . . . E2 5b

20m. A fine climb, low in the grade and usually cleaner that others hereabouts. Follow the crack that splits the overhang at the base of the slab to a good ledge on the right. Continue precariously up the slab, using the right arete when needed, to a break and an easier finish.
FA. John Eastham 1978

Pule Hill
Shooters
Heptonstall
Widdop
Earl Crag
Ilkley
The Chevin
Caley
Almscliff
Eastby
Crookrise
Rylstone
Simon's Seat
Brimham
Eavestones
Slipstones
Crag Willas
Goldsborough

Simple Simon

Gymkhana

Descent

About 40m

The right-hand side of the North face has a few worthwhile routes that weave ways up the jumbled series of blocks and faces.

❶ Simple Simon . . . . 🔲 **S 4b**
22m. Long and varied. Up the left edge of the flaky slab then move right to a long crack which leads to a ledge. Move right and pull over the roof following the crack and its steeper continuation.
FA. Frank Spence 1958

❷ Paws for Thought . . 🔲 **HVS 5b**
8m. The rounded arete has a sticky moment or two.
FA. Johnny Cutliffe 1997

❸ Gymkhana . . . . 🔲 **E1 5b**
18m. Varied and good value. Battle with the roof-crack on the front of the buttress then move round left and balance boldly up the rounded arete.
FA. Tony Barley 1971

❹ Low Nose Crack . . . . . . 🔲 **VS 5a**
16m. The crack splitting the nose is interesting.
FA. Allan Austin 1958

❺ The Naked Edge . . . 🔲 **E3 6a**
8m. The superb scooped arete passed on the approach is one of the best micro routes on grit.
FA. Jerry Peel 1978

South Face
The North Face has always been considered the buisiness end of Simon's Seat, though the South Face also has something to offer - short routes but on great rock and in a lovely setting.

❻ Corner Crack . . . . 🔲 **VDiff**
6m. The awkward groove on the left.
FA. The Waterfall brothers mid 1930s

❼ And She Was . . 🔲 **E3 6a**
8m. The left arete of the face is technical and unprotected.
FA. Derek Hargreaves 1988

❽ I'll Bet She Does. . . 🔲 **E3 6a**
8m. The centre of the buttress eases with height (if you can do the start and don't bottle it).
FA. Dave Musgrove (Jnr) 1995

❾ Straight Crack . . . . 🔲 **VS 4c**
8m. The smart crack on jams and chicken-heads.
FA. The Waterfall brothers mid 1930s

❿ Inaccessible Crack . . . . 🔲 **VS 5a**
6m. The hanging crack in the arete is accessed from the right.
FA. Alan Austin 1958

Straight Crack

Descent

The next routes are on the well cracked wall that faces north west and is liberally spattered with chickin' nuggets which are finger crimpin' good!

⑪ Left-hand Arete . . . . 🖼️ ☐ HVS 4a
6m. The right-hand arete (only kidding).

⑫ Out With the Old . . . . 🖼️ ☐ E1 5b
7m. Climb just right of the arete, trending slightly right to a trio of 'thank-God' bumps. Step left to finish.
FA. Andy Say 1989

⑬ Central Cracks . . . . 🔲 ☐ S 4b
7m. The trident of cracks is the best route on the face.

⑭ Right-hand Crack . . . . 🔲 ☐ S 4b
7m. The right-hand fissure offers more knob-tastic fun.

⑮ Chunky Chicken . . . . ☐ E1 5b
7m. The narrowing right-hand pillar without deviation.
FA. Dave Musgrove (jnr) 1995

Towards the right-hand side of the face is a wall half hidden behind a huge boulder.

⑯ Hidden Crack . . . . ☐ S 4a
10m. Climb the groove and crack to the top, move left then head up the bobbly slab.

⑰ Hidden Chimney . . . . ☐ VDiff
10m. The steep crack-line is a misnomer.

⑱ Open Face . . . . 🔲 🐔 🪓 ☐ HVS 5b
10m. Climb the scooped arete steeply to the break, move left and wobble up the warty wall without straying rightwards.
FA. Tony Barley 1991

	No star	☆	☆☆	☆☆☆
Mod to S	8	19	4	-
HS to HVS	20	32	17	7
E1 to E3	8	27	4	2
E4 and up	2	10	5	4

Brimham Rocks is set on the edge of the moor, just to the east of the central reaches of Nidderdale. It is, with good reason, an immensely popular tourist attraction owing to the amazing rock formations. This confusing array of blocks, towers and buttresses, threaded by myriad paths, have confused both walker and climber for years and the chances of getting completely lost are very real. Hopefully the following pages will point you in the right direction so that you can locate the many superb routes along the Main Edge as well as the few routes on the taller pinnacles. Some of the more important boulder problems have been described but there is plenty more at Brimham - see *Yorkshire Gritstone Bouldering - Vol. 1* (2008) for more details.

The view from Brimham House - go get lost! Photo: Chris Craggs

Conditions

Brimham is set at an altitude of 300m on the edge of the moor where it will catch any wind from the west or the north. Fortunately the rocks face all points of the compass, so it is usually possible to find some shelter and locals consider it a year-round venue. The section of rock that runs northwards from The Black Chipper faces north west and is surrounded by trees. It has become green over the years and is slow to dry, which is a great pity as there are some classic climbs. It tends to be humid and midgy over the whole area if there has been recent summer rain.

Approach

Brimham can be approached from Ripon, Grassington or Harrogate. The rocks are well signed when you get close. There is an extensive and pricey (unless you are a member) National Trust car park to either side of the track that runs into the centre of the rocks.

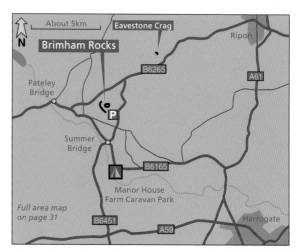

(Map) About 5km · N · Brimham Rocks · Eavestone Crag · Ripon · B6265 · A61 · Pateley Bridge · P · Summer Bridge · B6165 · Manor House Farm Caravan Park · *Full area map on page 31* · B6451 · Harrogate · A59

Side tabs: Fale Hill · Shooters · Heptonstall · Widdop · Earl Crag · Ilkley · The Chevin · Caley · Almscliff · Eastby · Crookrise · Eystone · Simon's Seat · **Brimham** · Eavestones · Slipstones · Crag Willas · Guisecliff

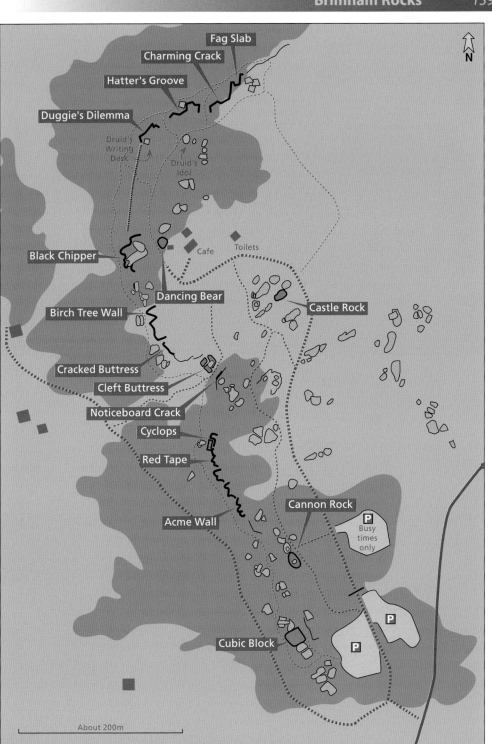

N

Fag Slab
Charming Crack
Hatter's Groove
Duggie's Dilemma
Druid's Writing Desk
Druid's Idol
Black Chipper
Cafe
Toilets
Dancing Bear
Castle Rock
Birch Tree Wall
Cracked Buttress
Cleft Buttress
Noticeboard Crack
Cyclops
Red Tape
Cannon Rock
Acme Wall
P Busy times only
P
P
Cubic Block

About 200m

Pule Hill · Shooter's · Heptonstall · Widdop · Earl Crag · Ilkley · The Chevin · Caley · Almscliff · Eastby · Crookrise · Hylstone · Simon's Seat · Brimham · Eavestones · Slipstones · Crag Willas · Goldsbrgh

Evening | 15 min | Green

Descent
(down gully)

Descent

Pig Traverse - 10m

Fag Slab

The most northerly of the regularly visited venues at Brimham are the slumped pieces of rock of the Fag Slab area. There are several worthwhile climbs here, though as the area faces north west, it tends to be green if the weather has been at all damp.

Approach (see map on page 139) - The shortest approach is by the path that runs past the cafe, the Dancing Bear and the Druid's Idol. Fag Slab is on the left 50m beyond this and is difficult to spot from above.

❶ Hourglass Chimney.... VS 5a
10m. The awkward rift is obvious from the name.
FA. Brian Evans 1956

❷ Bellyporker's Progress . V8
Layback the overhanging side of the arete. **E7** in old money.
FA. Nick Dixon 1990

❸ Allan's Crack Direct HVS 5b
12m. Climb the slab, trending left to the arete, and finish up this.
FA. (Start) Allan Austin 1958. FA. (Finish) Les Brown 1967

❹ Allan's Crack . . . . VS 4c
12m. Layback the left-leaning crack (good runners) until it is possible to move out right under the last of the bulges for a well positioned finish up the face. *Photo on page 22.*
FA. Allan Austin 1955

❺ Allan's Crack Right-hand . . . VS 4c
12m. From halfway up *Allan's Crack*, move right around the arete the step back left onto the edge. Finish by trending right.
FA. Tiny Marr 1994

❻ Little Funnel . . . . VS 5a
10m. The narrowing cleft is awkward until the good jams arrive.
FA. Allan Austin 1955

❼ Fag Slab . . . . S 4a
10m. Balance up the pleasant slabby groove then escape right. The finish might be a bit fluttery for the timid.

❽ Woodbine . . . . HVS 5b
10m. Climb the technically interesting slab to join the last moves of *Fag Slab Variant*.
FA. Johnny Adams 1967. Although he probably wasn't the first.

❾ Fag Slab Variant. . . . . . VS 4c
10m. The left-slanting overlap is a balancy pitch.
FA. Brain Evans 1956

❿ Silkcut. E3 6c
10m. Pull rightwards round the overlap with difficulty then sketch left until things ease. The start is around **V7**.
FA. Paul Clarke 1984. Long before bouldering mats.

⓫ Fag End. . . . . S 4a
10m. A short crack leads to a line of chipped holds.
FA. Harold Barraclough 1959. Before it was chipped.

⓬ Capstan Full Strength . . E3 5c
10m. Gain the right toe of the slab awkwardly then climb direct to finish over the roof.
FA. Francis Holland (at HVS 5b!) 1991. It was claimed again by Mick Johnson as Senior Service in 1997

17 Pig Traverse . . . . **HS 4b**
12m. Climb the cracks to the bulge then follow the break out to the right arete and a finish up the ridge.
FA. Allan Austin 1956

18 Reach for the Sty **E5 6b**
10m. Climb to the break then head left past the end of the overlap to a pocket. Finish to the left.
FA. Martin Berzins 1988

19 Sow's That **E5 6b**
10m. Follow the previous route to the end of the overlap then climb carefully rightwards on poor holds to finish.
FA. Al Manson 1988

20 Pig Slip Cow Punk **E6 6b**
10m. The sketchy slab to the break then more of the same on the upper slab.
FA. Nick Dixon 1990

21 Pig's Ear . . . . **HVS 5b**
10m. The arete throughout mostly by laybacking.
FA. Steve Rhodes 1988

22 Long Funnel . . . . **VDiff**
10m. The right-hand side of the deep rift behind the block gives good chimneying practice.
FA. Allan Austin 1956

23 Pathos **E3 6a**
8m. Stride onto the wall and climb to the horizontal break. The left-hand crack in the slab gives a technical finale.
FA. Al Manson 1980

24 Lithos . . . . **HVS 5b**
8m. Use the same start but follow the right-hand crack to a finish on the arete. A **Direct Start** is a technical **V4 (6b)**.
FA. Mike Hammill 1976. FA. (Direct Start) Al Manson, about the same time.

---

13 Narrowing Chimney . . . . **VDiff**
8m. The cleft with jammed blocks to a tough exit. The climbing style is best described as 'traditional'.

14 True Grit **E4 6b**
10m. The slanting leaning fissure crack is a tough nut to crack. The wider continuation up and left gives an easier finish.
FA. Ken Wood 1970

15 The Snuffer **E1 5b**
10m. The bell-shaped chimney from the dingy depths to daylight - character building stuff. It is also possible to start direct at **5c**.
FA. Baz Ingle 1961. FA. (Direct Start) Tony Marr 2007

16 Giggling Crack **E6 6c**
10m. The hilarious hanging rift, you will laugh till you cry.
FA. Jerry Peel 1976. Joe Brown laughed himself out of the top crack 1958

Pig Traverse
The right-hand of the slumped slabs has a prominent diagonal break rising rightwards across the face. The area has several popular face climbs and, round to the left, a set of arduous cracks that are often avoided.

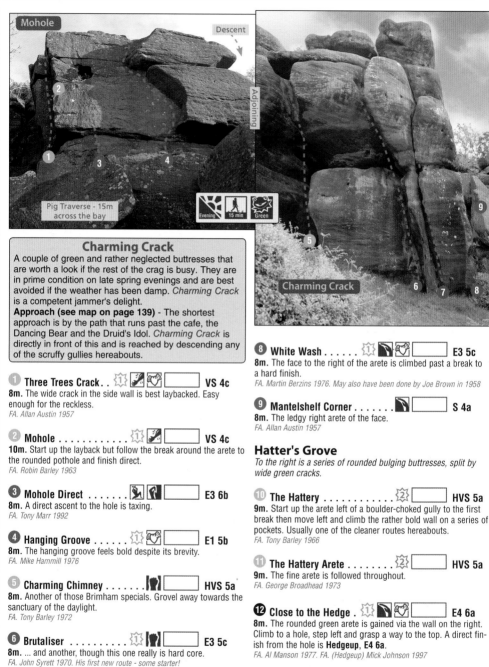

Mohole

Descent

Adjoining

Pig Traverse - 15m
across the bay

Evening | 15 min | Green

Charming Crack

Charming Crack

A couple of green and rather neglected buttresses that
are worth a look if the rest of the crag is busy. They are
in prime condition on late spring evenings and are best
avoided if the weather has been damp. *Charming Crack*
is a competent jammer's delight.

Approach (see map on page 139) - The shortest
approach is by the path that runs past the cafe, the
Dancing Bear and the Druid's Idol. *Charming Crack* is
directly in front of this and is reached by descending any
of the scruffy gullies hereabouts.

1 Three Trees Crack. . VS 4c
8m. The wide crack in the side wall is best laybacked. Easy
enough for the reckless.
FA. Allan Austin 1957

2 Mohole VS 4c
10m. Start up the layback but follow the break around the arete to
the rounded pothole and finish direct.
FA. Robin Barley 1963

3 Mohole Direct E3 6b
8m. A direct ascent to the hole is taxing.
FA. Tony Marr 1992

4 Hanging Groove E1 5b
8m. The hanging groove feels bold despite its brevity.
FA. Mike Hammill 1976

5 Charming Chimney HVS 5a
8m. Another of those Brimham specials. Grovel away towards the
sanctuary of the daylight.
FA. Tony Barley 1972

6 Brutaliser E3 5c
8m. ... and another, though this one really is hard core.
FA. John Syrett 1970. His first new route - some starter!

7 Charming Crack E2 5c
8m. The shady, leaning jamming crack is a little gem. As to the
grade - one of the last major Yorkshire sandbags gets its come-
uppance, perhaps?
FA. Joe Brown 1958

8 White Wash E3 5c
8m. The face to the right of the arete is climbed past a break to
a hard finish.
FA. Martin Berzins 1976. May also have been done by Joe Brown in 1958

9 Mantelshelf Corner S 4a
8m. The ledgy right arete of the face.
FA. Allan Austin 1957

Hatter's Grove

*To the right is a series of rounded bulging buttresses, split by
wide green cracks.*

10 The Hattery HVS 5a
9m. Start up the arete left of a boulder-choked gully to the first
break then move left and climb the rather bold wall on a series of
pockets. Usually one of the cleaner routes hereabouts.
FA. Tony Barley 1966

11 The Hattery Arete HVS 5a
9m. The fine arete is followed throughout.
FA. George Broadhead 1973

12 Close to the Hedge E4 6a
8m. The rounded green arete is gained via the wall on the right.
Climb to a hole, step left and grasp a way to the top. A direct finish from the hole is **Hedgeup, E4 6a.**
FA. Al Manson 1977. FA. (Hedgeup) Mick Johnson 1997

13 Last Crack HS 4b
8m. The right-angled corner can be green.
FA. Allan Austin 1955

Pule Hill · Shooter's · Heptonstall · Widdop · Earl Crag · Ilkley · The Chevin · Caley · Almscliff · Eastby · Crookrise · Brimstone · Simon's Seat · Brimham · Eavestones · Slipstones · Crag Willas · Goldsb'gh

Hatter's Groove

A green and neglected area, it does have a great selection of climbs but is perhaps best left for when the conditions are right. Fortunately, the routes are generally a bit cleaner than they look, so if in doubt, give them a go.
Approach - As for *Charming Crack* (opposite) or continue northwards round the edge from *Birch Tree Wall* following discontinuous paths through the trees.

14 Cracked Rib . . . . VS 5a
8m. Gain the hanging widening crack from the right. A direct approach is more like **5c**.
FA. Brian Evans 1957

15 Brief Crack . . . . HS 4b
8m. The jamming crack rising from the back left-hand corner of the ledge of The Pulpit.
FA. Allan Austin 1955

16 Graft Crack . . . . VS 4c
8m. The right-hand of the two cracks.
FA. Allan Austin 1955

17 Slippery Crack . . . . VS 4b
10m. A slippery start leads to good jamming above. High in the grade and worth **4c** in anything less than perfect conditions.
FA. Allan Austin 1955

18 Grit Expectations . . E4 6a
10m. The fine arete is climbed mostly on its right-hand side via the shallow groove and some useful pockets. Protection is there, but it is hard to place.
FA. Al Manson 1975

19 Hatter's Groove . . . HVS 5a
12m. A classic test-piece with a maddening move on it. Bridge the green groove awkwardly to the capstone where a good thread protects the taxing exit round the left edge of the boulder.
FA. Allan Austin (a shoulder and thread for aid) 1956. FFA. Joe Smith 1958

20 Hard Hat E1 5c
12m. The right-hand exit to *Hatter's Groove* is altogether harder.
FA. Tony Marr 1990

21 Easy Escape . . . . VS 4c
12m. Does what it says on the tin. Avoid the hard move of *Hatter's Groove* by crossing the right wall using the central break to finish up the wide easy crack just round the arete.

22 Grit Escape . . . . HVS 5b
10m. Climb the diagonal crack in the right wall until close to the arete, then continue up the left-hand side of this.
FA. Tony Marr 1993

23 Right-hand Arete . . . . HVS 5a
10m. The rounded right arete is followed until obliged to step right into the next route.
FA. Ken Tilford 1981

24 Lichen Chimney . . . . . . VDiff
10m. The widening crack is less lichenous than it used to be though it is still a bit grungy.
FA. Allan Austin 1955

Descent

Not much sun | 12 min | Green

Hatter's Groove - 75m

Grit Corner

Grit Corner and Duggie's Dilemma
Two short faces with a pleasant collection of easier climbs plus some harder offerings. The routes are generally cleaner than those further north.
Approach (see map on page 139) - Continue northwards round the edge from *Birch Tree Wall* following discontinuous paths through the trees.

4 Grit Bit . . . . **HVS 5c**
8m. Start up the groove and pass the bulge using a pocket. Finish up the arete.
FA. Tony Barley 1966

5 Pebbledash **E2 5c**
8m. Climb the crack that splits the narrow overhang. Avoid the block at the start.
FA. Tony Marr 1990

6 Overlapping Wall . . . . . **HS 4b**
8m. Cross the awkward overlap at its centre. Finish either by the easy chimney or, better, by the wall left of the chimney.
FA. Tony Marr 2005

7 Gully Arete . . . . **HS 4b**
6m. Balance up the lower arete and pull past the roof.
FA. Tony Barley 1972

8 No Doubt . . . . **VS 4c**
6m. Climb the left-hand side of the jutting rib and finish direct.

9 Duggie's Dilemma . . . . **VS 4c**
6m. The wall has an unprotected fun mantel at half-height.
FA. Allan Austin 1955

10 Spare Rib **E2 5c**
6m. The arete is short but scary.
FA. Bob Berzins 1977

11 Tight Chimney . . . . **Diff**
6m. The rift is best tackled when sober.

1 Gnome's Arete . . . . **HVS 5a**
10m. The slab and arete using some naughty holds.

2 Grit Corner . . . . **S 4a**
10m. Follow the groove until it begins to bear away right then finish direct up the groove above. Exiting rightwards is easier - **VDiff** - and rather less worthy.

3 Lunatic Rib . . . . **VS 4c**
8m. Climb the groove then layback round the nose on the left to reach easy ground.
FA. Ken Tilford 1981

Evening | 12 min | Green

Duggie's Dilemma

Black Chipper - 75m

Descent

Change in viewing angle

Afternoon 10 min

1 2 3 4 5 6 7 8 9

Black Chipper

Dogleg Crack

Pate Hill · Shooters · Heptonstall · Widdop · Earl Crag · Ilkley · The Chevin · Caley · Almscliff · Eastby · Crookrise · Brimham · Simon's Seat · Earlstones · Slipstones · Crag Willas · Goldsborough

Black Chipper

A rather retiring buttress with one classic climb. To its right are some shorter walls and ribs that have a selection of climbs that are not much more than extended boulder problems though, despite their diminutive size, most have awkward rounded exits and/or poor landings. The area gets plenty of sun and is quick-drying too.
Approach - To the left of *Birch Tree Wall* follow discontinuous paths past *White Rose Flake*.

❶ Natural Grit **E3 5c**
12m. Climb the wall to a ledge then move over to the *Black Chipper* thread, before finishing leftwards up the shallow ramp.
FA. Jerry Peel 1975

❷ Black Chipper. **E2 5b**
12m. After a tough start (5c?) follow pockets and slopers up to the break where a small thread (possibly also chipped?) and small cams protect the awkward (chipped) finish. Avoiding using the chipped hold, lest you be struck down, is nearer **5c**.
FA. Tony Barley 1966

❸ The Arch **E2 6a**
8m. A fiendish mantel leads to a narrow foot-ledge and another rounded mantel completes the fun.
FA. Ken Wood 1974

❹ For Crying Out Loud **E2 6b**
8m. The rib that bounds the right edge of *The Arch* and the technical wall above.
FA. Ian Dunn 1982

❺ Rotifer. **E3 6a**
8m. The arete is climbed with increasing trepidation.
FA. Bob Berzins 1977

❻ Dogleg Crack **E1 5c**
12m. Up the dog's leg to a ledge and a possible stance (for moral support - you will need it) then tackle the awful heart-rending wide crack above.
FA. Dez Hadlum 1960

❼ Ritornal **E1 5b**
6m. The arete to a rounded exit is a little gem.
FA. Bob Berzins 1980

❽ Inner State **E5 6c**
6m. A difficult independent line, straight up the centre of the wall. It was climbed on-sight using pads but still feels serious enough for the E grade. Some may think **V7/8**?
FA. James Ibbertson 2005

❾ Successor State **E4 6b**
6m. The next arete is also taxing, just less so.
FA. Richard Davies 1986

Across the slope to the right is a short wall with a prominent flake running up its centre but failing to reach the top.

❿ White Flag ...... **VS 5a**
6m. The left arete of the buttress to a rounded exit.
FA. Dave Musgrove 1990

⓫ White Rose Flake ...... **VS 5a**
6m. Climb to the end of the flake then finish with difficulty.
FA. Don Whillans (Red Rose Raider) late 1950s

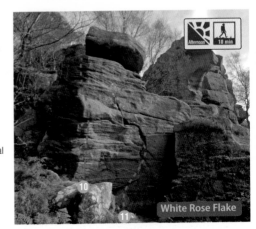

Afternoon 10 min

10

11

White Rose Flake

Pately Hill | Shooner's | Heptonstall | Widdop | Earl Crag | Ilkley | The Chevin | Caley | Almscliff | Eastby | Crookrise | Rylstone | Simon's Seat | **Brimham** | Eavestones | Slipstones | Crag Willas | Gordale'rgh

Birch Tree Wall

Brimham's tallest buttress has a selection of climbs as good as you could wish for. Apart from the classic buttress of *Birch Tree Wall* and the slippery chasm of *Lover's Leap Chimney*, there are plenty of other climbs to delight and tease.

Approach (see map on page 139) - The shortest approach is to follow the road to Brimham House then head down the broad valley past Cleft Buttress bearing right to locate the buttress.

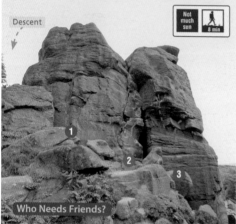

Descent

Not much sun | 8 min

Who Needs Friends?

❶ Who Need Friends . 〰 ▩ ▨ ☐ **E3 5c**
10m. Climb a flake to a break and continue to a flared horizontal (poor Friends - who needs 'em) then move left to reach a short jamming crack with some relief.
FA. Mike Hammill 1980

❷ Difficult Crack . . . . ▣ ☐ **VDiff**
8m. The flake-crack leads to a wide awkward cleft.

❸ Enigma . . . . 〰 ▩ ☐ **E1 5b**
12m. Climb to the roof and pass it on the right before moving carefully back left to a ledge. Balance up the final groove to safety. The ledge can be reached direct by a layback and a bit of a stretch.
FA. Ken Wood 1971

❹ Birch Tree Wall. . . . . . . Top 50 ▩ ☐ **VS 4c**
16m. The classic of the crag. Climb a groove then move rightwards to a ledge on the arete. Traverse the shelf (an ancient chipped hold, plus a huge cam and/or small wires might be of help) leftwards to the base of the left-trending groove. Balance up this to the top. A **Direct Start** is **6a** and a finish up the arete on the right is a little harder and bolder than the original finish. *Photo on page 26.*
FA. Brian Evans 1955. FA. (Direct Start) Al Manson 1978

❺ Love Bug . . . . 〰 ▩ ☐ **HVS 5a**
16m. Climb the crack in the left wall of the huge gully to its end then traverse the break left to the arete. Follow this with well positioned climbing. A **Direct Start** up the right-hand side of the lower arete is **5b**.
FA. Tony Barley 1970. FA. (Direct Start) Tony Marr 1994

Afternoon | 8 min

Descent

Birch Tree Wall

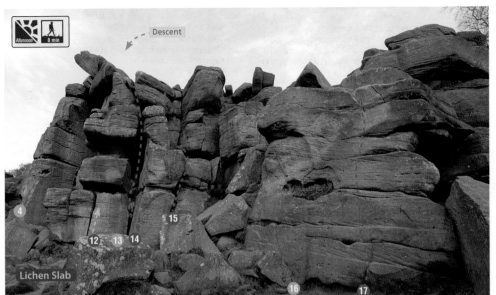

Descent

Lichen Slab

6 Left Wall . . . . 🔲 E5 6a
14m. The soaring left wall of the rift offers a sterling challenge. Climb the crack to its end then a thinner crack to its termination. From here poor pockets (and bold climbing) lead slightly rightwards to the top
FA. Mike Hammill 1977

7 Resurrection . . . . 🔲 E6 6b
14m. A hard pitch that links the cave of Lover's Leap Chimney with the finish of *Left Wall*.
FA. Dave Pegg 1989

8 Lover's Leap Chimney . . 🔲 VDiff 4b
16m. A venerable classic with the polish to prove it. Climb the very slippery crack on the left (hard - many fail here) to access the chockstone and a stance. Exit up the traditional left-hand cleft to an iron bar belay which is more like proper VDiff.
FA. Sidney Thompson 1930s

9 Lover's Leap Chimney Right 🔲 S 4b
16m. From the same start exit up the more taxing right-hand rift.

10 Ambidexter . . . . 🔲 HVS 5a
14m. A weird wandering route, though with some interesting climbing and more interesting positions. Climb to the top of the boulder in the back of the chimney via the crack on the right then balance right to join *Right Wall*. Climb to the overhang then move left before crawling up through the jammed boulders to an exit on the left. Told you it was weird.
FA. Tony Barley 1973

11 Right Wall . . . . 🔲 VS 4c
14m. A pleasant climb meandering up the right-hand wall of the chimney. Start left of the arete and climb to a large ledge before stepping left and following a crack then the continuation groove to a rightward exit.
FA. Dennis Gray 1957

12 Anniversary Arete . . . . . 🔲 V4 (6b)
The right arete of the widening crack.

13 Nameless Chimney . 🔲 HS 4b
14m. Around the arete is widening chimney that leads easily to ledges in its depths. It is the narrowing continuation crack that provides the point of the exercise.

14 Stepped Buttress . . . . . 🔲 E1 6a
14m. An eliminate but with some good moves. Climb the centre of the slab (**V2**) to a ledge then the narrow rib to a tough exit over the shelving capstone.
FA. Tony Marr 1996

15 President's Progress . . . 🔲 HVD
14m. Climb the short awkward chimney (avoidable on the right) to a platform then bridge the wide upper section.
FA. Harry Stembridge 1955

16 Left Edge . . . . 🔲 HS 4b
10m. A filler-in but while you are in the area. Climb to the bilberry-filled 'love-heart' then make tricky moves left to the gully. Continue up the crack on the right to a finish up an awkward slab, or if that is too much, crawl off right below it.

17 Lichen Slab . . . . 🔲 VDiff
8m. The centre of the polished slab is a popular beginners' climb, on the right end of the rope.

Pule Hill · Shooter's · Heptonstall · Widdop · Earl Crag · Ilkley · The Chevin · Caley · Almscliff · Eastby · Crookrise · Kyldstone · Simon's Seat · Brimham · Eavestone · Slipstones · Crag Willas · Goldsborough

Pule Hill
Shooter's
Heptonstall
Widdop
Earl Crag
Ilkley
The Chevin
Caley
Almscliff
Eastby
Crookrise
Rylstone
Simon's Seat
Brimham
Eavestones
Slipstones
Crag Willas
Godsbergh

Birch Tree Wall
round the corner

Descent

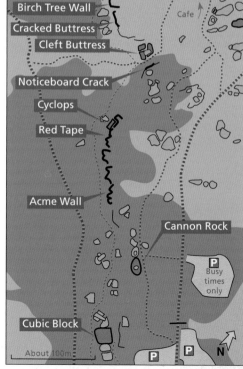

Birch Tree Wall
Cracked Buttress
Cleft Buttress
Noticeboard Crack
Cyclops
Red Tape
Acme Wall
Cannon Rock
Cubic Block
Cafe
P Busy times only
P P N
About 100m

Cracked Buttress

A quartet of worthwhile crack climbs tucked in behind the boulders. All have been popular for generations and so are a bit polished, and tricky exits add to the fun. The narrow walls between the cracks have been climbed and claimed but they are a bit too esoteric to be included here.

1 Parallel Cracks . . . . . . VS 4c
12m. The paired cracks on the far left give well protected jamming. The left-hand crack is the usual method of attack, finish left or, a little harder, right. The right-hand crack throughout gives a more sustained **4c** pitch.
FA. Allan Austin 1956

2 Central Crack . . . . VS 5a
12m. The crack starts from a sentry box and gives good climbing to a naughty finish up the widening and undercut crack. It is possible to avoid the last few moves by traversing the break leftwards to give a one star **HS 4b**.

3 Right-hand Crack . . . . VS 4b
12m. The best of the quartet gives classic jamming/laybacking (quite steep but fine once you commit to the moves) to a rest on a ledge on the left, and then more of the same to the top. It's a relief to find that the exit is reasonably straightforward.
Photo opposite.
FA. A.Marsden 1950

4 Cracked Corner. . . . . S 4a
8m. The flake-crack on the right has become harder, with a tricky polished start then easier climbing above.

Alicia Hudelson on *Right-hand Crack* (VS 4b) - *opposite* on the Main Edge at Brimham. Photo: Jamie Moss

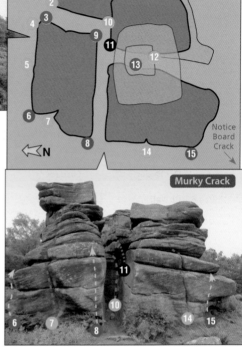

Cleft Arete

Descent reverse route 9

Cracked Buttress - 100m

Sun and shade | 5 min

Notice Board Crack

N

Murky Crack

Cleft Buttress

Part way down the shallow valley that runs down from Brimham House is the odd triple tower of Cleft Buttress. Although never a busy destination, the climbs here are good and the rock formations give an interesting setting. Most of the problems/routes have tricky starts and then easier finishes hence we have described most as problems although many were originally done as routes.

1 Gordon's Wall V2 (6a)
An exercise in tough pulls on sloping holds.
FA. Martin Berzins 1976

2 Syrett's Rib V1 (5b)
The left arete of the canyon.
FA. John Syrett 1976

3 Cleft Arete Left V0- (5a)
The left-hand side of the arete. Continue to the top for a **VS** tick.
FA. Gordon Higginson 1976

4 Cleft Arete Right V2 (5c)
The right-hand side is harder.

5 Womb with a View V2 (5c)
Link two short cracks and lots of sloping holds.
FA. G Milner 1988

6 Clingon V5 (6c)
The well named arete is as rounded as a really round thing.
FA. Alan Taylor 2006

7 Murky Crack .... VS 4c
12m. The awkward crack leads to right trending shelves and the top of the tower. Escape is problematical on first acquaintance.
FA. Allan Austin 1958

8 Murky Rib V3 (6a)
The left arete of the gully entrance on its left-hand side. Starting up the right-hand side and continuing to the top is **HVS 5b**.

The next collection of climbs are at the cross-roads in the centre of Cleft Buttress. Despite the rather claustrophobic setting the routes are worthwhile and often drier than you might expect.

9 Cleft Pinnacle .... S 4a
12m. Layback the inner arete (opposite *Lancet Crack*) then trend right to the summit plateau. Escape is by reversing the route.

10 Lancet Crack .... VS 5a
12m. Facing the southern entrance to the cleft is a fine climb up the thin crack and through the bulges above. Easier than it looks, apart from the start. It is often green.
FA. Allan Austin 1958

11 Stone Age Reveller E4 6b
12m. Layback the arete to reach the bulges then climb these with difficulty to enter the much easier groove above.
FA. Nigel Baker 1997

12 Druid's Reality .... HVS 5b
12m. Start under the capping boulder and climb to it then swing left rapidly to access the easy final groove of the last route.
FA. Alec Burns 1987

13 Cleft Buttress .... VDiff
12m. Opposite *Druid's Reality*, climb the wall to a ledge then improvise a way onto the top of the tower. Escape is tricky.

14 Perverted Crack ...... VS 5a
10m. The crack on the outer face give pleasure to those who like grinding fist-jamming - we know you are out there somewhere.
FA. probably Allan Austin late 1950s

15 Pair in a Cubicle V6 (6c)
Stretch and palm up the face just right of the crack.

Pule Hill
Shooter's
Heptonstall
Widdop
Earl Crag
Ilkley
The Chevin
Caley
Almscliff
Eastby
Crookrise
Rylstone
Simon's Seat
Brimham
Eavestones
Slipstones
Crag Willas
Guisecliff

Descent - scramble off the back

Cyclops - 100m

Notice Board Crack

Notice Board Crack

This is the wall overlooking Cleft Buttress with a conspicuous kinked crack in it. The bolts that supported the ancient NO CLIMBING sign can still be seen to the left of the wide crack.

Approach (see map on page 139) - The shortest approach is to follow the road to Brimham House then head down the broad valley until opposite Cleft Buttress.

❶ Notice Board Wall. .   **E2 5b**
8m. Climb the short crack to its end, get some gear in then trend left to reach the top via the scoop. Bold.
FA. Mike Raine 1981

❷ Take No Notice **E4 6b**
12m. The wall past the old bolts (wires over the heads or, better, giant cams in the break) to a high grope for a pocket.
FA. Steve Rhodes 1988

❸ Notice Board Crack .   **VS 4b**
12m. The kinked crack is an ancient and awkward classic. Traditionally graded VS, it's nearer HS with a suitably large cam.
FA. Sidney Thompson 1930s

❹ Long John's Rib . . . .   **HS 4b**
6m. The pleasant left arete.

❺ Acme Error. . . . . . .   **HVS 5a**
6m. Weave up the wall to a rounded exit
FA. Ken Tilford 1981

❻ Gordon's Proffer . . . .   **HVS 5a**
6m. The right arete has a high hard move round the nose, or sneak left under it to earn a **VS 5a** instead.
FA. Ken Tilford 1981

❼ Cyclops . . . .   **S 4a**
6m. The slabby wall to steeper moves past the 'eye'.

❽ Centre Point. . . . .   **Diff**
6m. Amble up the centre of the slab.

❾ Slab Arete . . . .   **VDiff**
6m. The right-hand arete of the face is worthwhile.

Cyclops

Red Tape - 40m

Cyclops

Between Cleft Buttress/Notice Board Crack and Cubic Block is a series of short buttresses and blocks hidden in the trees The first of these buttresses is clear of the trees and offers a few easier routes. It is best approached from Cleft Buttress, unless you are at Cubic Block in which case there is a crag-base path.

Red Tape

Cyclops - 40m

Red Tape to Acme Wall

Between the delights of the Cleft Buttress area and the Cubic Block are a whole series of buttresses hidden away in the trees, some of these are minor but the others are well worth a visit.

Approach (see map on page 139) - Either approach from the Cubic Block, or from Cleft Buttress and Cyclops. Either way, the crag-base path is tricky to follow through the thick vegetation.

40m right of Cyclops, and set back from the path, is a tall tower with a flat front face - Red Tape.

❶ Red Tape . . . . ⬜ **E3 5c**
12m. The centre of the face has a nice combination of long reaches and rounded holds. The apparent escape route to the right arete turns out to be a bad idea.

❷ No Red Tape . . . . ⬜ **V5 (6b)**
A sitting start up the hanging prow.

20m right of Red Tape is a squat rounded buttress split centrally by a deep chimney with a trio of chockstones.

❸ Merle . . . . ⬜ **S 4b**
8m. The rounded arete left of the deep cleft has a tricky start.

❹ Chockstone Chimney . . . ⬜ **Diff**
8m. Classic stuff with the expected jammed boulders.

❺ Hanging Crack . . . . ⬜ **E1 5c**
8m. The (wait for it) hanging crack in the right arete of the chimney is tricky to access.

Chockstone Chimney

Red Tape - 20m

Happy Days - 20m

20m right of Chockstone Chimney is a square buttress flanked on the left by a huge holly tree - Happy Days.

❻ R.P.T. . . . . 🔲🔲 **S 4a**
10m. Layaway up the leaning left arete by a pleasant sequence.

❼ The Belfrey . . . . 🔲🔲 **S 4b**
12m. The slanting rift gives a worthwhile and steep struggle until it is possible to exit rightwards onto ledges. Move right again and finish rightwards past a big soft thread runner.

❽ Happy Days Traverse . . . 🔲🔲 **V8**
From the groove on the left shuffle right to join *Happy Days.*

❾ Happy Days . . . . . . 🔲🔲🔲 **V5 (6b)**
Enter the hanging niche by a perplexing sequence of moves and a stretch to the break. For the **E3** tick use the high pocket to make more hard moves to the top.

❿ Bilge Bump . . . . . . 🔲🔲🔲 **V4 (6b)**
The acute right arete on its right-hand side is taxing, and starting from the ground rather then the boulder even more so.

⓫ Layback Crack . . . . 🔲 **S 4b**
7m. The wide and strenny crack splitting the right wall.

40m to the right, through the undergrowth, is the blunt nose of Acme Wall with a slabby block in front of it.

⓬ Acme Wall . . . . 🔲🔲🔲 **V3 (5c)**
The centre of the wall past the pocket. Quite high.

⓭ Appiewand . . . . 🔲🔲 **HS 4c**
6m. The thin crack left of the nose to a mantelshelf top-out.

Chockstone Chimney - 20m

Happy Days

⓮ Peerless . . . . 🔲🔲 **HS 5a**
6m. Hop off the block and up the blunt arete.

⓯ Forever Man . . . . 🔲 **V2 (5b)**
The wall just right of the arete.

⓰ The Rack . . . . 🔲🔲 **V7**
A mighty stretch up the centre of the wall.

Acme Wall

Happy Days - 40m

Cubic Block - 150m

Descent

East Face

The Cubic Block
A huge tilted chunk of gritstone that makes a good attempt at Yorkshire's answer to the Peak's mighty Higgar Tor. The Cubic Block is only seconds from the nearest car parking and has a great set of routes from mild and slabby to leaning, rounded and brutal.
Approach (see map on page 139) - A path leads out of the left-hand (south western) car park and bears to the right to reach the buttress in less than two minutes.
Descent - Scramble down blocks to the south.

1 Old Corner . . . . HVD
10m. The left-hand arete of the slabby face then the wide crack and bulges above.

2 Shorty's Dilemma . . . . . S 4a
10m. A line straight up the face starting from a conspicuous hole two metres right of the arete.
FA. Tony Marr 1988

3 Heather Wall . . . . S 4a
10m. From a short crack climb to and follow the diagonal crack/ ramp to the top.

4 Heather Wall Variant . . . . . . HS 4b
10m. Climb direct to the finish of the regular route then step right to a final mantelshelf.
FA. Tony Marr 1976

5 Great Slab . . . . HVD
10m. Head up the slab into the base of the diagonal slot then shuffle right and finish direct.

6 Square Route . . . . . HS 4b
10m. From a block climb straight up the sustained face.
FA. Tony Barley 1964

7 Cubic Corner . . . . HS 4b
10m. The right arete of the block is probably the best pitch here.
FA. Sidney Thompson 1930s

8 Idle Slabs . . . . Mod
6m. The easy angled slab opposite is a popular beginners' route.
The U-Tube, V8. Climb out of the hole in the slab.

9 Thin Line . . . . HVS 5a
10m. From the boulders climb the face just right of the arete, low in the grade with a modern selection of cams.
FA. Tony Barley 1963

10 Stone Wall . . . . . . HVS 5b
12m. Climb the face direct to a deep break, move up and right and finish direct. There is good gear where it is most needed, but it still manages to feel bold, and it is tough for the short.
FA. Tony Barley 1974

11 Rough Stuff . . . . HVS 5b
12m. A direct line from the thin crack at ground level cutting through the 'rainbow'.
FA. Tony Barley 1989

12 Rough Wall . . . . VS 5a
12m. The classic of the face with a tough but well protected moves. Climb to the overlap and pull leftwards through it.
FA. Allan Austin 1957

13 Rough Neck . . . . VS 5a
12m. A direct line up the face and overlap right of *Rough Wall*.
FA. Tony Barley 1989

14 Moss Side . . . . VS 4c
14m. Trend right following the arete to a ledge, step left and finish awkwardly.

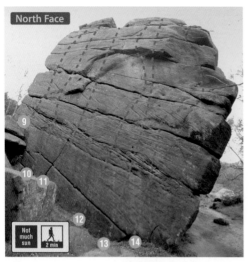

North Face

15 No Joke . . . . ⛰🔲🔲 **V5 (6b)**
From the break, reach a sharp crimp to gain the break above.

16 Joker's Wall Start . . . . . ⛰🔲 **V3 (6a)**
The steep wall past the pocket is the start of the next three routes.

17 Joker's Wall Arete . ⛰🔲🔲 **E3 6a**
14m. The leaning wall just right of the arete.
FA. Hank Pasquill 1974

18 Joker's Wall. . . . . . ⛰🔲🔲 **E4 6a**
14m. The original route of the wall is devious and pumpy - a right comical affair for most. From the ledge at 4m, move right, up and back left to a shelf. Access this with difficulty then escape rightwards.
FA. John Syrett 1971

19 Joker's Wall Crack . ⛰🔲🔲 **E4 6b**
12m. The hideous hanging crack offers a direct finish for those with telescopic arms and in the mood for a good fight.

20 Joker's Wall Right . . . . 🔲 **V5 (6b)**
An independent problem direct to the traverse on *Joker's Wall*.

21 Minion's Close . . . . ⛰🔲 **V3 (6a)**
The wall just left of the crack. Easier than the crack for some.

22 Minion's Way . . . . . ⛰🔲🔲 **HVS 5c**
12m. A couple of pulls on cruel jams leads to a ledge for a breather, then an easier layback to finish. **VS 4c** for grit gurus.
FA. Allan Austin 1957

23 Wisecrack . . . . ⛰🔲🔲 **HVS 5c**
18m. A fine extension to *Minion's Way* along the near horizontal break, with some excellent jamming. Only 5a after the start.
FA. Tony Marr 1993

24 The Overhanging Flake . ⛰🔲 **V5 (6b)**
Climb the steep flake to a ledge.

25 The Bottom Line ⛰🔲🔲🔲 **E7 6c**
12m. Climb the flake leftwards then scale the bulges and evil hanging orifice. Good gear and no holds about sums it up.
FA. Dave Pegg 1989

26 Beatnik . . . . ⛰🔲🔲 **E3 5c**
12m. Climb the right edge of the yellow wall then the bulges until it is possible to escape leftwards.
FA. Robin Barley 1963

27 Cave Chimney . . . . ⛰🔲 **HVD**
12m. The gloomy cleft on the right of the face.

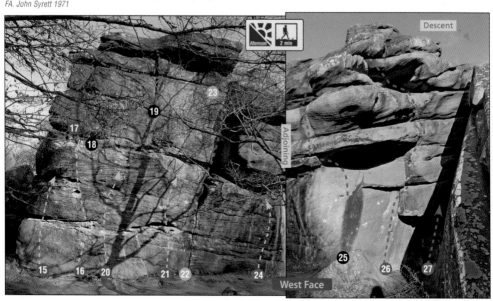

Descent

Adjoining

West Face

Descent

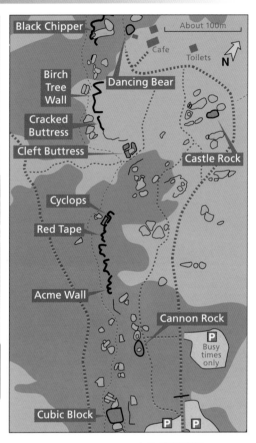

Black Chipper

Birch Tree Wall

Dancing Bear

Cracked Buttress

Cleft Buttress

Castle Rock

Cyclops

Red Tape

Acme Wall

Cannon Rock

P Busy times only

Cubic Block

About 100m

Cafe

Toilets

N

P   P

Cannon Rock

A fine tower named because of the cannon hole, a narrow tunnel that pierces its upper section. The tower is situated to the left of the track a couple of minutes walk from the parking and is set back a short distance.

1 Mon's Meg . . . . **HVS 5a**
10m. The bulging nose gives an interesting and committing exercise in rounded grippings. Big gun, big bang.
FA. Dave Musgrove 1974

2 Maloja . . . . **VS 4c**
12m. Get onto the ledge at the base of the open groove and climb it right then left. Finish past the cannon hole.
FA. East Yorkshire MC members 1950s

3 Frensis . . . . **VS 5a**
12m. Power up the paired jamming cracks to their termination then shuffle right and finish with a taxing mantelshelf.
FA. Allan Austin 1956

4 Frensis Direct **E1 5b**
12m. The continuation provides a fitting finale - low in the grade but awkward enough to keep you working.
FA. Allan Austin 1957

Castle Rock

5 Hawk Traverse . . . . **HS 4b**
22m. A wandering pitch that visits some exciting spots at an amenable grade, care with rope work required. Climb the short wide crack on the left and traverse right into *Desperation Crack*. Up this a short way then continue the traverse below the bulges until the final section of *Jabberwok* can be reached. Finish up the chimney.
FA. Brian Evans 1959

6 Desperation Crack . . . . **HVS 5b**
14m. The slanting widening fissure is a classic of its genre. The lower section is steady enough until things turn pear-shaped, then abandon all technique and swim for your life.
FA. East YMC member early 1950s

7 Swan Arcade **E4 6a**
14m. A bold outing up the wall between the two main cracks. A fingery lower section leads to the bulges, move right and cross them at their widest point to a final difficult move. This is always a tough outing, and broken flakes on the overhangs have compounded the difficulties.
FA. Mike Hammill 1976

8 Jabberwok . . . . **VS 4c**
14m. A good climb, up the central feature of the face. Climb the reachy and fingery wall left of the diagonal crack where the odd broken hold has made things trickier (the crack is a harder **VS 4c**) to the bulges then move right to access the base of the chimney. Finish up this.
FA. A.Marsden 1950

9 Picnic **E2 5c**
12m. A good route, though not the stroll in the park the name suggests. Climb the thin crack and the groove above, at its top move right to a small cave. The pullover from here is taxing.
FA. John Syrett 1973

Descent scramble off the back

Castle Rock

This is the imposing squat tower that sits in an open valley just to the left of the road as it approaches Brimham House and the toilet block. It has one of the tallest faces in the whole area and is home to a fine set of rapid drying and sunny climbs.

Approach - Head down the main track towards the cafe and the crag will soon appear on the left, forming the right-hand side of the wide grassy valley that runs down towards Cleft Rock.

🔟 Picnic Variation . . . . 🔲 HVS 5a
14m. A bit of a cop-out though with good climbing and plenty of variety. Climb *Picnic* to where it moves right but instead traverse left under the bulges to reach the final chimney of *Jabberwok*.
FA. Allan Austin 1956

⓫ Cakewalk . . . . 🔲 VS 5a
10m. Climb the short awkward crack and wall above until an unsatisfactory escape rightwards become available.
FA. Alan Austin 1956

⓬ Rainy Day . . . . 🔲 HVS 5c
12m. Climb the wall on the right of the crack to ledges then move left before finishing direct.
FA. Jeff Appleyard 1971

The final pinnacle described is just to the west of the cafe.

⓭ Dancing Bear . . . . 🔲 HVD
7m. The south west face is well travelled. Descend by reversing it.

⓮ Tender Homecoming 🔲 E8 7a
9m. The big rounded arete on the block behind the Dancing Bear. Start on the left. A fall from the final moves would be serious and the route hasn't yet attracted much attention from boulderers.
FA. Nick Dixon 1990

Dancing Bear

One of the best-known of the formations at Brimham is just to the west of the cafe. The two routes covered here are from opposite ends of the grade spectrum.

⓮ On pinnacle behind

Dancing Bear

	No star	1	2	3
Mod to S	2	1	1	1
HS to HVS	3	3	2	-
E1 to E3	-	6	3	2
E4 and up	-	-	-	3

Eavestones is a bit of a Lost World, once a lightly wooded valley with pretty lakes and waterside walks, over the years it has been neglected and become choked with rhododendrons and other greenery. There are almost 150 routes here, though many of them have been as good as lost and the whole place sees little traffic. Here is a selection of the best (and cleanest) climbs, call in and give the place a try, you might enjoy it. If you want further details, consult *YMC Yorkshire Gritstone (1998)*.

Conditions

The valley is deeply incised and very sheltered. This means it can be hot and humid in the summer, though it provides a sheltered retreat from Brimham on bitter days - it can be ten degrees warmer on The Fort than up on Cannon Rock! The best time to visit is April/May before the trees are heavy with leaves but the rhododendrons are in full bloom.

Approach

East of the turning off the B6265 to Brimham Rocks is a minor turn to the north signed to Eavestone. Follow this down to the farm then bear right and take the road down into the valley. On the right is limited parking by a footpath sign. The Fort Buttress can be glimpsed from here through the trees rising from the lake.

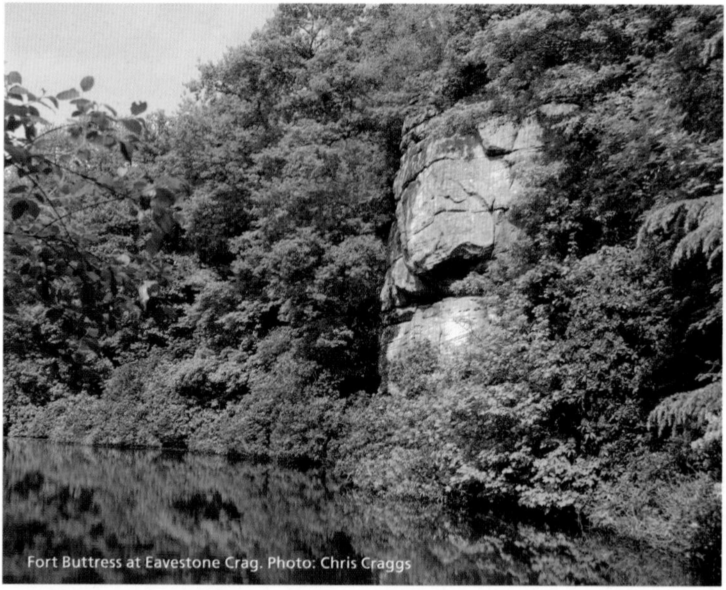
Fort Buttress at Eavestone Crag. Photo: Chris Craggs

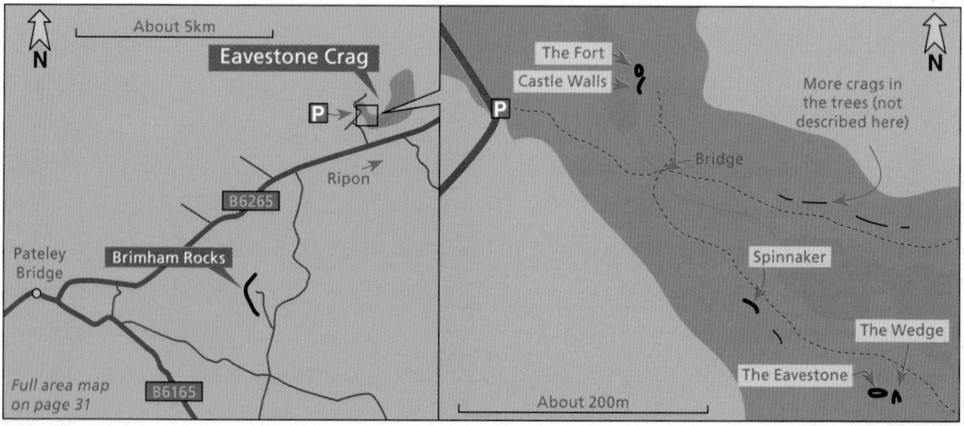
N
About 5km
Eavestone Crag
P
Ripon
B6265
Pateley Bridge
Brimham Rocks
B6165
Full area map on page 31
The Fort
Castle Walls
P
N
More crags in the trees (not described here)
Bridge
Spinnaker
The Wedge
The Eavestone
About 200m

Pule Hill | Shooter's | Heptonstall | Widdop | Earl Crag | Ilkley | The Chevin | Caley | Almscliff | Eastby | Crookrise | Rylstone | Simon's Seat | Brimham | Eavestones | Slipstones | Crag Willas | Goldsborough

Dave Musgrove on the first ascent of *The Alamo* (E2 5b) - *page 160* - on the Fort at Eavestone Crag. Photo: Musgrove collection

Lots of sun | 3 min | Sheltered | Green

Change in viewing angle

Castle Walls

The Fort

The sunny walls on the northern side of the Upper Lake are the closest to the parking and have an interesting set of climbs that are cleaner than most in the valley.
Approach - Follow the path down to the lake, cross a foot-bridge then turn left and weave through the shrubbery to reach a clearing beside the pinnacle of The Fort.
Descent - From the top of The Fort cross the tree-bridge to the main edge (airy) then descend a narrow gully to the right to arrive back at the gear.

❶ Portcullis . . . . 〔2〕☐ **S 4a**
22m. A mini-expedition, interesting and devious with considerable splash-down potential. From the beach, traverse out left to the base of cracks and climb these to the roofs then traverse left again (a rounded hand-traverse or wobbly crawl) to reach the base of a chimney. Head up this then finish up the exposed cracks just to the right.
FA. Tony Barley 1989

❷ Excalibur . . . . 〔1〕◥ ◪☐ **E2 5c**
16m. An exciting line up the front face of the buttress. Start as for *Portcullis* but climb the flake in the right arete of the first groove. At the roof move left into the steep crack above and follow this to its end. A wild and pumpy hand-traverse leads back right to finish just left of the arete.
FA. Tony Barley 1989

❸ The Alamo . . . . 〔3〕◪☐ **E2 5b**
14m. A great climb, always clean and usually dry, up the right-hand edge of the front face. Climb to the bulges then head up the crack on the left to pass these and gain the slabbier front face of the buttress, right of the bounding rib. Finish direct.
Photo on page 159.
FA. Dave Musgrove 1989

❹ Oubliette . . . . 〔3〕◪☐ **E2 5b**
12m. Makes the most of the right-hand side of the buttress. Climb the bubbly wall to the roof then move left and pass the overhang using the crack of *The Alamo*. Above the roof move back right to climb the hanging face via a series of short cracks.
FA. Tony Barley 1967

The Castle Walls

The short walls to the right of The Fort have a selection of sheltered routes and, although not brilliant, they are worth a few minutes of your time if in the area.
Descent - There is a narrow gully just to the left.

❶ Castellan . . . . **HVS 5b**
8m. The slanting crack in the wall to the right of the foot of the descent gully give a pumpy little pitch. Gaining the upper crack is especially hard.
FA. Tony Barley 1971

❷ Battlement **E3 6a**
8m. The slabby rib is bold and delicate, small cams around to the left just about give protection when it is really needed.
FA. Dave Musgrove 1990

❸ The Dirty Rascal **E1 5c**
10m. Climb a short crack then balance up to the thin overlap. Move out left to gain the shallow scoop right of the arete. Finish up this.
FA. Tony Barley 1989

❹ The King of the Castle **E2 5c**
9m. A more direct finish with a fingery pull required to get past the overlap. Nice technical moves.
FA. Dave Musgrove 1989

❺ Rampart . . . . **HVS 5b**
10m. The right-hand arete is climbed left then right to pass the nose, with a finish up the right-hand side. A start on the right-hand side via the open groove is **Ditch, HVS 5c**.
FA. Dave Musgrove 1989

❻ Casement Crack . . . . **VDiff**
8m. The wide crack that bounds the wall.
FA. Dave Musgrove 1990

❼ Dungeon . . . . **S 4a**
10m. The right-hand of the wide cracks is a dingy affair. Climb it past a cave to the upper chimney system.
FA. Tony Barley 1989

❽ Stockade . . . . **VS 4c**
10m. Gallop up the right arete of the chimney on its lake-side, trending right to finish.
FA. Tony Barley 1989

❾ Merlon **E1 6a**
10m. The wall two metres right of the arete has a bouldery start to reach better holds in the break. From here, finish direct.
FA. Robin Barley 1990

❿ Crenellation **E1 5c**
10m. The wall right of centre has a tricky move to the break, undercut off this and stretch for the final holds.
FA. Tony Barley 1989

⓫ Machicolation . . . . **VS 4c**
8m. The leaning right arete of the wall.
FA. Tony Barley 1989

⓬ Arrow Slit . . . . **HS 4b**
6m. The short cracks before the jungle takes over.
FA. Tony Barley 1989

The Wedge

15m gap

The Eavestone

The Wedge
The prominent jutting axe-edge buttress of the Wedge is obvious from its name. It has a small collection of climbs that stay relatively clean.
Approach - See The Eavestone approach opposite.

❶ The Thin End . . . . 🛈 ☐ **HVS 5a**
10m. The arete is climbed on its left-hand side to a steep finish over the capping blocks. Easier than first appearances suggest.
FA. Tony Barley 1965

❷ Fat Chance. . . . . 🛈 ☐ ☐ **E3 5c**
10m. The right-hand side is altogether more taxing. Tricky 'barn-door' laybacking reaches a good ledge. Finish over the blocks or escape right.
FA. Dave Musgrove (Jnr) 1990

❸ Wedgewood . . . . 🛈 ☐ ☐ **HVS 5a**
12m. Start just right of the green streak and climb the wall to reach the left-trending ramp-line. Move out right to the cracks in the wall and finish steeply up these. Pumpy but well protected.
FA. Tony Barley 1965

❹ Taper . . . . 🛈 ☐ **HS 4b**
12m. Climb the groove then access the ramp on the left. Balance across this, crossing *Wedgewood*, to reach the blocky cracks right of the arete and finish steeply up these.
FA. Tony Barley 1967

❺ The Heel . . . . 🛈 ☐ **S 4c**
10m. From the recess on the right, climb steeply leftwards to reach the base of a crack. Bridge up this pleasantly. Nice climbing which would get two stars if it were done a bit more often.
FA. Robin Barley 1965

❻ Bunkered . . . . 🛈 ☐ ☐ **E2 6a**
8m. Make steep and technical moves into a hanging groove then move left and finish up the rib.
FA. Tony Barley 19891

The Eavestone

❼ Evenso . . . . 🛈 ☐ ☐ ☐ **HVS 5a**
10m. The left-hand side of the square rib on the uphill side of the Eavestone gives a bold little pitch.
FA. Tony Barley 1967

❽ Eavesdropper . . . . 🛈 ☐ **HVS 5a**
10m. The right-hand rib is usually cleaner and gives a fine pitch.
FA. Tony Barley 1967

❾ Crazy Paver . . . . . . 🛈 ☐ ☐ ☐ ☐ **E2 5c**
16m. A weaving line up the left-hand side of the north east face. From near the left edge, climb up and right then hand traverse out right to reach a ledge beside a tall flake. Pull leftwards through the bulges and sprint up the face on positive but well spaced holds.
FA. Tony Barley 1989

8
9
10
The Eavestone
11   11   12 - Spinnaker - 80m   13

Change in viewing angle

The Eavestone

A good set of routes on this bulky block. The grades and star ratings assume that the routes are clean - bear in mind that they probably won't be.

Approach - Turn right just before the foot-bridge that leads across to The Fort and follow the southern shore of the Lower Lake for five minutes, past Spinnaker buttress, until the crag appears on the right, just after a small stream crosses the path.

🔟 Eavestone Wall . . . 　　　　　　 E3 6b
16m. A fine route up the centre of the wall with a tough, but safe, moves. Climb straight up the face (reachy, rounded and bold) to a ledge just right of the fragile flake. Reach the thin crack up and right with great difficulty then continue up this to a rightward exit.
FA. Tony Barley (1 sling) 1989. FFA. Kim Greenald 1990

⓫ Eavestone Crack . . . . . . 　　　　　 E4 6a
14m. A great climb up the left-hand crack in the narrow west face of the Eavestone. Mantel onto the shelf from the left then climb to the bulges. Stretch left to the base of the crack and thug up this to reach easier ground.
FA. Dave Musgrove (at the 4th attempt) 1989

⓬ Genesis . . . . 　　　　　　 E5 6b
14m. A fine outing up the right-hand crack. Mantel onto the ledge from the right then gain a higher ledge with difficulty. Head up and left to the first decent holds then shuffle right on slopers to access the crack which is climbed strenuously on gradually improving jams.
FA. Dave Musgrove 1990. A 6:30am start was needed to beat other suitors.

⓭ Life Begins at Forty. 　　　　　　 E6 6c
20m. The big white wall round to the right gives a taxing pitch. Climb the crack in the left-hand rib then trend right past the overhang to a flake-crack. Move right again to a second flake above the bulges and use this to commit to the upper wall, then finish direct by more hard climbing. The direct finish is one of Yorkshire's more blatant 'last great problems'.
FA. Bob Smith 1991. Northumbrian raider strikes southwards and takes two big ground-falls into the Eavestones' mulch in the process.

The rest of the routes at Eavestones are located to either side of the extensive body of the water that is the Lower Lake. The northern side of the lake has half a dozen buttresses with some good routes and bouldering too, though these are not described here. Details can be found in YMC Yorkshire Gritstone (1998).

One final route worth mentioning is passed on the way to the Eavestone - see the map on page 158.

⓮ Spinnaker . . . . 　　　 S 4a
18m. A great route. From the left edge of the buttress traverse out right round the arete to reach a ledge above the roofs. Trend up and right, past another ledge to reach a shallow groove which leads to the top of the tower. A short Diff down-climb is the easiest way off the back. *Photo below featuring Dave Spencer.*
FA. Tony Barley 1989

Spinnaker
14

	No star	✪	✪✪	✪✪✪
Mod to S	35	7	1	-
HS to HVS	35	19	10	1
E1 to E3	12	19	9	4
E4 and up	4	4	0	4

A fine little cliff, not unlike a northern version of Burbage, though admittedly a little further from the road and therefore (a bit) quieter. The routes are only short - up to about eight metres high - and, although the crag is often regarded as a bouldering venue, the landings are often quite poor. Soloing the longer routes certainly requires a steady head. Recent years have seen an increase in the popularity of the cliff and the almost inevitable corresponding increase in problems of parking, erosion and litter. It only requires a little forethought and care to be part of the solution rather than the problem.

Conditions

The crag faces south west and can get very hot in the summer. It has long been known as a good winter venue, as long as the sun is out and the wind is in the right direction (preferably from the north) otherwise the place can be Baltic. The crag dries quickly and, apart from the odd stubborn streak, takes virtually no drainage.

Approach

From Masham, take the minor road that runs west through Fearby and Healy up in to Colsterdale, keeping right after Healey. Just after a steep uphill section after leaving Healey, there is parking on the right, around the entrance of the track that leads up to West Agra Farm - PLEASE PARK WITH CONSIDERATION. About a dozen cars can be slotted in here with care. Follow the track towards the farm, but where this bears right, continue along the line of the wall to a gate/stile. After the gate, turn hard right and follow the path up the side of the wall until vague tracks lead leftwards to the right-hand end of the rocks - about 15 minutes from the car.

Middle of winter and the parking is full!
Photo: Chris Craggs

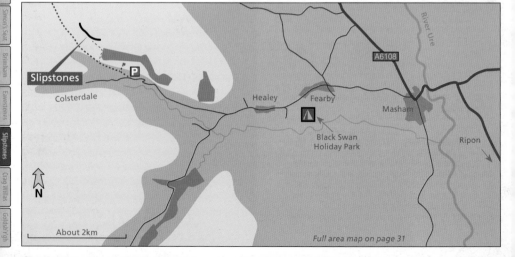

Full area map on page 31

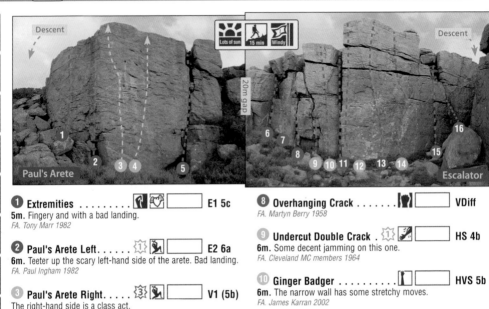

Descent

Descent

20m gap

Paul's Arete

Escalator

1 2 3 4 5 6 7 8 9 10 11 12 13 14 15 16

1 Extremities .... 🔲 **E1 5c**
5m. Fingery and with a bad landing.
FA. Tony Marr 1982

2 Paul's Arete Left ...... 🔲 **E2 6a**
6m. Teeter up the scary left-hand side of the arete. Bad landing.
FA. Paul Ingham 1982

3 Paul's Arete Right ..... 🔲 **V1 (5b)**
The right-hand side is a class act.
FA. Paul Ingham 1982

4 Steve's Wall .... 🔲 **V1 (5b)**
Up the centre of the wall trending rightwards.
FA. Steve Brown 1982

5 Heather Crack .... 🔲 **Diff**
FA. Martyn Berry 1957

6 Roofed Corner .... 🔲 **Diff**
FA. Martyn Berry 1957

7 Little Corner. .... 🔲 **Diff**
4m. The right-hand side of the tiny recess.
FA. Martyn Berry 1958

8 Overhanging Crack ...... 🔲 **VDiff**
FA. Martyn Berry 1958

9 Undercut Double Crack . 🔲 **HS 4b**
6m. Some decent jamming on this one.
FA. Cleveland MC members 1964

10 Ginger Badger .... 🔲 **HVS 5b**
6m. The narrow wall has some stretchy moves.
FA. James Karran 2002

11 Not So Tight Chimney .. 🔲 **HVD**
FA. Geoff Milburn 1960

12 Breakwind Arete .... 🔲 **HVS 5c**
FA. Phillipe Osbourne 1995

13 Space Trukin' .... 🔲 **E1 5b**
8m. Climb the blunt rib past a suspect flake.
FA. Ian Dunn 1982

14 Escalator .... 🔲 **HVS 5b**
8m. A fine climb up the middle of the face to reachy moves.
FA. Tony Marr 1964

Descent

The Far Left
A series of short, steep walls and the slabby back to the Beldin Block. The routes here don't see as much attention as the more impressive offerings over to the right, a good spot for a bit of peace and quiet - maybe. Despite the apparent lack of traffic, there are some good routes here.

Escalator

Jenny Binks

17 18 19 20 21 22 23 24

Beldin Block
The front face of the block presents a tall face with the longest routes at Slipstones.

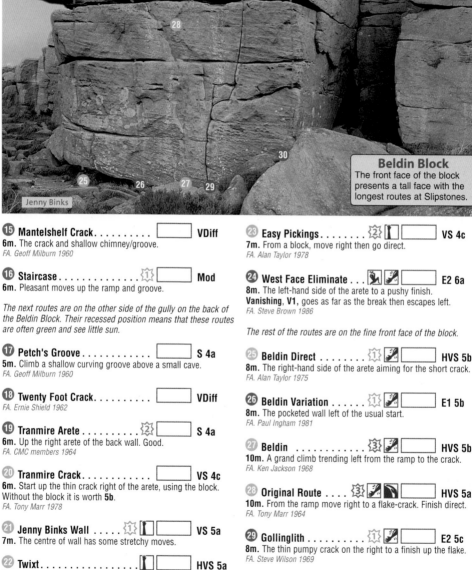

15 Mantelshelf Crack . . . . VDiff
6m. The crack and shallow chimney/groove.
FA. Geoff Milburn 1960

16 Staircase . . . . Mod
6m. Pleasant moves up the ramp and groove.

The next routes are on the other side of the gully on the back of the Beldin Block. Their recessed position means that these routes are often green and see little sun.

17 Petch's Groove . . . . S 4a
5m. Climb a shallow curving groove above a small cave.
FA. Geoff Milburn 1960

18 Twenty Foot Crack . . . . VDiff
FA. Ernie Shield 1962

19 Tranmire Arete . . . . S 4a
6m. Up the right arete of the back wall. Good.
FA. CMC members 1964

20 Tranmire Crack . . . . VS 4c
6m. Start up the thin crack right of the arete, using the block. Without the block it is worth **5b**.
FA. Tony Marr 1978

21 Jenny Binks Wall . . . . . VS 5a
7m. The centre of wall has some stretchy moves.

22 Twixt . . . . HVS 5a
7m. An eliminate up the wall just to the right.
FA. Alan Taylor 1999

23 Easy Pickings . . . . VS 4c
7m. From a block, move right then go direct.
FA. Alan Taylor 1978

24 West Face Eliminate . . . E2 6a
8m. The left-hand side of the arete to a pushy finish.
Vanishing, V1, goes as far as the break then escapes left.
FA. Steve Brown 1986

The rest of the routes are on the fine front face of the block.

25 Beldin Direct . . . . HVS 5b
8m. The right-hand side of the arete aiming for the short crack.
FA. Alan Taylor 1975

26 Beldin Variation E1 5b
8m. The pocketed wall left of the usual start.
FA. Paul Ingham 1981

27 Beldin . . . . HVS 5b
10m. A grand climb trending left from the ramp to the crack.
FA. Ken Jackson 1968

28 Original Route . . . . HVS 5a
10m. From the ramp move right to a flake-crack. Finish direct.
FA. Tony Marr 1964

29 Gollinglith E2 5c
8m. The thin pumpy crack on the right to a finish up the flake.
FA. Steve Wilson 1969

30 Tachyon E2 5c
8m. The right arete of the face finishing round on the gully wall.
FA. Alan Taylor 1999

Pate Hill | Shooter's | Heptonstall | Widdop | Earl Crag | Ilkley | The Chevin | Caley | Almscliff | Eastby | Crookrise | Rylstone | Simon's Seat | Brimham | Eavestones | Slipstones | Crag Willas | Guisecliff

Lots of sun | 15 min | Windy

Descent

3

12

16 17 18

1 2 4 5 14 15

6 8 9 11 13

7 10

Beldin Block

Agra Block
The right-hand of the pair of blocks is capped by a long narrow overhang. It has a good selection of climbs in the orange zone plus some worthwhile bouldering.

1 Zoom .... HVS 5c
7m. Link the flake and final crack. Tricky and strenuous.
FA. Tony Marr 1966

2 Atomic E3 6b
7m. Up the centre of the wall, step left and finish with difficulty.
FA. Ian Dunn 1982

3 Atomic Right-hand E3 6b
7m. A right-hand exit is hard.
FA. Hugh Harris 1994

4 Barnley Crack .... S 4a
6m. The awkward left-hand crack.
FA. Geoff Milburn 1960

5 Barnley Wall .... HS 4b
6m. Up the centre of the narrow back wall with a mantel start.
FA. Steve Wilson 1966

6 Ulfers Crack .... VDiff
6m. The awkward right-hand crack.
FA. Geoff Milburn 1960

7 Forever Onward E1 5b
6m. The centre of the right-hand side wall to hard move high up.
FA. Paul Ingham 1988

8 Timeless Divide V2 (6a)
The arete is a good problem. A right-hand start is **V5**.
FA. Paul Ingham 1983. FA. (RH Start) Ian Cummins early 1980s

9 Agrete V2 (5c)
Stretch to the black flake then head left to finish up the arete.
FA. Tony Marr 1980

10 Agra Direct Start V2 (5c)
Head straight for the left-hand end of the traverse.
FA. Tony Marr 1981

11 Agra .... HVS 5b
8m. Pull past the overlap then traverse out left to a good ledge. The centre of the roof requires a bit of a tussle. **The Wimp's Finish** heads all the way to *Ulfer's Crack* to avoid the roof, **VS 4b**.
FA. Tony Marr 1965

12 Agra Righ-hand ..... HVS 5b
8m. From the same start climb direct then move right to the roof.
FA. Paul Ingham 1980

13 Narrow Margin E2 6a
8m. Pull past the overlap and follow the pockets to the roof.
FA. Tony Marr 1992

14 Wisecrack Direct Start .. V5 (6a)
Hard (chipped) moves access the base of the crack. Jump off or continue up the original version to a high finish.
FA. Ian Cummins 1980s

15 Wisecrack E1 6a
6m. Gain the hanging crack from the right.
FA. Paul Ingham 1982

16 Alan's Arete .... VS 4c
6m. Balance up the right side of the arete. The left-hand side is **5b**.
FA. Alan Taylor 1980

17 Shine On .... VDiff
5m. The short lived layback.
FA. Martyn Berry 1958

18 Mantel On .... S 4b
4m. Gain the ramp awkwardly.
FA. CMC members 1964

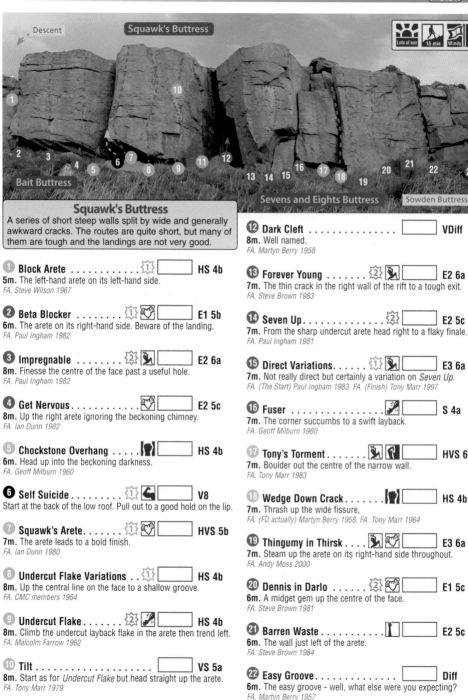

Descent

Squawk's Buttress

Bait Buttress

Sevens and Eights Buttress   Sowden Buttress

Squawk's Buttress

A series of short steep walls split by wide and generally awkward cracks. The routes are quite short, but many of them are tough and the landings are not very good.

1 Block Arete . . . . HS 4b
5m. The left-hand arete on its left-hand side.
FA. Steve Wilson 1967

2 Beta Blocker E1 5b
6m. The arete on its right-hand side. Beware of the landing.
FA. Paul Ingham 1982

3 Impregnable E2 6a
8m. Finesse the centre of the face past a useful hole.
FA. Paul Ingham 1982

4 Get Nervous E2 5c
8m. Up the right arete ignoring the beckoning chimney.
FA. Ian Dunn 1982

5 Chockstone Overhang . . . . HS 4b
6m. Head up into the beckoning darkness.
FA. Geoff Milburn 1960

6 Self Suicide V8
Start at the back of the low roof. Pull out to a good hold on the lip.

7 Squawk's Arete . . . . HVS 5b
7m. The arete leads to a bold finish.
FA. Ian Dunn 1980

8 Undercut Flake Variations . . HS 4b
8m. Up the central line on the face to a shallow groove.
FA. CMC members 1964

9 Undercut Flake . . . . HS 4b
8m. Climb the undercut layback flake in the arete then trend left.
FA. Malcolm Farrow 1962

10 Tilt . . . . VS 5a
8m. Start as for *Undercut Flake* but head straight up the arete.
FA. Tony Marr 1979

11 Flakeout Arete . . . . HVS 5a
8m. The left-hand wall of the gloomy chimney.
FA. Phillipe Osbourne 1995

12 Dark Cleft . . . . VDiff
8m. Well named.
FA. Martyn Berry 1958

13 Forever Young E2 6a
7m. The thin crack in the right wall of the rift to a tough exit.
FA. Steve Brown 1983

14 Seven Up E2 5c
7m. From the sharp undercut arete head right to a flaky finale.
FA. Paul Ingham 1981

15 Direct Variations E3 6a
7m. Not really direct but certainly a variation on *Seven Up*.
FA. (The Start) Paul Ingham 1983. FA. (Finish) Tony Marr 1997

16 Fuser . . . . S 4a
7m. The corner succumbs to a swift layback.
FA. Geoff Milburn 1960

17 Tony's Torment . . . . HVS 6a
7m. Boulder out the centre of the narrow wall.
FA. Tony Marr 1983

18 Wedge Down Crack . . . . . . HS 4b
7m. Thrash up the wide fissure,
FA. (FD actually) Martyn Berry 1958. FA. Tony Marr 1964

19 Thingumy in Thirsk E3 6a
7m. Steam up the arete on its right-hand side throughout.
FA. Andy Moss 2000

20 Dennis in Darlo E1 5c
6m. A midget gem up the centre of the face.
FA. Steve Brown 1981

21 Barren Waste E2 5c
6m. The wall just left of the arete.
FA. Steve Brown 1984

22 Easy Groove . . . . Diff
6m. The easy groove - well, what else were you expecting?
FA. Martyn Berry 1957

23 Edge Route . . . . Mod
6m. Up the blocky buttress.

Pule Hill

Shooters

Heptonstall

Widdop

Earl Crag

Ilkley

The Chevin

Caley

Almscliff

Eastby

Crookrise

Rylstone

Simon's Seat

Brimham

Eavestones

Slipstones

Crag Willas

Goldsbrough

Squwak's Buttress

Descent

Lots of sun   15 min   Windy

Sowden Buttress

Ripper

Marr's Buttress

Not much sun

Sowden Buttress

Sowden Buttress is a detached block that stands in front of the cliff and has routes on all sides. Those on the front are excellent, those on the back tend to be green, easy and not described here. Right again is Ripper Buttress with its leaning and rather smooth front face.

1 Right Arete . . . . VDiff
4m. The right arete of the back wall is the usual descent.

2 Problem Wall . . . . HVS 5b
5m. The centre of the north-facing wall.
FA. Paul Ingham 1982

3 Left Wall . . . . VDiff
5m. The curving groove.
FA. Geoff Milburn 1960

4 Sowden Left-hand E1 5b
6m. The wall and arete.
FA. Paul Ingham 1982

5 Sowden . . . . HVS 5a
6m. The flake in the left-hand side of the face leads to a tricky exit.
FA. Malcolm Farrow 1962 or Mike Railton 1964 (depends who you ask).

6 Sinbad E3 6b
6m. Take the flake to its end then trend right past a pocket.
FA. Dave Paul 1983

7 Space Plucks E3 6a
6m. The wall has a couple of useful pockets.
FA. Paul Ingham 1983

8 Forthright E2 5c
5m. The blunt rib on its left side.
FA. Steve Crowe 2000

9 Dixon's Dilemma . . . . VS 4c
5m. The wall behind the block. Avoid using the block.
FA. Nick Dixon 1984

10 Witton Wall . . . . S 4b
4m. The awkward crack in the right-hand side of the wall.
FA. Mike Railton 1964

11 Halfway Chockstone . . . . Diff
4m. The chimney at the top of the gully, exit left past the boulder.
FA. Martyn Berry 1958.

12 Central Bay Route . . . . VDiff
4m. The stepped groove in the right-hand side of the gully.
FA. Martyn Berry 1958

13 Leany Meany E1 5c
8m. Climb the arete to the horizontal break, then trend right to pockets and a stretchy finish. The arete direct is **Old Peculiar**, also **E1 5c** but a touch harder than the original.
FA. Paul Ingham 1980. FA. (Old Peculiar) Tony Marr 2003

14 Killer E4 6b
8m. Start up a shallow groove then trend left using a set of pockets to a scary top out.
FA. Dave Paul 1983

15 Ripper E1 6a
7m. The right arete of the block contains a shallow groove, work out a way up this. Fine climbing. *Photo on page 165.*
FA. Paul Ingham 1980

Pule Hill | Shooters | Heptonstall | Widdop | Earl Crag | Ilkley | The Chevin | Caley | Almscliff | Eastby | Crookrise | Rylstone | Simon's Seat | Brimham | Earlestones | Slipstones | Crag Willas | Goldsborough

Marr's Buttress and Siamese Blocks

Marr's is the flat-fronted buttress with a prominent wide crack splitting its left-hand side. The Siamese Blocks are the vaguely similar twin towers further to the right, both capped with narrow overhanging blocks. They are home to several good boulder problems of the arete variety.

1 Picnic Wall . . . . Diff
4m. The easy chimney that cuts in behind the buttress.
FA. Martyn Berry 1957

2 Cummin's Route V1 (5b)
The centre of the narrow wall left of the crack.
FA. Paul Ingham 1982

3 Christopher Robin . . . . . VS 4b
5m. The wide crack is a worthwhile thrash.
FA. Geoff Milburn 1960

4 Right Wall V1 (5c)
The wall just right of the crack.
FA. Tony Marr 1983

5 Marr's Route . . . . VS 5a
6m. Follow the flake to the roof then use a good hold to make scary moves out rightwards over the roof.
FA. Eric Marr and Tony Marr 1964. The misplaced apostrophe is traditional.

6 Da's Route . . . . VS 5a
6m. Head up the shallow 'feature' by the green streak. Pull the roof direct, or sneak off right - tut, tut.
FA. Steve Crowe 1994

7 Moderator . . . . Mod
4m. The blocked chimney splitting the right side of the buttress.
FA. Martyn Berry 1958

8 Pa's Route . . . . S 4b
5m. The centre of the square pillar.

Next are the twin pillars of the Siamese Blocks home to some good bouldering (as long as you like aretes).

9 Friday 13th V2 (6a)
The left side of the left arete of the left-hand buttress is good.
FA. Steve Brown 1982.

10 Sunday 20th V4 (6b)
The left arete on its right-hand side past a high pocket is better and scary too.
FA. Paul Ingham 1983

11 Slipway V4 (6a)
The right-hand arete on its left-hand side starting from the left.
FA. Richard Davies 1990s

12 Siamese Bridge . . . . Diff
4m. A bit of 'classical' work up the wide rift between the blocks.
FA. Martyn Berry 1958

13 Right-hand Twin V2 (5c)
The slabby side of the next arete. Quality moves.
FA. Tony Marr 1980

14 Leaning Wall V5 (6b)
The arete on the steep side is a bit of a different ball game.
FA. Alan Taylor 1980

15 Strictly Personal V3 (6a)
The right arete on its left side, though pockets round right help.
FA. Paul Ingham 1983

16 Brush Up V1 (5b)
The short wall right of the arete.
FA. Paul Ingham 1983

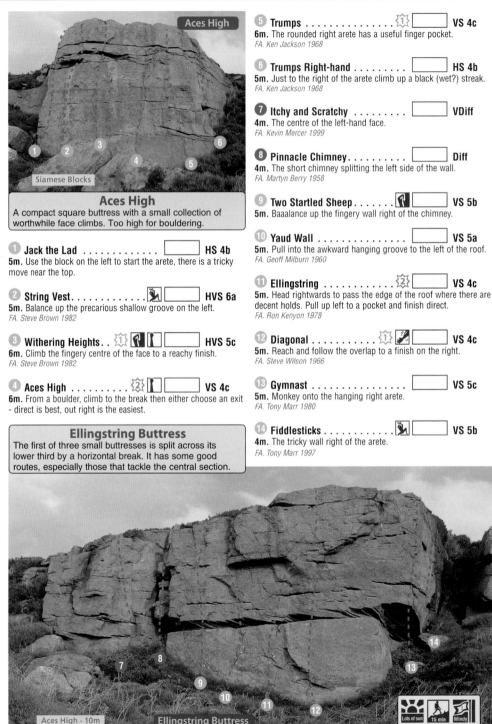

Aces High

Siamese Blocks

Aces High
A compact square buttress with a small collection of worthwhile face climbs. Too high for bouldering.

1 Jack the Lad . . . . **HS 4b**
5m. Use the block on the left to start the arete, there is a tricky move near the top.

2 String Vest . . . . **HVS 6a**
5m. Balance up the precarious shallow groove on the left.
FA. Steve Brown 1982

3 Withering Heights . . . . **HVS 5c**
6m. Climb the fingery centre of the face to a reachy finish.
FA. Steve Brown 1982

4 Aces High . . . . **VS 4c**
6m. From a boulder, climb to the break then either choose an exit - direct is best, out right is the easiest.

Ellingstring Buttress
The first of three small buttresses is split across its lower third by a horizontal break. It has some good routes, especially those that tackle the central section.

5 Trumps . . . . **VS 4c**
6m. The rounded right arete has a useful finger pocket.
FA. Ken Jackson 1968

6 Trumps Right-hand . . . . **HS 4b**
5m. Just to the right of the arete climb up a black (wet?) streak.
FA. Ken Jackson 1968

7 Itchy and Scratchy . . . . **VDiff**
4m. The centre of the left-hand face.
FA. Kevin Mercer 1999

8 Pinnacle Chimney . . . . **Diff**
4m. The short chimney splitting the left side of the wall.
FA. Martyn Berry 1958

9 Two Startled Sheep . . . . **VS 5b**
5m. Baaalance up the fingery wall right of the chimney.

10 Yaud Wall . . . . **VS 5a**
5m. Pull into the awkward hanging groove to the left of the roof.
FA. Geoff Milburn 1960

11 Ellingstring . . . . **VS 4c**
5m. Head rightwards to pass the edge of the roof where there are decent holds. Pull up left to a pocket and finish direct.
FA. Ron Kenyon 1978

12 Diagonal . . . . **VS 4c**
5m. Reach and follow the overlap to a finish on the right.
FA. Steve Wilson 1966

13 Gymnast . . . . **VS 5c**
5m. Monkey onto the hanging right arete.
FA. Tony Marr 1980

14 Fiddlesticks . . . . **VS 5b**
4m. The tricky wall right of the arete.
FA. Tony Marr 1997

Aces High - 10m

Ellingstring Buttress

Lots of sun | 15 min | Windy

Ellingstring Buttress

Stainthorpe's Wall

Double Mantelshelf

Lay-by Buttress

Stainthorpe's Wall

These two buttresses are also known as Buttress Sixteen and Buttress Seventeen which is a little dull. Both are split at mid-height by a horizontal break and both have a selection of climbs that are on the border-line between short routes and highball problems.

15 Fearby . . . . VS 4b
6m. Using a boulder, climb the face just right of the VDiff arete.
FA. Geoff Milburn 1960

16 Stainthorpe's Wall E1 5b
6m. Start left of the streak and move right past it to finish via a pocket and shallow groove. A **Direct Start** is **V1 (5c)**.
FA. Dave Stainthorpe 1980. FA. (Direct Start) Tony Marr 1965

17 Alan's Wall . . . . HVS 5a
6m. A direct finish to *Stainthorpe's Wall* utilising the thin flake.
FA. Alan Taylor 1999

18 Only Sixteen V3 (6a)
A worthwhile more direct start to *Stainthorpe's Wall*.
FA. Paul Ingham 1982

19 Fascionationby E2 5c
6m. Enter the hanging groove and wobble up it using creaky finger-flakes to start. Can be done as a highball **V3**.
FA. Paul Ingham 1983

20 Jug Handle Pull Up . . . . VDiff
5m. Step off the boulder and climb the left arete of the buttress. (The same arete is **4b** without the boulder).
FA. Geoff Milburn 1960

21 Wall Centre . . . . VS 4c
5m. The centre of the buttress to a reachy finish.

22 Happy Daze . . . . VS 4c
5m. Start by the central arete and trend left up the wall to a finish on small pockets.
FA. Alan Taylor 1979

23 Double Mantelshelf . . . . VDiff
5m. The stepped groove by a pair of swift mantels.
FA. Geoff Milburn 1960

24 Out on Bail . . . . HVS 5c
5m. Bridge up the shallow groove and then head up the wall using a tiny broken flake and a one-finger pocket.
FA. Ian Henderson 2000

25 Right Edge . . . . HVS 5c
4m. The right arete is quite a tease.
FA. Tony Marr 1980

Pule Hill · Shooter's · Heptonstall · Widdop · Earl Crag · Ilkley · The Chevin · Caley · Almscliff · Eastby · Crookrise · Rylstone · Simon's Seat · Brimham · Eavestones · Slipstones · Grag Willas · Goldsbr'gh

Stainthorpe's Wall

Lay-by Buttress

Adjoining

Overhanging Arete

Lay-by Buttress

A short block clearly identified by the black drainage streak running down its centre. There are some good boulder problems here though they are pretty tough. Across the slope is another short square block with some popular, and easier, boulder problems.

1 Hand Traverse . . . . Diff
6m. Swing along the break to just short of the arete.
FA. Geoff Milburn 1960

2 Rock Over V0- (4c)
A tiny route up the centre of the tiny wall.
FA. Steve Crowe 1995

3 Lay-by Arete V8
The arete starting on the right and finishing round to the left.
FA. Paul Ingham 1985

4 Lay-by Arete Direct V9
Stay on the right-hand side all the way.
FA. Ian Cummins 2001

5 Lay-by V3 (6a)
The central flake-crack is the original classic of the wall.
FA. Alan Taylor 1976

6 Little Baldy V5 (6c)
A desperate eliminate heading straight to the bullet-hole. Using holds on the flake of *Lay-by* is taboo.
FA. Ian Cummins 1985

7 Rock On Left-hand V3 (6a)
Gain the slot then stretch left to use the bullet-hole to finish.
FA. Paul Ingham 1981

8 Rock On. V2 (5c)
From the same start as *Rock On Left-hand*, go direct.
FA. Paul Ingham 1980

9 Rock Off V1 (5b)
The right-hand rib.
FA. Paul Ingham 1980

10 All Off V0 (5a)
Up the tiny face using a small flake.
FA. Paul Ingham 1980

11 Ten Foot Moderate . . . . . . Mod
The short lived and slightly awkward wide crack.
FA. Martyn Berry 1958

12 Twenty Something V0- (4c)
Up the side wall just left of the arete.
FA. Steve Crowe 1994

13 Overhanging Arete V2 (6a)
Steep pulls up the leaning arete starting from the left.
FA. Steve Wilson 1966

14 Reason and Rowan V3 (6a)
Leap for the thin pocket in the wall then do the same to the top.
FA. Andy Banks 2001

15 Flaky Wall V1 (5b)
Follow the flakes up the steep wall.
FA. Tony Marr 1970

16 Left Wall . . . . HVD
4m. The blunt rib that bounds the face.

17 Two Chockstones . . . . Diff
On the right is a wide awkward crack with the expected chocks.
FA. Martyn Berry 1958

Steptoe

18 Super Fury Animal V12
A flying dyno from a low side-pull all the way to the boulder edge.
FA. Steve Dunning 2001

19 Sidewinder V6 (6b)
The centre of the wall under the overhang is crimpy
FA. Steve Crowe 2002

20 Exocet. V11
From a sitting start, undercut the overlap and heave off a shoddy sloper. Sidling left into *Sidewinder* is only **V9**!
FA. Steve Dunning 2002

Pale Hill
Shooters
Ripon stall
Widdop
Earl Crag
Ilkley
The Chevin
Caley
Almscliff
Eggley
Crookrise
Brimham
Simon's Seat
Brimham
Eavestones
Slipstones
Crag Willas
Goldsborough

Overhanging Arete | Curving Slab | Steptoe | The Arch

Steptoe
Behind the tilted block of Curving Slab, is a long low wall capped by a narrow overhang along its right-hand side, home to the hard-core. To the right is a short smart wall with some nice problems of a more amenable grade.

㉑ Stipule **V9**
An eliminate dyno up the edge of the wall. No arete allowed.
FA. Steve Dunning 2002

㉒ Curving Crack Arete . . . . **V1 (5b)**
Do the left edge of the crack from a sitting start.

㉓ Curving Crack . . . . **VS 4c**
4m. The tricky overhanging crack is fun.
FA. Geoff Milburn 1960

㉔ Bert Wells . . . . **V2 (5c)**
The flake just right of the gap without touching the arete.
FA. Paul Ingham 1983

㉕ Centre Left . . . . **V2 (5c)**
Start 2m right of the gap. Climb the overlap using a finger slot.
FA. Tony Marr 1983

㉖ Steptoe . . . . **V3 (6a)**
The middle of the wall with escalating difficulties.
FA. Steve Brown 1982

㉗ Tiptoe . . . . **V1 (5b)**
The arete has a tricky start. The right side of the arete is **V2**.
FA. Tony Marr 1965

㉘ Micro Corner . . . . **V6 (6b)**
Behind the *Stepoe* block is this mini-classic, easily recognised from its name.
FA. Steve Brown or Paul Ingham 1982

㉙ Welcome Wall . . . . **VB (4b)**
The centre of the left wall has a tricky top-out.
FA. Paul Ingham 1982

㉚ Stereo Android . . . . **V0- (4c)**
Keep left of the arete throughout.
FA. Paul Ingham 1982

㉛ Tommy's Dilemma . . . . **VB (3c)**
Climb the centre of the narrow slab to the right of the arete.
FA. Geoff Milburn 1960

㉜ Gypsy Wham . . . . **VDiff**
5m. The centre of the slab passing the half-height ledge.
FA. Geoff Milburn 1960

㉝ Tea Party Slab . . . . **V0 (5a)**
Keep just to the right of the mid-height ledge to get the tick.
FA. Tony Marr 1965

㉞ Question of Balance . . . . . . **V2 (5c)**
Start off the left end of the ledge and climb left of a small pocket.
FA. Tony Marr 1965

㉟ Right Edge . . . . **V1 (5b)**
Climb the slab to the right of the small pocket.
FA. Tony Marr 1965

Curving Slab
Below the cliff is slumped slab with a collection of routes that is easier that is usual for grit. Not surprisingly they are very popular, as the trampled ground testifies.

Steptoe
Curving Slab

The Arch

A bevy of taxing and superb problems on the last bit of rock on the crag, fortunately it is the first section reached on the approach, so drop that mat and get going.

① Davies Ramp V4 (6a)
The slabby ramp on the front face gives a little gripper. The block and/or arete are out of bounds.
FA. Richard Davies 1985

The next three routes are variations on a theme and share holds.

② Simple Sally V7
A hard direct version of *Davies Ramp* up the centre of wall direct, via a solitary good crimp to access the ramp.
FA. Dave Slater 1994.

③ Holeshot V9
Start up the middle of the face until forced right past a pocket and out towards the arete and a high finish. *Photo opposite.*
FA. Ian Cummins 2000

④ Anniemutt V10
Climb *Holeshot* but continue direct where it scuttles off right.
FA. Steve Dunning 2001

⑤ Cypher V13
The striking arete has a desperate start, then gets harder still before finally easing.
FA. Ben Moon 2002

⑥ The Arch . . . . V14?
The line through the arch will doubtless be done some day.
FA. Someone good 20 ..?

⑦ Chockstone Pull Up . . . . Diff
3m. The block-choked crack doesn't really fit in here.
FA. Martyn Berry 1958

⑧ Dry Slap V4 (6b)
Climb the wall by pulling hard on a very slopy sloper, or crimp past it on the right (cheating some say).
FA. Ian Cummins 1985

⑨ Supple Wall V7
The blunt arete is climbed, starting on its right side and spiralling round to the left where a pocket lurks.
FA. Ian Cummins 1985

⑩ Slanting Flake Left-hand . . . V2 (5c)
From *Slanting Flake* rock up and left to gain a thinner flake.
FA. Paul Ingham 1983.

⑪ Slanting Flake V0 (4b)
Hand traverse the flake to its termination then mantel away.
FA. Geoff Milburn 1959

Pule Hill · Shooter's · Heptonstall · Widdop · Earl Crag · Ilkley · The Chevin · Caley · Almscliff · Eastby · Crookrise · Rylstone · Simon's Seat · Brimham · Eavestones · Slipstones · Crag Willas · Goldsborough

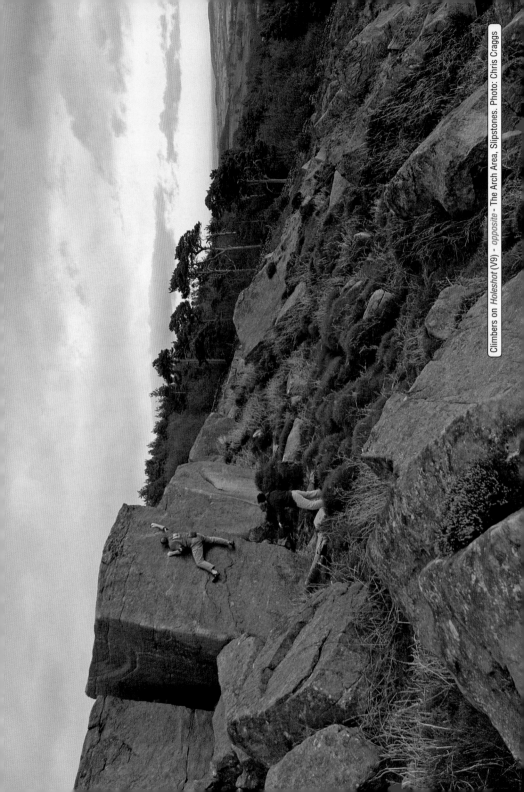

Climbers on *Holeshot* (V9) - *opposite* - The Arch Area, Slipstones. Photo: Chris Craggs

	No star	☆	☆☆	☆☆☆
Mod to S	10	17	-	-
HS to HVS	5	10	-	-
E1 to E3	3	5	-	-
E4 and up	1	2	-	-

This small crag is about as remote as you could wish for, set in a position of splendid isolation to the west of Reeth in Swaledale. Although not very extensive, or very high, the cliff and associated boulders are composed of good quality gritstone. A single star system has been used to indicate the more worthwhile climbs. The cliff is also known as Healaugh.

Conditions

Crag Willas is set at an altitude of 500m on the southern slopes of Great Pinseat. The cliff faces south and so gets all the sun that is going, though it is also exposed to the worst of the weather and seems to catch the wind, which is why the flue from the lead smelting works was installed here.

Approach

There are two regularly used approaches that both start from the minor road that runs between Fleetham in Swaledale and Langthwaite in Arkengarthdale.

Approach 1 - A short distance north of Fleetham, the road crosses Surrender Bridge over Old Gang Beck. Park here and follow the good track up the north side of the stream to the extensive mine workings 1.5km up the valley. Turn right and follow the flue steeply up the hill until the crag eventually appears - 30 to 40 minutes from the car.

Approach 2 - Alternatively, continue on the main road to parking where a good track branches left, signed 'Public Bridleway'. Follow this as it weaves steadily up the hill to a vague junction by Shooting Butt No 8. Turn left and follow the path as it loops left round the hill past the line of shooting butts and, where these end, continue along the path and the crag appears over on the right - 20 to 30 minutes from the car.

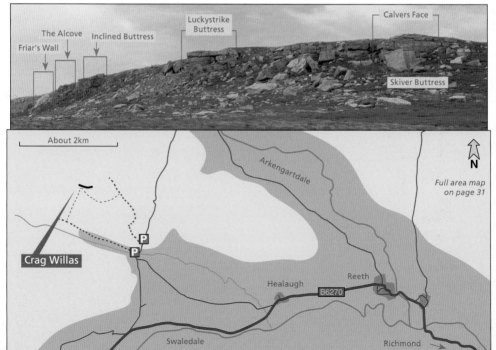

Jamie Moss on *Marzuka* (VB 4a) - *page 183* - Crag Willas. Photo: Jamie Moss (ST)

Low-angled Slab

The Alcove

Friar's Wall

The Alcove

At the far left of the crag is a large block with a pale, easy angled slab. The steep left-hand wall has some worthwhile climbs. To the right is The Alcove with a tipped block on the left and a short groove rising from a rock ledge on the right.

1 King Kone . . . . VO (5a)
Start from a boulder and climb past a useful pocket to an awkward finish. Escaping left at the top is **4c**.

2 Mr Wobbly . . . . VO (5a)
The shallow groove just left of 'JT', to a tricky finish up the crack.

3 On The Level . . . . . VO (5a)
Start up the shallow groove with 'JT' and follow the rising breaks all the way to the end of the block.

4 The Dare's On You . . . . VO (5a)
Start up the chimney and move right to the ledge. Step back left onto the hanging slab and make a thin move to the top.

5 Call me Al . . . . VS 4c
5m. Climb the short arete to the shelf then climb the wall above.

6 Bruce's Arete . . . . VS 4b
5m. Climb a groove to the ledge then step right and climb the arete on its right side.
FA. Bruce Perry 1978

7 Friardays . . . . VO (5a)
The left arete on its right-hand side.

8 Friarfold . . . . VB (4b)
The flaky wall, one metre right of the arete.

9 Fry Up . . . . VO+ (5b)
Head up the wall three metres right of the arete and just left of a thin flake.

10 Friar Tuck . . . . VO (5a)
Start left of the carved 'MC' intials and climb the face using the brittle flakes.

11 Hush V1 (5c)
Start just left of the initials 'MC' and using a pointy left finger-flake climb direct.

12 Ye Olde Friars . . . . VO (5a)
From the small ledge trend left using the drill hole to reach flake holds above 'MC'.

13 Gangue Way . . . . VB (4b)
Hop on to the small ledge just left of the arete and climb the scoop and arete. Accessing the initial ledge from the right is **5a**.

14 Gable End . . . . VO- (4c)
The right-hand arete is climbed on its right-hand side and has a tricky start.

15 The Pig . . . . VO+ (5b)
The south-facing side wall is climbed near its right edge.

Friar's Wall

A large boulder with a steep sunny face tilted towards the valley. The tiny routes are amongst the most popular here with good reason - amenable grades, good rock and a lovely setting.
First Ascents - the North East England guide attributes these routes to "Ron Kenyon 1978" though myself and Swaledale Outdoor Centre members were climbing here in the late 1960s and we were not the first.

The Alcove

Friar's Wall

The Alcove - 30m

Inclined Buttress

This is actually a collection of four small buttresses gathered together under the heading of the most obvious feature here. The routes are boulder problems on the left and some hard routes further right.

1 The Griddle . . . . 🔆 🏃 [____] **V3 (6a)**
The shallow left-facing groove in the centre of the face.

2 Magic Music . . . . 🔺 [____] **VB (4c)**
The short arete to the right.
FA. Ron Kenyon 1978

3 Paul Daniel's Wears a Wig . 🔺 [____] **VB (4c)**
The wall one metre right of the arete.
FA. Mark Turner 1990s

4 Karl's Arete . . . . 🔆 [____] **V0 (5a)**
The left hand arete of the next buttress.
FA. Karl Lunt 1991

5 Fall Arete . . . . 🔆 💪 [____] **V0 (5a)**
Pull onto the hanging right-hand arete.
FA. Ron Kenyon 1978

6 Autumn Wall . . . . . 🔆 🏃 🐾 [____] **V4 (6b)**
The wall to the right of *Fall Arete* is hard and fingery. Finish just right of the beak and no bridging back.
FA. Steve Crowe 1990s

7 An Inclination to Solitude. . . 🔆 [____] **HVS 5b**
5m. Climb the green streak using the short crack to finish.
FA. Bob Bennett 1990s

8 Peace in the Valley . . . . . . 🏃 [____] **E1 5c**
4m. Start in the recess on the right and climb up and out left (no bridging) then swing left to join *An Inclination to Solitude*.
FA. Steve Crowe 1995

9 The Emerald Isle . . . . . 🔺 🐾 [____] **E5 6a**
7m. Climb the steep left arete via two large ledges.

10 Blood Red Streets. . 🔆 🐾 🔺 [____] **E6 6c**
7m. Use a short flake to reach the wide break. Continue up the bulging wall past another break to an easier finish.
FA. Steve Crowe 1997

11 Sinn Fein. . . . . 🔆 🐾 [____] **E5 6b**
7m. The right-hand arete eventually eases.
FA. Steve Crowe 2001

The rest of the routes are on the shorter face round to the right.

12 Alfalfa. . . . . 🔆 ❘❘ [____] **VS 4c**
5m. The wall one metre right of the arete passing a break. Easier than it looks.
FA. Karl Lunt 1990s

13 Clover at Your Feet . . . . [____] **HVD**
5m. The wall and the shallow rightward-facing groove.
FA. Ron Kenyon 1978

14 Twin Cracks . . . . [____] **HVD**
5m. The twin cracks (obvious really) to the right.
FA. Ron Kenyon 1978

The easy arete to the right is the best way down.

Between The Alcove and Inclined Buttress, and immediately to the left of the upper section of the flue, are the Flue Buttresses, home to ten or so short serious routes that are not described here.

Pule Hill · Shooter's · Heptonstall · Widdop · Earl Gay · Ilkley · The Chevin · Caley · Almscliff · Eastby · Crookrise · Brylstone · Simon's Seat · Brimham · Eavestones · Slipstones · Crag Willas · Goldsborough

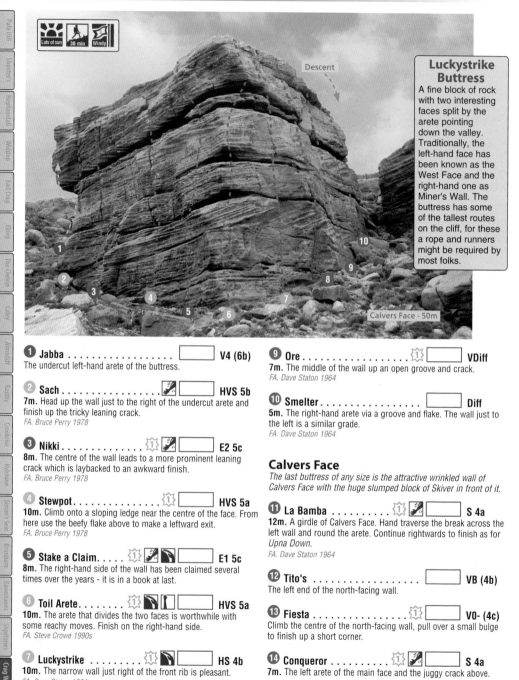

Descent

Luckystrike Buttress

A fine block of rock with two interesting faces split by the arete pointing down the valley. Traditionally, the left-hand face has been known as the West Face and the right-hand one as Miner's Wall. The buttress has some of the tallest routes on the cliff, for these a rope and runners might be required by most folks.

Calvers Face - 50m

Side tabs: Pule Hill, Shooter's, Heptonstall, Widdop, Earl Crag, Ilkley, The Chevin, Caley, Almscliff, Eastby, Crookrise, Kyloe, Simon's Seat, Brimham, Eavestones, Slipstones, Crag Willas, Goldsbrgh

1 Jabba . . . . [ ] **V4 (6b)**
The undercut left-hand arete of the buttress.

2 Sach . . . . [ ] **HVS 5b**
7m. Head up the wall just to the right of the undercut arete and finish up the tricky leaning crack.
FA. Bruce Perry 1978

3 Nikki . . . . [ ] **E2 5c**
8m. The centre of the wall leads to a more prominent leaning crack which is laybacked to an awkward finish.
FA. Bruce Perry 1978

4 Stewpot . . . . [ ] **HVS 5a**
10m. Climb onto a sloping ledge near the centre of the face. From here use the beefy flake above to make a leftward exit.
FA. Bruce Perry 1978

5 Stake a Claim . . . . . [ ] **E1 5c**
8m. The right-hand side of the wall has been claimed several times over the years - it is in a book at last.

6 Toil Arete . . . . [ ] **HVS 5a**
10m. The arete that divides the two faces is worthwhile with some reachy moves. Finish on the right-hand side.
FA. Steve Crowe 1990s

7 Luckystrike . . . . [ ] **HS 4b**
10m. The narrow wall just right of the front rib is pleasant.
FA. Dave Staton 1964

8 Galena . . . . [ ] **S 4a**
8m. The wall 2m to the right of the front rib is also worth doing.
FA. Dave Staton 1964

9 Ore . . . . [ ] **VDiff**
7m. The middle of the wall up an open groove and crack.
FA. Dave Staton 1964

10 Smelter . . . . [ ] **Diff**
5m. The right-hand arete via a groove and flake. The wall just to the left is a similar grade.
FA. Dave Staton 1964

Calvers Face
The last buttress of any size is the attractive wrinkled wall of Calvers Face with the huge slumped block of Skiver in front of it.

11 La Bamba . . . . [ ] **S 4a**
12m. A girdle of Calvers Face. Hand traverse the break across the left wall and round the arete. Continue rightwards to finish as for *Upna Down.*
FA. Dave Staton 1964

12 Tito's . . . . [ ] **VB (4b)**
The left end of the north-facing wall.

13 Fiesta . . . . [ ] **V0- (4c)**
Climb the centre of the north-facing wall, pull over a small bulge to finish up a short corner.

14 Conqueror . . . . [ ] **S 4a**
7m. The left arete of the main face and the juggy crack above.

15 Green Dragon . . . . [ ] **S 4a**
8m. The shallow groove and crack to the right of the arete gives a good pitch with a fingery start and a juggy finish.
FA. Dave Staton 1964

Calvers Face

Towards the right-hand side of the cliff is this fine wall, arguably the best bit of rock on the cliff. For budding geologists it provides a classic example of current bedding. It has a pleasant set of little routes that can all be ticked in a short session - solo or with a rope.

16 Marimba .... VS 5a
8m. Climb the face to the break and make a delicate move up into a scoop. Finish up and left.
FA. Dave Staton 1964

17 Marimba Direct ...... V0+ (5b)
The sketchy wall to the right gives a variation start.

18 Upna Down .... S 4a
7m. The right-hand side of the face to a ledge and a finish using a good pocket.
FA. Dave Staton 1964

The final routes described are on the big fallen block that sits in front of the cliff.

19 Grafter V4 (6b)
The slanting arete gives a pumpy uphill hand-traverse.

20 Rondo .... VDiff
3m. Tackle the awkward slanting crack. Solid at the grade.

21 Eliminate .... V0+ (5b)
The left-hand side of the main arete, resisting the temptation to move round onto the slab.

22 Tarantella V0 (5a)
Boldly climb the left arete of the slab on the front face.
A **Direct Start** is nearer **V2 (5c)**.
FA. Ron Kenyon 1978

23 Skiver V1 (5b)
The bold and precarious centre of the slab. Not too difficult, but the rock is just a little crusty - take care to to the top.

24 Mazurka .... VB (4a)
The right arete of the slab has an awkward last move.
Photo on page 179.
FA. Ron Kenyon 1978

Skiver Block
The large slumped block that sits in front of the edge is the last bit of the cliff to be described. Its front face has some good precarious slab climbs, and the slightly gritty texture means the routes are a little more harrowing than they look. A spotter is useful/essential depending on your outlook.

Skiver Block

	No star			
Mod to S	7	3	-	-
HS to HVS	4	3	1	-
E1 to E3	7	10	-	1
E4 and up	5	3	-	-

The only crag in the Yorkshire section which isn't actually in Yorkshire, Goldsborough Carr is an isolated set of buttresses overlooking open countryside to the south of Upper Teesdale in County Durham. Although not very extensive, and not especially high, the cliff has an intense set of climbs. Many should be considered as extended boulder problems due to the undercut nature of the two main buttresses which gives the routes hard starts at a bouldering height with easier climbing above. Visitors from afar are rare up on these wild moors, though if you are passing, a couple for hours spent here should blow your forearms away. There are a dozen or so belay stakes above the crag if you decide you want to lead the routes, but for most a pad or two will do for the starts on Thornbird and Thin Wall Buttresses.

Conditions
The crag faces south into the wilderness of Cotherstone Moor, it takes no drainage and is very exposed to the weather.

Approach
There is roadside parking below the short North Face rocks of Goldsborough Carr. From Barnard Castle, drive up Teesdale on the B6277 (south side of the river). After Cotherstone take either of the two left turns that run up Baldersdale. From West Briscoe continue for a couple of kilometres to roadside parking by a path that runs up towards the right-hand end of Goldsborough Carr. The best climbing is round to the right on the South Face, ten minutes from the car.

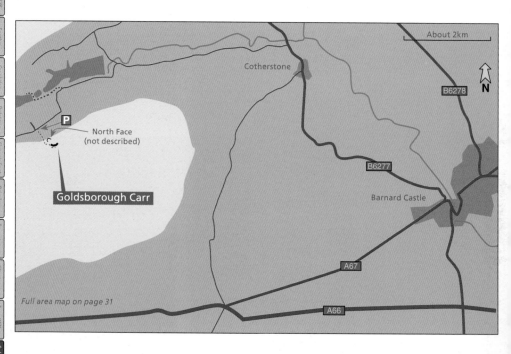

Full area map on page 31

The undedrcut start of *Fiddler's Arete* (HVS 5b)
- *page 189* - typical of much of the climbing at
Goldsborough Carr. Photo: Chris Craggs

Hubris

The first walls on the sunny side of the hill, they are only short, but despite this it has are some nice problems, (generally) good landings and a superb aspect.

1 The Swaledale Morris Men . S 4b
3m. The left arete of the face.

2 Y-Crack . . . . VDiff
3m. Take the Y-shaped crack at the left-hand end of the buttress.
FA. Eden Valley MC members 1970s

3 Finger-crack . . . . VB (4c)
The spidery crack with a thin finger-jam move.
FA. Eden Valley MC members 1970s

4 System of a Brown V4 (6b)
The arete of the chimney, avoid the block in the chimney.
FA. Ian Cummins 2002

5 Ravock Chimney . . . . S 4a
4m. The chimney is tricky to enter.
FA. Eden Valley MC members 1970s

6 In Search of Cheap Bananas V4 (6b)
Monkey up the arete right of the chimney.
FA. Ian Cummins 2002

7 Enigma Direct V4 (6b)
Pull straight into the groove and follow it to the top.
FA. Ian Cummins 2002

8 Enigma V3 (6a)
The original version gains the groove from the right via a hard move. Finish direct.
FA. Paul Carling early 1980s

9 Old Moss V2 (5c)
As for *Enigma* but continue direct up the face/arete.

10 Cotherstone Reiver V1 (5b)
Layback onto a solitary foothold and stretch.

11 Corner Crack . . . . Diff
4m. The short angular corner.
FA. Eden Valley MC members 1970s

12 Holstein Friesian V4 (6b)
The shallow groove in the right-hand wall of the corner.
FA. Paul Smith 1980s

13 Flake and Crack . . . . S 4b
5m. The name should be all the description you need.
FA. Eden Valley MC members 1970s

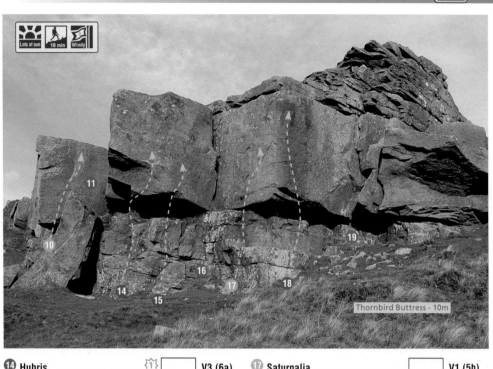

Thornbird Buttress - 10m

⑭ Hubris . . . . **V3 (6a)**
Pull rightwards to gain the hanging side wall.

⑮ Hubris Right-hand . . . . **V5 (6b)**
The wall just to the right.
FA. Ian Cummins May 2004

⑯ Cenopod Corner . . . . **VDiff**
4m. The next angular corner; no more than three pegs allowed!

⑰ Saturnalia . . . . **V1 (5b)**
The wall just right, the landing is not too friendly.

⑱ Ian's Arete . . . . **V6 (6c)**
The right-hand side of the jutting arete to a highball finish.
FA. Ian Cummins 2000

⑲ Hunder Crack . . . . **S 4a**
6m. Start hunder the crack, climb it and the wall above.
FA. Eden Valley MC members 1970s

Blackton Reservoir and Baldersdale seen from Goldsborough Carr.

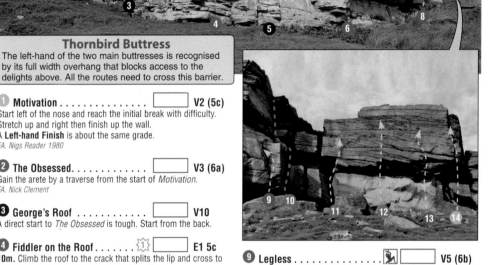

Thornbird Buttress
The left-hand of the two main buttresses is recognised by its full width overhang that blocks access to the delights above. All routes need to cross this barrier.

1 Motivation . . . . [ ] **V2 (5c)**
Start left of the nose and reach the initial break with difficulty. Stretch up and right then finish up the wall.
A **Left-hand Finish** is about the same grade.
FA. Nigs Reader 1980

2 The Obsessed . . . . [ ] **V3 (6a)**
Gain the arete by a traverse from the start of *Motivation*.
FA. Nick Clement

3 George's Roof . . . . [ ] **V10**
A direct start to *The Obsessed* is tough. Start from the back.

4 Fiddler on the Roof . . . . [ ] **E1 5c**
10m. Climb the roof to the crack that splits the lip and cross to good holds on the lip. Heave over and its all over.
FA. Dave Bowen 1970s

5 Klute . . . . [ ] **E6 6c**
10m. Cross the overhang via a pair of crusty finger pockets then from the lip udge left to a groove and finish up this.
FA. Paul Smith 1980s. Named after a grim Durham nightclub.

6 Green Nigel . . . . [ ] **E2 6a**
10m. From a ledge under the overhang, stretch round the lip to a jug then trend left up a shallow ramp to finish precariously just to the left of the wide pale streak.
FA. Ian Cummins 1983

7 The Thornbird . . . . . [ ] **E2 6a**
10m. Start as for *Green Nigel* to the jug then climb the wall via a thin crack. Excellent and exciting.
FA. Paul Carling early 1980s

8 The Long Reach . . . [ ] **V6 (6c)**
10m. Taxing for the tall and harder for the short. Climb the undercut arete then layback and stretch for the ledge. For the full **E4** tick finish up the leaning arete.
FA. Paul Carling early 1980s

9 Legless . . . . [ ] **V5 (6b)**
10m. Up the hanging groove to the ledge. For the **E4** version continue right of the arete to a juggy finale.
A sit-start is **Clamp Master**, **V9**.
FA. (Clamp Master) Tom Newman 2006

10 Tute Crack . . . . [ ] **S 4a**
6m. The left-hand crack to a ledge and short groove above.
FA. Eden Valley MC members late 1970s

11 Yale . . . . [ ] **VB (4b)**
The right-hand crack and wall above. A right-hand start is **4c**.

12 Lock Out . . . . [ ] **VB (4c)**
The centre of the wall has a snappy start.
FA. Eden Valley MC members late 1970s

13 Borstal Breakout . . . . [ ] **V3 (6a)**
The wall just left of the arete, with an overhanging start.

14 Loups Arete . . . . [ ] **V1 (5a)**
The short hanging crack which splits the arete.
FA. Eden Valley MC members late 1970s

Thin Wall Buttress

The is 'the other' fine buttress here and again has a good set of climbs, on the 'tough starting sequence' theme. The leaning sheltered bay on the far right is home to a plethora of tough boulder problems, link-ups and desperate eliminates. These are not listed here - check out *Climbing in North East England* (2003)

1 Maggie's Wall . . . . VDiff
5m. From the ledge, wander up the side wall.

2 Topal's Wall . . . . VS 4c
5m. From the ledge, trend right (tricky to start) to finish close to the arete as for *Fiddler's Wall*.

3 Rock Art V10
The taxing wrinkled side wall on tiny sloping holds.
FA. Ian Cummins 2005

4 Fiddler's Wall V6 (6c)
The wall left of the arete has a hard start then eases.
FA. Nick Clement 1980s

5 Fiddler's Arete . . . . HVS 5b
The hanging left arete gives a good pitch. The start is a fierce pull onto the wall - **V1**. *Photo on page 185.*
FA. Stew Wilson late 1970s

6 Fiddler . . . . HVS 5a
8m. Right of the arete, pull onto the wall then step left and balance up to better holds and a ledge. Finish straight up the arete.
FA. Eden Valley MC members 1970s

7 Fiddler Direct E1 5b
6m. Use the same start as *Fiddler* but head straight up the wall.

8 Low-level Traverse . V6 (6b)
The clue is in the name - pump along the low break all the way from the left of *Fiddler's Arete* to *Jumping Jack Flash*.

9 Barney Boys V3 (6a)
Mantle on the left-hand edge of the narrow shelf on the face then balance up to reach better holds. Finish right of the bulge.
FA. Nick Clement 1986

10 The Scoop V4 (6b)
The super slim groove in the centre of the wall eases.
FA. Nick Clement 1986

11 Confectionary Debris . . . V9
The last gap on the wall just had to be done.
FA. Ian Cummins August 2003

12 Thin Wall Special V2 (5c)
Power up to the thin crack where a quick layback reaches rounded holds. Weave between the heather to the top for the **E2** tick.

13 Jumping Jack Flash . . . V3 (6a)
The leaning right-hand arete is photogenic. A tricky start reaches better holds then trend right up the hanging arete until the wall can be accessed. Finish carefully on rounded holds - **E2**.

The overhanging and ever-dry bay on the right is home to a host of tough link-ups, only the most obvious route is listed here.

14 Beth's Traverse . V9 (6c)
From a start sitting in the back of the cave, follow the sustained finger-traverse to finish up *Jumping Jack Flash*.
Prelude, **V11** is the extended start.
FA. Ian Cummins 1990s. FA. (Prelude) Ian Cummins 2005

North York Moors

Alan James enjoying perfect autumn conditions on *Tippling Wall* (HVS 5a) - *page 206* - a Scugdale classic. Photo: Chris Craggs

Alan James climbing *Sphinx Nose Traverse* (S 4a) - *page 217* - at the Wainstones. Photo: Chris Craggs

The North York Moors have always been a bit of a climbing backwater, lacking any major cliffs or renown national classics, the area has been largely overlooked by the 'scene'. Despite this, and as the locals have long been aware, there are many fine cliffs and excellent climbs tucked around the edges of the valleys that cleave the rim of the plateau making up the National Park. Even considering the lack of cachet, a flick through the first ascent list of the climbs hereabouts reveals some real aficionados who honed their skills on these rocks and then went on to write their names large in the history of UK climbing.

We only have room to cover a small selection of the available climbing on five of the more popular cliffs; try one of these as a taster and the likelihood is that you will want to explore this intriguing area further.

All the cliffs described here are Jurassic sandstone - there are also some esoteric limestone cliffs in the area that we haven't included though they are also not without interest. The rock is younger than the other cliffs in this book, but it is tougher than this fact might suggest - hard sandstone with great friction and stacks of iron hard edges - a fine medium.

A winter day stretching the muscles on Scugdale's micro-classics or a high summer afternoon storming Ravenscar's big routes are the more obvious ways to be introduced to the North York Moors - you should enjoy the experience!

Fossil seashell at Highcliff Nab

Colin Binks and Bruce Perry dodging the showers on *North West Direct* (VS 4c) - *page 229* - Highcliff Nab. Photo: Chris Craggs

Scugdale

Wainstones

Raven's Scar

Highcliff Nab

Park Nab

Ethics and Style

The quiet cliffs of the North York Moors have a long history of bold ascents by talented locals and occasional visitors; many routes were originally done as solos after a quick top-rope inspection. Soloing remains a popular way of enjoying the shorter climbs, though holds do occasionally snap so a circumspect approach and/or spotters are sensible precautions.

The development of modern gear has tamed many of the once-serious climbs, though the repeated insertion and removal of gear can rapidly erode placements, especially when the climber ends up weighting it. If the climb is too hard for you it maybe best to leave it until you are ready to do it in good style rather than risk trashing the only runner placement with repeated falls.

Soft Rock and Top-roping

The cliffs on the North York Moors are of generally high quality sandstone but its granular nature means it can easily be damaged by inappropriate use. A weighted rope running over the cliff edge will rapidly saw into the rock. If you must top-rope then please be aware of the consequences - make sure you extend the top krab over the edge using a second rope or slings, and make sure you pad this at the point it goes over the edge with an empty rucksack or the like.

None of the cliffs have suffered the erosion that has become a problem in some other areas of the UK due to overuse, though the right-hand end of the Scugdale cliffs is heading that way. Please minimise your impact so the climbs are still available for the next generation of climbers to enjoy.

Access

Like everywhere in the UK, access across the North York Moors has had its problems over the years, though the individual cliffs listed here have enjoyed open access for most of the time - let's try and keep it that way.

Parking - don't block other peoples' access, get right off the road if possible and, if the parking really is full, maybe it is worth trying somewhere else.

Litter/Fires/Dogs - the potential problems here should be obvious - the sign at Scugdale is quite explicit, no dogs at the cliff means exactly that! Organised groups could help by taking a big plastic bag to the cliff and bringing back any litter they find. Please read any access information carefully and take great care not to infringe any restrictions. If in doubt contact the BMC (page 9) or check the access section of the BMC website **www.thebmc.co.uk**.

Roseberry Topping seen from the Cleveland Hills

Alan James at the top of the awkward *Twin Cracks* (HS 4b) - *page 232* - at Park Nab. Photo: Chris Craggs

Scugdale

Wainstones

Raven's Scar

Highcliff Nab

Park Nab

Mountain Rescue
In the event of an accident requiring the assistance of Mountain Rescue:

Dial 999 and ask for 'POLICE - MOUNTAIN RESCUE'

All mountain rescue incidents in Yorkshire fall under the responsibility of the Yorkshire Constabulary. If in doubt request Yorkshire Police Operations Room.

Tourist Information Offices
If you are short of ideas of what to do on a wet day or need accommodation, take a look at the **www.visitnorthyorkshiremoors.co.uk** or visit the **Moors Centre (National Park Centre), Danby, Whitby.   Tel: 01439 772737**

Camping
Most climbers tend to make day-visits to climb on the North York Moors, though there are campsites scattered throughout the area. Generally these tend to be over towards the coast or in the south east and many offer static caravans for hire.

Cote Ghyll Caravan & Camping Park (see map on page 198)
Osmotherley, Northallerton, North Yorkshire DL6 3AH.   Tel: 01609 883425
A large site north of the village. Also has static caravans for hire.   **www.coteghyll.com**

Not Camping
Cottages, bed and breakfast, hotels and bunk-houses are all widely available in the area, especially towards the coast.
Youth Hostels - There is a Youth Hostel in Osmotherly which is ideally situated for the climbing. There are five other Youth Hostels in the area, though these are on the southern edge of the National Park or out towards the coast - **www.yha.org.uk**
Cottages - The area is littered with cottages for hire and, if you are in a group, this can be a very cost-effective and pleasant way of staying in the area. A good way to start is putting "North York Moors Cottages" into Google.

Some good sites are **www.northyorkmoors-stay.co.uk**, **www.sykescottages.com**, **www.iknow-yorkshire.co.uk**

Getting Around
All the crags in this section are easily reached by car and the approach descriptions are written assuming you have access to a car. However, if you are trying to get to the crags by public transport this may help:
Buses - The Tourist Information Centre is the preferred method of obtaining timetables and local knowledge, but the website **www.showbus.co.uk/timetables** lists the various operators in the area, and where to obtain timetable information.

Climbing Shops
Nevisport - 100 Newport Road, Middlesborough, TS1 5JD   Tel: 01642 248916
Nevisport - 8 St Sampson's Square, York YO1 8RN   Tel: 01904 639567
www.nevisport.com

Food and Drink
There are many pubs and cafes in the areas covered by this book. The following is a selection of the favourite apres-climb pubs contributed by readers of UKClimbing: **The Jet Miners** in Great Broughton, **The Black Horse** in Swainby, **The Anchor** in Guisborough.
More pubs listed at - **www.pub-explorer.com**

Climbing Walls
The following are climbing walls that are within striking distance if you get rained-off.

Rock Antics - Extensive lead and bouldering wall.
Newton Aycliffe Leisure Centre, DL5 4EH.   Tel: 01325 320683   www.rockantics.co.uk

Rock City (page 2) **-** 16m high lead wall and extensive bouldering areas.
Hawthorne Avenue, Hull, HU3 5JX.   Tel: 01482 223030   www.rockcity.co.uk

The Climbing Wall - 14m tall concrete leading wall.
The Dolphin Centre, Darlington, DL1 5RP.   Tel: 01325 388406

Homeward bound after a day at Highcliff Nab. Photo: Chris Craggs

	Routes	up to Sev	HS to HVS	E1 to E3	E4 and up
Scugdale	*121*	50 ✓✓✓	55 ✓✓✓	14 ✓✓	2 ✗
Wainstones	*60*	24 ✓✓✓	21 ✓✓✓	14 ✓✓	5 ✓
Raven's Scar	*38*	4 ✓	19 ✓✓	11 ✓✓	4 ✓
Highcliff Nab	*19*	4 ✓	3 ✓	8 ✓✓	4 ✓✓
Park Nab	*37*	11 ✓✓	13 ✓✓	13 ✓✓	- ✗

Quality and range of routes in different grade bands: ✓✓✓ - Excellent   ✓✓ - Good   ✓ - Okay   ✗ - Not worth a visit

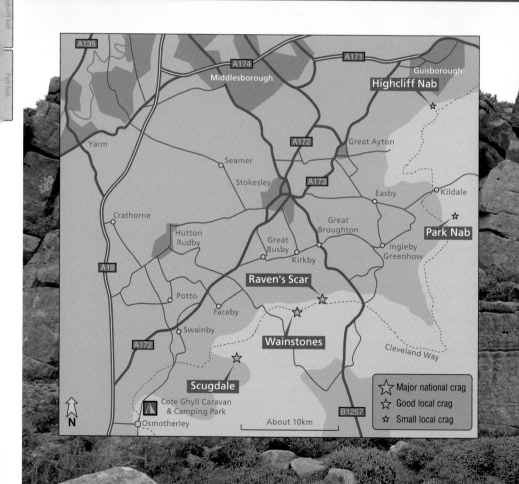

Scugdale

Wainstones

Raven's Scar

Highcliff Nab

Park Nab

Approach	Sun	Dry	Green	Shelter	Windy	Summary	Page
8 - 10 min	Lots of sun					A delightful and extensive crag with over 100 routes to go at, many of them in the lower grades. Though only short, the rock is of great quality throughout and the setting is sunny.	200
25 min	Sun and shade				Windy	A couple of mini-pinnacles and a good sized edge with an extensive repertoire of excellent climbs. Factor in the superb outward views and the reason for the crag's popularity is obvious.	212
15 min	Not much sun		Green		Windy	The most impressive cliff in the area with some great climbs up powerful lines. Sadly the crag faces north and is not often in condition but if you time it right, a great day out is guaranteed.	220
20 min	Not much sun		Green		Windy	A well positioned little crag with a nice set of climbs. The recent felling of trees at its base has opened the crag up and it is less green than it used to be.	226
5 min	Afternoon				Windy	A mini-outcrop with some good routes, the exposed setting is good on midgy days. Sadly the crag's best feature fell down a few years ago.	230

Scugdale

Wainstones

Raven's Scar

Highcliff Nab

Park Nab

Alan James stretched out on *Stewker* (E1 5c)
- *page 204* - Scugdale. Photo: Chris Craggs

	No star	☼	☼☼	☼☼☼
Mod to S	32	13	5	-
HS to HVS	24	24	7	-
E1 to E3	7	3	4	-
E4 and up	1	1	-	-

This lovely little edge is the most popular venue on the North York Moors and with good reason. An easy approach, a sunny aspect and an excellent collection of climbs across the grades all add to the attraction of the place. The crag is not very high and this has led to it being somewhat overlooked in the past, but what it does offer tends to be on beautifully featured rock, with excellent holds, cracks and breaks.

It isn't all sweetness and light though, many routes are tricky to protect, holds do occasionally snap and the landings are often poor. This combination has led to some serious accidents here in recent years, so please TAKE CARE.

Scugdale is the name of the valley. There are actually two crags here: Scot Crags and Barker's Crags. Only Scot Crags are covered in this book.

Access

The landowner has requested that NO DOGS be taken up to the crag, in the interest of preserving access to this great little crag, please do as he asks.

Conditions

The crag faces south west and gets the sun for most of the day - it can get hot here in summer. Scugdale faces the prevailing winds and offers little shelter if the weather does turn. It can be a great venue in the middle of winter when a low sun warms the rock.

Approach

From the A172, turn south into Swainby and drive through the village, turning left (signed 'Scugdale Road') on the minor road (ford) that runs up the valley. Follow this for around 5km until the crag becomes visible above and left. There is limited parking for about 4 well-parked cars here and a couple of other tight spots nearby. Please park carefully and get your car right off the road, leaving room for wide farm vehicles to pass. A path leads directly up the hill from the parking spot. NOTE: Traffic accidents on the narrow approach roads have been on the increase, often involving climbers versus locals. The routes will still be there in five minutes, and if you do have an accident, it will be guaranteed to ruin your day, and somebody else's too, so slow down!

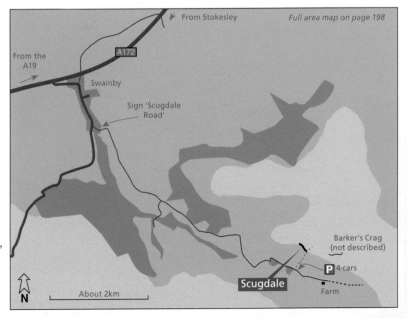

From Stokesley

Full area map on page 198

A172

From the A19

Swainby

Sign 'Scugdale Road'

Barker's Crag (not described)

P 4 cars

Scugdale

Farm

About 2km

N

Alan James on *Zeta Wall* (VS 4c) - *page 208* - a nice but deceptive little crack-climb at Scugdale. Photo: Chris Craggs

Scugdale Buttress

Romulus and Remus

Uncles and Parson's Nose

Scot Buttress

Adam and Eve

Drunken Buttress

Barker's Buttress

Holly Tree Buttress

Beginners' Slab

Descent

Descent

Lots of sun

10 min

20m gap

Uncles

Parson's Nose

Uncles and Parson's Nose
Two small buttresses on the far left with an interesting collection of routes. This area is usually very quiet and the views to the west are excellent.

1 Aunties . . . . **VS 5a**
5m. The tricky left arete of the tower. No bridging backwards.

2 Rake's Progress . . . . **Diff**
5m. Trend right across the face to a fluted finale.

3 Uncles. . . . . **VS 4c**
6m. A short crack leads to the final wall, with its trio of pockets.

4 Straight and Narrow . . . . . . **VDiff**
8m. The right-hand edge of the buttress is pleasant.

5 Parson's Chimney . . . . **Mod**
4m. The tiny chimney on the left.

6 Hand Jive . . . . **VS 5b**
4m. Fingery climbing leads to a tricky exit. Avoid using the arete.
FA. Tony Marr 1972

7 Jivers' Wall . . . . . . **VS 4c**
5m. Stretchy and fingery moves up the centre of the wall.

8 Bop Route . . . . **S 4a**
5m. The arete of the front face leads to a shallow groove.

9 Bopped . . . . **VS 5a**
5m. Battle the bulge on the front of the buttress.
FA. Tony Marr 1978

10 Zoot Route . . . . **VDiff**
5m. A good little number up the wall and groove left of *The Nose.*
FA. Arthur Evans 1950s

11 The Nose . . . . **HVS 5b**
4m. Tackle the jutting snout on its right side. Short but sharp.
FA. Johnny Adams 1965

Scot Buttress

A smart looking buttress, probably the best at this end of the cliff. It is easily recognised by the converging cracks of *Bawbee* and *Blaeberry* - all very Scottish. The side wall of the buttress has three recognised routes.

1 **The Vallum** . . . . S 4a
5m. The left edge of the wall leads to a short wide crack.

2 **Hadrian's Wall** . . . . . . HS 4b
5m. Foot-traverse the short slanting crack, then climb direct up the middle of the wall.

3 **Corner Direct Left-hand** . . . . . . S 4a
6m. Head directly up the left-hand side of the arete.

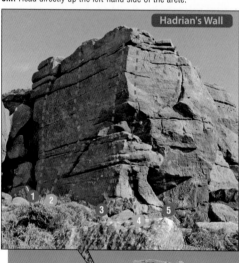

Hadrian's Wall

4 **Corner Direct Right-hand** . . . HS 4b
6m. Climb into the recess of the nook and finish up the arete.

5 **Nook and Cranny** . . . . S 4a
7m. Climb right of the previous route to the nook, traverse right to the flake of the cranny and finish up this.
FA. Arthur Evans 1950s

6 **Nook and Cranny Direct** HS 4b
7m. Start under the final flake-crack of the normal route, pull over the bulge and finish smartly up the cranny-crack.

7 **Highland Fling** E1 5b
7m. The blunt rib leads to a tiny groove - scary. The cranny is to be avoided to get the grade.

8 **Bawbee Crack** . . . . HVD
7m. Step off the block and climb the tricksome crack past the rattly chockstone of the 'Bawbee'.

It is possible to climb the lower wall between the cracks at 4c-ish, using the ramp, until squeezed out of existence.

9 **Blaeberry Crack** . . . . Diff
7m. The left-slanting crack is followed to the junction.

10 **Blaeberry Buttress Direct** . . . . . HS 4b
7m. Straight up the wall immediately right of the slanting crack.

11 **Blaeberry Buttress** . . . . Mod
6m. Interesting and mild. Climb blocky ground then head diagonally left all the way to *Blaeberry Crack* using the sloping shelf for hand-holds.

Descent

Descent

Scot Buttress

Descent

Descent

The Prow

Romulus and Remus

Romulus and Remus

A pair of slabby faces on the left, split by a deep chimney. The right-hand buttress is crossed by a substantial ledge at half-height.

1 Wolf Wall . . . . S 4b
5m. The thin crack just right of the bounding groove.

2 Wolf Whistle . . . . HS 4b
6m. Nice climbing up the centre of the steep slab.

3 Woodpecker Wall . . . . . S 4a
7m. Climb the lower arete then the pocket-spattered face above.

4 Romulus . . . . HS 4b
7m. The rounded arete that forms the left edge of the chimney.

5 Tiber Chimney . . . . Mod
7m. The narrowing cleft has the odd loose block.

6 Tiber Wall E1 5c
7m. Power through the overhang and finish up the slab. No bridging back at the grade.
FA. Ron Lake 1971

7 Remus . . . . VS 4c
8m. Follow mini-ramps leftwards to the mid-height ledge. Continue up the wall at the back to a reachy finale. The left arete gives an easier finish (**4c**) and the right-hand side is (**5a**).

The next buttress starts with a short wall high on its left.

8 Halyards . . . . VDiff
5m. The left-hand arete is pleasant.

9 Little by Little. . . . . VDiff 4a
5m. The little groove in the centre of the wall.

The Prow

The jutting blade of rock that is tackled front on by *The Prow* is the best feature in this area, though there are other worthwhile routes to either side.

10 Main Mast Crack. . . . . . S 4b
5m. The short steep groove is harder than it looks - honest.
FA. Arthur Evans 1950s

11 Stewker. E1 5c
7m. Tackle the centre of the side wall by linking a layaway and a pocket by a long reach. The holds are okay but the landing isn't - the route has been responsible for a fair few helicopter rides!
Photo on page 199.
FA. Tony McLean 1978

12 Prowess E3 6b
7m. Layback the left-hand side of the arete. Scary.
FA. Tony Marr 1988

13 The Prow. E1 5a
7m. Climb the narrow arete to a hard finish. 'Lifting a fridge' type moves might be found of help.

14 Galley Chimney . . . . Mod
7m. The rift passing a big jammed block.

15 The Heads . . . . HS 4b
7m. The right arete of the chimney. Start either side of the lower arete, and finish on the side wall of the chimney - without touching the other side.

16 The Bulkhead . . . . VS 4c
7m. The leaning crack gives a good little pitch with a stiff finale.

17 The Keel . . . . HVS 5a
6m. Climb a short crack and the ensuing flake to a taxing exit.
FA. Tony Marr 2002

Descent

Adam and Eve

23

18

20

19

21

10

17

14 15 16

13

22

The Prow

Adam and Eve

Another 'odd couple'; like Romulus and Remus. A short and tall buttress sit together. Adam is tiny, but Eve is altogether more impressive, with her jutting axe-edged arete.

Descent

19

22

26

24   25

Adam and Eve

18 Jill's Delight . . . . ⬜ **Diff**
4m. The face just left of the angular arete.

19 Right-hand Side . . . . ⬜ **Diff**
4m. The right-hand side of the arete.

20 Evens/The Fig Leaf . . . . ⬜ **VS 4c**
5m. Opposite *Adam,* and at the top of the gully, use the pocket to reach the groove above. Some nice moves in a gloomy setting.

21 Curving Arete . . . . ⬜ **VS 4c**
6m. The bow-shaped arete that bounds the north face.

22 Jack's Delight . . . . ⬜ **VS 4b**
8m. From the toe of the tower, trend left to the centre of the face then go direct up pockets. Good climbing but bold (i.e. a solo!).

23 Eve Left-hand . . . . . ⬜ **E1 5a**
8m. The left-hand side of the arete is sustained and unprotected.
FA. Tony Marr 1975

24 Eve Right-hand . . . . ⬜ **E2 5b**
8m. The right-hand side of the arete is even harder.
FA. Dave McKinney 1978

25 Hob Nobs . . . . ⬜ **E4 6a**
8m. Straight up the face one metre right of the arete.
FA. Paul Smith 1988

26 Serpent . . . . ⬜ **E4 6a**
8m. Climb to the tiny right-trending crack, follow it for a couple of moves until pockets up and left can be reached. Exit rapidly.
FA. Ian Carr early 1980s

The Pulpit and Drunken Buttress
On the left are the stacked block overhangs of the Pulpit, and to the right the large leaning tower of Drunken Buttress, with a slab on the left flank, and overhanging front and right-hand faces. There are several excellent short routes hereabouts.

❶ The Pulpit .... 🔲 **E1 5b**
6m. Follow the easy crack then hand traverse the break below the overhang to a tough finish on the nose.
FA. (Thread for aid) J.Elliot 1958. FFA. Stew Wilson 1965

❷ Lazing on a Sunday Afternoon 🔲 **HVS 5b**
6m. A short sharp finish up the left arete.
FA. Ian Dunn 1980

❸ The Choir............. 🔲 **VDiff**
6m. Balance up the rounded arete right of The Pulpit.

In the gully between The Pulpit and Drunken Buttress is a small set of routes whose names appear to have changed with time.

❹ Lost Arete/Halleluja Chorus ... 🔲 **VS 5a**
6m. Climb the short scoop and the left-hand side of the arete.
FA. Tony Marr 1972

❺ Anvil Chorus .... 🔲 **VS 5b**
5m. The right side of the arete has a tough start through a bulge.
FA. Tony Marr 1972

❻ Forgotten Wall/Haec Dies .. 🔲 **VS 4c**
5m. Straight up the centre of the wall. Strenuous.
FA. Tony Marr 1971

❼ Forgotten Arete/The Choir .... 🔲 **HVS 5a**
5m. The right side of the wall leads to a tricky finish.

To the right is the large slumped block of Drunken Buttress, it has high quality climbs on all sides.

❽ Seamy Side .... 🔲 **Diff**
6m. The pleasant arete on the left-hand side of the block.
FA. Arthur Evans 1950s

❾ Bottoms Up .... 🔲 **HS 4b**
7m. A bit of an eliminate up the centre of the slab. Holds on adjacent routes may have to be used, just don't tell anyone.
FA. Eric Marr 1962

❿ Hangover........... 🔲 **VS 4c**
7m. A powerful layback start up the flake gains the very pleasant slabby groove above. A mini-classic.
FA. Arthur Evans 1950s

⓫ Tippling Wall Left-hand .... 🔲 **HVS 5b**
7m. An old problem that gives a good variation up the left-hand side of the wall, linking decent holds by reaches.

⓬ Tippling Wall .... 🔲 **HVS 5a**
7m. The valley face of the block gives a fingery climb with the holds gradually increasing in size up to the high break. A direct finish is best, though the harassed may wish to sneak off left.
See photos on page 20 and 190.
FA. Arthur Evans 1950s

⓭ Tippling Arete ...... 🔲 **E1 5b**
7m. Head up the right edge of the wall using some snappy feeling ironstone edges to the final roofs and a sprint finish.
FA. Paul Ingham 1978

⓮ Humbug...... 🔲 **E4 7a**
6m. Climb the wall with extreme difficulty following a hairline crack and some shallow pockets - no using the adjacent block. Finish directly straight over the capping overhang. The hardest climbing on the crag - by miles! **V9-ish** above a mat.
FA. Paul Smith 1988

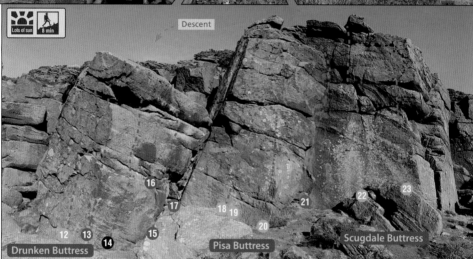

15 The Shelf **E2 5c**
6m. Access the shelf on the wall with difficulty (watch your back and/or ankles) and make one more hard pull to easier ground.
FA. Alan Taylor 1977

16 Tippling Traverse . . . . . **V4 (6b)**
A pumpy traverse around the base of the buttress from *Plumb Line* to *Hangover*, or in the opposite direction.
FA. Tony Marr 1979

17 Plumb Line . . . . **S 4a**
8m. The awkward tilted crack leads to the top of Drunken Buttress, finish up the left edge of the slab on the right.

18 Pisa Buttress . . . . **VS 5a**
8m. Climb straight up the fingery wall to the break, trend right to reach a sloping ledge awkwardly then finish direct.

19 Gravity Wall Direct . . . . **HS 4c**
8m. A hybrid, but offering the best climbing on the face. Start up the previous climb and finish up the next one.

Pisa and Scugdale Buttress
Pisa is the right-leaning buttress with the bulk of Drunken Buttress slumped against it (obviously in need of support). Right again is Scugdale Buttress, the main section of which is round to the right.

---

20 Gravity Wall . . . . **HS 4b**
8m. Start up the arete and climb to the break then trend left crossing the face to finish at its top left edge.

21 Galileo's Gully . . . . **S 4a**
8m. Bridge the outside of the chimney. Delving into the depths is a scruffy **Diff**.

22 Tooth and Nail . . . . **HS 4c**
8m. Climb the wall aiming for the thin hanging crack, then follow it on improving holds.
FA. J.Elliot 1958

23 Supine . . . . **VS 5a**
7m. From a block climb straight up the arete. Some of the holds feel a bit snappy.

Scugdale Buttress and Barker's Buttress

Two of the better buttresses on the cliff with a good variety of routes of a decent length. Virtually all the climbs here are worth doing.

❶ Scugdale Chimney Eliminate

.... 🔲🔲 **VS 4c**
8m. Worthwhile and high in the grade. The narrow rib left of the chimney with a powerful pull over the overhang (good but worn runner slots below). Originally it started up the chimney.

❷ Scugdale Chimney .... 🔲🔲 **VDiff**
8m. The banana-shaped chimney is a classic of its type.

❸ Scugdale Wall .... 🔲🔲 **VS 4b**
8m. Climb the fingery flat wall right of the chimney until it bends over to meet you.
FA. Nick Dixon 1980

❹ Zeta Wall. .... 🔲🔲 **VS 4c**
8m. Pull into the odd zig-zag crack system in the wall and follow it on improving holds. Harder than it used to be due to erosion of the ground at the base of the wall. *Photo on page 201.*

❺ Deviator .... 🔲🔲 **HVS 5c**
6m. A tricky little critter up the corner and shallow groove above. Finish direct or out to the left.
FA. Eric Penman 1960

❻ Nameless Crack .... 🔲🔲 **S 4a**
5m. The widening crack just to the right doesn't see much attention, can't imagine why.

To the right is a fine striated wall, the left-hand side of Barkers' Buttress. All the routes on it are worth doing.

❼ Cubs' Climb .... 🔲 **Diff**
5m. A short offering, exiting via a tiny groove.

❽ Kitten's Climb .... 🔲🔲 **VDiff**
6m. Climb the short crack then head up the wall, trending left.

❾ Pup's Climb .... 🔲🔲 **S 4b**
7m. Climb the left-trending flake-crack to its end then head up the face direct, to finish at a tiny notch.

❿ Bonzo .... 🔲🔲🔲 **HVS 5b**
7m. Straight up the wall with a tricky move using a letter-box hold to get past the blankest section. Probably only VS if you actually lead it. *Photos opposite.*

⓫ Pets' Corner. .... 🔲🔲 **VS 4b**
7m. Pleasant moves up the wall and tiny crack left of the arete. One of the best routes on the cliff.

⓬ The Arete. .... 🔲 **VS 4c**
7m. Straight up the edge.

⓭ Whippet Wall .... 🔲🔲 **VS 4c**
7m. Climb the narrow side wall direct to finish up a short flake.
FA. Arthur Evans 1950s

⓮ Barker's Chimney .... 🔲 **Diff**
6m. The short chimney in the main angle.
FA. Arthur Barker early 1930s

Descent

Barker's Buttress

The next two routes show the full breadth of the orange spot grade.

15 Pluto . . . . HS 4b
6m. The left side of the wall. A tough start past the bulge.

16 Pluto Variant . . . . . HVS 6a
6m. The right-hand side of the wall is rather artificial at the start - no bridging allowed.
FA. Johnny Adams 1970

17 Cat Walk . . . . VDiff
6m. Step off the large boulder on the right, then climb until a traverse left can be made to finish up either *Barker's Chimney* or *Pluto* (harder).

18 Hyena . . . . S 4a
5m. From the boulder, climb the short steep arete.

19 Cerberus Crack . . . . HS 4b
5m. The wide leaning crack is short but tricky.

20 Peke's Perch . . . . S 4a
5m. The rib leads to a thin crack.

It doesn't really matter which way you do it! (L to R) Colin Binks, Alan James and Chris Craggs demonstrating three different methods of doing *Bonzo* (HVS 5b) - *opposite*.

Scugdale

Wainstones

Raven's Scar

Highcliff Nab

Park Nab

Holly Tree Buttress

As the years roll by the tree gets ever bigger and the routes around it disappear under the spiky foliage. The routes to either side of the tree are included for completeness, though their current condition might preclude doing all the routes on the crag in a day.

Holly Tree Buttress - Left

1 Pingers Left-hand . . . . [ ] **VS 5b**
6m. The left-hand side of the wall, finishing up a shallow groove. The arete should be avoided, unless you are struggling.
FA. John Chambers early 1960s

2 Pingers . . . . [ ] **VS 5a**
6m. Climb directly up the centre of the wall using small pockets (a mono on a VS - wild!) and flakes. There are variations galore.
FA. Fred Lightfoot early 1960s.

3 Pingers Right-hand . . . . . . [ ] **VS 5c**
6m. The wall right of *Pingers* can be climbed avoiding holds on the parent route. It is tricky - both the climbing and the avoiding.
FA. Kelvin Neal late 1970s

4 Prickly Rib . . . . [ ] **S 4b**
7m. Climb the wall just left of the holly tree to finish up the left-hand side of the rib, or as close as the holly allows.

5 Holly Tree Chimney . . . . [ ] **HVD**
8m. Climb up and across a slab under the roof (secateurs and body armour required) to finish up the chimney.

6 Touch and Go . . . . . [ ] **E2 6b**
6m. Climb to the roof and pull over left of the nose, fingery, powerful and bold. The landing is a bit sharp.
FA. Tony Marr 1989

7 Holly Tree Wall . . . . [ ] **VS 4b**
6m. The narrow wall and thin crack passing right of the bulge.

8 Holly Tree Hover . . . . [ ] **VS 5a**
6m. An illogical finish pulls left to the short wall above the roof.
FA. J.Elliot 1959

9 Saint's Wall . . . . [ ] **S 4a**
6m. The awkward crack passing a niche. Prayers may be needed.

10 Oak Tree Wall . . . . [ ] **HS 4a**
6m. A short groove leads to moves right then climb the shallow cracked groove to a rounded exit.

Across the gully to the right is a slabby buttress.

11 The Mantelshelf . . . . . . [ ] **S 4c**
6m. The slippery slab leads to a bulge which is passed by a gut-busting mantel. Continue to the top. Long graded a taxing Diff.

12 Humpty Dumpty . . . . [ ] **HS 4b**
6m. The steep right-hand rib via a good red jug - no deviations!

Holly Tree Buttress - Right

The Mantelshelf

Beginners' Slab

The final pair of buttresses are popular with beginners and not just because they are the nearest pieces of rock to the car park! All the routes have got harder over the years due to polishing and erosion - clean those boots!

1 Cicatrice/Central Route .... HVD 4a
4m. The centre of the tiny wall to a thin crack and a tricky sloping exit.

2 Slashed Wall .... VDiff
4m. Climb the left-trending grooves on the right of the wall.

3 The Gash .... Diff
4m. The tiny chimney bounding the tiny wall.

4 The Arete Finish ...... HS 4b
7m. From the top of *The Gash*, step onto the delicate arete on the right, up this to finish up a shallow groove.
FA. Tony Marr 1988

5 Razor Wall .... HS 4c
8m. Head up the left-hand side of the wall to a ledge then the continuation by fingery climbing. Also known as *Sweeney Todd*.

6 Razor Rib .... HVD
8m. A classic little outing. Climb the left-hand side of the arete then the left-slanting flake-crack.
FA. Arthur Evans 1956

7 Gillette .... VS 5a
8m. Layback up the right-hand side of the arete and mantel onto the ramp. Finish up the rib.
FA. Eric (Spider) Penman 1960

The next routes are on the narrow right-hand face of the buttress, and, although tiny, the routes are serious undertakings.

8 The Strop .... VDiff
8m. From the gully on the right access the gangway and follow it leftwards around the arete to find a finish.

9 Suds .... HVS 5b
5m. The thin crack above the left-hand end of the gangway.
FA. Johnny Carter 1959

10 Tension E1 5c
5m. The fingery wall and right-hand crack off the gangway. The landing is grim.
FA. Johnny Carter 1959

11 Alpha .... VDiff
7m. The awkward lower wall leads to the foot a of a steep ramp, balance up this to the top.

12 Beta .... VDiff
7m. Branch right up the centre of the slab. This can also be started from the next climb by trending left.

13 Gamma .... HVD 4a
7m. Trend right then climb the arete to the top. It can be started direct at **4c**.
FA. Tony Marr 1971

14 Curtain Call .... Diff
5m. Start right of a wide crack. Follow a line of flakes up the slabby wall.

15 Curtain Crack .... VDiff
5m. Climb the vertical crack.

16 Curtain Corner .... VDiff
5m. The last arete on the cliff climbed on its left-hand side.

To the right, beyond the wall is the excellent (and neglected) Barker's Crag, extending for several hundred metres. If Scot Crags are too busy for your liking, this place should better fit the bill. There are well over a hundred routes to go at and they cover the grade spectrum form Moderate to E5, with a couple of buttresses offering popular bouldering. Full details can be found in Climbing in North East England (2003).

	No star	[1 star]	[2 star]	[3 star]
Mod to S	9	12	2	1
HS to HVS	9	10	2	-
E1 to E3	4	6	2	2
E4 and up	1	4	-	-

The Wainstones is one of the original climbing venues of the North York Moors, the old guys were attracted by the twinned mini-towers of the Needle and the Steeple as well as the superb aspect of the crag. Over a hundred years on, the place is still well worth a visit. There is a good spread of grades to go at, the rock is excellent hard sandstone and the setting is a delight. Despite all the attractions the Wainstones are a lot less popular than they used to be, maybe it is a fashion thing.

Conditions
The main section of the crag faces south west and gets loads of sunshine and wind a-plenty too. The left-hand side of the crag is equally exposed to the wind but only gets the sun late in the afternoon in the summer. The whole crag takes little drainage and dries rapidly after rain.

Approach
There are two commonly used approaches, a short and brutal one, and a more leisurely version. For the former, head out of Great Broughton and take the minor road off a bend just south of the village. Drive straight towards the hills and park care-fully at the end of the lane. A good track winds steeply up through the forest until a fence on the edge of the open moor is reached. Cross this and flog up the final steep slope to the cliff. Alternatively, park in the large car park near the top of Hasty Bank, on the B1257. Cross the road and follow either the steep path through the trees or the Cleveland Way path a little further up the road. Either way soon reaches a good track that undulates west through the upper edge of the trees, passing under Raven's Scar to intersect the other approach right under the Wainstones.

It is also possible to climb up the ridge and follow the flagged path along the crest (Cleveland Way), passing above Raven's Scar, to arrive on top of the cliff. This is the preferred route to take home because of the stunning views.

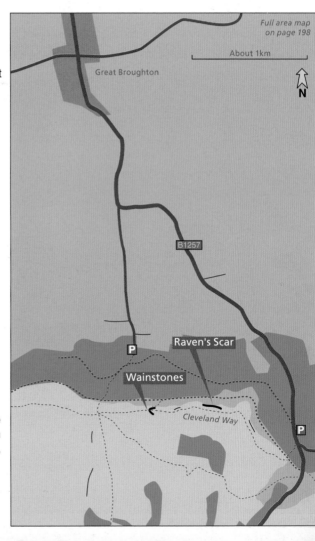

Mark Binney traversing out to the arete on the excellent *Sphinx Nose Traverse* (S 4a) - *page 217* - The Wainstones. Photo: Chris Craggs

Broughton Buttress

Broughton Buttress

The left-hand side of the cliff is the least popular, the routes are short and they don't get much sunshine so tend to be green. Good on hot days though.

1 Broughton Ridge. . . . . ⬚ VDiff
6m. Hop onto the polished arete from the left. Direct is **5a**.

2 Bench Mark Crack. . . . . ⬚ HS 4b
7m. The short corner is tricky.
FA. Arthur Barker late 1920s

3 Bench Mark Wall . . . .⬚ E1 6a
7m. The tiny groove just right is almost always green.
FA. Paul Ingham 1982

4 Psycho Syndicate . . ⬚ E4 6b
8m. The desperate wall via a couple of peg scars.
FA. Paul Ingham 1984

5 Tiny's Arete Direct . . . . ⬚ HVS 5b
8m. The taxing arete is started from the left.
FA. Chris Shorter 1977

6 Tiny's Dilemma Direct. . ⬚ HVS 5a
8m. Climb the wall avoiding the crack to the right.

7 Tiny's Dilemma . . . . ⬚ S 4b
8m. Climb the cracked corner until it is possible to stride left onto a good foothold. Continue direct.

8 Morning Wall. . . . .⬚ S 4a
6m. Balance up the centre of the delicate slab to a ledge and finish through the notch above.

9 Rookery Nook. . . . . ⬚ VDiff
9m. A widening chimney to the ledge, move left under the roof to join the final moves of *Tiny's Dilemma*.

The Sheep Walk is the wide slanting gully that splits the cliff at this point. The next routes are at the top right side of the gully.

10 Green Wall . . . . ⬚ HS 4c
5m. Climb the wall (steep) using a thin crack. Often less green than it looks.
FA. Bill Dell 1958

11 Sheep Walk Slab . . . . . ⬚ Mod
8m. A diagonal traverse heading up and right to finish up the short chimney on the right.
FA. Arthur Barker late 1920s

12 Flake, Wall and Crack. . . . . ⬚ HS 4b
6m. Start from a flake protruding from the lower end of the Sheep Walk. Clamber onto a ledge then climb the cracks above.

13 Solomon's Porch. . . . . ⬚ HS 4b
6m. Start around the arete at the wide crack. Climb this until the arete on the left can be reached for a finish. A start up the arete is about the same grade.
FA. Phillip Horne 1945

14 Lurch . . . . ⬚ VS 5a
6m. Leap and lurch up the arete just to the right. Loss of a holds has made this harder than it used to be.
FA. Tony Marr 1968

15 Humpty Dumpty . . . . ⬚ VDiff
6m. From a finger-shaped block, climb the short slab then the sweet jamming crack above.
FA. Phillip Horne 1945

Descent

The Steeple and The Needle
A couple of fine if diminutive spires that
are one of the attractions of the crag -
summiting both of them is a 'must do' on
a first visit. The top block of the Needle is
reputed to wobble in a high wind.

North West Face

16 Steeple Groove . . . . 🗒 [____] **HVD**
8m. The polished groove between the blocks leads towards the
summit of the Steeple. Sadly W.Bennison beat you to it!

17 Steeple Face . . . . . 🗒 👋🏽 🦉 [____] **E1 5b**
9m. From the top of the blocks climb the centre of the steep
tower with increasing difficulty. Bold - avoiding the arete is hard.
FA. B.Mankin 1955

18 Steeple Chimney . . . . . 🗒 👐 [____] **VDiff**
9m. Use blocks to enter the chimney splitting the south face of
the Steeple. Inside is secure but a thrash, outside is less of a battle but bolder.

19 Centre Fold . . . . 🦅 [____] **HVS 5c**
8m. Sketch up the centre of the face right of the chimney until the
ledge on the arete can be reached. Finish up the arete.
FA. Tony Marr 1979.

20 Chop Yat Ridge . . . . 🗒 🐟 🦅 [____] **S 4a**
8m. Start at the foot of the west ridge of the Steeple. Climb the
ridge to a horizontal break at 3m, then move right and climb the
steep fingery face to easier ground.

21 Steeple Gap . . . . [____] **Mod**
7m. The easy polished groove to the right of *Chop Yat Ridge*
leads to a junction with the upper part of *Steeple Groove*.
FA. Maurice Wilson 1957

Between the Steeple and the Needle is Needle Gap, the rest of the
routes described here are on the Needle.

22 Main Route . . . . 🗒 🐟 [____] **Diff**
8m. From below the huge block, climb the arete to a ledge. Move
left and climb the south face - polished. Beware, the descent is
problematical.
FA. Arthur Barker 1928

23 North Route . . . 🗒 🐟 🐟 🦉 [____] **E1 5a**
8m. Climb a thin flake and make a long reach to pass the awkward bulge (flat holds and bold), continue using the sharp arete.
FA. Brian Evans 1959

24 West Face Direct . . 🗒 👋🏽 🦉 [____] **E4 6b**
8m. Impressive climbing past the horizontal crack and up the
shallow groove in the centre of the wall. Bold and technical.
FA. Dave Paul 1980

South West Face

Lots of sun

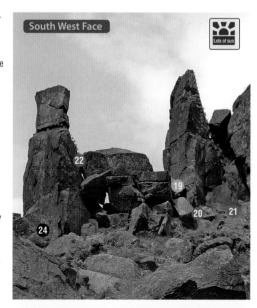

Summit Buttress and Ling Buttress

The main south west-facing section of the Wainstones starts with a couple of nice buttresses, one steep and undercut and the other more slabby.

❶ Summit Crisis **E2 5c**
12m. Climb the deep groove then finger traverse the thin crack rightwards to the good holds on *Bird Lime*. Continue right to the arete and finish up (or down) *Little Bo-Peep*.
FA. Tony Marr 1997

❷ Bird Lime **E3 5c**
8m. From atop a jutting block, pull onto the wall and climb rightwards (brittle flakes) to a pocket. Head leftwards to the top. Bold!
FA. Miles Mosely 1965

❸ Little Bo-Peep . . . . **VS 4b**
12m. Excellent and airy. Climb the block in the gully then step up and traverse left out to the far arete; the tall can reach a useful foothold, the short will have to dangle. Finish up an exposed shallow groove.
FA. Tony Evenett 1951

❹ Miss Muffet . . . . **VS 4c**
8m. Follow *Little Bo-Peep* to the start of its traverse. Gird your loins then head up the steep shallow groove above. Short lived but strenuous and graded Severe for years.

❺ Cantilever . . . . **VDiff**
8m. Climb up the slab in the gully (as for the previous climbs) then continue up and over the outside of the big chockstone.

❻ Peel Out **E4 6b**
8m. The desperate leaning wall of the gully is climbed using a series of shallow undercut finger-flakes. Finish up the arete.
FA. Ian Dunn 1978. Named after Chris Shorter's tumble from the last move when a hold snapped. Fortunately (!) he landed on his sister who slept below.

❼ Ling Arete . . . . **HVS 5a**
8m. The right arete of *Peel Out,* on its left side, via a series of small steps. Awkward and with poor protection until a good jug marks the start of easier climbing.
FA. Franco Cookson 2007

❽ Ling Buttress . . . . **S 4a**
10m. Climb into an A-shaped niche, stride awkwardly out of this onto the arete on the left then continue up this. A good climb, sustained and well protected. A direct version is a little harder.
FA. Arthur Barker late 1920s

❾ Groove and Crack . . . . . . **S 4a**
10m. Start in a right-slanting corner at the base of the buttress. Climb the corner and a short tricky groove (harder if the big ledge is avoided) then trend left to finish up the short steep and awkward crack to a shelving exit.
FA. Jack Devenport 1939

❿ Ling Corner . . . . **HS 4a**
10m. Follow *Groove and Crack* until it starts to head left. From here continue straight up the left-hand side of the steep arete.

⓫ Falcon Rib . . . . **Diff**
10m. Up the right side of the slabby rib to ledges, then head up and left to finish up the short narrow chimney in the right wall of *Ling Buttress*.

Descent

Change in viewing angle

The Sphinx

The Sphinx

The central feature of the face is the jutting headstone of the Sphinx. There are a couple of real classics here plus some less popular outings. Surprisingly, and unlike most rocks named after a Sphinx, this really does look like one, and from both sides too.

① The Direct Start . . . **E2 5c**
10m. The wall with the mouth feature provides a technical direct start to either of the next pair of routes.
FA. John Cheesmond 1960

② West Sphinx Climb . **E2 5b**
11m. From under the nose, move up left to below the overhang (poor improvised gear) and make a hard pull over. Move up to reach a thin horizontal crack and runners. Teeter left along this then escape up the arete.
FA. Harry Hall 1959

③ West Sphinx Direct . **E3 5b**
10m. Superb bold and engrossing, and only a bit harder than the 1959 original version. Follow *West Sphinx Climb* as far as the thin horizontal crack. Make a long move up to a pocket then slink off right to the forehead slab. Substantially harder for the short, especially the reach for the eye.
FA. Paul Ingham 1979

④ Black Knight **E5 6c**
10m. A desperately technical outing that scales the chin via the peg-scarred crack that forms the 'Douglas dimple'.
FFA. Steve Brown (2 peg runners) 1986

⑤ Terrorist **E4 5c**
10m. Pull into the hanging groove right of the chin then move slightly right and head up the wall by sustained fingery climbing.
FFA. Paul Ingham (1 peg runner) 1979

⑥ Walk on the Wild Side . . **E3 5c**
10m. A squeezed line up a short capped groove. Climb the groove and up the face (fingery and harrowing) to reach a flake. Sprint up this to the break (runners!) then finish straight up the face.
FA. Martin Parker 1992

⑦ East Sphinx Direct . . . . **HVS 5a**
10m. Pull up to the hanging crack in the centre of the South Face and climb it and the wider continuation. Head up this to the crest and the airy summit. All over after the first few moves.
FA. Harry Hall 1959

⑧ East Sphinx Climb . . . . **HVD**
10m. Slight but pleasant. Start from a block in the gully and shuffle left along the ledges to a good crack, which leads to a spike and the top.

⑨ Sphinx Nose Traverse . . . . . **S 4a**
14m. Excellent, a real midget gem. Follow *East Sphinx Climb* (or *East Sphinx Direct*) but traverse left, heading for the eye, on a continually surprising set of holds, onto the exposed arete hanging in space. Step round onto the forehead and reach for the flutings. Lovely stuff. *Photo on page 192 and 213.*
FA. Cliff Fielding 1954

Bilsdale Buttress and Main Wall

Another pair of pleasant buttresses with a collection of worthwhile lower grade routes in a sunny sheltered situation. As might be expected they are popular.

❶ Jackdaw Wall E2 6a
7m. The smooth wall is climbed leftwards from a fingery layaway. The landing is poor, as is the gear.

❷ Jackdaw Ridge . . . . HVD
10m. Follow the ridge (not much gear) until ledges lead leftwards.

❸ Jackdaw Gully . . . . Diff
10m. The left-slanting groove gives a good beginners' pitch.

❹ Christopher . . . . HS 4b
9m. Climb the gully for a couple of metres then cross the right wall under the roof (small cams) making awkward moves out to the right to gain the security of a shallow groove. Finish up this.
FA. Christopher Columb 1956

❺ The Bulge Super Direct E2 5b
8m. Start under the shallow groove and climb the wall on its right by technical and bold moves to slabbier ground. Sticking with the groove is **Wilson's Groove** a bold and precarious **E3 6a**.
FA. Eric Penman 1959. FA. (Wilson's Groove) Dave Wilson 1982

❻ The Bulge . . . . VS 4c
9m. From a block in the left branch of *Dusty Gully* climb the steep wall to a horizontal finger-crack. Traverse this leftwards past the bulge until an awkward step gains the slab. Heading straight up before the finger-traverse is **The Bulge Direct, VS 4c**.
FA. Arthur Barker late 1920s

Dusty Gully is the twin forked rift and beyond this is Main Wall.

❼ The Slab Climb Variation S 4a
9m. From an embedded flake climb straight up the edge of the slab with a tricky mantel, finish up steeper rock.

❽ The Slab Climb . . . . HS 4b
9m. A nice outing though protection is lacking. Climb the centre of the slab by at least one mantelshelf. Finish up a short groove.

❾ Central Route . . . . HVS 5b
9m. Start up *The Slab Climb* but branch right to a good foothold close to the next route. Continue by a decisive mantelshelf.
FA. "An unknown climber from Halifax" 1959

❿ Wall and Ledge . . . . VDiff
10m. Start from a block and climb the prominent crack system to the top of the huge flake. Move up to a higher ledge and finish up a short shallow groove. Well worth doing.
FA. Arthur Barker late 1920s

⓫ Ridge Route . . . . S 4a
12m. Pull up to a ledge on the arete (phew - beefy) then continue to join the previous climb as it comes in from the left.
FA. Jack Devenport 1939

⓬ Ridge Route Right-hand . . . HVS 5a
12m. Pull onto the ledge as for *Ridge Route* then continue laybacking up the right side of the arete throughout. Artificial, but it has its moments.
FA. Tony Marr 1972

⓭ Concave Wall . . . . HVS 5b
11m. From the ledge on *Ridge Route*, step right into the centre of the slab and climb direct by precarious climbing, with a particularly tricky move to get stood in the mid-height break. The break offers good gear (awkward to place) and a finger-hold. *Photo opposite.*
FA. Stan Shout (1 peg runner) 1965

⓮ Garfit Eliminate E1 5b
18m. A wanderer, though with good moves and positions. Follow *Concave Wall* past its hard move, stride across the gully then climb diagonally across the steep face until the final steep crack of *Virgin Wall* offers an escape.
FA. Ken Jackson 1967

Garfit Buttress
The crag's last gasp is the tall steep tower of Garfit Buttress, home to some of the harder routes. The lack of protection on many climbs, and the capping roofs, ensure that some are exciting and exacting outings.

15 Mousehole Gully. . . . . **Diff**
10m. The awkward rift can be tackled at a variety of depths - deeper is generally easier.

16 Lemming Slab . **E4 5c**
10m. The centre of the front face. Climb directly past two ledges, with a tricky move to reach a horizontal crack. Step slightly left (not as far as the arete) and climb direct to the second break and a projection. Continue in the same line by further hard moves. Escaping out to the arete is a grade easier and less worthwhile.
FA. Kelvin Neal 1990s. FA. (Direct Finish) Paul Ingham 1980

17 Ali Baba **E2 5c**
10m. Climb the shallow groove precariously on sloping holds to reach the overhang and runners, including a fat thread. Climb direct or slightly right to finish. The escape out right is a cop-out, otherwise the route is high in the grade.
FA. Terry Sullivan (3 pegs - well it was freezing) 1960
FFA. Tony Marr (finished to the right) 1965. FA. (Direct) Paul Ingham 1977

18 Sesame **E2 5b**
10m. Climb *Ali Baba* boldly to the overhang then follow the slanting rift rightwards to finish up a wide vertical crack
FA. Terry Sullivan (in a blizzard!) 1960

19 Virgin Wall/Garfit Face . . . . . **HVS 5a**
8m. Start from the gully on the right edge of the buttress, stretch left for a flat hold then swing boldly onto the front face. Climb up to the wide vertical crack (*Sesame*) for a finish. Crossing the wall a little higher is easier and less exciting.
A **Direct Start** from the boulder is **E1 5c**.
FA. Johnny Clark 1956. The route's name was censored for many years - how times change! FA. (Direct Start) Tony Marr 1980

The final routes are round to the right on the back of the block.

20 Lofty's Ease . . . . **S 4a**
6m. From a block, climb the right-hand side of the arete. Reachy.

21 Tom Thumb . . . . **Diff**
4m. The centre of the short wall at the back of the buttress.

Below the crag is an extensive collection of boulders that have long been popular for whiling away the hours or honing techniques. Details of 40 of the best problems available here can be found in Climbing in North East England (2003).

Alan James balancing up *Concave Wall* (HVS 5b) - *opposite* - The Wainstones. Photo: Chris Craggs

Scugdale
Wainstones
Raven's Scar
Highcliff Nab
Park Nab

	No star	☆	☆☆	☆☆☆
Mod to S	-	1	3	-
HS to HVS	5	10	1	3
E1 to E3	1	8	-	2
E4 and up	-	3	-	1

An impressively situated crag with a big feel about it, Raven's Scar wouldn't be out of place up on the edge of the Kinder plateau in amongst the steep dark cliffs hidden away up there. Many of the climbs follow strong natural lines and the cliff is the tallest in the area, it is just a great shame it doesn't face south or even west, then it would see the attention it really deserves. On the majority of the routes the gear is generally good, a selection of larger cams will be found especially useful.

Conditions
The crag faces almost due north and is best on summer evenings when it gets the late sun. It is definitely not a winter venue when it becomes green and unpleasant. Raven's Scar is also worth considering on very hot days when the Wainstones are baking.

Approach   See map on page 212
Park near the top of Hasty Bank, on the B1257, south of Great Broughton, in the large car park to the left of the main road. Cross the road and follow either the steep path through the trees, or the Cleveland Way path which starts just a little further up the road. Either way soon reaches a good track that undulates west though the upper edge of the trees, passing under Raven's Scar where a stile gives access to the steep path running up to the cliff. It is also possible to continue following the path up the ridge and then on the flagged path along the crest (Cleveland Way), until you are above Raven's Scar, from there paths lead down round either end to get to the climbing. If there are sunbathers in the team it might be best to make a base on top of the cliff in the sun and descend into the shade to do battle when suitably organised.

Homeward bound from Raven's Scar along the Cleveland Way. Photo: Chris Craggs

Tiptoeing along the exposed traverse of *Forest Face* (HS 4b) - *page 224* - Raven's Scar. Photo: Chris Craggs

Left-hand Walls

The left side of the cliffs has some good climbs, the best of which follow striking lines, the superb long corner line of *Satchmo* being the prime example.

❶ Evening Wall . . . . **HS 4b**
11m. Climb the right wall of a chimney slot to a bilberry ledge. Finish up the good crack in the wall up and left.
FA. Tony Marr 1979

❷ Thrasher . . . . **VS 4c**
11m. Thrash over the juggy roof then trend right to ledges. Finish up the pleasant right-trending slabby ramp.
FA. Geoff Fixter 1961

❸ Suede Shoe Shuffle. . . . **HVS 5c**
11m. Monkey up into the hanging notch in the roof then climb the buttress above which is easier, at least in decent footwear!
FA. Chris Shorter (solo in his Hush Puppies) 1978

❹ En Passant. . . . . **S 4b**
12m. The long groove in the left arete of the recess is a fine climb at the grade when clean. The top is often a bit grassy.
FA. Cleveland MC members mid 1950s

❺ Afterthought. . . . . **HVS 5a**
12m. Climb the centre of the slab, skirting the left edge of the green streak, to finish up the centre of the upper wall.
FA. Paul Ingham 1979

❻ Lazy Bones . . . . **HS 4b**
12m. The long groove that runs up the back left-hand corner of the recess is a good pitch and an impressive line at the grade.
FA. Terry Sullivan 1955

❼ Grooves-ology . . . . **VS 5a**
12m. Start up *Lazy Bones* but move right to the fine long flake-crack and follow it throughout. Good climbing with good gear.
FA. Vic Tosh (3 pegs for aid) 1961. FFA. Tony Marr 1965

❽ Stardust. **E1 5b**
12m. A flake-crack leads to the ledge shared with *Grooves-ology*. Climb the right-hand peg-scarred crack to the top.
FA. Terry Sullivan (4 pegs for aid) 1957. FFA. Bob Hutchinson 1977

*The wall to the right was originally an aid climb on home-made bolts. It is now free - **Screwed, E4 6b** - but being hard, serious and devious, it is sees little attention.*

❾ Satchmo **E1 5c**
14m. The superb long leaning groove gives a great piece of climbing, sustained, though with good protection, and a hard move high up (well, apart from the move to get off the ground). Well worth calling in for when the conditions are right.
FA. Terry Sullivan (6 pegs for aid) 1956. FFA. Tony Marr 1970

❿ Ch-Ching **E7 6c**
16m. The arete is hard and worthwhile but will be so much better when it gets the finish it really deserves.
FA. Francis Montague 1996

⓫ Stratagem **E4 6b**
16m. Originally called *Ella*, this ancient aid route would be a Millstone masterpiece were it shipped down there. Climb the initial overhang and follow the crack to a ledge (beware nesting birds - puke, puke). The slanting crack gives a sustained technical battle to a taxing exit. There may be a peg runner in place.
FA. Terry Sullivan (6 pegs for aid) 1961. FFA. John Redhead 1977

⓬ Sunshine Slab . . . . **VDiff**
10m. A pleasant finish after a devious approach. Climb past a huge jammed boulder in the gully then move left to the deep slabby groove and finish up this.
FA. Richard Whardell 1954

⓭ Sunny Delight. **E1 5b**
8m. Follow *Sunshine Slab* until it heads for the main groove then climb the rounded and poorly protected arete. Scary.
FA. Tony Marr 1979

Satchmo

En Passant — Satchmo — Ahab — Forest Face — Fever Pitch

Descent

⑭ Little Gem . . . . ▧▢ **HVS 5b**
8m. Head up the right wall of the big gully to a good ledge, then pull into the short hanging crack with difficulty.
FA. Tony Marr 1994

⑮ Too Young To Fly . . . . ⛶▢ **HVS 5a**
10m. Shin up the right-hand side of the arete to reach a large grassy ledge. On the right is a crack, close to the upper hanging arete, finish up this. Tricky.
FA. Chris Shorter 1977

⑯ Loose Ends . . . . ⛶▢ **E1 5c**
10m. Pull onto the arete as for *Too Young to Fly* and shuffle right until an elongated pocket can be reached by harsh cranking on the prominent nipple. Head up the steep wall into a left slanting groove that leads to the big grass ledge, then escape up the groove at the back of the ledge.
FA. Tony Marr 1985

⑰ Ahab . . . . ⛶▧▢ **HS 4b**
14m. A fine climb up a good line. The bottom of the groove is blank, so hand traverse in from the left and pull into the main groove. Continue, passing a ledge to the final corner-crack. The **Direct Start** is a problematic but short lived **V2 (6a)**.
FA. John Hickman (the regular start) 1954

⑱ Rock Bottom . . . . . ⛶▧▮▢ **E3 6b**
12m. Start as for *Ahab* (the *Direct Start* is most fitting) then climb the wall past a mouth, making desperate moves to the break. Continue to a good ledge (used as a stance on the first ascent). Access the upper wall using a jutting boss to pass the roof and continue direct.
FA. Chris Shorter, John Redhead (alt leads) 1977

The jutting arete just to the right has two worthwhile problems.

⑲ Hard On . . . . ⛶▢ **V1 (5c)**
The shallow groove just right of the corner gives a nice problem.
FA. John Redhead 1977

⑳ Rock On . . . . ⛶▢ **V3 (6a)**
The suitably flexible can access the jutting beak on its left side.
FA. Alan Taylor early 1980s

㉑ Jonah . . . . ⛶▧▢ **VS 5a**
12m. From just right of the arete, climb up and left through the roof with difficulty. Finish up *Ahab*.
FA. Tony Marr 1964

㉒ Moby Dick . . . . ⛶▢ **HS 4b**
12m. From the gully right of the buttress, balance left above the roof then climb the wall to a good ledge. Gain the undercut upper wall with difficulty and climb this to an exit round the rocking block that caps the wall.
FA. Cleveland MC members mid 1950s

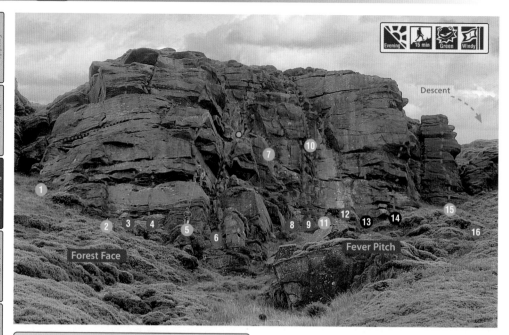

Central Walls

An imposing set of climbs up steep open faces and with great outward views. Like the rest of the cliff, visits need to be linked to a spell of good weather. The best of the climbs here are very good indeed, be prepared to be surprised at their quality.

① Forest Face . . . . **HS 4b**
22m. A devious and exciting classic. Care with the rope work is needed for maximum enjoyment. Start at the foot of the gully on the left of the buttress. Exit right from the recess and follow ledges rightwards (easy but increasingly exposed) to reach a thin crack. Climb this (awkward) and its continuation, to an eventual rightward exit. Excellent. *Photo on page 221.*
FA. Terry Sullivan 1958

A roof cuts across the crag at one quarter height, the next four routes find ways past this.

② Red Light. . . . . **HVS 5a**
14m. Climb the groove to ledges then weave through the overhangs to reach a thin crack-line. Follow this to a large lying down type of ledge then, when recovered, finish up the exposed arete on the right.
FA. Tony Marr 1979

③ Naught for your Comfort **E1 5c**
16m. Climb to and through the roof and press on past the right-hand edge of a second roof to reach the traverse on *Forest Face.* Head boldly through the upper overhangs to finish.
FA. John Redhead (finishing up Forest Face) 1977.
FA. (as described) Paul Ingham 1979

④ Hooker **E2 5c**
16m. Follow the thin crack, 6m left of the arete, to the roofs. Hard climbing (a fierce pull on an iron blob) gains the big pocket above, then trend right to an easier groove and ledges. Pull through the bulges and finish up a short wall.
FA. Paul Ingham 1979

⑤ Harlot's Groove . . . . . . **VS 4c**
18m. A fine climb up the big arete that is the chief feature of the centre of the cliff. Climb the left side of the arete to ledges then pull up to the hanging flake/groove with difficulty. Continue to higher ledges where more tricky climbing is needed to access the A-shaped cracks. Finish right, then left.
FA. Terry Sullivan 1959

⑥ Tumble-down Dick . . . . **Diff**
18m. A great beginners' route and one of the area's better winter climbs on the rare occasions when it is cold enough. Start by climbing the open gully/groove to a commodious platform - awkward belays. For the second pitch climb up the steeper corner to reach the moor.
FA. Richard Whardell 1954

⑦ Tumble-down Crack. . . . . . . **VS 5a**
18m. From the top of the grass bank, climb the thin corner-crack on the left to the large ledge and a belay. Bridge the leaning groove on the right (steep but only 4b) until it is possible to escape right onto easier ground.
FA. Cleveland MC members mid 1950s. The Original Start (to the left) is poor and grassy, the described version includes the old Right-hand Start.

⑧ The Omen **E1 5a**
18m. A good climb with a bold feel. Climb *Tumble-down Crack* until it is possible to pull out right and ascend to a break. Continue up steep rock to reach a shallow groove and from the top of this finish straight up the face.
FA. John Redhead 1977

9 Spell Bound . . . ⬡ 🪓 🠗 🦅 ▢ **E2 5b**
18m. A bold and pumpy outing starting up the steep wall right of the corner to reach a ledge. Continue up a groove to the bulges then pull over leftwards to access the arete. Climb this in an exposed position, gradually easing towards the top.
FA. Tony Marr 1992

The big green groove is much better than it looks (except after wet weather). Both variations are worth doing.

10 Waterslide Left-hand. . . ⬡ 🪓 ▢ **HS 4b**
18m. Climb the wall just to the left of the green streak and continue up the left-hand groove directly above. A good line though it is inclined to be green and gritty early in the season.
FA. Tony Marr 1994

11 Waterslide . . . . ⬡ 🦅 ▢ **HS 4b**
18m. The right-hand version is usually cleaner but isn't well protected. Follow the *Left-hand* to the ledge at the foot of the left-hand groove. Move across right then follow the right-hand groove throughout - steep to start but gradually easing with height. The **Right-hand Finish** involves traversing the big horizontal break all the way out to the right arete, with no change in grade.
FA. Alan Chester 1954. FA. (Right-hand Finish) Terry Sullivan 1957

12 Fever Pitch . . . . . . Top 50 🠗 🦅 ▢ **E2 5b**
16m. Another big pitch with excellent bold climbing. Start at the right-hand side of the green streak at a shallow groove. Climb to the bulges then trend right through these to a crack. Swing swiftly back left and pull onto a ledge right on the arete. Finish up a thin crack splitting the top wall.
FA. Terry Sullivan (as Vigilante, an aid route) 1964. FFA. John Redhead (except the finish) 1977. FA. (as described) Chris Shorter 1978

13 Gangrene. . . . . ⬡ 🧗 ▢ **E4 6b**
16m. An impressive line up the centre of the wall. Climb the steep lower wall leftwards to the overhangs. Pass these and continue up the face, slightly rightwards, by sustained hard climbing.
FA. Chris Shorter 1978

14 Three Screaming Popes ⬡ 🦅 ▢ **E6 6c**
16m. The soaring arete is approached through the large bulges then climbed on its left-hand side throughout. The route has a compelling line but the subtle blend of difficulty and boldness means it sees little attention.
FA. Terry Sullivan (As Vendetta, an aid route) 1964. FFA. Chris Shorter 1992

15 Broadway . . . . ⬡ 🠗 ▢ **HVS 5b**
12m. The narrow buttress on the right side of this section of the cliff eases with height. Rounded climbing.
FA. Terry Sullivan late 1950s

16 Airlift . . . . ⬡2 🠗 ▢ **S 4a**
14m. Across the grassy descent gully is a jutting buttress. Start at the foot of the front face and climb up and left to the left-hand side of the arete. Up this to the highest break, then move back round to the right for a fine exposed finish. *Photo adjacent.*
FA. Terry Sullivan late 1950s

To the right the cliff continues for some distance and is home to another thirty-odd routes, many of which are worthwhile. Like the rest of the crag, visits are best reserved for dry spells. Full details will be found in Climbing in North East England (2003).

Tony Marr on the superbly positioned *Airlift* (S 4a) - *this page* - Raven's Scar. Photo: Mike Took

	No star	☆	☆☆	☆☆☆
Mod to S	2	1	1	-
HS to HVS	-	3	-	-
E1 to E3	2	2	3	1
E4 and up	-	-	3	1

Highcliff Nab sits in a splendid position just to the south of Guisborough with great views south and west across the North York Moors and north and east towards the distant conurbation of Teesside and the North Sea. The best routes at Highcliff are technical and bold wall climbs with the prominent arete of *Magic in the Air* being the showpiece of the crag. The walls to either side of this arete have been tackled by various routes over the years, often climbed in separate halves, or with high side runners, but now moistly done direct and in a pure style. For slightly more amenable challenge *Scarecrow Crack* is the one to head for and there are also a few good easier routes towards the right-hand side of the crag.

Conditions

The crag faces north and west and is at its best on warm summer evenings after a dry spell. It is also a useful retreat on hot days. The felling of the trees that used to grow close to the base of the crag have made conditions here much more pleasant than they used to be. A breeze will keep the midges away now and the more open aspect means that the cliff gets a chance to dry after damp weather, although sections, especially to the left, still stay green.

Approach

There is limited parking at the end of the minor road that runs south through Hutton Village, south west of Guisborough, ending at the gate across the track to the crag. This is a quiet residential area - please park considerately. The road is used by LARGE timber lorries, if their access is restricted in any way you will find your car has been moved!

Go through the gate and follow the tarmaced road uphill to a T-junction. Turn left and follow the main track (avoid the right turn to the farm) until the trees are exited, a gate bars the track and the cliff is visible up and right. Follow the track up the hill then branch left to reach the grassy base of the cliff - 20 minutes walk. An alternative approach is the direct version, short and sharp, from parking in Ilkley Grove or Gothland Grove at the southern end of Guisborough. Just follow the public footpath up to the moor and the crag.

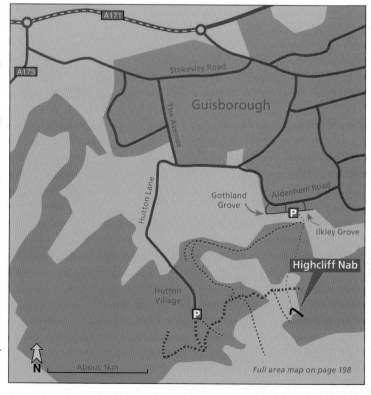

Full area map on page 198

Descent

The northerly aspect of the crag encourages lichen growth, the harder routes may need a LIGHT brushing before an ascent.

Left of the routes described here are another forty or so climbs that have become increasingly overgrown over the years - these are listed in Climbing in North East England (2003).

❶ Wombat **E1 5b**
16m. The imposing corner is approached via the slab and gives a beefy, well protected pitch. The exit is inclined to be grassy.
FA. Terry Sullivan (aid) 1961. FFA. Les Brown 1966

❷ Trampled Underfoot . . . **E1 5b**
22m. A good strenuous outing which links *Wombat* with the finish of *Magic in the Air* via a tough traverse under the roofs.
FA. Rick Graham (1 peg) 1977. FFA. Ian Dunn 1982

❸ Esmerelda **E7 6c**
20m. An astounding route that follows the old bolt holes up the steep side wall of the buttress. Technically hard climbing and limited protection ensure it sees few successes.
FA. Terry Sullivan 1962. As the aid route Quasimodo using large curtain hooks for bolts. FFA. Paul Smith (at E6 6b - 1pt) 1988 FFA. Richard Waterton 1995

❹ Magic in the Air **E6 6b**
20m. The superb, bold and technical arete is the best route on the cliff and maybe in the whole area. Follow the arete on its right-hand side throughout. A pre-placed and pre-clipped runner over to the right, in *Stargazer*, reduces the grade to **E5 6b**.
FA. Nick Dixon (with side-runners) 1982. FA. (without side-runners) Francis (Monty) Montague 1991

❺ Desperate Den **E6 6c**
20m. Start at a carved cross and make desperate moves up the wall to reach holds and runners on *Stargazer*, finish up the wall above passing the right-hand edge of the roof. The start is currently a bit dusty.
FA. Steve Brown (starting up Magic in the Air) 1983. FA. (Direct Start) Tony Marr 2001

❻ Stargazer **E3 5c**
20m. Devious but excellent. Start up *Scarecrow Crack* and traverse out left on good holds in the break. Use small edges to pull up and left to better holds and a finish up the crack in the arete. **Stargazer Super Direct, E4 6a**, is the direct line above the traverse and is now incorporated in *Desperate Den*.
Photo on page 227.
FA. Paul Ingham 1979. FA. (Super Direct) Nick Dixon 1983

❼ Scarecrow Crack . . . **E1 5b**
20m. The wide twisting crack is the best line on the cliff and it gives a suitably impressive tussle. Laybacking or offwidth techniques work, large cams are a real help too.
FA. D.Holliday 1954. The story goes that he spotted the route when flying past the crag in his jet.

❽ Puffs Parade **E1 5c**
20m. The blunt rib is climbed on spaced holds - bold! Finish up *Scarecrow Crack*, or rightwards up *Queer Street*.
FA. Dave Ladkin 1972

❾ Moonflower Super Direct **E5 6b**
20m. Start right of the initials and balance up the blunt rib to its top (small wires out left). Step left onto the large ledge and finish up the scooped wall. Originally the route started up the carved initials before moving right and then finishing up *Queer Street*.
FA. Nick Dixon 1981. FA. (Moonflower) Dave Paul 1981

❿ Queer Street **E1 5a**
22m. Climb the flake right of the arete then pull left onto the wall, and head under the overhang to access the shallow groove round the arete. Finish up this. A bold outing.
FA. Tony Marr, Ken Jackson (alt leads- the belay at the stance was the only gear on the route) 1972

Highcliff Crack

Descent

⓫ Highcliff Crack . . . . . . S 4b
20m. The fine groove was one of the first routes on the cliff and remains well worth doing. It is awkward in places but well protected throughout. An excellent outing.
FA. The Barker brothers 1930s

⓬ Rockhopper E3 5b
18m. Just to the right of *Highcliff Crack*, climb the rib rightwards to ledges. Step right and climb the steep and bold arete.
FA. Dave McKinney 1977

⓭ Flake Crack . . . . VS 4c
18m. The deep groove gives a good pitch - powerful, sustained and a lot better than it looks. Bridge, jam and haul on those (occasionally wobbly) jugs then exit right at the top.
FA. Terry Sullivan 1961

⓮ Heart Throb Crack. . . . . HS 4c
18m. The wide crack is guaranteed to get the pulse rate up. An awkward start leads to a niche and then ledges. The chockstone is most easily passed on the right then finish up grassy cracks.
FA. Cleveland MC members early 1950s

⓯ Highcliff Chimney Direct . . . S 4a
16m. Squirm the narrow chimney direct. A finish up the right arete is nicer but avoids part of the real challenge.
FA. The Barker brothers 1930s. FA. (The Arete Finish) Tony Marr 1992

⓰ Highcliff Chimney - Ordinary . . VDiff
18m. Start up the groove in the arete and climb it to ledges which lead left to the chimney. Continue up this passing the chockstones and making a rightward exit.
FA. The Barker brothers 1930s

⓱ Scarface E1 5c
12m. The thin crack in the upper wall.
FA. Unknown (3 pts aid) 1959. FFA. Tony Marr 1992

⓲ North West Route . . . . . HVD 4a
20m. Climb a tricky groove and slab rightwards to a small ledge on the arete. Move around the corner (stay high) then move right again and climb the flake-crack to the top.
FA. The Barker brothers 1930s

⓳ North West Direct . . . . . VS 4c
12m. Climb sandy rock to jugs then the thin crack to the exposed corner on *North West Route*. Finish up the thin crack in the arete to a tricky exit. *Photo on page 193.*
FA. (the start) John Carter 1960. FA. (the finish) John Smith 1970

North West Direct

	No star			
Mod to S	7	4	-	-
HS to HVS	2	7	4	-
E1 to E3	2	1	-	-
E4 and up	-	-	-	-

A tiny cliff in a lovely setting, with a good selection of climbs, and only a short (but steep) hike from the road. Although not very tall, many of the routes are action packed and a couple of hours here is guaranteed to give you a good work out. The most impressive feature of the cliff used to be the large jutting buttress tackled by the classic of *Shere Khan*. Sadly this collapsed in 1995 and now lies scattered down the slope. It didn't even have the good grace to stay in large chunky blocks to give some decent bouldering.

Park Nab from the approach path. Photo: Chris Craggs

Conditions

The crag faces west and makes a great afternoon venue. It catches the wind and takes no drainage so is one of the fastest drying crags in the area but there is no shelter in the event of rain.

Approach

The crag is situated high on a hillside to the south of Guisborough and south east of Great Ayton. From the A172 Stokesley ring road, turn onto the A173. On a bend in the road pick up a minor road that runs to Easby. Drive through the village, then after 2km turn left towards Kildale. Just before you get to Kildale, there is a right turn to Bilsdale. Drive up this to the crest of the hill where there is a large parking area on the right. The crag is clearly visible for much of this approach drive and is reached by a steep five minute walk.

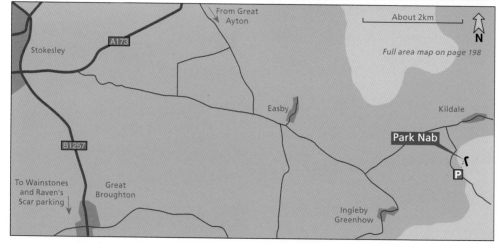

Lion's Jaw

To the right is the open corner that is all that remains of the cliff's best feature, the tall jutting buttress that was home to the superb Shere Khan. A thunderstorm in 1995 saw the destruction of the buttress, the debris lies scattered down the hillside. Within a couple of months the newly created gaps had been plugged though the new routes are lesser offerings than their forebears.

5 A Step Class .... HVD
5m. Sprint up the pleasant angular arete.
FA. Graeme Sayer 1995

6 Forked Crack .... VDiff
5m. The escapable groove and crack
FA. Graeme Sayer 1995

7 Baloo .... HS 4b
5m. Climb the right arete of the slab.
FA. Graeme Sayer 1995

8 Grumble in the Jungle ..... VDiff
6m. The chimney-crack is a little awkward.
FA. Graeme Sayer 1995

9 Twister E3 5c
8m. The bold arete used to be a bit close to the chimney, but not since the chimney chose to move away.
FA. Ian Dunn 1982

10 Twin Cracks .... HS 4b
6m. It's all in the name. Inferior eliminate versions exist; left only is **5a**, right only is **4c**, or maybe it's the other way round - you try and decide. *Photo on page 195.*

11 Dynamo .... HVS 6a
6m. The narrow wall is climbed trending slightly leftwards.
FA. Johnny Adams 1960s

1 Dangle .... HVS 5c
6m. Power through the centre of the roof, and watch your back.
FA. M Binks 1971

2 Lion's Jaw .... HVS 5b
6m. The strugglesome fissure splitting the right side of the roof. The hanging arete immediately right is **Lion King**, a tough **5c**.
FA. E Derwin late 1950s

3 Zero Route .... HVS 5a
5m. Climb the hard little right-hand wall, trending right.
FA. Terry Sullivan late 1950s

4 Cook's Gully .... Mod
5m. The left-hand fissure. Variations exist.

Descent

Twin Cracks

12 Ladies Gully Left . . . . ☆ ☐ **Diff**
6m. An easy climb, or a viable descent for the competent.

13 Right Crack . . . . ☐ **S 4a**
6m. The nearby twin is quite a bit harder.

14 Pinnacle Crack Left-hand . . . ☆ ☐ **Diff**
6m. Climb blocks then the curving crack to a groove.

15 Pinnacle Crack Right-hand . . . . ☐ **S 4a**
6m. A variation finish up the widening overhanging crack.

16 Pinnacle Face . . . . ☆ 🏃 ☐ **E1 5b**
7m. After a boulder problem start (6a?), head up the narrow left-hand face of the Pinnacle using the right arete when needed. An indefinite and escapable line which looks better than it really is.
FA. Chris Woodall 1972

17 Chairman's Climb . . . . . ☆ 🧗 ☐ **HVS 4c**
7m. The wide crack gains a ledge. Finish up the leaning wall by combining a useful pocket hold and the arete. Low in the grade. Climbing the left arete instead, and avoiding the ledge, is **5a**.

18 Chockstone Chimney . . . . . . 🚶 ☐ **Diff**
6m. The stepped crack leads to a narrow chimney.

19 Wall Bar Buttress . . . . . ☆ ✎ ☐ **S 4a**
8m. Pleasantly powerful moves up the line of wall bars between the cracks. *Photo on page 231.*

20 Picture This . . . . ☆ 🏃 ☐ **HVS 5a**
7m. Climb to a ledge up and right, gained by a tricky mantel, and finish up the vague rib above.
FA. Tony Marr 1960s

21 Scoop Chimney . . . . . . ☆ 🚶 ☐ **VDiff**
7m. Climb the wide crack into the scoop then finish up either of the continuation cracks in the back.

22 Pessimist . . . . ☐ **E3 5c**
7m. The jutting arete is technical and unprotected. Heading right gives a rather easier (**5b**) alternative.
FA. Johnny Adams 1960s. FA. (Right-hand exit) Paul Ingham 1977

23 Hara-Kiri . . . . ☆ 🖐 ☐ ☐ **HVS 5a**
8m. A fine climb. Stretch up the thin crack then move right along the break where a layaway and another stretch gains the top. A **Direct Start** is **5b** but needs a good spotter.
FA. John Hickman 1950s

24 Long Bow . . . . ☆ ☐ **VS 4c**
7m. The curving and awkward crack (especially entering the upper section) gives worthwhile climbing.

25 Bowstring . . . . ☆ 🖐 ☐ **HVS 5a**
6m. Straight up the thin seam to the wide finish of *Long Bow*.

26 The Bitter End . . . . ☆ 🏃 🖐 ☐ **HVS 5c**
6m. Pull leftwards on the wall to reach a good slot then finish up the face above this. A **Direct Start** to the slot is **6a**.
FA. Tony Marr 1965. FA. (Direct Start) Ian Cummings 1979.

27 The End . . . . ☆ ☐ **VS 5a**
6m. The arete is the end of all things (in the NYMoors section....)

Afternoon | 5 min | Windy | Descent

Northumberland

Mark Glaister climbing, Emma Medara belaying, on the magnificent *The Trouser Legs* (E2 5c) - *page 287* - at Ravensheugh. Photo: Glaister Collection

Climbers enjoying the classic of *Sunset* (S 4a) - *page 260* - on Sunset Buttress, Peel Crag. Photo: Chris Craggs

Northumberland manages to remain one of the few relatively unspoilt corners of the UK, far enough from most of the major population centres not to be used as a quick-hit, it requires a bit of effort to get there and to get the most out of the place; long may it remain so. I was brought up in the North East, but have lived for many years on the edge of the ever-busy Peak District. Because of this, trips to Northumberland always feel like a homecoming - the wide open spaces, broad skies and delightfully varied cliffs make the place very special.

Geoffrey Winthrop Young (1876-1958) captured the essence of the County (he was a poet of some renown) when he wrote the introduction to the first guide to Northumberland, published well over half a century ago -

"There is no nobler county than that of Northumberland as it rolls processionally northward to the Border in great waves of coloured and historic moorland, cresting upon the skyline into sudden and surprising crags, which crown for us the magnificent walking with admirable rock climbs. May the growing tide of northern climbers flow onward as great heartedly."

From the austere Whin Sill crags tucked below the Roman Wall to the hidden delights of Kyloe in the Woods, the lofty Ravensheugh to the ever-popular Bowden crags and plenty of places in between; Northumberland has masses to offer the itinerant climber. Enjoy the peace and the solitude; respect these great cliffs and their lovely little climbs.

Causey Quarry | Crag Lough | Peel Crag | Callerhues | Great Wanney | E. Woodburn | Sandy Crag | Ravensheugh | Simonside | Drake Stone | Corby's | Bowden Doors | Back Bowden | Kyloe In | Kyloe Out | Berryhill

Ethics and Style

Northumberland has a history of bold ascents from long before the days of padded mats and sophisticated protection. Many of the routes are devoid of protection and treated nowadays as highball boulder problems, but most were originally done as solos, often ground up. Obviously, your style of ascent is up to you, but keep in mind the comments below about soft rock and top-roping. The main thing is to enjoy your climbing and be honest with yourself about what you want to achieve and what you have achieved. For most people an onsight ascent of a route at HVS will be more satisfying than a pre-practiced E2.

Soft Rock and Top-roping

The sandstone of Northumberland is of superb quality but it does not have the robustness of millstone grit or the volcanics of the west and north of the UK. On some popular boulder problems the significant holds are wearing away at an alarming rate now that the tough rock surface has been eroded. Ropes running across the edge of the cliff can cause thousands of year's wear in a few minutes, so if you must top-rope, make sure you extend the top krab over the edge using a second rope or slings, and make sure you pad this at the point it goes over the edge with an empty rucksack or the like. The rock is a finite resource and it is up to us to preserve it, and these great routes, for future generations.

Access

Like everywhere in the UK, access in Northumberland has had its problem spots. We haven't included any of the cliffs that lie in the military training grounds of the Otterburn Moors because of limited access, even though some of them are pretty good.

Warning sign, Otterburn

Military Firing Range. Keep out when red flags or lights are displayed or barriers closed.

Danger Do not touch any military debris. It may explode and kill you.

Elsewhere the usual issues have raised their heads over the years, the blocking of access through thoughtless parking being pre-eminent amongst these. However, due to continuing negotiations and strict adherence to agreements by climbers, the vast majority of venues have unrestricted access at present. Individual crag access is covered in each of the crag sections. Please read this information carefully and take great care not to infringe any restrictions. If in any doubt contact the BMC (page 9) or check the access section of the BMC website **www.thebmc.co.uk.**

Parking - It is all a matter of common courtesy, don't block access, get right off the road if possible and, if the parking is full, try to find somewhere else.

Litter/Fires/Dogs - It should be obvious.

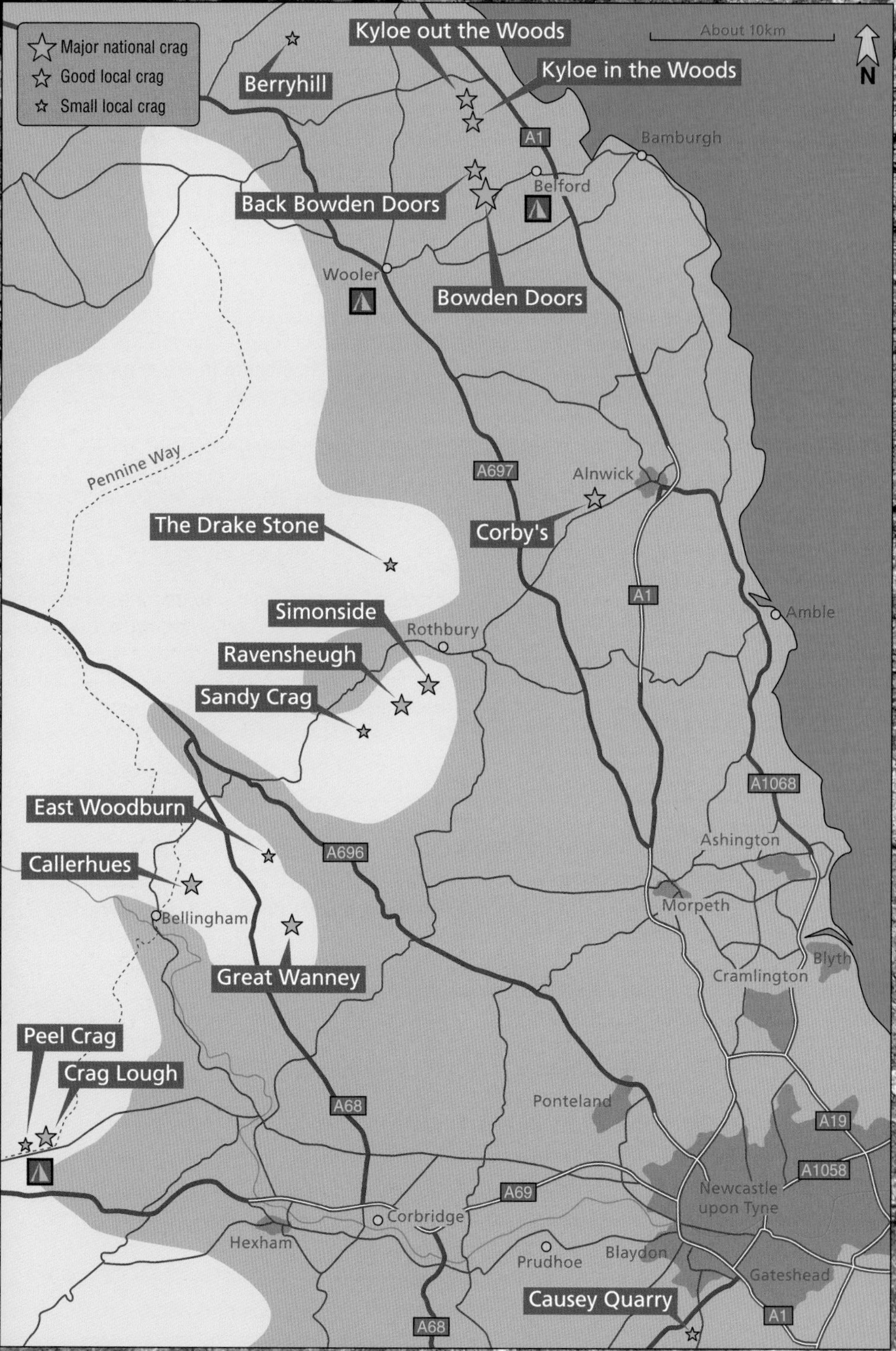

Legend:
- ☆ Major national crag
- ☆ Good local crag
- ☆ Small local crag

About 10km

N

Kyloe out the Woods
Kyloe in the Woods
Berryhill
Bamburgh
A1
Back Bowden Doors
Belford
Bowden Doors
Wooler
Pennine Way
A697
Alnwick
The Drake Stone
Corby's
A1
Simonside
Rothbury
Ravensheugh
Amble
Sandy Crag
East Woodburn
A696
A1068
Callerhues
Ashington
Bellingham
Great Wanney
Morpeth
Peel Crag
Blyth
Crag Lough
Cramlington
A68
Ponteland
A19
A1058
A69
Newcastle
upon Tyne
Corbridge
Hexham
A68
Prudhoe
Blaydon
Gateshead
Causey Quarry
A1

Berryhill · Kyloe Out · Kyloe In · Back Bowden · Bowden Doors · Corby's · Drake Stone · Simonside · Ravensheugh · Sandy Crag · E. Woodburn · Great Wanney · Callerhues · Peel Crag · Crag Lough · Causey Quarry

Causey Quarry · Crag Lough · Peel Crag · Callerhues · Great Wanney · E. Woodburn · Sandi Crag · Ravensheugh · Simonside · Drake Stone · Corby's · Bowden Doors · Back Bowden · Kyloe In · Kyloe Out · Berryhill

Mountain Rescue

In the event of an accident requiring the assistance of Mountain Rescue:

Dial 999 and ask for 'POLICE - MOUNTAIN RESCUE'

All mountain rescue incidents in the Northumberland fall under the responsibility of Northumberland Constabulary. If in doubt request Northumberland Police Operations Room.

Tourist Information Offices

If you are short of ideas of what to do on a wet day or need some accommodation, take a look at www.visitnorthumberland.com or at any of the local Tourist Information Offices. They have much more useful information than it is possible to include in these pages. A few of the T.I. Offices most central to the climbing are listed below.

Heather, Back Bowden

Alnwick   01665 511333
Bellingham   01434 220616
Corbridge   01434 632815
Hexham   01434 652220
Once Brewed   01434 344396
Otterburn   01830 520093
Rothbury   01669 620887
Wooler   01668 282123

Camping

There are many campsites in Northumberland and websites that list them. A search for "Northumberland Campsites" will produce loads of results. The ones listed below are some of the more central for climbers. Their approximate locations are marked on the map on the previous page, and on appropriate close-up maps.

Winshields Farm Campsite, Hadrian's Wall (see map on page 250)
Winshields Farm, Military Road, Bardon Mill, Hexham, NE47 7AN.   Tel: 01434 344243
Good for the climbing under the Roman Wall and on the southern cliffs. Close to the Twice Brewed pub.   **www.winshields.co.uk**

Highburn House Caravan & Camping Park, Wooler
Wooler, Northumberland, NE71 6EE.   Tel: 01668 281344
Site is located on the western outskirts of village, pleasant and inexpensive.
www.highburn-house.co.uk

South Meadows, Belford (see map on page 312)
South Meadows, Belford, NE70 7DP.   Tel: 01668 213326
Good for the Bowden/Kyloe areas and close to Belford itself (shops and pubs).
Very large and quite pricey.   **www.southmeadows.co.uk**

Climbing on the Brain

It was back in the early 1990s on the way to Skye, we stopped off at East Woodburn to break the journey north. I took this photograph, put the camera on a rock then soloed the route behind Colin.

Late the next day we stopped on Rannoch Moor to take a shot of the Buchaille in all its glory when I had a sudden revelation - the camera was still on the rock! I phoned Sherri who was in Middlesborough (a lot nearer than me) and gave her precise instructions which included 'park by the No Climbing sign' (oops). The whole area was enveloped in mist, but follow the instructions she did, and sure enough it was still sat there - waiting. The photographs survived their unexpected bivouac but Sherri missed her Sunday dinner.

Colin Binks on *Woodburn Wall* (E1 5b) - *page 276* - East Woodburn. Photo: Chris Craggs

Left margin (vertical tabs): Causey Quarry · Crag Lough · Peel Crag · Callerhues · Great Wanney · E. Woodburn · Sandy Crag · Ravensheugh · Simonside · Drake Stone · Corby's · Bowden Doors · Back Bowden · Kyloe In · Kyloe Out · Berryhill

Not Camping

Cottages, bed and breakfast, hotels, caravans and bunk-houses are all widely available in the area. More information can be found from the Tourist Information Offices.

Youth Hostels - There are YHAs in Wooler, Byrness (Otterburn), Keilder, Grindon and Once Brewed. Check - **www.yha.org.uk**

Cottages - The area is littered with cottages for hire and, if you are in a group, this can be a very cost-effective and pleasant way of staying in the area. A good way to start is putting "Northumberland Cottages" into Google. Good sites are **www.northumbria-cottages.co.uk**, **www.northumberlandcottages.com**, **northumbria.sykescottages.co.uk**

Getting Around

All the crags in this section are easily reached by car and the approach descriptions are written assuming you have access to a car. If you are trying to get to the crags by public transport here is a list of contacts which may help, though bear in mind Northumberland is extensive and thinly populated, plus the cliffs are a long way apart.

Buses - The Tourist Information Centres are the preferred method of obtaining timetables and local knowledge, but the website **www.showbus.co.uk/timetables** lists the various operators in the area, and where to obtain timetable information.

Trains - Two railway lines skirt the edge of the area; the main coastal route north from Newcastle (stopping at Berwick) and the cross-country line stopping at Hexham. For timetable information go to **www.nationalrail.co.uk**

Climbing Shops

Track 'n' Terrain - Elvet Bridge, Durham City. *See advert on page 11.*
Tel: 0191 3843758   **www.tracknterrain.com**

Tiso Newcastle - 100-104 Grainger Street, Newcastle, NE1 5JQ.
Tel: 0191 222 0020   **www.tiso.com/uk_shops/newcastle/**

LD Mountain Centre - 34 Dean St., Newcastle, NE5 1PJ.
Tel: 0191 232 3561   **www.ldmountaincentre.com**

Food and Drink

There are many excellent pubs and cafes in the areas covered by this book. Wentworth Cafe in Hexham car park is a 'greasy spoon' which sells cheap mugs of tea and the best bacon butties ever.

The following is a small selection of the favourite après-climb pubs contributed by readers of UKClimbing: **The Salmon** and **The Bluebell** in Belford, **The Gate** in Forestburn and **The Star** in Harbottle. More pubs listed at - **www.pub-explorer.com**

Climbing Walls

The Newcastle Climbing Centre (opposite) - New wall (2008) in an old church.
St. Marks Church, 285 Sheilds Road, Byker, Newcastle, N6 2UQ.   Tel 0191 2656060

Berghaus Wall - An interesting and popular bouldering wall.
Eldon Leisure, Eldon Square, Newcastle, NE1 7XY.   0191 2771277

Sunderland Wall (opposite) - 23m high lead/top-rope wall plus a bouldering area.
Doxford Works, Sunderland, SR4 6TQ.   Tel: 0191 5144234   **www.sunderlandwall.co.uk**

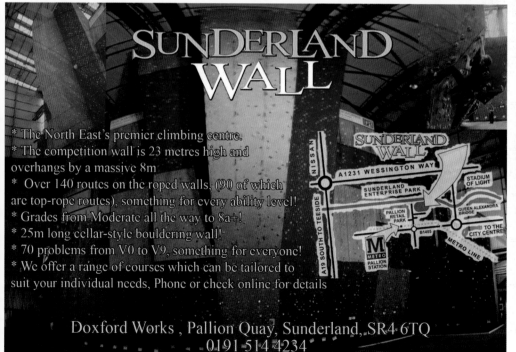

Crag	Routes	up to Sev	HS to HVS	E1 to E3	E4 and up
Causey Quarry	24	4 ✓	13 ✓✓	4 ✓	3 ✓
Crag Lough	41	17 ✓✓✓	19 ✓✓✓	3 ✓	2 ✓
Peel Crag	25	8 ✓✓	7 ✓✓	9 ✓✓	1 ✗
Callerhues	48	1 ✗	9 ✓✓	22 ✓✓	16 ✓✓
Great Wanney	45	14 ✓✓	12 ✓✓	9 ✓✓	10 ✓✓
East Woodburn	21	6 ✓	5 ✓	10 ✓✓	- ✗
Sandy Crag	19	- ✗	8 ✓✓	3 ✓	8 ✓✓
Ravensheugh	83	12 ✓✓	22 ✓✓✓	25 ✓✓✓	24 ✓✓✓
Simonside	63	19 ✓✓✓	24 ✓✓✓	12 ✓✓	5 ✓
The Drake Stone	14	3 ✓	6 ✓	3 ✓	2 ✓
Corby's	43	9 ✓	21 ✓✓	11 ✓✓	2 ✗
Bowden Doors	97	8 ✓	32 ✓✓✓	33 ✓✓✓	11 ✓✓✓
Back Bowden	53	3 ✓	3 ✓	23 ✓✓✓	24 ✓✓✓
Kyloe in the Woods	70	12 ✓	22 ✓✓✓	25 ✓✓✓	11 ✓✓
Kyloe out the Woods	59	15 ✓✓	27 ✓✓✓	10 ✓✓	7 ✓
Berryhill	26	10 ✓	10 ✓✓	3 ✗	3 ✗

Quality and range of routes in different grade bands: ✓✓✓ - Excellent ✓✓ - Good ✓ - Okay ✗ - Not worth a visit

Approach	Sun	Dry	Green	Shelter	Windy	Summary	Page	
3 min	Not much sun	Dry in the rain		Sheltered		An old quarry in a deep wooded gorge. The place is much used by the locals as a quick-hit venue and is worth one visit if you are passing. Very sheltered and dry in light rain.	246	Causey Quarry
20 min	Evening				Windy	An extensive and tall north-facing crag composed of dolorite. It has a good selection of lower grade routes though it is never popular. Treacherous in the wet.	250	Crag Lough
10 min	Evening				Windy	Crag Lough's smaller sibling, more accessible, sunnier and (a little) more popular, especially the right-hand end of the cliff - Sunset Buttress.	257	Peel Crag
40 min	Lots of sun				Windy	A small remote crag, of excellent rock, in a sunny setting. The crag is a fair walk from the road and has long had esoteric grades - but not any longer!	262	Callerhues
20 min	Evening		Green		Windy	A tall north-facing sandstone wall looking out over a dark forest. Great Wanney has one of the longest histories in Northumberland. Great in hot weather with many excellent routes.	268	Great Wanney
5 min	Lots of sun					Only a small selection of routes but worth calling in for if you are passing. Short and sunny.	274	E. Woodburn
50 min	Afternoon		Green		Windy	A compact crag, but remote of access and often not in prime condition. Only a small selection of routes, but what a selection.	278	Sandy Crag
50 min	Afternoon		Green		Windy	Possibly the finest crag in the County. A bit of a haul and only gets the afternoon sun but, under the right conditions, a great day is assured. Home to a prime selection of jamming cracks.	284	Ravensheugh
30 min	Afternoon				Windy	A classy crag in a lovely situation, with an excellent selection of routes, many in the lower and mid grades. Exposed so can be windy and, despite a northerly aspect, it is quick drying.	294	Simonside
10 min	Sun and shade					"The biggest boulder in Northumberland" or so the story goes. A small selection of climbs across the grades. Generally not well protected.	302	Drake Stone
2 min	Evening			Sheltered		A fine set of routes but the roadside setting has led to some problems with erosion. Please respect the place.	304	Corby's
2 -5 min	From mid morning				Windy	Northumberland's most famous crag; extensive, a fine outlook, afternoon sun and a great set of climbs across the grade spectrum. It can be busy - no surprises there then.	312	Bowden Doors
5 min	From mid morning			Sheltered		The shy and secluded other Bowden. The undercut nature of the cliff means it is popular with boulderers. There are plenty of high quality routes here too but mostly hard ones.	324	Back Bowden
15 min	Sun and shade	Dry in the rain	Green	Sheltered		A magical (an overused but wholly appropriate epithet) crag, popular with boulderers, hence the unsightly chalk that never washes off. Needle-infested top-outs add to the spice.	332	Kyloe In
10 min	Afternoon			Sheltered		Despite the name, the crag is being overtaken by the encroaching woodwork. Lovely climbs in a sunny setting, with many classics to go at. Some erosion problems on the easier routes.	340	Kyloe Out
10 min	Lots of sun					A small and rather soft crag, in a secluded setting. Not many routes, though the best are really rather good. Permission from land owner required to climb there.	348	Berryhill

Causey Quarry
Crag Lough
Peel Crag
Caletheses
Great Wanney
E. Woodburn
Sandy Crag
Ravensheugh
Simonside
Drake Stone
Corby's
Bowden Doors
Back Bowden
Kyloe In
Kyloe Out
Berry Hill

	No star	☆	☆☆	☆☆☆
Mod to S	2	2	-	-
HS to HVS	7	4	1	1
E1 to E3	1	2	1	-
E4 and up	1	2	-	-

Not one of the North East's prime venues, but the cliff's accessibility, largely ever-dry nature and general steepness means it is worth at least one visit if you are passing by, if only to tick the classics. Even in poor weather the *Low Level Girdle* is a good bet for a heart-warming work-out and it is only a three minute downhill walk from the car.

Limited first ascent information is available. The crag was first developed by Nev Hannaby, Albert Rosher, Eric Rayson and Geoff Oliver in the 1960s.

Conditions

The crag is tucked away in a deep gorge, it faces north west and doesn't get much sun because of its aspect, recessed position and the tree cover. The trees overhang the crag and can keep light rain off in the summer when the canopy is dense. The unstable slopes above the cliff and generally soft rock mean that this is an unsuitable venue for abseiling.

Sign, Causey Gorge

Approach

The quarry is hidden in a deep valley between Sunniside and Stanley (County Durham) to the south west of Newcastle. From Sunniside, follow the A6076 towards South Stanley until a large white pub (The Causey Arch) is reached on the left. Turn right, over the railway into the Causey Park Picnic Area and park here. Head out of the southern end of the car park and follow signs towards the Causey Arch and the gorge, branching right to drop into the gorge then turn left to reach the crag in less than 5 minutes from the car.

There is limited parking in the valley bottom, even nearer to the cliff, although the amount of debris around the area suggests it is best to park back up the hill in the main car park.

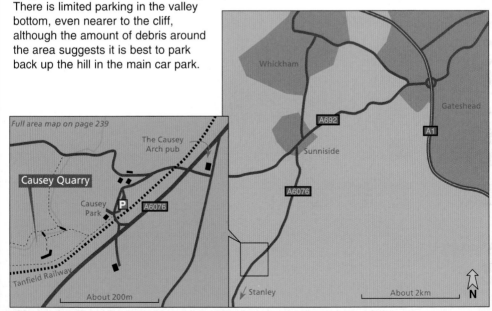

The Main Wall

The section of cliff that faces the approach path is the show-piece with some superb steep and pumpy routes. Some of the exits are a bit grotty, although there are several conveniently placed trees. The central part of the face is steep enough to stay dry during light rain.

1 Quarry Wall . . . . VS 4c
14m. Follow the wide crack through bulges to a ledge on the left. Continue up a pocketed crack then step right for a steep finish through the juggy bulges.

2 Overhanging Wall . . . . HVS 5b
14m. Some good climbing although unfortunately the hard moves are avoidable by stepping right into the chimney.

3 Crack and Chimney . . . . S 4b
14m. A good line up the disjointed chimney system that bounds the left edge of the Main Wall.

4 The Mauler E3 5b
16m. Climb a rib to ledges then hand traverse right (hand over the bulge) before trending left up the wall (bold) to a position below the big roof. Step out right and trend left to finish. Often dirty after rain.

5 Mauler Roof E5 6b
16m. From under the roof, shuffle left then surmount it directly.
FA. George Hayden 1980s

6 Mangler . . . . HVS 5a
18m. The beckoning crack-line gives a great route; pumpy but with good gear, and well worth calling in for. *Photo page 247.*

7 Perplexity E6 6c
18m. A thin crack leads to the overhang, cross the centre of this on small holds and make hard moves to reach flat holds on the left. Head up the centre of the wall which eases gradually.
FA. Paul Linfoot 1980s

8 Dangler E3 5c
18m. A line of old peg pockets lead to the overhang; cross this rapidly leftwards using the nose to a rest, then head back right until a line of better holds can be followed leftward to the top. A direct version is a little harder.

9 Strangler E4 6b
18m. A right-hand start to *Dangler*. Tackle the wall and roof direct to reach its easier upper section.

10 Hangover E1 5b
16m. Climb the wall and crack to the stacked overhangs and pull strenuously through these to reach easy (and broken) ground.

The next few routes offer some half-decent climbing though the rubble slope above adds little to the experience. A rope fixed from the trees above to the edge of the cliff might help. Lengths are given to the top of the solid climbing.

11 Letterbox Wall E1 5b
10m. A short jagged flake leads to a smooth section of rock passed using the useful letter-box. Above this things soon turn a bit grotty.

12 Route 2.5 . . . . HVS 5a
8m. The groove and overhang lead to the choss-field above.

13 The Arete . . . . HS 4b
8m. Start with a mantelshelf, then head up the arete. Bold.

The Right-hand Area

The right-hand end of the face is based around a couple of tall open corners. Some of the routes here - especially those to the left - have horrible exits, though the best of the rest are worth doing.

⑭ Wall Route Three . . . . [ ] **S 4b**
10m. Climb the crack to the right of the arete to a standing position on a big flake. Step left to access the grotty slopes.

⑮ Hanging Crack . . . . [ ] **VS 4b**
14m. Head up the long groove until blocked by an overhang. Exit rightwards up a crack. A **Direct Finish** is **VS 4c**.

⑯ Causey Crack . . . . 🔄 [ ] **VS 4c**
14m. An excellent route up the crack in the wall right of the groove. Climb the crack with a deviation to a ledge on the right. Continue past a niche and up the crack above.

⑰ A Means to an End . . . . [ ] **VS 4c**
14m. Gain the ledge above the overhang then continue up the arete to the top.

⑱ Diagonal Direct . . . . 🔄 [ ] **HS 4b**
12m. Climb the crack and wall rightwards to the ledges of *Diagonal*. Climb onto the big flake from the left (or direct if you are feeling lucky) and finish up the wall.

⑲ Diagonal . . . . 🌦 [ ] **Diff**
16m. From the top of the slope, follow ledges up and left past the arete to a finish above *Causey Crack*. Easy but scary.

⑳ Telstar Crack . . . . 🔄🖊 [ ] **VS 4c**
12m. Follow the crack-line just to the left of the corner.

㉑ Telstar Corner . . . . 🔄 [ ] **S 4a**
12m. Head up the main groove to the a position below the roof, then hand traverse out left to join *Telstar Crack*.
The **Direct Finish** requires a bit of butch undercutting - **VS 4b**.

㉒ Right-hand Wall . . . . [ ] **VS 5a**
12m. Climb *Telstar Corner* to a small flat-topped block on the right and traverse past this to a ledge. Pull up left to another ledge then finish through the overhang on large holds. A rightwards escape below the final roof is **4c**.

㉓ Right-hand Wall Direct . 🔄🖊 [ ] **HVS 5b**
14m. To the right of the corner, climb to a niche then through the overhang above to join and finish as for *Right-hand Wall*.

㉔ The Low-level Girdle . . . . . 🖊 [ ] **V1 (5b)**
80m. The traverse along the base of the wall gives a good pump and is almost always dry.

	No star	✪	✪✪	✪✪✪
Mod to S	5	5	5	2
HS to HVS	-	8	7	4
E1 to E3	-	3	-	-
E4 and up	1	-	-	1

An austere crag with a long climbing history - the most impressive cliff in Northumberland some would argue. The well-preserved remains of the Roman Wall and the superb views northwards add to the ambience of the place. There is a lot of good climbing here, much of it in the lower grades, often up strong natural lines.

But ... (there is always a 'but') the crag is north-facing and set at a height of 500m; conditions can often best be described as a little 'fresh'.

The rock is a layer of fine grained dolorite (basalt) that was injected between older rocks 295 million years ago, and underlies much of northern England. On cooling, the rock formed pillars that give the crag its characteristic blocky structure. This means that there can be large loose areas of rock and the fine grained texture leads to it being impossibly slippery if conditions are at all wet. The cliff is called Highshield Crag on some maps.

Conditions

Cool on hot days, freezing on cold ones, and best avoided if at all damp. A great place to escape the heat on hot summer days.

Approach

There is a Pay and Display (National Trust) car park at Steel Rigg, just north of the B6318 and Once Brewed Youth Hostel. A path leads out of the south east corner of the car park and follows the Roman Wall down into the dip then branches left in front of Peel Crag. The path continues indistinctly parallel to the escarpment, to reach Crag Lough in about 20 minutes from the parking. If the ground underfoot is at all damp then it is better to approach over the top, along the main path beside the Roman Wall.

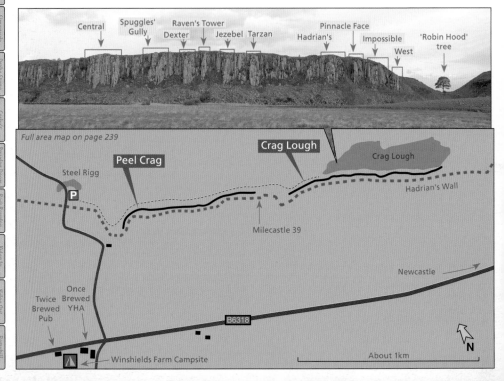

Full area map on page 239

Central Buttress

The most extensive buttress on the cliff and just about the furthest decent piece of rock from the car park. The NMC Northumberland Climbing Guide (2004) lists over 25 routes; here are ten of the best as a sampler.
Access - The crag often has birds nesting on it in the spring - check the BMC RAD for the current situation.

1 Stephenson's Rocket . . . E4 5c
22m. A fine climb up the hanging pillar up and right of the tree. Climb the rib then the groove to the roof and pull leftwards into the hanging groove. Up this to its top then continue up the thin crack on the right, above which things ease.
FA. Bob Smith 1980

2 Main Wall Route Two HVS 5a
30m. Start left of the toe of the buttress and climb a groove and overhang to access the face. Up this - technical and sustained - to a good ledge. Finish via the steep cracks up and right. An alternative (and original) finish is to move out left and mantel the rib.

3 Main Wall . . . . 50 HS 4b
34m. A great classic. It can be done in two pitches. From the toe of the buttress, trend up and right to the rib and climb this past awkward moves to reach the base of the wider upper crack system. Climb this - tricky at the overhang - and finish up a short wall at the back of the final ledge.
FA. Marcus Beresford Heywood early 1900s

4 Great Chimney . . . . HS 4b
26m. The long groove in the back left-hand corner of the bay leads, with sustained interest, to a huge rock blocking the way. Good holds and a swift mantel lead to easier ground.
FA. Marcus Beresford Heywood early 1900s

5 Impossible Wall . . . E4 6b
26m. The big smooth wall was originally an aid route and now gives a fine free climb. There is a hard move early on but interest is well maintained. Difficult climbing leads to a thin crack at the top of which is a small resting ledge. Continue up a black groove then a second one on the left which is climbed until the face on the right can be crossed to reach the arete and then easier ground.
FFA. Jeff Lamb early 1970s

To the right of the smoothness of Impossible Wall are three tall pillars bounded by four steep grooves - these are the Organ Pipes. There are some interesting routes here, following strong lines, but like a lot of the cliff, they could do with more traffic.

6 Left Organ Pipe . . . . . . HVS 5a
24m. The left-hand groove gives a fine sustained pitch with an awkward chimney, some good jamming to reach a big flake and a finish up the grooves just to the right. The central section of the routes is a bit vegetated at present.
FA. Tony Moulam c1945

The other two Organ Pipe grooves have good lines but sadly the Central Organ Pipe, HS is wide and awkward and the Right Organ Pipe, HS is vegetated.

7 Neglect . . . . HVS 5a
24m. A bit green, but has some good climbing, a bit like the whole crag really. Head up the wall to the right of *Right Organ Pipe* and bridge the shallow groove to reach a high roof. Pull over this to easier ground.
FA. Nev Hannaby 1960s

Deep Chimney
descent route (Mod)
Care required

🔵 Grad's Groove . . . . 🔳🔳🔳 VS 4b
22m. The front of the buttress is split by a steep groove, climb this to a ledge then continue up the easier chimney above.
FA. Brian Cooke c1945

🟡 Crystal . . . . 🔳🔳 HVS 5a
22m. A little devious but with excellent, varied and exposed climbing. Head up the awkward left-leaning groove, then move left and climb *Grad's Groove* until holds lead out right. Climb the crack and continuation flake to a small ledge, then move delicately right into *Y Climb* to finish. The **Direct Version** is a good **HVS 5b.**

🔟 Y Climb . . . . 🔳🔳🔳 HVS 5a
14m. ... why not? The diverging cracks in the west wall are worth doing. Gain the single lower crack from the right by a swing on a dubious flake then jam the gradually-easing cracks above.
FA. Albert Rosher 1950s

Dexter Buttress and Raven's Tower

🔴 Spuggies' Gully . . . . 🔳🔳 VDiff
20m. The cleft in the crest of the buttress leads with interest to a choice of chimneys leading to a ledge with huge blocks and a tree belay. Scramble off.

🔵 Back Alley . . . . 🔳🔳 Diff
20m. Start up the slope on the right, climb a short crack, then traverse left into the long chimney. Follow this until a squeezy escape through leftwards is possible. Finish easily.

🔵 Block Chimney . . . . 🔳🔳 Diff
17m. On the left is a chimney with the expected item. Climb to and under it then move out right and climb the giant's staircase.
FA. Andy Frazier 1950s

Dexter Buttress and Raven's Tower
A trio of interesting and clean buttresses with a good spread of grades, an excellent area for a first encounter with Crag Lough.

🔵 Chariot Race . . . . 🔳🔳🔳 E3 5c
17m. Gallop up the front face of the tower, starting up a groove just right of the chimney and climbing out right to the arete, then back left to access the upper groove.
FA. Jeff Lamb late 1970s

🔵 Why Not Direct . . . . 🔳🔳🔳 HVS 5b
22m. The long smooth-looking groove gives a fine pitch with some hard climbing in the lower section of the groove.

🔵 Why Not . . . . 🔳🔳 VS 5a
22m. Climb the corner to a ledge then continue in the same line until the top of the huge flake is reached. Move left and finish up the groove above.
FA. Albert Rosher mid 1950s

🔵 Dexterity . . . . 🔳🔳 S 4a
20m. Start up the corner as for the previous two routes, but follow the ledge out to the right-hand arete. Climb this, trending left to reach a large ledge, then finish up the exposed cracks in the right-hand side of the final wall.

🔵 Crescent Cracks . . . 🔳🔳🔳🔳 VS 5a
16m. Climb cracks and blocks to a niche then pull over the roof using the pair of curving cracks. Follow cracks to the top.
FA. Albert Rosher mid 1950s

🔵 Raven's Tower . . . . 🔳🔳 VS 4b
16m. Start as for *Crescent Cracks* to the niche, then move out right and climb the pleasant cracks in the right arete throughout.

Jezebel and Tarzan

These two narrow buttresses each has its own low-grade classic. The other routes are worth a look while you are here.

① Woodentops......... E1 5b
14m. The thin cracks splitting the smooth face up and left were an old aid route. Climb the cracks for a short distance then move right to the arete. Up this until tricky moves can be made back left to the upper section of the crack and a sprint finish.
FFA. Bob Smith 1981

② Jezebel .... Top 50 Diff
24m. An excellent beginners' route, interesting and devious. Follow the wide blocky crack to ledges then move right and climb cracks to the top of a huge block. Move left and climb the wall to enter a chimney, then meander up this.

③ Jezebel Direct .... VS 4b
22m. Climb the grooves and cracks straight up the right-hand side of the Jezebel Buttress, joining the original route up to the huge block, then step out right and head up another groove.

④ Sinister Corner......... S 4a
22m. Start up the clean groove on the right and climb this to ledges. Move out right across the wall to the sinister groove and continue up this almost to its top at which point an escape out left is possible.

⑤ Tarzan's Mate.......... S 4a
22m. An interesting trip up the left-hand side of the narrow buttress. Climb a short steep crack on the left (making the route **VDiff**) or, better, the steep groove in the front of the buttress. From the ledge continue up a series of grooves trending left until the easier rocks lead rightwards to the top.
FA. Marcus Beresford Heywood 1907

⑥ Tarzan .... Top 50 S 4a
26m. A devious little expedition twisting its way up the buttress. Start on the right in a bay and climb up to the right until it is possible to traverse left across the rift to reach the base of a narrow chimney. Up this to its top (hard work) at which point *Tarzan's Mate* is met. Finish up this.
FA. Marcus Beresford Heywood 1907

⑦ Evasion Groove ... HVS 5a
22m. Follow *Tarzan* to the foot of the narrow chimney (or start direct - more in keeping at **4c**) and climb up and right to a ledge at the foot of a deepening groove with a hanging tongue of rock. Climb the groove with escalating difficulties, bridging past 'the tongue' to reach easy ground.

Appian Way · – ~
Descent Route

Change in viewing angle

Evening   20 min   Windy

Causey Quarry | Crag Lough | Peel Crag | Callerhues | Great Wanney | E. Woodburn | Sandy Crag | Ravensheugh | Simonside | Drake Stone | Corby's | Bowden Doors | Back Bowden | Kyloe In | Kyloe Out | Berryhill

❶ Ash Tree Wall . . . . 🔦 [____] **S 4a**
14m. The series of cracks running straight up to the prominent tree give a good pitch but could do with a bit more traffic to keep the greenery at bay.

❷ Hadrian's East . . . . 🔦 👤 [____] **VDiff**
18m. The blocky wall three metres left of the chimney leads to a hanging rift at half-height. Finish awkwardly up this, ignoring the grass ledges.

❸ Hadrian's Chimney . . . . 👤 [____] **S 4b**
18m. The cleft splitting the front of the buttress has considerable difficulties accessing the hanging upper section. Originally called *Bloody Crack* with good reason.
FA. Marcus Beresford Heywood 1907

❹ Hadrian's Rib . . . . 🔦 👤 [____] **VS 4c**
18m. The blocky rib to the right of the chimney gives an interesting pitch. It is reachy and a bit escapable, but worth doing all the same.

Hadrian's Buttress
The first buttress left of the Pinnacle and the descent gully of Appian Way is the broad bulk of Hadrian's Buttress. It has the classy Hard Severe of the same name (possibly the most popular route on the crag) and a few other outings of interest.

❺ Hadrian's Buttress . . . . 🔦 ◀ [____] **HS 4b**
18m. A great climb in a sunnier setting than most around here and one of the most popular outings on the cliff. A recent rockfall has changed the route a little but it is still well worth doing. Start on the right and climb the left-hand of a pair of clean cracks until a resting ledge on the left can be reached. Step back right and climb the continuation crack then progress by a couple of classical mantelshelf moves. Finish easily. *Photo on page 251.*

❻ Hadrian's Recess . . . . . 🔦 👤 [____] **S 4a**
16m. The right-hand crack splits at eight metres and leads to a good rest. The wider continuation leads awkwardly to the top.

Pinnacle Face to West Buttress

The quartet of buttresses and faces nearest the car park are the most popular venues on the cliff - especially with the top-roping brigade. There are some good climbs hereabouts with *Pinnacle Face* being especially notable; it is amongst the best VS climbs on the cliff.

1 Pinnacle Face . . . . **VS 4c**
14m. One of the classics of the crag with spectacular and photogenic positions. Start on the left (or by climbing over the pinnacle) and tackle the roof at the top of the initial groove - direct is thuggy, on the right is technical. The exposed face above gives a superb finish.

2 Bracket . . . . **VDiff**
16m. The crack system just round the arete from *Pinnacle Face* is climbed starting up a polished ramp. Another good climb with a choice of finishes.

3 Impossible Slab **E3 5c**
18m. A direct line up the smooth left-hand flank of the face. Climb to the flake then continue linking thin cracks by hard sustained climbing. A slab? I don't really think so.

4 Route Two . . . . **VDiff**
20m. The left flank of Impossible Buttress. Start up the right-hand groove in the nose and follow the ledge/flake leftwards round the corner and across to the chimney that bounds the buttress. Up this for a short distance until the left arete can be accessed. Finish up this in a great position.

5 Route One . . . . **HVS 5a**
18m. A great climb that unlocked the secrets of the Impossible Buttress. Start as for *Route Two* but follow the crack system directly up the front of the buttress to a rest on the right. A tricky high step up and left reaches better holds and the top. There are left and right-hand variations that avoid the hard moves, but are no easier. How strange is that?
FA. Tony Moulam mid 1940s

6 Route Three . . . . **VS 5a**
16m. On the far right-hand side of the buttress is a steep groove leading to a crack. Climb these to a rest on the right then access the groove left of some hanging blocks with difficulty. Once established, better holds lead back right to a steep finish.
FA. Albert Rosher mid 1950s

7 Face Route . . . . **S 4a**
15m. Trend right then follow the crack that runs up towards the jutting block of the monolith. From here, footholds trend left up the face, and where these run out head straight up the cracked face to easier ground and then the top.

8 Wall and Crack . . . . **Diff**
10m. Climb the chimney to half-height then move left and climb the face. The crack direct is harder.

9 West Corner . . . . **S 4a**
10m. The groove right of the arete to a ledge. Finish to the right.

10 West Chimney . . . . **Mod**
8m. The juggy rift is the last, or first, route on the cliff.

	No star	☆	☆☆	☆☆☆
Mod to S	3	3	1	1
HS to HVS	-	5	1	1
E1 to E3	-	7	1	1
E4 and up	-	-	1	-

The western extension of Crag Lough has a similar ambience, though in general the cliff is less impressive, more vegetated and even less popular than its big brother. On the plus side, it is only a short walk from the car park and Sunset Buttress (nearest to the parking) gets the sun from shortly after midday until it sets. Again, the altitude and aspect mean that the cliff is best saved for use as a high summer venue. Loose blocks do occur and the rock is fine grained and so can be a nightmare if conditions are at all damp. The best routes here stay clean but many of the less popular outings are being reclaimed by nature.

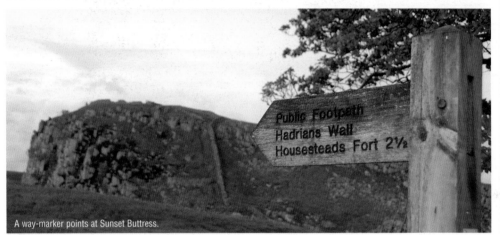

A way-marker points at Sunset Buttress.

Conditions
Cool on hot days, freezing on cold ones, and best avoided if at all damp. A great place to escape the heat on hot summer days. Sunset Buttress often makes a good afternoon venue.

Approach   See map on page 250
There is a Pay and Display (National Trust) car park at Steel Rigg, just north of the B6318 and Twice Brewed Youth Hostel. A path leads out of the south east corner of the car park; follow the Roman Wall down into the dip then branch left in front of the crag to arrive at Sunset Buttress in about five minutes from the car.

Peel Crag catching the evening sun, seen from the path by the car park.

To the left of the first buttress described here are another forty or so routes with some good climbs amongst them, though they are rather scattered in the wilderness. A copy of the NMC Northumberland Guide will reveal all.

Tiger Wall and Central Wall

This wall has a selection of the best Extremes on the crag. Generally they are clean and on good rock. The area of rock tackled by *Rock Island Line* and its near neighbours is especially worth a visit.

❶ Kamikaze Sex Pilot .   **E2 5c**
18m. The left-most piece of rock is a smooth wall, split in its upper part by a thin crack - this is the line. Originally a hard peg route, perhaps A5, so it was a lot harder to aid than to free.
FA. Callum Phillips early 1980s

❷ Tiger's Overhang . . . . .   **VS 4c**
18m. Climb the cracked wall to reach the arching overhang which is passed by bridging and stiff pulls on the substantial holds that lurk just above the roof. More crack climbing gains the top.
Photo on page 261.

❸ Tiger's Chimney . . . . . .   **VDiff**
20m. The steep left-facing groove leads to the hanging chimney to the right of the arching roof. Finish up this; don't look down.

❹ Grooves . . . .   **HS 4a**
22m. Worthwhile at the grade but tough. Start under a tall niche just left of the arete of the buttress. Climb cracks to and through the niche to reach a small ledge, then continue until a tricky move can be made rightwards into the base of a widening crack. Gird your loins and set about it to reach a substantial tree belay.
Photo on page 261.
FA. Albert Rosher 1950s

❺ The Intruder **E2 5c**
22m. Makes the best use of the left side of the wall. Head straight up into the odd hanging recess in the left-hand side of the roofs. Bridge through this and follow the thin cracks to the top, avoiding gravitating into *Rock Island Line.*
FA. Bob Smith 1979

❻ Rock Island Line **E1 5b**
22m. The best route on the crag. Climb the cracks that fall from the centre of the prominent steeped overhangs to a position in the hanging corner. Swing out left to bypass the roof and reach the hanging crack in the headwall. Finish up this with gusto.
FA. Probably Albert Rosher 1950s

❼ Parental Guidance .   **E2 5c**
22m. A weaving line up the centre of the buttress. Climb the face to a small overhang with a broken tip and move right around this into the groove of *Trilogy*. Exit left and climb into the hanging black groove with difficulty. Powerful moves up the groove, and over the roof, reach easier ground at last.

❽ Trilogy **E2 5b**
22m. A good line up the long groove that bounds the right-hand section of the smoothest part of the wall. Climb leftwards out of the mini-cave at the foot of the face, then follow the groove throughout by sustained and interesting climbing.

❾ Certificate X **E1 5a**
22m. Climb rightwards out of the mini-cave to access the arete and climb this, eventually trending left into the groove of *Trilogy*. A short way up this, a break leads right to twinned hair-line cracks which are followed with difficulty to better holds. Finish more easily up the groove.
FA. Albert Rosher 1950s

Jester

Blasphemy Wall

Cassey Quarry

Crag Lough

Peel Crag

Callerhues

Great Wanney

E. Woodburn

Sandy Crag

Ravensheugh

Simonside

Drake Stone

Corby's

Bowden Doors

Back Bowden

Kyloe In

Kyloe Out

Berryhill

10 Green Line . . . . 🔲🔲🔲 **E1 5b**
14m. From a block, climb the cracks - bold and hard to start - to reach easier climbing then the ledges. Scramble off.

11 Ritual . . . . . . 🔲🔲🔲🔲 **E4 6a**
20m. Climb the black groove to the inverted staircase, move right then pull through onto the wall. Climb the thin crack to a jug (old peg) where desperate moves up and right reach more holds. Finish straight up the crack.
FA. Bill Wayman 1980s

12 Ace of Spades . . . . 🔲🔲🔲 **HVS 5a**
20m. Climb easy ground to reach the crack splitting the upper wall. Step into it from the left then jam on.

13 Sacrifice . . . . 🔲🔲🔲 **E3 6a**
20m. The black groove on the right (an old aid climb - **Chocolate Diedre**) is followed to the overhang which is crossed on the left with difficulty. Easier crack climbing awaits the successful.

14 Jester . . . . 🔲🔲🔲 **VS 5a**
20m. Jocular fun starting up a green, right-facing groove capped by a jagged black overhang. Climb the groove then move right to pass the overhang by a swift layback. Continue up easier ground taking care to avoid the huge pile of stacked and jammed blocks just to the left.

Jester and Blasphemy Wall
The first walls beyond the Sunset Buttress area have some worthwhile climbs separated by scruffier terrain. All the listed routes are good but *Overhanging Crack* is the outstanding classic of the area.

15 Blasphemy Wall . . . . 🔲🔲 **HVS 5a**
22m. Climb the arete right of a 10m high pillar of stacked blocks until it is possible to traverse left to the top of the pillar. Step right and climb the wall until holds lead out to the arete for a nicely positioned finale.

16 Albert's Wall . . . . 🔲🔲 **E1 5a**
18m. An eliminate but with some good varied climbing taking a direct line up the left-hand side of the face. Any contact with *Overhanging Crack* is to be avoided to maintain the grade.
FA. Probably Albert Rosher 1950s

17 Overhanging Crack . 🔲🔲🔲🔲 **VS 4c**
18m. Classic. The fine crack in the right-hand side of the face is approached by interesting moves up the lower wall. The crack gives some good jamming and gradually eases with height.
FA. Albert Rosher 1950s

Sunset Buttress

The buttresses closest to the car park are the most popular in the area and not just because they see more sun than the rest of the cliff. In general the routes are pleasant, if a little unremarkable, though *Sunset* itself is well worth doing.

1 Ulysses . . . . VDiff
16m. The isolated buttress on the left gives a pleasant pitch. Start just right of the rowan and climb up to a groove where an awkward move out left gains the slabby front of the buttress. Finish up this.

2 Chockstone Chimney . . . Diff
24m. Climb the open groove into a grassy bay (some loose rock) then trend left to the base of the actual chimney, corked by the chockstone. Climb this to the top.

3 Sunset Direct . . . . HVS 5a
22m. The blocky arete left of *Sunset* gives a good, if rather artificial, pitch. Start up a shallow clean-cut groove and at its top move over left onto the crest to reach a ledge. Continue up the outer edge ignoring any potential escape routes, and the slightly dubious nature of the pillar you are climbing.

4 Sunset . . . . S 4a
24m. The classic of this part of the crag, with good climbing and a sunny aspect. Thought by some to be the best Severe between Hadrian's Wall and the border. From the lowest point of the buttress, follow the grooves up and right to a high ledge below the overhang. Gain the groove to the left of the overhang either directly, or via a short traverse from the right, and finish up this.
Photo on page 236.
FA. M.Heywood 1912

5 Twin Cracks . . . . VS 5a
20m. Start up the obviously-named feature(s) to reach a square rock-scar, pass this awkwardly to reach a breather in a niche to the right, then continue up the cracks above.

6 Jackdaw . . . . Diff
18m. The blocky crack forms an easier start to the next route and is only included because it is quite popular.

7 Layback Buttress . . . . VDiff
18m. A nice start up the curving layback crack leads to more mundane ramblings through the trees via a wide crack and the short arete above.

8 Route 1 . . . . VDiff
16m. The groove cutting up the first piece of rock passed is quite pleasant.

Ruby Robinson on the left on *Tiger's Overhang* (VS 4c) and another climber on *Grooves* (HS 4a) - *page 258* - at Peel Crag. Photo: Nick Smith

	No star	✦1✦	✦2✦	✦3✦
Mod to S	1	-	-	-
HS to HVS	1	6	1	1
E1 to E3	5	14	2	1
E4 and up	1	10	3	2

A small cliff, up to about 10m high, in a superbly wild setting - up on the moors to the north east of Bellingham. The dark grey sandstone has an excellent texture with plenty of creases, pockets and nodules for climbing but there are still blank sections making most of the routes technical and demanding, often with sloping top-outs.

The reputation for stiff grades and the long walk-in tend to make Callerhues less popular than many cliffs hereabouts.

Grades

The routes are largely the work of locals Bob and Tommy Smith who graded the routes back in the 1970s when the trend was to give short routes low adjectival grades. Since then, the national trend has tended to upgrade short hard routes and this has made the grades at Callerhues look extremely harsh. For some reason no guidebook has really bothered to re-assess the grades properly before now. In this book, to cries of "southern softies" from the locals, we have tried to give grades more in line with modern thinking. It is likely that we will not have got this correct for every route but hopefully the shock of starting up a VS which turns out to really be an E2 should be a thing of the past. Please let us know of any anomalies you find via the Rockfax Databases - **www.rockfax.com**.

Conditions

The crag faces south and catches all the sun that is going, it is also exposed to south westerlies so it can get a bit blowy up here at times. It is rapid drying though lack of traffic means that some of the routes can be a bit lichenous.

Approach

Callerhues Crag is approached from limited parking at Blakelaw Farm, which is reached by a private road that branches north off the Bellingham to West Woodburn road, a short distance north east of Bellingham. Permission to park amongst the farm buildings is normally freely given; ask at the building with the sign that announces "Never Mind the Dog, Beware of the Wife" on the gate; you will be told where to leave your car and of any potential access problems on the moor or at the crag. Follow the Pennine Way through the farm then up the hill towards the copse of Linn Plantation. The path bears right through a gate at which point the crag can clearly be seen.

The best approach is to stick with the Pennine Way for another ten minutes or so until just beyond a fenced enclosure

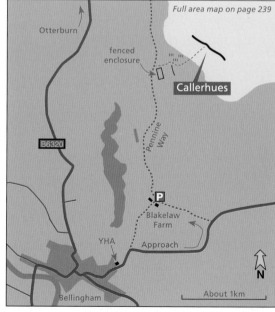

then follow vague tracks which soon fizzle out. The direct approach from here is a bit rough and damp; scrambling up onto the rocky outcrop on the right (Little Callerhues) offers a drier approach - about 30 to 40 minutes from the car.

Tom Gilbert on *Boulevard* (E3 6b) - *page 264* - a hard test-piece at this remote cliff. Photo: Jamie Moss

Descent · Detached Wall · Descent

Lots of sun | 40 min | Windy

1 · 2 · 3 · 4 · 5 · 6 · 7

Left-hand Buttresses

Some interesting routes on great rock, short in stature but not impact. The climbing tends to be fingery and technical, often allied to grasping rounded exits. Although many of these routes are short and have little or no gear, they are all a bit too high to be considered as actual boulder problems.

1 Arkle **E1 5a**
7m. The side wall of the recess. Bold and thin climbing.
FA. John Earl 1978

2 Side Walk . . . . **HVS 5a**
7m. Solo up the left arete of the wall. One technical move.
FA. Bob Smith 1978

3 Boulevard **E3 6b**
7m. A thin flake leads to the seam and a very thin section. **V5** above a mat. *Photo on page 263.*
FA. Steve Blake 1978

4 Curbside **E3 6a**
7m. Link the seams and the flake to reach a hard finishing move.

5 Footpath **E2 5c**
7m. The central line has a taxing mantelshelf to stand on the seam.
FA. Bob Smith 1978

6 Paving **E1 5b**
6m. Climb the wall to reach a short crack and a belly-flop finish.
FA. Bob Smith 1978

7 Quarrel Arete **E2 5c**
7m. Pass the roof to good holds then finish up the fingery rib.
FA. Bob Smith 1978

8 Tom's Peeping **E1 5b**
7m. Twin cracks lead to a desperate direct (**5c**) exit, or a **5b** version if you step right to the top of *Monocle*.
FA. Bob Smith 1978

9 Monocle **E2 5c**
7m. Gaining and standing on the seam are both tricky. Solo.
FA. Bob Smith 1978

10 Copper's Nark . . . . **HVS 5b**
7m. The crack also has a tricky top-out but some good gear.
FA. Bob Smith 1978

11 Crouching the Mahogany **E5 6b**
8m. The left side of the face has two desperate moves to connect a decent hold. A highball **V8** above mats.
FA. Bob Smith 1984

12 Weeping Fingers **E2 5c**
8m. The slim flaky groove is excellent and has runners. Save a bit for the technical last move.
FA. Bob Smith 1978

13 The Storyteller . . . **E5 6b**
8m. The centre of the face is hard. A (very) highball **V7**.
FA. Bob Smith 1978

14 Task Master . . . . **HVS 5b**
7m. Climb the shallow groove on some lovely holds. Exit right onto the slab at the top. The left-hand crack is a much harder exit.
FA. Bob Smith 1978

15 The Whip **E1 5b**
7m. Climb the wall to enter the open scoop.
FA. Bob Smith 1978

Descent · Descent

20m gap

7 · 8 · 9 · 10

11 · 12 · 13 · 14 · 15

Tom's Peeping

Task Master · Central Buttress - 40m

Central Buttress

The chunk of rock in the centre of the cliff has some outstanding climbs, although the left-hand side wall can be a bit dirty. Under its right-hand side the landing is especially soft. The routes are generally steep and strenuous, plus the majority have testing exits onto the bald top of the buttress.

❶ Dolcis Arete **E4 6a**
7m. The left arete to a hard finish.
FA. Tommy Smith 1978

❷ Rain Drops. **E2 5b**
8m. The shallow groove right of the arete, to a leftwards exit.
FA. Tommy Smith 1978

❸ Shadow Players . . . **E4 5c**
9m. The wall on small holds to a gripping and unprotected exit.
FA. John Boyle 1990

❹ Pot-Hole Wall. **E5 6a**
10m. Climb the flake to a ledge then move left and use the pot-hole to reach another harrowing exit.

❺ Shoe Horn . . . . **HVS 5a**
12m. Starting from the right, climb the shallow scoop to a hole. Continue up and right to finish.
FA. Bob Smith 1978

❻ Tossin' a Wobbler . . **E3 5c**
12m. Pull left out of *Callerhues Crack* and climb to and through the roof, then wobble up the fingery wall to a hasty exit.
FA. Bob Smith 1978

❼ Callerhues Crack . . . . . **HVS 5a**
12m. The classic HVS of the crag, and on this one the grade has always been about right. Follow the flakes rightwards strenuously, to finish via any combination of the twin cracks.
Photo on page 5.

❽ Twin Hats **E3 5c**
12m. The cracked arete leads to the ledge, head rightwards to the hanging crack which finishes too far short of the top.
FA. Bob Smith 1978

❾ Ned Kelly. **E3 5c**
12m. Head up the hanging groove then pull rightwards into the crack. Climb this until it fizzles out, then the problems begin - and it was all going so well.
FA. Bob Smith 1978

Second Born

The frighteningly steep right-hand side of Central Buttress.
Further right, past the chimney, is a tall and impressive wall.

1 **Second Born** E6 6c
12m. The leaning crack through the biggest of the bulges is about as impressive as they come, sustained and powerful, though at least with a soft landing.
FA. Bob Smith 1985

2 **Callerhues Chimney** . . . HVS 4c
12m. The classic rift on the right is often dirty.
FA. John Earl 1976

3 **Rice Krispies** E4 5c
12m. The left side of the wall, right of the chimney, starting up the thin crack which is less helpful than the wall to its right. Finish back left.
FA. Tommy Smith 1978

4 **Toshiba Receiver** . . E4 5c
10m. Hard climbing up the thin features on the right-hand side of the face.
FA. Allan Moist 1984

Tom, Dick and Harry

A series of walls, cracks and aretes with three short but imposing
(i.e. wide and steep) cracks towards the right-hand side.

5 **Cold Start** E3 6b
8m. Desperate moves reach the beckoning flake - occasionally.
FA. Bob Smith 1978

6 **Green Fluff.** E4 6b
10m. Wrestle with the bulging undercut arete then move left.
FA. Bob Smith 1978

7 **Dulalai T.A.P.** E5 6b
10m. From a ledge, get to the good pocket then swing right to the twin diagonal cracks. Sprint up these.
FA. Bob Smith 1984

8 **Sheer Temptation** . . E6 6b
10m. The steep attractive arete is started on the left and finished on the right, or maybe flat on your back.
FA. Bob Smith 1985

Descent

19 20 21 22 23 24 25

The Throughbred

Right-hand Buttresses

An interesting set of walls stretching away right until the crag fizzles out. There is quite a selection of butch cracks here and some more open stuff. The cliff finishes with the jutting snout of *The Thoroughbred* and its excellent collection of climbs - queuing not normally needed for these boys! If treated as boulder problems they should be considered 'highballs' so bring a mat or three.

9 The Mongrel E4 6a
10m. The side wall is climbed right to left, finishing up the arete.
FA. Bob Smith 1978

10 Flake Corner . . . . HS 4b
8m. The left corner of the recess is a worthwhile easier route.

11 Polo . . . . VDiff
8m. The wide right-hand rift, finishing either side of the block.

12 Micro E3 5c
9m. The slanting flake-crack leads rightwards, then tricky moves have to be made rightwards into the 'lift-shaft' to finish.
FA. Bob Smith 1978

13 Tom E1 5b
8m. The left-hand of the trio of tough cracks.

14 Dick . . . . HVS 5a
8m. The sinuous central crack.

15 Harry E1 5b
8m. The right-hand crack doesn't quite reach the ground.

16 Hanging Crack E2 5c
8m. The upper part of the wall is split by a hanging seam. Boulder up to reach the seam and climb it to a steady exit.
FA. Bob Smith 1970s

17 Chouca E4 6b
8m. The pocketed right-hand side of the wall.
FA. Bob Smith 1988

18 Bracken Crack E1 5b
8m. The crack with the bilberry bushes has a gruesome upper part.

The Thoroughbred

The final buttress has an imposing jutting snout - The Throughbred.

19 Cut and Dried E2 5b
10m. The pocketed left arete is approached by the rib and scoop.
FA. Bob Smith 1978

20 White Rock E2 5b
10m. Climb the easy rib then balance out right to the flake.

21 The Lurcher E3 5c
8m. Lurch up the leaning groove and exit to the right.
FA. Bob Smith 1978

The stepped shrubby slab to the right is **Country Downfall**, *Diff.*

22 The Hyena E2 5c
10m. A hanging crack reaches a hole then finger-holds lead rightwards to a steep and pushy finish.
FA. Bob Smith 1978

23 New Kids on the Rock . . E5 6b
10m. The double diagonal overlaps are climbed with difficulty to the finish of *The Hyena*.
FA. John Boyle 1990. Someone else gets a look in.

24 The Thoroughbred . . E5 6b
10m. Jump for finger-holds then move right and climb to the crack splitting the beak. Finish through this with difficulty.
FA. Tommy Smith 1978

25 Horse Play E4 6a
8m. The centre of the right-hand wall has a dyno for most, and a hard mantelshelf exit.
FA. Bob Smith 1979

Lots of sun 40 min Windy

	No star	⚑	⚑⚑	⚑⚑⚑
Mod to S	3	6	3	2
HS to HVS	3	7	-	2
E1 to E3	4	1	3	1
E4 and up	-	4	3	3

A fine crag with many excellent climbs across the grade range, including a great set of hard classics and some high quality easier routes. Great Wanney has been climbed on for over a hundred years and it remains a popular venue when the conditions are right.

Conditions
The crag is set on a high moor and faces north. It is usually a summer venue as it can be cold and is often green and lichenous after rain. The crag gets the evening sun and makes a good evening or hot weather destination.

Approach
There are two approaches. Either park by the eastern end of Sweethope Lough and follow the footpath (often wet) up the moor to the crest of the ridge, then drop over and descend to the foot of the cliff (30 mins). Or park on the minor road to the north of the cliff (1.8 miles west of the junction) where a major track heads into the forest. Follow this, avoiding any branch tracks, until the path pops out of the trees right in front of the crag (20 mins).

Full area map on page 239

East Buttress

The eastern end of the main edge consists of a fine trio of buttresses; a slabby right-hand one a tall smooth central one and a left-hand one capped by a huge roof. Some of the best routes on the crag are located here and the upper grades are especially well represented.

① Eastern Traverse. . . . . . . 🔲 🔲   **HS 4b**
12m. Start in the gully on the left and reach the break that runs under the roof awkwardly. Follow it (exposed) round into *Great Chimney* to finish.

② East Buttress Direct. 🔲 🔲 🔲   **E3 5c**
14m. Follow the shallow pocketed groove out to the arete and balance up this to the break and runners. The short roof-crack on the left gives a safe tussle to a heathery finish.
FA. Bob Hutchinson 1970s

③ Thunder Thighs . . . 🔲 🔲 🔲   **E5 6b**
14m. The centre of the wall is bold and hard, a dynamic approach may be needed. Fortunately, the imposing roof-crack has holds and runners.
FA. Bob Smith 1980

④ Idiot Wind . . . . 🔲 🔲   **E4 5c**
14m. Bold and high in the grade. Climb the unprotected arete with trepidation to the break. Move left to jugs on the edge of the roof and pull onto the final wall strenuously. Finish more easily.
FA. Bob Hutchinson 1976

⑤ Great Chimney . . . . 🔲 🔲   **VDiff**
14m. The tall rift just left of the fence is a long standing classic. Sustained and a little awkward, but well protected.
FA. Geoffry Winthrop Young 1902

⑥ Obverse Direct . . . . . . 🔲 🔲   **HS 4c**
14m. The steep crack right of the chimney leads to a rest. Climb the slab rightwards and exit using the protruding block.

⑦ Absent Friend. . . . . 🔲 🔲   **E5 6b**
15m. Superb climbing up the left edge of the buttress. Climb the old peg pockets then follow the crack and holes and the continuation crack to the overhang, before pulling out leftwards onto the side wall with difficulty. Finish rightwards up this.
FA. Bob Smith 1981

⑧ Crisis Zone . . . . . . 🔲 🔲 🔲   **E7 6c**
15m. The direct finish to *Absent Friend* is awesome. From the base of the crack, break right onto the leaning headwall and climb this (ancient bolt) directly.
FA. Hugh Harris 1991

⑨ Endless Flight . . . . 🔲 🔲   **E5 6a**
16m. Start up *Absent Friend* (originally an easier start from the right was used) but traverse the upper break to the arete (thread). Climb it on the left then on the right to a break, runners and then easier climbing. The brilliant **Direct Start - E8 7a** follows shelving rock then pinch-grips the arete to reach the thread on the original.
FA. Bob Hutchinson 1978. FA. (Direct Start) Andrew Earl 2004

The side wall is climbed directly by **Policy of Truth,** *E6 6c starting from the centre of the higher horizontal break.*

⑩ Boundary Corner. . . . . . . 🔲 🔲   **VDiff**
15m. The long groove is a popular outing. Pass the big jammed block awkwardly then finish through the bowels of the cliff for the easiest exit.
FA. Geoffry Winthrop Young 1902

Great Wall

This fine smooth wall is home to a great HVS, *Great Wall*, and the superb HS of *Idiot's Delight*. There are other worthwhile offerings too. The buttress is above the point where the northern approach track arrives at the crag.

⑪ Hawk Slab . . . . **HVS 5a**
12m. Climb the slabby arete past a grassy ledge to a finish on the right of the final steeper section.

⑫ Dove's Nest Crack . . . . **HVS 5a**
12m. The narrowing leaning chimney gives a character-building battle to pass the steepest section.

⑬ Patchett's Plunge **E3 5b**
12m. The rib gives a good pitch that is poorly protected unless some lateral deviousness is employed - in which case it isn't worth the E3 tag.
FA. Hugh Banner 1970s. Jim Patchett had plunged on an earlier attempt.

⑭ Idiot's Delight . . . . **HS 4c**
14m. A great climb up a fine line. Follow the slabby right-trending groove to a rest in a cave (complete with seasonal bird's nest). Traverse out left to reach the easier upper section of *Patchett's Plunge* and finish up this in a fine position.
FA. Hugh Banner 1960s

⑮ Loony's Lament . . . . **HVS 5b**
14m. A reasonable climb up a decent line but often overlooked. The groove can be a bit ferny if there has been no recent traffic. Climb onto a ramp and follow it leftwards into the steeper groove. Up this to the bird-nest cave on *Idiot's Delight* then finish up the steep crack that rises from this to a grassy exit.

⑯ Great Wall . . . . **HVS 5b**
14m. A great climb linking a series of features up the right-hand edge of the smoothest rock - a true Northumbrian classic. Climb the groove in the right-hand edge of the face then move right to access a thin crack. Up this until forced out right to a ledge hidden just around the arete. Finish up the overhanging groove.
Photo on page 269.
FA. Hugh Banner 1971. The story goes that Banner had done every route on Cloggy except for ....

⑰ Great Wall Direct Finish
. . . . **E5 6a**
14m. From where *Great Wall* moves right continue up the mini-ramp running left across the wall, finishing with a long reach from indifferent holds, miles above the gear - exciting stuff.
FA. John Syrett 1979

⑱ Fox's Hole . . . . **Diff**
20m. Link two corners with some quality grass rambling.
FA. Geoffry Winthrop Young 1902

⑲ Karabiner Crack . . . . **VS 5a**
6m. The short groove at the left end of the ledge is quite taxing.

⑳ Spare Rib **E4 6a**
6m. The blunt rib is technical and bold.

㉑ Bilberry Wall . . . . **VS 4c**
8m. Climb the shallow groove and thin crack until a short traverse out left can be made to a finish close to the arete.

Central Gully

Causey Quarry
Crag Lough
Peel Crag
Callerhues
Great Wanney
E. Woodburn
Sandy Crag
Ravensheugh
Simonside
Drake Stone
Corby's
Bowden Doors
Back Bowden
Kyloe In
Kyloe Out
Berryhill

Central Gully and Main Wall

A deep-cut rift bites into the cliff with good hard climbs on the walls and some easier stuff in the depths. The routes are sheltered but also inclined to be green. Main Wall is the clean west-facing sheet of rock round to the right.

4 Central Gully East . . . . ☐ **Diff**
14m. The left-hand corner-crack in the back of the gully is accessed using the convenient tall flake. Continue up the groove.
FA. Geoffry Winthrop Young 1902

5 Central Gully West . . . . ☐ **S 4a**
14m. The right-hand version is steeper and more awkward.

6 Northumberland Wall . . Top 50 ☐ **E2 5c**
14m. A great climb up the groove and crack cleaving the right wall of the gloomy recess - honest hard work and well protected throughout. Climb the leaning groove then continue up the con-creted crack above until it fizzles out. Finger traverse right then pull for the top. A **Direct Finish** is only a little harder.
FA. Bob Hutchinson 1976

7 Osiris . . . . ☐ **E3 5c**
14m. Gain the crack above the roof and follow it up onto the arete. Swap sides then finish up the bold arete.
FA. John Earl 1980

8 Pharaoh's Face. . . . . ☐ **E3 5c**
16m. Climb a short crack then continue past the overhang to reach a shrubby ledge. Move left onto the exposed arete to finish.
FA. Hugh Banner 1970s. With a hanging stance and graded VS!

9 Main Wall . . . . ☐ **S 4a**
16m. Worthwhile, with pleasant open climbing, protection is a bit lacking. Start on the right and follow holds up and left to ledges. Move back right and finish up passing a useful flake.

10 Lichen Chimney . . . . ☐ **Mod**
14m. The long groove that bounds the wall on the right.

1 Nose Chimney . . . . ☐ **VDiff**
14m. Traverse into the hanging chimney from the left (or struggle direct - **S 4b**) then continue to a grassy ledge. The upper part is an awkward width - big gear might help.

2 The Last Retreat . . . . . . ☐ ☐ **E4 6a**
14m. Access the hanging nose above the first roof from left or right then climb the right-hand side of the arete to ledges. Continue up the right-hand side of the final arete.
FA. Bob Smith 1978

3 Nosey Parker . . . . . ☐ ☐ ☐ **E5 6a**
15m. A bold line up the slim ramp on the left wall of the gully. Use the right-hand start of *The Last Retreat* but continue up the wall to the mid-height ledge. Move right and climb the ramp and the wall above (good holds to the left) - precarious and bold.
FA. Bob Hutchinson 1978. Steve Blake was sniffing around.

Central Gully   Main Wall

Jacob's Ladder

Jacob's Ladder and West Buttress

These two buttress on the right-hand side of the crag have a few decent climbs but no major classics.

7 Jacob's Ladder . . . . VDiff
12m. The long groove gives a fine pitch at the grade. The upper section can be climbed using classic chimneying techniques.

8 Stairway to Heaven E5 6a
12m. The bold upper arete is approached via the centre of the lower face. It is hard to start and committing to continue.
FA. John Wallace 1986

9 Rake's Progress . . . . VDiff
12m. Climb the right-hand edge of the lower face to access the hanging groove and continue up this - a bit heathery - to the rift behind the huge flake. Finish though the shrubbery or out left.

10 Broken Wing E3 5c
12m. The wall left of the long corner has a hard move high up.
FA. Bob Hutchinson 1978

11 Raven's Nest . . . . VDiff
12m. The long groove gives a fine well protected pitch to a fun subterranean exit under the capping boulders.
FA. Geoffrey Winthrop Young 1902

12 Thin Ice E4 6a
12m. The easy crack just right leads to a shallow technical groove then pleasant face climbing high on the wall.
FA. Bob Smith 1980

13 Golden Virginia E1 5b
14m. A thin crack leads to the ledge. Use the block to access the wall, up this and exit through a notch.

14 California Crack . . . . HVS 5a
14m. An intimidating line. Climb the rib to the break then head up the wall to the roof. Escape round the exposed left arete.
FA. Hugh Banner 1970s

15 Arete and Groove . . . . VDiff
18m. The jutting prow leads to pastures new. Escape up the groove away to the right.

1 The Brute . . . . HVS 5a
10m. The well named leaning groove is climbed with difficulty.

2 Enery's Ammer E2 5b
10m. The vague open groove is protected by double overhangs. Pull past these on good holds then climb the groove precariously.

3 Sweethope Crack . . . . . HS 4b
10m. Pull past the left end of an overlap then trend right to the base of the the steep groove. This has some tricky moves passing the overlaps, then eases.

4 Squeezy Bill . . . . VDiff
10m. The blocks (or cracks to either side) lead to the base of the chimney. This is awkward but short lived.

5 Rake's Crack E1 5b
12m. The long groove and crack in the arete give a fine pitch, sustained, well protected and with a hard finish.
FA. Hugh Banner 1970s

6 Rake's Arete . . . . VDiff
14m. Climb the flaky rib until things turn mean and the best course is to head over to *Jacob's Ladder* to exit.
A **Direct Finish** is a serious and rounded **E3 5c**.

West Buttress

Evening | 20 min | Windy | Green

	No star	⚁	⚂	⚃
Mod to S	4	1	-	1
HS to HVS	3	2	-	-
E1 to E3	2	5	3	-
E4 and up	-	-	-	-

Also known as Staniel Heugh, this nice little crag, with four small buttresses, in a sunny setting, is great for a short day if you are in the area. There are only about 20 routes here, and the best of these are in the mild Extreme range, but the competent can tick all of the appropriately graded climbs in a couple of hours, or less. The best routes tackle roof features on the two largest buttresses, although there are also decent lines to be found on the clean walls and aretes.

Access

There used to be problems at this crag but since CRoW the situation has improved. Bear it in mind when parking your car and at the crag and please report any problems.

Conditions

The crag is on an exposed hillside in a sunny situation. The rock is good quality sandstone and it takes virtually no drainage so is rapid drying. Year-round climbing is possible when the weather is being kind.

Approach

Tun off the A68 and drive into East Woodburn village. A minor road heads north and after about a kilometre there is a gated right turn (signed Blakelaw). Driving up here, the crag is visible on the left, park directly below it (room for a couple of cars - get well off the road) and walk straight up the moor - 5 minutes.

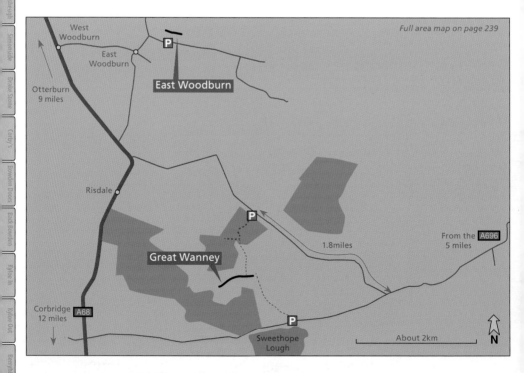

Full area map on page 239

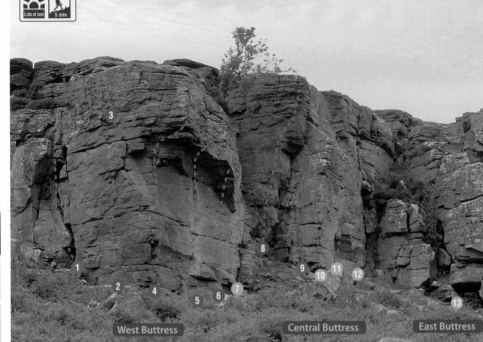

West Buttress

Central Buttress

East Buttress

1 Old Ash Crack. . . . . [ ] **Diff**
8m. The narrow cleft at the left-hand side of the face.

2 Woodburn Wall. . . . . . . [ ] **E1 5b**
10m. The centre of the side wall gives a great micro-pitch, with excellent protection in the frequent horizontal breaks.
Photo on page 241.
FA. Gordon Thompson and/or John Grey 1970s

3 Woodburn Wall Direct [ ] **E2 5c**
10m. The direct finish bumps up the grade and the pump.

4 Oliver went a Huntin'. . . [ ] **E2 5c**
10m. Climb the right-hand side of the arete to the capping roof then lean out right and make hard moves to reach and climb the hanging nose. *Photo on page 275.*
FA. Mark Savage 1990s

5 Ridsdale Wall . . . . [ ] **E1 5b**
10m. The centre of the front face leads to the roof which is crossed with urgency.
FA. Gordon Thompson and/or John Grey 1970s

6 The Arbitrator. . . . . [ ] **E1 5b**
10m. A parallel line to *Ridsale Wall*. Tackle the right-hand side of the roof at its widest point.
FA. Karl Telfer 1980s

7 Foxey . . . . [ ] **VS 4c**
10m. The rib that forms the right-hand side of the wall, heading for the capping rowan.

8 Autobahn. . . . . [ ] **E2 5c**
10m. The right-trending arete is steep and pushy. A good jug at half-height offers a shake-out.
FA. Paul Linfoot and/or Andy Winter 1990s

9 Green Slab. . . . . [ ] **VDiff**
10m. The slightly-green slab is climbed rightwards until it is possible to step round the arete. Finish up the short crack on the left.
FA. Gordon Thompson 1960s

10 The Arete. . . . . [ ] **HS 4b**
10m. Nice moves up the squeezed-in arete with good positions.

Central Buttress

East Buttress

Far East Buttress

⓫ Green Wall . . . . ⌂ ⚡ [____] **HVS 5b**
10m. The centre of the pocketed wall is even less green than the slab. Climb to its crest, then move right to finish up the groov
FA. Gordon Thompson 1960s

⓬ Pattie's Route . . . . [____] **VS 5a**
10m. The right-hand side of the wall leads straight into the base of the final groove of *Green Wall*. Stride out right to a block and finish up the short crack.

The next routes are on the jutting buttress with a clean west face, crossed low down by a narrow overhang.

⓭ Flying Scot. . . . . ⟋ [____] **HVS 5a**
8m. The left-hand side of the wall is unremarkable.

⓮ Capstone Wall . . . . ⌂ ⚡ ▮▯ [____] **E1 5b**
10m. A good route up the centre of the side wall with a reachy start and pumpy finish.

⓯ Death Wish . . . . ⌂ [____] **E1 5b**
12m. The arete is perhaps a little too dramatically named but is a nice enough pitch. Finish up the short wall above the overhang.
FA. Paul Linfoot and/or Andy Winter 1980s

⓰ The Pandemonium Carnival ▮▮ [____] **E1 5b**
14m. Climb the cracks in the left-hand side of the front face of the buttress, then cross the roof with a pocket and difficulty.

⓱ Capstone Traverse . . . . [____] **S 4a**
18m. Climb the central groove to the overhang then creep left under it and round the arete. Finish up the side wall or cop-out and escape off left.

⓲ Capstone Direct . . . ⌂ ◀ ⟍ [____] **E1 5c**
12m. The central groove leads easily to the capping roof, which is where the problems lurk. Scale it using the thin crack.
FA. Gordon Thompson and/or John Grey 1970s

⓳ Stilton . . . . [____] **VDiff**
8m. The left edge of the short buttress is pleasant enough.

⓴ Cheese Wedge . . . . [____] **S 4a**
8m. A thin crack points the way. Finish up the tiny wall above.

Cassey Quarry | Crag Lough | Peel Crag | Callerhues | Great Wanney | E. Woodburn | Sandy Crag | Ravensheugh | Simonside | Drake Stone | Corby's | Bowden Doors | Back Bowden | Kyloe In | Kyloe Out | Berryhill

	No star	⚝	⚝⚝	⚝⚝⚝
Mod to S	-	-	-	-
HS to HVS	1	3	3	1
E1 to E3	-	2	-	1
E4 and up	1	2	2	3

Sandy Crag (marked as Key Heugh on some maps) has a small selection of climbs but there are some real gems amongst them. The longish approach means that the place is never busy, though the extra effort involved in making a visit here on the right day will be repaid many times over. The routes are amongst some of the tallest on Northumbrian sandstone and are well divided between hard bold aretes and safe but strenuous cracks.

Conditions

The crag is set on a high exposed hillside and faces west. It is basically a summer venue as it can be cold and is often green and lichenous after rain. The crag gets the afternoon sun but its remoteness ensures there is little traffic so the climbs tend to feel a bit adventurous especially when compared to popular venues such as Corby's, Bowden and Kyloe. As with many of the less-travelled Northumberland crags, the routes often feel quite hard for the grade.

Access

The local warden, Stuart Whitfield, has requested that climbers phone him, or leave a message, on 01669 640272 (current 2008) before venturing onto the moor. The moor is occasionally used for shooting on Saturdays in August and September but this shouldn't affect access.

Approach

There is parking for 6 cars south of the B6341 Otterburn to Rothbury road, just north of Elsdon, at which point the crag can clearly be seen. Follow the footpath down to the stream, over the wide wooden bridge and towards the hidden lake of Darden Lough, keeping left at the only junction. A pair of prominent large pine trees mark the gate into the fence around an old plantation (currently deforested). Continue following the fence round, past its south east corner, then drop down into the narrow valley containing Darden Burn and head for the crag - a bit of a grind. Aim out left to where the heather has been burnt off and keep going uphill until the left edge of the cliff can be reached by narrow tracks leading back out right. The chaos of huge boulders, neck-high heather and bottomless pits directly below the cliff are best avoided.

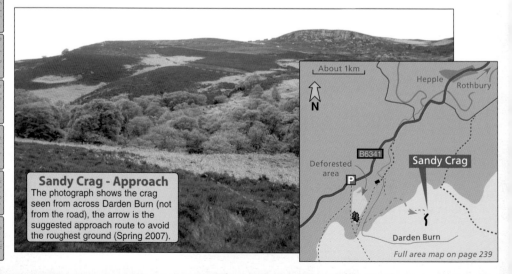

Sandy Crag - Approach
The photograph shows the crag seen from across Darden Burn (not from the road), the arrow is the suggested approach route to avoid the roughest ground (Spring 2007).

About 1km
N
Hepple
Rothbury
B6341
Sandy Crag
Deforested area
P
Darden Burn

Full area map on page 239

Causey Quarry · Crag Lough · Peel Crag · Callerhues · Great Wanney · E. Woodburn · Sandy Crag · Ravensheugh · Simonside · Drake Stone · Corby's · Bowden Doors · Back Bowden · Kyloe In · Kyloe Out · Berryhill

VincentButtress

④ Question Mark Crack... VS 4c
16m. Layback round the head-shaped flake, and its smaller continuation, until it is possible to move left into the grassy groove. Finish easily up this.
FA. Probably College Club members 1950s

⑤ Raven's Nest Crack. VS 5a
16m. The fine (if a touch wide) fissure shooting straight up the crag gives a cracking pitch - steep, sustained and well protected, with enough large gear to hand.

⑥ Raven's Nest Chimney.. HS 4b
18m. The soaring rift is better than it appears and is well worth a look if you are into chimneys. The climbing is steady as far as the blocking chockstone then more awkward to a scruffy exit. The raven has relocated about 30m south.

❼ Victim of Circumstance . E5 6a
18m. A scary outing up the top third of the stunning arete. The lower section MUST be the best unclimbed line in the County (or is that Country?). Climb *Raven's Nest Chimney* to the chockstone then move out right and across to the arete where a harrowing move reaches easier climbing up the scalloped arete.
FA. Hugh Harris 1990

❽ Pall Arete E3 6a
6m. The short technical arete leads to the heather fields above.
FA. Bob Smith 1979

The scruffy corner that borders Angel Fingers is the line of **Rake End Crack***, S 4a. The finish up the crack in the right wall of the top corner raises the quality of the outing, a tiny bit. A traverse of the lower break of the walls to either side of* **The Vertical Vice** *is* **The Jaws***, VS 5a. Although well recommended, the grubby approach up* **Rake End Crack** *and past the huge raven's nest on the second pitch means there are better things to do here at the moment.*

❾ Angel Fingers..... Top 50 HVS 5b
20m. Rumoured to be the best HVS in Northumberland, there is only one way you will find out. A hard start on the left reaches finger-locks and runners then the crack unfurls in a most appealing fashion. The final crack has tricky moves to start, laybacking from the left is one solution. *Photo on page 279.*
FFA. John Earl 1974. The in-situ wooden wedges suggested that he was not the first.

❿ Goldfinger .... HVS 5b
20m. No more than a right-hand finish to *Angel Fingers* but well worth the effort if you have done the regular route. Follow *Angel Fingers* to the break then climb the arete to access the hanging groove just right of the upper arete. Finish up this.
FA. Bob Hutchinson 1977

⓫ Living on Borrowed Time E5 6a
22m. The blunt central arete of the crag is approached from a short way up the crack on the right to reach a ledge. Climb boldly up the right-hand side of the arete, eventually using a long fluting, then moving back left. The short upper groove of *Goldfinger* brings welcome relief.
FA. Hugh Harris 1990

Vincent Buttress
The first piece of rock reached is a fine jutting arete that has classic hard routes on either side. Twenty metres to the right, across the heather, is another fine arete. Queues are rare for this particular trilogy.

❶ Leonardo.............. E6 6b
12m. Layback up the desperate leaning groove left of the arete. It has both runners and holds, but not a deal of either. When these run out, escape leftwards past the snapped flake to reach easy ground. The obvious **Direct Finish** still awaits.
FA. Bob Smith 1985

❷ Vincent E5 6a
12m. The fine and harrowing arete is approached from the right and followed with increasing trepidation to where the artist's 'ear' used to be, then finish direct. Low in the grade but never forget, that's low in the grade Northumbrian style!
FA. Bob Hutchinson 1978

❸ Salvation E4 5c
14m. Another big, bald, jutting arete, 20m to the right of *Vincent* (not shown on topo - but impossible to miss). Climb the arete until forced left then finish direct
FA. Bob Hutchinson 1976

To the right are some rather indeterminate walls, home to half-a-dozen routes. These are rather scruffy except for the right-slanting fissure to the right of a block-filled rift, which is followed by **Fang Crack***, VS 5a - just about worthy of a star. Beyond here the crag increases in size and features some fine lines, they are what makes the effort expended in the walk up worthwhile.*

Angel Fingers

Raven's Nest Crack

Sandy Crack

⑫ The Vertical Vice ..... ⟨1⟩ 🍴 ⬜ **HVS 5a**
22m. The central fissure is a bit of a 'climb-me' line, though the current state of the raven's nest means it is best avoided in the spring. Easy climbing leads to the narrows where the expected tussle ensues to reach the big break. Accessing the hanging bell-shaped crack is the final obstacle, awkward and scary moves finally reach easier ground.
FA. Probably College Club members 1950s

⑬ Sandy Crack .... Top⟨50⟩ ✏️ ⬜ **E2 5c**
22m. The stunning soaring crack is a mega-classic, as good as any route of its length in the UK. Pull through the tough roof-crack to reach the ledge then jam the narrowing crack with escalating difficulties (great cam protection) until the break arrives. Move right and back left to access the final short crack.
Photo on page 283.
FFA. Bob Hutchinson 1974. Another one that had been pegged by persons unknown back in the Iron Age.

⑭ Greenford Road ... ⟨3⟩ 🏞️ 🔪 ⬜ **E5 6b**
22m. The elegant hanging groove in the impressive hanging arete right of *Sandy Crack* gives a serious piece of climbing. Climb the roof of *Sandy Crack* then move right and make difficult moves up to the dubious security of the groove. Continue warily up the groove to the big break and an easy finish up the fluted arete. The **Direct Start** up the overhanging arete is steep, sustained and unprotected, it weighs in at **E8 6b**.
FA. Tommy Smith 1980. FA. (Direct Start) Karl Telfer (with runner in Sandy Crack) 1989, Mark Savage (without) 2003

Sandy Crack
Although not very extensive this is the show-piece of the crag, the trio of soaring aretes and steep cracks of varying widths - all of which are worth doing if you are up to the challenge - though the wide spread of grades might be a bit of a problem.

Caussy Quarry / Crag Lough / Peel Crag / Callerhues / Great Wanney / E. Woodburn / Sandy Crag / Ravensheugh / Simonside / Drake Stone / Corby's / Bowden Doors / Back Bowden / Kyloe In / Kyloe Out / Berryhill

Far Right

To the right of the main section of the cliff are some shorter walls. These see even less activity than the rest of the cliff, though the climbs are not without interest.

❶ Corporal Punishment... 🖾🎏 ☐ **E4 6b**
10m. Kick off from the slab and climb the arete to the break, then make desperate moves up the leaning upper section to the big break and an easier finish.
FA. John Earl 1985

❷ The Slit .... ☆1 🕴 ☐ **VS 4c**
8m. The widening and steepening crack has its moments.

❸ Classroom Worm .. ☆ 🕴🎏 ☐ **E4 6a**
10m. Move right from *The Slit* and climb the thin crack in the wall until it is possible to gain the arete on the right. Swing rightwards round this and climb the diagonal crack to a tricky exit.
FA. Bob Smith 1980

❹ Time and Motion .. ☆2 🎏🕴 ☐ **E7 6c**
10m. The innocuous looking arete has no runners, no holds worthy of the name and a big drop below it. The climbing is sustained and the hardest section is near the top.
FA. Joe Webb 1991. Above six very concerned spotters.

❺ Christmas Crack .... 🕴 ☐ **VS 4c**
10m. The wide crack is very tricky to access because of the jutting nose. Once past this it eases to just plain awkward. Unlike its Stanage namesake, and *Christmas Curry* on Tremadog, this one rarely sees queues on 25 December.

Carpe Diem
Late September 1979, the climber's magazine of the day - Rocksport - featured an article on some remote outcrop in Northumberland, Sandy Crag. The article was illustrated with photographs of some stunning looking crack-lines. Three days later (the weekend) saw us flogging up the moor to the crag. Six routes were dispatched including the classic of *Angels Fingers* (HVS 5b) and *Sandy Crack* (E2 5c). The photo to the right was taken just before I took a fall - fortunately the cammed hexes held. Although Friends were available in 1978, I couldn't afford them!

Chris Craggs heading for a tumble on *Sandy Crack* (E2 5c) in 1979 - *page 281* - Sandy Crag. Photo: Craggs Collection

	No star	☆	☆☆	☆☆☆
Mod to S	10	2	-	-
HS to HVS	7	6	5	4
E1 to E3	13	6	2	4
E4 and up	3	10	6	5

Ravensheugh is perhaps Northumberland's most enigmatic venue; a super crag in a magnificent setting and with a truly stunning set of climbs, but despite all this, it sees little traffic. The lack of popularity is probably due to the crag being quite a way from the road, the routes being in the middle and upper grades, and the crag not getting the sun until well into the afternoon. However, time your visit correctly and a great day's climbing is guaranteed.

Conditions

The crag is on an exposed hillside facing north west. It is best considered as a summer venue as it can be cold and is usually green after rain. If you turn up, and it's a bit grotty, it is only a short amble back to Simonside, which somehow always manages to feel more amenable.

Approach

Park at the Simonside Forest car park, which is reached from Rothbury via Great Tosson. Head west out of the car park up the barred trail (orange route) and follow this as it winds steadily uphill, eventually branching right by a mobile phone mast. Continue to the next junction and turn left along an undulating track, passing signs to the Little Church Cave. 600m from the junction is a left turn that rises steadily up a small gully to pop out of the trees at which point Simonside appears ahead. Head towards the crag to reach the major forest track cutting across the hillside, and turn right. Ignoring the junction towards Selby's Cove, follow the track to the right of the trees to reach a stile onto open moor where narrow paths lead through the heather to the cliff - 50 minutes from the car.

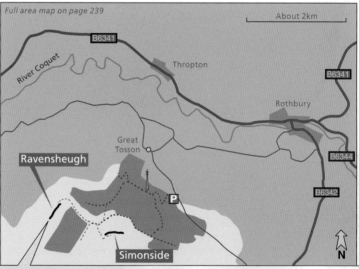

Full area map on page 239

Parallel Cracks — East Buttress — First Pinnacle — The Bay — Second Pinnacle — Western Walls

Chris Craggs approaching the crutch moves on *The Trouser Legs* (E2 5c) - *page 287* at Ravensheugh, under the watchful eye of Graham Parkes. Photo: Craggs Collection

Parallel Cracks

Parallel Cracks

The far left-hand wall is short but is composed of excellent hard sandstone and gets the sun earlier than much of the cliff. Its crest is a great sunbathing/ picnic spot which catches enough breeze to keep the insects away on hot summer days. Although only short, these are quite a taxing set of climbs, and this includes the easy ones.

1 Rubberneck . . . . HVS 5b
6m. The centre of the left-hand wall.

2 Dark Passage V2 (6a)
16m. A low-level traverse of the wall to beyond *Big Daddy*.

3 Left Parallel Crack . . . . . . VDiff
6m. The left-hand of the near parallel cracks. Awkward.

4 Central Parallel Crack . . . . . VDiff
6m. The central and right-trending fissure. Very awkward.

5 Limbo V2 (5c)
6m. The centre of the wall has taxing moves to get stood on the good flake hold. Finish direct.
FA. Steve Blake 1978

6 Arete-shun E1 5b
6m. Layback the arete to a hard final pull.

7 Right Parallel Crack . . . . . VDiff
6m. The right-hand of the trio of wide cracks is awkward; no surprises there then.

8 Little Idi V1 (5b)
6m. Trend left up the wall using the 'expando-flake' carefully.

9 Big Daddy V5 (6b)
Spring up the wall to the right, using a thin flake for the take-off.

The right-hand end of the wall has a short fingery left-trending problem V1 (5c). Across the slope and past the descent gully is the first buttress of the main edge - East Buttress.

East Buttress

The left-hand section of the main part of the cliff is an attractive rippled buttress. Unfortunately it is steeper and blanker than it looks so the majority of the routes are serious undertakings. The classic of *Pendulum* redresses the balance a little.

10 Pete's Ploy E2 5b
8m. The left wall of the buttress is rounded and bold.

11 Plumbline E5 6a
10m. The rounded arete is technical and bold (as in no gear).
FA. John Earl 1977

12 The Judas Hole . . . E5 6a
10m. Poorly protected climbing up the crescent-shaped groove and wall just left of the crack of *Pendulum*. The 'hole' of the route name does accept gear but only begrudgingly.
FA. Bob Smith 1979

13 Pendulum Direct . . . VS 4c
10m. Follow the crack throughout. It eases with height.

14 Pendulum . . . . VS 4c
10m. Gain the base of the main crack from the thinner crack to the right by a tricky traverse. Continue up it.
FA. Allan Austin1960s. Second, Dave Roberts, took a swinger on the first move.

15 Hanging Chimney . . . . . S 4b
10m. The angle of the buttress. Hard exiting the bottleneck.

16 Billy Biscuit . . . E5 6a
10m. Another of those excellent, tough, rounded and serious aretes. A dyno may be needed to link the half-decent holds.
FA. Bob Smith 1979

17 Lapse of Reason . . . E5 6a
10m. The blunt rib in the centre of the face, trending slightly right to a harrowing finish
FA. Hugh Harris 1989. The on-sight solo gave the name.

18 Easter Grooves E2 5b
12m. Start up the arete, then move right and follow the ramp and groove to steeper rock until it is possible to get left onto a shelf on the arete. Finish more easily.

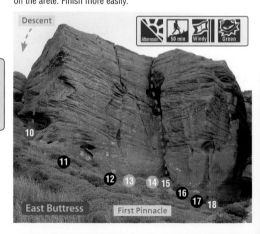

East Buttress First Pinnacle

19 Verbal Abuse . . . .  **E2 5c**
12m. From the gully, move up and then out right to access the left
arete of the front face. Finish up this. The **Direct Start** needs a triple jump approach and some serious slapping. Pretty ungradeable
really but something around **V9** or **V10** is probably close.
FA. Bob Smith 1989s. FA. (Direct Start) Nick Dixon 1996

20 Baluster Crack . . . . **HVS 5b**
14m. Magnificent! The compelling crack system in the left side of
the valley face of the First Pinnacle is worthy of the walk up on its
own. A description would be superfluous, suffice to say a right-
hand finish is more in keeping with the fun lower down.
FA. Allan Austin 1960s

21 The Sandrider **E3 5c**
14m. The right-hand crack system leads up and left then bolder
moves are needed to climb rightwards up the wall to the base of
the crack splitting the final overhang. Finish through this.
FA. Bob Hutchinson 1974

22 Castaway **E6 6a**
14m. Where *Sandrider* heads left, continue up a short crack then
boldly climb the wall slightly rightwards and back left to reach
respite and runners in the finishing crack.
FA. Tim Gallagher 1989

23 The Trouser Legs **E2 5c**
16m. The West Face classic. Climb into the hanging groove with
difficulty (runners) then move right - with difficulty to access the
crutch. Continue - still with difficulty to ledges and an escape right
up the easier cracks. A **Direct Start** (from the right) is **5c**.
Photo on page 285 and 234.
FA. Hugh Banner1960s. Success on a return-match after a fall a week earlier.

24 Agape **E6 6a**
14m. Serious climbing plugging a large gap. From good runners on
Trouser Legs head up left to a hole, then back right to a rest. The
leaning wall on sloping holds leads to a harrowing rounded finish.
FA. Richard Davies 1989

25 Easter Crack . . . . **VDiff**
6m. The north east arete of the tower offers the easiest way up,
for summit tickers - and down, for escapees.

The large block in the gully to the right is Intermediate Buttress.

26 Pussyfoot . . . . **VS 5a**
8m. Claw a way onto the the right-hand edge of the face then
trend left to the ledge and the finish of *Catwalk*. The thin crack of
Felix is just right and is a more fitting finish.

27 Catwalk . . . . **VDiff**
8m. Start on the ramp on the right and follow it leftwards passing
the arete awkwardly. Finish up the cracks on the front face.

28 Felix . . . . **VS 5a**
8m. Start along *Catwalk* but tackle the thin slanting technical
crack to a rounded exit.

First Pinnacle
A fine sandstone tower with
an array of grand climbs on its
bulbous faces. *Baluster Crack*
is as good as any of the Peak's
vaunted jamming cracks, and
if you want hard and bold, look
no further.
Descent - Down-climb **Easter
Crack** over on the north east
arete.

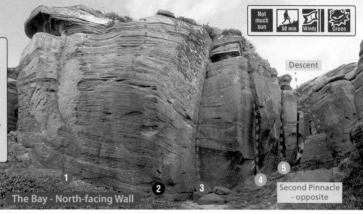

The Bay - North-facing Wall

The Bay

Behind the Second Pinnacle is a pair of short walls, facing each other and with a nice collection of worthwhile routes. One side gets plenty of sun and the best of the collection are described here. **Descent -** Reverse down the blocky groove to the right - **Backdoor, Mod.**

Descent

Second Pinnacle - opposite

1 **Octopus** **E3 6b**
8m. The technical shallow groove on the left. Finish rightwards.
FA. John Earl 1978

2 **Reiver** **E7 6c**
8m. The committing rounded rib is sketched (if at all) on a set of poor and well spaced holds.
FA. Noel Crane 1996

3 **Smarty Pants** **E2 5c**
8m. The prominent groove gives a nice technical pitch.

4 **Half Minute Crack** . . . . . **VS 5a**
8m. The slanting jamming crack is fun.
FA. Allan Austin (in less than 30 seconds!) late 1960s

The tiny hanging groove just right is **Chasing Sheep, E3 6b.**

5 **One Boot Crack** . . . . . . **VS 5a**
8m. The boot-width crack is awkward if you wear two rock shoes.

Second Pinnacle
The rest of the climbs in The Bay are on the opposite wall which is actually the South Wall of the Second Pinnacle.

6 **Layback** . . . . **VDiff**
8m. The wide and awkward crack is also the normal descent.

7 **The Nark** . . . . **VS 4c**
8m. Hop onto the slab and climb the creased wall, trending left.

West Buttress

Descent down here

Second Pinnacle - South-facing Wall

Descent down
Route 6 - Layback

Not much sun | 50 min | Windy

Green

12
13
14
The Bay
16
15
17

Second Pinnacle - East Face

Second Pinnacle

Another fine free standing tower of sandstone ringed by a great selection of routes. The front face is especially impressive but there are good climbs on all sides, and a few more on the short wall of The Bay directly behind the tower. Most of the routes on the pinnacle manage to feel hard for their given grade. **Descent** - Reverse down **Layback, VDiff,** the wide crack splitting the inside face of the pinnacle.

❽ Dawes' Route **E5 6c**
8m. The broad blunt rib is fiercely technical; it eases with height.
FA. Johhny Dawes 1996

❾ The Squealer **E2 5c**
8m. The right wall gives a much easier approach to the rib.

❿ Scoop Crack . . . .   **HS 4b**
8m. Good moves up the cracked scoop feature.

⓫ Cat's Whiskers . . . .   **HVS 5b**
8m. Nice climbing up the right-hand (uncracked) scoop.

⓬ Hot Bricks **E1 5c**
8m. The wall right of the north east arete on indifferent holds.

⓭ East Wall . . . .   **S 4a**
8m. Trend right to a dirty ledge in the centre of the face and finish direct from here, with a choice of lines.

⓮ Sunny Sunday **E2 5c**
10m. Wander up the centre of the face starting from the pointed block at it base. Dirty, unprotected and rarely climbed.

⓯ Crocodile Arete . . .   **E7 6c**
16m. The stunning north east arete of the tower gives a magnificent pitch. A dynamic start gains the first break then continue up the rest of the arete staying on its right-hand side throughout.
FA. Andrew Earl 2003

⓰ Old Man River **E4 6a**
18m. Lacking in line but with some good climbing. Cross the roof as for *Honeymoon Crack* then follow the diagonal crack leftwards past the arete. Continue up the arete (hard) on its slabby side to a ledge, then finish up and leftwards.
FA. Paul Stewart, Steve Blake c1978. With a hanging belay above the lip.

⓱ Honeymoon Crack .   Top 50   **E3 6a**
16m. The superb crack rising above the huge overhang is a must. Battle with the overhang to reach the crack (get the heavy metal thrown up on a bandoleer once established?) then plug away up the crack and its wider continuation up and left.
The start was originally done with a shoulder, lowering the grade to a rather uphill **E1 5b.**
FA. Geoff Jackson (with a shoulder) late 1960s. FFA. Bob Hutchinson 1976

⓲ Trial Separation . . .   **E4 6b**
18m. Climb the undercut right arete using a trio of large and spaced pockets to pass the initial overhang. Continue past a break to ledges then finish up the arete on the left.
FA. Bob Smith 1987. Another audacious solo.

Evening | 50 min | Windy

Green

16
17
15
18
Second Pinnacle - West Face

Second Pinnacle - North Face

Causey Quarry / Crag Lough / Peel Crag / Callerhues / Great Wanney / E. Woodburn / Sandy Crag / Ravensheugh / Simonside / Drake Stone / Corby's / Bowden Doors / Back Bowden / Kyloe In / Kyloe Out / Berryhill

Second Pinnacle - West Face

The west-facing wall of the Second Pinnacle gets more sun and is consequently cleaner than the other faces. There are some fine climbs with the emphasis on rounded holds and bold top-outs, though *The Crescent* should entertain those who don't like exposed routes - a speleological delight.

❶ Rock and Roll Star .   **E5 6a**
16m. Climb the wall on slopers and poor pockets to the break (bold) then move out left and finish up the arete.
FA. Bob Smith 1984

❷ Candle in the Wind **E3 5c**
18m. Devious but excellent, and another one that is high in the grade. Access the left-hand of a pair of flaky cracks and climb this to the ledge of the Balcony. Get onto the ledge with difficulty then move left and finish up the shallow scoop right of the arete - bold and rounded.
FA. Bob Hutchinson 1975.

❸ Gates of Eden. .   **E2 5c**
16m. High in the grade. Climb the centre of the wall using the right-hand flake-system to a mini-cave. Move left and gain the Balcony with difficulty. Move up from its right-hand end to gain the hanging crack and finish up this with some reachy moves.
FA. John Earl 1975

❹ Paradise Lost **E5 6b**
14m. The direct finish to *Gates of Eden*. Exit directly from the cave to a rounded and worrying finish up the rib.
FA. Hugh Harris 1991

❺ Borstal Boy **E1 5b**
12m. Climb the wall to a jutting nose and cross this on good holds to the base of a ramp. Finish delicately up the left arete.
FA. Bob Smith 1980s

❻ The Crescent . . . .   **S 4b**
12m. Start up the crack to the first ledge then move right and hand traverse the edge of the crack until access to the wider curving continuation crack is possible. Pull into this and wriggle though the cliff to reach *Layback* on the opposite face and finish up this - bizarre.

❼ Crescent Wall. . . . . . .   **VS 4b**
12m. Good varied climbing. Up the wide curving crack until the ledge at the base of the groove on the left can be reached. Finish up the wall right of the groove using a suspect flake carefully.

❽ Wide Eyed and Legless   **E4 5c**
10m. Another bizarre route and well named. Make scary progress by bridging between the two sharp aretes until it is possible to escape onto the tower, or to the main edge.
FA. Bob Smith 1979

To the right an awkward scramble between the aretes of Wide Eyed... leads round into the Bay at the back of the Second Pinnacle. Right of this is the impressive bulk of West Buttress with its compelling crack-lines and bolder face routes.

West Buttress

❾ Cave Crack. . . . .   **VS 4c**
12m. The gloomy rift on the right of the narrows is a struggle until the Second Pinnacle is near enough to bridge across to for a little respite. Finish awkwardly.

❿ Ravensheugh Crack. . . .   **HVS 5a**
12m. Another of the superb jamming cracks that the crag abounds with. A tricky groove leads to a ledge then move right and motor up the soaring crack-line.
FA. Dave Roberts, Hugh Banner (alternate leads!) 1960s

Descent down Layback
(previous page)

Trial Separation

West Buttress

Second Pinnacle - West Face

⓫ First Among Equals. E6 6b
12m. The disappearing groove above the start of *Ravensheugh Crack* gives a fine pitch of escalating difficulty and seriousness.
FA. Hugh Harris 1989

⓬ Childhood's End E4 6a
14m. Start round to the right and climb leftwards to gain the base of the shallow left-trending groove. Climb this, sustained and excellent, until the groove fizzles out and a tricky little traverse scoots left into the upper section of *Ravensheugh Crack*.
FA. Bob Hutchinson 1978

⓭ Wild West Show HVS 5a
14m. A shallow groove leads to the break, swing left (or stomach traverse) and pull up to access the base of the fine crack. Climb this to its end then finish up the slab.
FA. Hugh Banner 1960s

The next five routes climb the slabby right-hand end of the buttress. The routes are delicate and poorly protected.

⓮ Redskin E3 5b
10m. A steep start up the leaning scoop leads to the base of the slab. Pull over and pad to the top.
FA. Bob Smith 1980s

⓯ Hang em' High E5 6a
14m. Start as for *Redskin* then continue directly up the wall using small pockets to a precarious exit onto the slab. Climb this, trending leftwards to top out as for *Wild West Show*.
FA. Graeme Read 2007

⓰ Sitting Bull E3 5b
10m. Start just right of a jutting nose, climb to a ledge and pass the bulge using pockets. Finish up the slab.
FA. Bob Smith 1980s

⓱ Buckskin VS 4c
12m. A worthwhile mini-expedition that links *Moccasin* with a finish beyond *Redskin*, by some pleasant diagonal padding.
FA. Bob Smith 1980s

⓲ Moccasin Slab HVS 5a
8m. Bridge up until it is possible to hop onto the base of the slab then finish straight up it pleasantly.
FA. Bob Smith 1980s

Not much sun | 50 min | Windy | Green

Western Walls

Beyond the tall imposing mass of West Buttress, the crag continues in a less impressive fashion, though it does have a nice selection of short routes that are invariably quiet. The first piece of rock is a squat jutting pillar.

1 Bonneville **E3 6c**
6m. Hop abord and sprint up the taxing jutting arete.
FA. Bob Smith 1985

2 Penfold . . . . **V8 (6c)**
The direct start to *T.C.* with your left-hand on the arete.

3 T.C. **E3 5c**
6m. Start up the groove of *Mole* and traverse left along the break where a useful pocket allows the top to be reached.

4 Mole . . . . **S 4a**
6m. The groove in the first of the angles.

5 Just Arrested **E2 5b**
8m. Start up *Mole* but head right past a ledge to a groove.

6 Just Ice **E3 6a**
8m. Basically a direct start to the finishing groove of *Just Arrested*, starting below and right of the groove.
FA. Steve Crowe 1997

7 Out On The Wall Gully . . . . **Diff**
10m. Climb the chimney right of the block, then the right wall.

8 Overpowered **E5 6c**
8m. Taxing moves up the leaning wall left of the prow.
FA. Andrew Earl 2001

9 Pink Lane **E1 5b**
8m. Pull onto the crinkly left wall of the groove, then traverse towards the arete and a ledge. Move back right to finish.
FA. Bob Hutchinson 1977

10 Facing Facts **E2 5c**
6m. Straight up the wall from the start of *Pink Lane*.

11 Little Leaner . . . . . **VS 5a**
6m. Climb the left wall of the little leaning corner to good holds, then use these to finish to the right.

12 Bede Crack . . . . **S 4a**
6m. The angle is worth doing despite the vegetation.

13 Grease **E4 6a**
8m. Start up *Bede Crack* but traverse right along the lip of the roof to a pocket, making bold and fingery moves to finish.
A **Direct Start** using some poor pockets is **6b**.
FA. Steve Blake 1978

14 Mimic **E3 5c**
6m. Pull through the bulge then move right to the rounded arete.
FA. Steve Blake 1978

15 St. Cuthbert's Crack . . . **VS 5a**
6m. The next groove westwards is tricky.

16 Slab Corner . . . . **VDiff**
8m. The angle between the steep wall and the slab.

There are another 30 odd routes scattered along the edge, most of these are in the lower grades, and there are some interesting bits and pieces. The NMC Northumberland Climbing Guide (2004) lists all of these.

The most significant trio of routes are to be found on Plumber Buttress, which is about 100m west of Slab Corner.

17 The Apprentice E4 6b
8m. Start up the blunt left arete and gain the hanging green groove up and right.
FA. Graeme Read 2006

18 The Magician E7 7a
8m. The amazing main arete of the wall. A highball **V9**.
FA. Andy Earl, Chris Graham (both solo) 2007

19 The Plumber E5 6b
8m. The right wall of the buttress on surprisingly poor holds and a complete lack of polish.
FA. Bob Hutchinson 1978

A 'fair day' at Ravensheugh, looking towards distant Cheviot. Photo: Chris Craggs

	No star	⚀	⚁	⚂
Mod to S	18	6	2	1
HS to HVS	7	12	3	2
E1 to E3	2	6	3	1
E4 and up	-	2	1	2

A fine cliff in a lovely setting, though tilted a bit too much towards the north for maximum user-friendliness. The setting and collection of amenable routes means that Simonside has possibly the longest climbing history of any crag in Northumberland - the rocks were first explored around 1900 and the crag even had a small guidebook by the 1920s. If the conditions are right you will probably end up sharing the place with other teams, though the 60+ routes are quite spread out so there is always plenty to do.

Conditions

The crag is on an exposed hillside and faces north, though some of the buttresses jut well out of the hillside and get the after-noon sun. It is usually considered a summer venue since it can be cold and windy up here, though it does dry rapidly after rain.

Approach   See map on page 284

Park at the Simonside Forest car park, which is reached from Rothbury via Great Tosson. Head west out of the car park up the barred trail (orange route) and follow this as it winds steadily uphill, eventually branching right by a mobile phone mast. Continue to the next junction and turn left along an undulating track passing signs to the Little Church Cave. 600m from the junction is a left turn that rises steadily up a small gully to pop out of the trees, at which point the cliff appears ahead. Head towards the crag to reach the major forest track cutting across the hillside, and locate tracks heading up the steep slope to the cliff.

Climbers enjoying the fine upper slab of *Delicatessen* (VS 4c) - *page 298* - and the dramatic setting of Simonside Photo: Chris Craggs

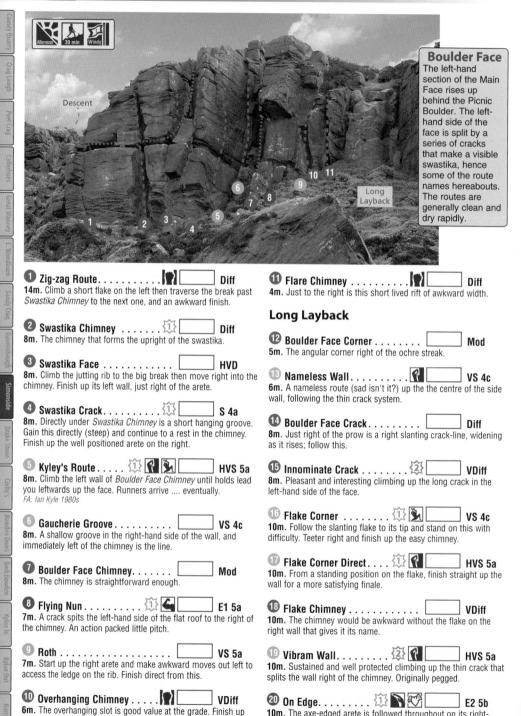

Boulder Face

The left-hand section of the Main Face rises up behind the Picnic Boulder. The left-hand side of the face is split by a series of cracks that make a visible swastika, hence some of the route names hereabouts. The routes are generally clean and dry rapidly.

1 Zig-zag Route . . . . Diff
14m. Climb a short flake on the left then traverse the break past *Swastika Chimney* to the next one, and an awkward finish.

2 Swastika Chimney . . . . Diff
8m. The chimney that forms the upright of the swastika.

3 Swastika Face . . . . HVD
8m. Climb the jutting rib to the big break then move right into the chimney. Finish up its left wall, just right of the arete.

4 Swastika Crack . . . . S 4a
8m. Directly under *Swastika Chimney* is a short hanging groove. Gain this directly (steep) and continue to a rest in the chimney. Finish up the well positioned arete on the right.

5 Kyley's Route . . . . . HVS 5a
8m. Climb the left wall of *Boulder Face Chimney* until holds lead you leftwards up the face. Runners arrive .... eventually.
FA. Ian Kyle 1980s

6 Gaucherie Groove . . . . VS 4c
8m. A shallow groove in the right-hand side of the wall, and immediately left of the chimney is the line.

7 Boulder Face Chimney . . . . Mod
8m. The chimney is straightforward enough.

8 Flying Nun E1 5a
7m. A crack spits the left-hand side of the flat roof to the right of the chimney. An action packed little pitch.

9 Roth . . . . VS 5a
7m. Start up the right arete and make awkward moves out left to access the ledge on the rib. Finish direct from this.

10 Overhanging Chimney . . . . . VDiff
6m. The overhanging slot is good value at the grade. Finish up the open groove above.

11 Flare Chimney . . . . Diff
4m. Just to the right is this short lived rift of awkward width.

Long Layback

12 Boulder Face Corner . . . . Mod
5m. The angular corner right of the ochre streak.

13 Nameless Wall . . . . VS 4c
6m. A nameless route (sad isn't it?) up the the centre of the side wall, following the thin crack system.

14 Boulder Face Crack . . . . Diff
8m. Just right of the prow is a right slanting crack-line, widening as it rises; follow this.

15 Innominate Crack . . . . VDiff
8m. Pleasant and interesting climbing up the long crack in the left-hand side of the face.

16 Flake Corner . . . . VS 4c
10m. Follow the slanting flake to its tip and stand on this with difficulty. Teeter right and finish up the easy chimney.

17 Flake Corner Direct . . . . HVS 5a
10m. From a standing position on the flake, finish straight up the wall for a more satisfying finale.

18 Flake Chimney . . . . VDiff
10m. The chimney would be awkward without the flake on the right wall that gives it its name.

19 Vibram Wall . . . . HVS 5a
10m. Sustained and well protected climbing up the thin crack that splits the wall right of the chimney. Originally pegged.

20 On Edge E2 5b
10m. The axe-edged arete is followed throughout on its right-hand side - bold and balancy. The narrow wall just right again is **On the Brink, E3 5c.**

Long Layback

The main feature of the crag is the well named wide crack-line that still succumbs most easily to a bold and pushy feeling layback. There are some worthwhile and popular easier routes here and also a collection of high-quality desperates that see a little less attention. The routes are generally clean and rapid drying.

Innominate Crack

㉑ Long Layback Crack   **VS 4c**
12m. One of the classics of the cliff - a great line and with bold sustained laybacking being the order of the day. Very big cams might help but only if you can stop to place them.

㉒ AKA Mr. Vegas .   **E7 6c**
12m. The blank wall has sustained climbing. There is a decent hold under the slim overlap from where to assess your options, then it is all or nothing to the top.
FA. Mark Savage 1999 (upper section) 2004 (lower section)

㉓ Command Performance   **E4 6b**
12m. The central line on the wall gives an excellent pitch. Follow small holds to the overlap then trend rightwards for a breather and runners under the roof. Undercut past the edge of this then climb the wall boldly to reach easier ground.
FA. Bob Smith 1980

㉔ Over the Edge. **E3 5c**
12m. Layback the right arete to runners under the overhang then move round the arete and access the thin crack; climb this with difficulty. Excellent and with decent gear, after the start.
FA. Geoff Lamb 1978

㉕ Dirty Corner . . . .   **VDiff**
10m. The deep cleft often isn't as dirty as you might expect.

㉖ On the Border. **E3 5c**
10m. The steep groove in the right wall of the chimney is worth doing when it is clean and dry - sadly it usually isn't either.

㉗ Dry Run. **E2 5b**
10m. The arete is climbed direct, or reached from *On the Border*.

㉘ Staircase Chimney . . . .   **Diff**
10m. The narrow rift is awkward and often a bit shrubby.

Long Layback

'A' Buttress
The left-hand of the three taller buttresses has an excellent set of climbs which can conveniently be split at the large ledge, helping to give a mountain feel to the climbs. Generally the rock is clean and rapid drying.

① **The Privy** . . . . **HVS 5a**
15m. The left-hand side of the buttress. Climb the centre of the face via a shallow groove then move left and pull over the bulge on pockets. The second slab is accessed awkwardly and its arete followed until the final section of *Giant's Stair* can be reached for a finish.

② **Giant's Stair** . . . . **VS 4c**
15m. A worthwhile outing up the right edge of the buttress. Start via the right-slanting flake, then move left a little and climb the bum-shaped crack through the bulge. Hop onto the second, rather green, slab via its undercut right arete and finish up the centre of the third slab.
FA. John Earl 1970s

③ **Great Chimney** . . . . **Diff**
16m. A fine climb at an amenable grade following a strong line. Climb the chimney until it is possible to tunnel through to reach an expansive stance. A corner-crack leads to a smaller ledge then beyond this continue up the narrow chimney to reach the moor.

④ **'A' Buttress Left-hand** . . . . **VDiff**
8m. An alternative start to the next route.

⑤ **'A' Buttress Direct** . . . . . **VDiff**
18m. Worthwhile and interesting, though not hugely direct. From the foot of the buttress, head up with a jig right to pass the bulge then continue on rounded holds before heading left under the mushroom to reach the ledge and a stance. The crack leads up and left to join the final section of *Great Chimney*.

⑥ **'A' Buttress Right-hand** . . . . **S 4a**
8m. A right-hand start up the steep wall and short crack/groove.
Photo on page 301.

The next routes start from the commodious belay ledge and climb the rock above its right-hand side.

⑦ **The God Machine** . . **E3 5c**
12m. The tilted and photogenic arete that hangs over the ledge is gained via the rounded rib below. If you fall, don't bounce!
FA. Mark Savage 2002

⑧ **The Wind Tunnel** . . . . **HVS 5a**
12m. The large scooped groove is approached via the rather crusty slab. Climb boldly to a steep finish.

⑨ **Aeolian Wall** . . . . **VS 5a**
12m. Climb straight up the slab heading for a large 'ear'. Mantel over this then head through the bulges to reach the flanges that form the right edge of the big scoop. Follow these to the top.
FA. John Earl 1970s

⑩ **Delicatessen** . . . . . **VS 4c**
12m. A nicely varied classic. Cross the slab rightwards just above the overhangs (delicate) then climb up to the fine crack which gives a fittingly fine finish. A **Direct Start** is possible from the grass slope below *Chockstone Crack* via a groove and short traverse, at **HS 4b**. *Photo on page 295.*
FA. Malcolm Lowerson 1959

The steep wall to the right of Delicatessen is climbed by **Golden Days, E1 5a** *on the left and* **Gimme Wings, E4 6a** *up the centre.*

⑪ **Chockstone Crack** . . . . **Diff**
10m. The straight and deep cleft on the right of the tall wall.

⑫ **Archer's Chimney** . . . . **Diff**
8m. The next deep chimney reached by a sporting grass bank.

Buttress Face

Less popular than the rock to the left, though these short but smart walls do see some action. There is a neat mixture of aretes, faces and cracks here, though there isn't too much for the slab aficionado.

The front of the next subsidiary buttress has three closely spaced cracks, all of which are worth doing.

13 Sagittarius . . . . **VS 4c**
10m. The left-hand crack is probably the pick of the trio.
FA. Geoff Jackson early 1970s

14 The Quiver . . . . **VS 5a**
10m. Wobble up the central crack passing the half-height roof with difficulty.
FA. Geoff Jackson early 1970s

15 Wide Eyed and Witless . . . . **VS 4c**
10m. The thin right-hand crack passing a mini-peapod.

Buttress Face

16 Quartz Buttress . . . . **HVS 5a**
12m. Start up cracks in the left-edge of the wall to the roof then move right above the lowest overhang to access a small ledge round the right-hand arete. Finish direct - a fine outing.
FA. Hugh Banner 1970s

17 Regular Nightmare **E4 6a**
10m. Climb the ramp and wall to reach the roof, swing left, pull over and head up the wall above.
FA. Bob Smith early 1980s

18 Blood on the Rooftops . . **E5 6b**
10m. The blunt arete on the right is hard to start and bolder above. From the break, power though the roof to reach the wall.
FA. Joe Webb 1992

19 Gillette **E3 5b**
10m. The sharp left arete gives a fine but bold pitch.
FA. Karl Telfer 1979

20 Cut Throat **E4 6a**
10m. The front face of the tower is another good one with little in the way of gear and a fearsome fall-out zone.
FA. Bob Smith 1980

21 The Stoic **E2 5c**
10m. Grit your teeth and get up that right-hand arete.
FA. Bob Hutchinson 1979

22 Loophole Crack . . . . **S 4a**
10m. The corner-crack is a pleasant easier route.

23 Les Perchass . . . . **HVS 5b**
10m. The left-hand of a pair of thin cracks is tricky to start.
FA. George Michelson 1972

24 Nee Perchass . . . . **VS 5a**
10m. The right-hand crack.
FA. John Earl 1972

25 Broken Toe . . . . **HVS 5a**
10m. Power through the overlap and climb the wall.

26 Cairn Crack . . . . **VDiff**
9m. The crack is okay despite the rather grassy upper part.

27 Cairn Slab . . . . **S 4a**
8m. Hop over the roof and climb the slab rightwards then direct.

28 Cairn Scoop . . . . **VDiff**
8m. The open groove to a steeper finish.

29 Cairn Crack West . . . . **VDiff**
8m. The crack is the last feature of the wall.

30 Sunset Wall . . . . **S 4a**
8m. The wall, leftward traverse and crack round to the right are most easily reached up the gully, though crawling under the overhangs at the end of the terrace will also get you there.

Possible continuation climbs
See previous page for route
numbers and descriptions.

Buttress Face

Descent

Descent

'D' Buttress

'B' Buttress

'B' and 'D' Buttresses

'B' Buttress is the centre of the three taller buttresses
- the ancients avoided the temptation to call it A-nother
Buttress. It is less popular than 'A' Buttress though it
does have some good climbing. It is possible to easily
finish up one of the short routes on Buttress Face to
extend the pleasure. Right again is 'D' Buttress, the last
piece of rock described here. Seekers of solitude might
want to explore West End Buttress which is even further
west, close to the main path to the top of Simonside.

1 'B' Buttress Direct . . . . .   **HS 4b**
16m. Gain the scoop in the centre of the slab from the left (delicate) or from the right (strenuous) and pad up the ledge then step
right where steeper rock leads to easy ground.

2 'B' Buttress Chimney . . .   **S 4b**
16m. The deep rift is a struggle to a sentry box and more of a
struggle above, a thread runner is some consolation. From the top
of the pillar, step right and finish as for *Cairn Wall*.

3 Bee Bumble **E5 5c**
10m. The rounded arete to a steep and gripping finish. A (distant)
runner in the chimney reduces the grade to **E3**.
FA. Karl Telfer early 1980s

4 Cairn Wall . . . .   **S 4a**
20m. An interesting line starting up the right side of the tall tower
standing close to the buttress. Climb to and up the groove that
bounds the tower to its summit. Climb the short steep wall to a
higher ledge then step up and traverse round the arete to finish
up the top of the groove of *Lightning Wall*.

5 Lightning Wall . . . . . .   **HVS 5a**
12m. Trend left across the gully wall to reach the hanging crack
and follow it until a couple of tricky moves gain the ledge to the
left. Move back right and balance round to gain the green groove,
finish up this.
FA. John Earl 1970s

6 Stormbringer . . . . .   **HVS 5a**
14m. Head up to the flake in the centre of the wall then press on
by steep sustained climbing passing the wide break and a small
overhang to reach the right-hand end of the upper ledge.

7 Thunder Crack **E1 5b**
12m. The steep crack springing from the hollow in the right-hand
side of 'D' Buttress is approached easily then gives a short tussle
on solid jams. Good sport.
FA. Hugh Banner early 1970s

8 Master Plaster **E2 5b**
14m. The wall to the right of *Thunder Crack* is steep and pushy.
Climb to the flutings and press on to the break before moving
round left to finish.
FA. Graham Telfer 1980s

9 Dirty Thor't **E3 5c**
14m. The centre of the wall to the right of *Thunder Crack* gives
another steep and pushy pitch heading for the right-hand set of
flutings and finishing direct.
FA. Martin Doyle 1978

10 'D' Buttress Crack . . . .   **VS 4c**
8m. The short crack high on the right-hand side of the buttress is
reached by the steep fingery wall below.

	No star	☆	☆☆	☆☆☆
Mod to S	-	1	2	-
HS to HVS	1	5	-	-
E1 to E3	1	1	1	-
E4 and up	1	1	-	-

Reputedly Northumberland's biggest boulder; this interesting little venue is in a lovely setting and has enough at each grade to pass a couple of hours for most folk. Doing all the routes here in one visit would be quite an impressive achievement though.

The block faces all directions with the slabby east face and steep west face giving the best climbing. The routes generally are short and sharp and protection is lacking on many of the climbs, although there are some cracks that give the odd runner. Belaying on top of the block requires a bit of ingenuity. The easiest way down is via the chipped ladder and easy angled ramp of *Tourist Route* on the east face. Probably the most impressive feature of the rock is the current bedding formed when the rock was originally deposited.

Chris Craggs solo on *Plymouth Hoe* (S 4a) - *opposite* - the best protected route on the crag. Photo: Sherri Davy

Conditions

Sun or shade can be found at most times of the day and, being high on a hill, the crag tends to get enough of a breeze to keep the midges away. Some of the routes are a bit lichenous, a circumspect approach is best on the unprotected slabby climbs that rely almost exclusively on sloping holds. The outward view is superb.

Approach

The boulder is located high on the hill overlooking the small village of Harbottle which is 10 miles west of Rothbury and best reached by turning off the B6341 just past Flotterton. Drive through Harbottle (the boulder can be seen high up and left) to parking on the left in a nice shady Forestry Commission car park. A good track heads up the hill towards Harbottle Lake which is hidden over the brow of the hill. Follow the main path until it flattens out then head left via rough tracks to arrive at the boulder - an easy 10 minutes from the car.

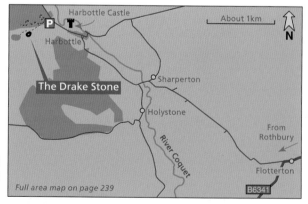

Full area map on page 239

East Face

West Face

North Face

---

① Cape Horn 🔲🔲🔲 **VS 4c**
10m. The slabs on the left-hand side of the east face are climbed trending leftwards to finish up the arete. Unprotected and spooky.

② Tourist Route 🔲🔲 **Mod**
7m. The ramp and then the line of chipped buckets is the easiest way up (and down) the block. Unprotected.

③ Garden Hoe 🔲🔲 **VS 4b**
7m. Head up the slab on a series of rounded holds.

④ Plymouth Hoe 🔲🔲 **S 4a**
7m. The finger-crack gives the best line on the boulder.
FA. Bob Hutchinson 1977

⑤ Pieces of Eight 🔲🔲🔲 **HVS 5b**
7m. The rounded arete is climbed until a move left gains the top. Worthwhile but serious and originally graded Hard Severe!

⑥ Good Hope 🔲🔲 **HVS 5b**
7m. The left arete of the west face is tricky - another serious one.

⑦ Sol Pelicanos 🔲🔲 **E2 5b**
8m. The flake in the upper part of the wall is gained from the break which is accessed by a short traverse from the arete.
FA. Cliff Robson 1995

⑧ The Pelican 🔲🔲 **E1 5b**
8m. The right-hand side of the face has a tough start then eases.

⑨ Hispaniola 🔲 **HVS 5a**
10m. The left arete leads to runners in the break, head up the wall to finish.

⑩ The Golden Hind 🔲🔲 **VS 5a**
10m. Climb the fingery wall and shallow groove to a finish up the fluted slab.
FA. Bob Hutchinson 1977

⑪ Lubbers' Hole 🔲🔲 **S 4a**
14m. Devious but excellent. Start up the thin crack of *Sir Francis* then traverse the break leftwards to the groove of *The Golden Hind*. Up this to the next break then swing round the leaning arete to an easier finish.
FA. Andrew Phillipson 1958

⑫ Sir Francis 🔲🔲🔲 **E3 5c**
10m. A fine climb up the crack and bold wall above. From the top of the crack trend slightly rightwards - a small flake helps.
FA. Bob Hutchinson 1970s

⑬ Rhumba 🔲🔲 **E4 5c**
10m. From the diagonal overlap, trend left to the break, then direct to holds in a higher break. Trend boldly rightwards to finish.
FA. Andy Moss 1983

⑭ Powder Monkey 🔲🔲 **E4 5c**
10m. The right-hand side of the south face is climbed rightwards then back left on spaced holds to reach a creaky flake and a precarious finish.
FA. Bob Smith 1983

	No star	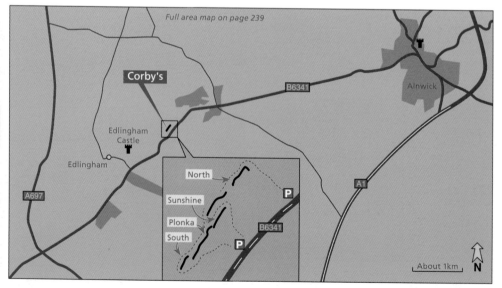 ☆	☆☆	☆☆☆
Mod to S	6	2	1	-
HS to HVS	6	11	2	2
E1 to E3	5	4	1	1
E4 and up	-	2	-	-

Corby's is a lovely cliff in an idyllic setting, with a good spread of routes, afternoon sun and splendid views over towards the Cheviot - there is little wonder that the crag has long been popular.

Access

The accessibility and quality of the crag has lead to some problems.
The rock at Corby's is softer than at many Northumberland venues and it is suffering from inappropriate use - please be aware of the problems and act accordingly.

Abseiling - The area above South Buttress is a popular abseiling venue and the severe degradation of the cliff top is evident for all to see. The thin vegetation has gone, replaced by loose sand, which washes down the crag with each wet spell. Put simply, this is not a good place for repeated group use. Indoor walls, bridges and quarries make better abseiling venues where less damage is likely to be done.

Top-roping - Although pretty much part of climbing nowadays, top-roping needs to be done with some common sense. For example, the cliff edge above *Audacity* is already deeply grooved from people ticking this great classic. If you really must top-rope it (the gear is excellent you know) ensure the ropes hang over the cliff edge and that they are padded.

Conditions

The crag faces north west and gets the afternoon and evening sun, it is also surprisingly sheltered. The cliff takes remarkably little drainage considering the extensive hillside above the crag and can be a good bet at any time of the year if the weather is being kind.

Approach

Corby's lies just below the B6341 Alnwick to Rothbury road a short distance north east of Edlingham. There is extensive parking (and a convenient bench) on the left near the top of the steep hill when heading towards Alnwick. Paths lead round either end of the cliff to reach its grassy base.

Colin Binks on *Ranadon* (E2 5b) - *page 306* - one of
the best pitches at Corby's. Photo: Sherri Davy

North Buttress

This is the show-piece of the crag with some fine and long climbs, often with hard finishes. *Audacity* and *Ranadon* are the classic ticks but all are worth doing. The crag base makes a superb picnic area, so it is perhaps best to visit the wall late in the day to make the most out of late afternoon sunshine.

Erosion - Please avoid top-roping these routes if possible since the cliff top is eroding badly.

1 Friday's Child . . . . 🌙📷 [ ] **E3 5c**
14m. The left-hand side of the main section of the face. Follow flakes steeply to the break then the fluting to the cave (often occupied by smelly birds). Pull into the hanging groove from the right and exit it to the right with difficulty.
FA. John Earl 1973

2 Ash Wednesday . . . 🌙📷📷 [ ] **E4 6a**
14m. A tough climax high on the wall. Climb out of the right-hand side of the hollow and up the fingery wall to the break. Cross the roof and climb juggy rock to the headwall and climb this via the solitary (and shallow) fluting to finish.
FA. Bob Smith 1979

3 Ranadon . . . . 🌙📷📷 [ ] **E2 5b**
16m. A fine climb, interesting and varied, with a well positioned finish. Climb the broad rib (good holds for the right hand) to the roof and make fingery moves to jugs which lead easily to the final roof. Once committed, it all falls nicely into place.
Photo on page 305.
FA. Martin Doyle 1977

4 Man Friday . . . . 🌙📷 [ ] **VS 4c**
20m. Devious but with some nice climbing, although the bird's nest doesn't add a lot to the experience. Climb the large flake then traverse the break leftwards to a second one that gives access to the cave. Continue the traverse out to the arete and a rather grotty finish.
FA. Ken MacDonald 1970s

5 Audacity . . . . 🌙📷📷 [ ] **HVS 5a**
16m. The classic of the crag; a fine line with good and well protected climbing throughout. Climb the flake and/or the wall just left to the break, move left a little then pull over using the flutings to gain the upper wall. Move right to skirt the overhangs then finish up the pleasant left-trending groove. **Please avoid top-roping this route; the cliff top is getting very eroded from badly placed top-ropes.** *Photo opposite.*
FA. Ken MacDonald 1971

6 Tenacity . . . . 🌙📷 [ ] **E4 6a**
16m. The final crack will test your determination. Start up *Audacity* but break right and climb the wall via a fluting before moving right to dirty ledges. The final crack gives a tenuous and strenuous piece of laybacking, only the weak are spurned.
FA. Jeff Lamb 1977

7 Cauliflower Lug . . . . . . 📷📷 [ ] **E3 6a**
12m. Leap through the lower overhangs to grasp the 'lug' then, once established, step right and climb the shallow groove and wall to the old tree.
FA. Bob Smith 1980

8 Plumbline . . . . 📷📷 [ ] **VS 4c**
12m. A direct line up the right-hand side of the face, tackling the bulges and short slab to a tree belay.

Causey Quarry
Crag Lough
Peel Crag
Callerhues
Great Wanney
E. Woodburn
Sandy Crag
Ravensheugh
Simonside
Drake Stone
Corbys
Bowden Doors
Back Bowden
Kyloe In
Kyloe Out
Berryhill

The right-hand side of North Buttress is a lot less imposing and has some pleasant easier climbs.

9 Easy Rider . . . . | | **S 4a**
12m. Climb the rounded arete to the dangling branches of the oak, then traverse out right to the arete to finish.

10 False Impression . . . . | | **VS 5a**
10m. The wall leads to a quick pull through the bulges.

11 Black Wall . . . . . . | | **HVS 5a**
10m. Follow the flakes to the roof and pass this with some forcefulness. Used to be a bit of a sandbag at VS 4c.
FA. Ken MacDonald 1970

12 Misunderstanding . . . . . | | **S 4a**
12m. The pleasant slab can be climbed anywhere at an amenable grade. The topo shows one of the easier versions of the route.

13 Cake Walk . . . . | | **Diff**
14m. Climb the groove on the right then follow good holds away left to eventually reach the trees.

14 Amorous Antics . . . . | | **E3 6b**
10m. Make taxing moves through the overlap then finish up the groove in the slab.
FA. Bob Smith 1981

15 Boulder, Crack and Slab . . . . . | | **VDiff**
12m. The name says it all.

Colin Binks on *Audacity* (HVS 5a) - *opposite*. Photo: Chris Craggs

Sunshine Superman

Sunshine Superman

A short wall of good rock at the left-hand end of the Upper Tier. It is less popular than other sections of the cliff, but there are some action packed little routes here.

1 Bogeyman .... **VS 5a**
8m. The short steep crack on the far left is good value.
FA. Ken MacDonald 1970s

2 Birdie .... **HVS 5a**
10m. Climb the wall just right of the crack by unobvious moves.

3 Super Spooky **E2 5c**
10m. The wall has small, well spaced holds.
FA. Bob Smith 1982

4 Hole in One .... **VS 4c**
10m. Follow the good holds rightwards then make a big reach for the next set of holds and scuttle back left to finish up the final section of the crack.
FA. John Earl 1970s

5 Corbeau. **E1 5a**
10m. The wall is steep and pumpy, though the holds are generally good. Protection is in short supply.
FA. Bob Hutchinson 1973

6 Sunshine Superman ... **HVS 5a**
10m. Thrilling climbing linking great holds by powerful moves. From the final niche, either step left and power through the bulges, or escape out right to evade the roofs.
FA. Ken MacDonald 1970s

7 Point Blank **E3 6a**
10m. The fingery bulging wall leads to a solitary fluting which is used to make the hard moves to reach the top.
FA. Steve Blake 1978

8 Tiger Feet **E1 5a**
10m. That's neat; a good climb with a well positioned finish. Climb the juggy arete to the bulges, stretch for holds then layback the fluting with conviction.
FA. Steve Blake 1977

9 Ken's Caper .... **HVS 4c**
12m. Start as for *Tiger Feet* but at the overhang traverse out right past the arete and gain a rest on the lip of the big overhang. Finish up the face.
FA. Ken MacDonald c1970

10 Gibbon's Gambol **E2 5c**
12m. Well named. Reach the right-hand end of the flake in the roof and ape left along it until it is possible to grope round the lip with difficulty. Finish easily up the slab. A **Direct Start** with no change in grade misses out most of the simian antics.
FA. Bob Hutchinson 1974

11 Wonderland .... **S 4a**
12m. Climb the wide leaning crack and its easier continuation.

12 Crossover .... **S 4a**
16m. Climb the front of the buttress until the angle eases then head left, crossing *Wonderland*, and meandering out to a finish up the airy arete.

13 The Plonka. .... **S 4a**
12m. A mini-classic, well worth doing. From the left edge of the cave, follow the diagonal crack leftwards to a junction with *Wonderland*. Finish up this, or better, continue left up the face.
Photo on page 311.
FA. Ken MacDonald c1970

Tiger Feet

Sunshine Superman

Descent

9
13
10 11
12
14 15 16 17

The Plonka

---

14 Missed Opportunity . . . . ⬜ **HVS 5b**
10m. Climb the fluted slab to the overhangs where undercuts enable tricky moves up and right to reach a thin flake-system. Finish direct from this.

15 Scotsman's Way . . . . ⬜ **VS 4c**
10m. Climb the left-slanting flakes then cross the hanging shield of rock on the right to reach the blunt arete. Follow the flakes to a rounded top-out.

16 First Opportunity . . . . . . ⬜ **S 4b**
10m. The compelling but awkward crack-line is a good bet for your first encounter with off-widthing, perhaps.

17 Overunder . . . . ⬜ **HS 4b**
10m. Start on the front of the buttress and follow the flakes up and left under the trio of bulges until it is possible to get out right onto the front. Finish direct. It is also possible to pull strenuously over the bulges lower down at **VS 5a**.

The Plonka
The central and right-hand section of the Upper Tier have some nice routes, including the classic that gives the area its name. It tends to be a popular venue.
Erosion - This is another section of the crag which is suffering from erosion. Please try and avoid abseiling and top-roping here.

18 Temptation . . . . ⬜ **VS 5a**
10m. An enticing tapering thin flake above the bulge beckons. Approach it steeply, use it gently, then finish on rounded holds.
FA. Ken MacDonald 1970

19 Prediction . . . . ⬜ **VS 5a**
10m. Follow the slanting slab to its top then make tricky moves up and left to access a second slab. Wander up this to the top.

20 Chicken Run . . . . . . ⬜ **VS 4c**
10m. The rounded buttress just left of the descent gully. A good flake leads to easier angled terrain. Continue direct - a bit bold feeling - or scuttle off right, to calls of "chicken!"
FA. Bob Smith c1979

Descent

17 18 19
20

Temptation

South Buttress
The first piece of rock reached when using the southern approach has long been popular, partly because of some good routes and partly because of its accessibility.
Erosion - This section of the crag is suffering especially badly from erosion as the cliff edge vegetation has been worn away. Please try and avoid abseiling and top-roping here.

1 Bluebird . . . . . ⑫ 🦋 E3 6a
10m. The jutting arete of the buttress has steep and bold moves to pass the bulge and gain the flutings above.
FA. Steve Blake c1978

2 Misrepresentation. . ⑫ VS 4c
10m. The flake to the right of the arete gives a good pitch. Climb steeply to it, then layback and bridge to its top where a rounded exit awaits.
FA. Ken MacDonald c1970

3 Nut's Wall . . . . ⑫ VS 4c
10m. Climb the open groove to reach the thin flake on the left. Up this steeply then make a tricky move out right to reach a good resting ledge. Finish direct.
FA. Ken MacDonald c1970

4 L.P. . . . . ⑫ VS 4c
10m. Good climbing, devious and interesting. Pull over the bulge on pockets then follow the ramp rightwards before moving back left a little and finishing direct.
FA. Ken MacDonald c1970

5 Reject E1 5b
10m. Fills the gap up the wide rib. Pull through the bulges then climb the bold wall to ledges. Move right a short way, finish direct.
FA. Bob Smith c1979

6 Bloody Sunday . . . . ⑫ VS 5a
12m. Start just right of the rounded cave and climb flakes until moves right reach a better crack. Up this to ledges then move left a couple of metres to find the easiest finish.
FA. Ken MacDonald 1970

7 Two Tree Chimney. . . . . Diff
12m. The well wooded rift has some (easy) rock climbing too.

8 Little X . . . . ⑫ VS 5a
6m. Start below and left of the 'X' and make tricky moves to and past it. Harder variations are available. Finish more easily above.

9 Mr. Jones . . . . Diff
12m. The right arete of the cliff on well worn holds to a ledge. Finish up the right-trending ramp.

Jamie Moss catches the evening light on *The Plonka* (S 4a) - *page 308* - at Corby's. Photo: Jamie Moss (ST)

	No star	☼	☼☼	☼☼☼
Mod to S	10	7	2	2
HS to HVS	13	9	5	5
E1 to E3	16	10	5	2
E4 and up	2	5	1	3

Perhaps the archetypal Northumbrian crag, Bowden Doors has everything; over 150 routes right across the grade spectrum, wonderful rock, easy accessibility, a great outlook, the afternoon sun and loads of bouldering. With all this it is hardly surprising that the place gets popular; if you find it a bit busy then it is always worth heading further along the crag to find a more peaceful spot.

Access
Although the rock is superb quality sandstone, it is easily damaged by ropes running over the edge. If you must top-rope here, PLEASE do your utmost to protect the rock by ensuring that your belay rope is draped well over the edge of the crag and well padded by a rucksack or similar. The same applies to leaders, winching multiple seconds up routes.
The southern end of the crag and the normal approach are not on Access Land. The farmer has made the very reasonable request that people don't park in front of the gate to the field, and that they don't bring any dogs with them - please respect his wishes.

Conditions
The crag faces west and gets the sun all afternoon. To some degree, it is in the rain shadow of the distant Cheviots and so it is often drier here then you might expect. Bowden is in a breezy situation and takes little drainage so it is rapid drying. Please avoid climbing here when the rock is wet or damp since that makes the sandstone more brittle.

Approach
Bowden Doors is just north of the B6349 Belford to Wooler road. Follow the road from Belford west and, just over a crest in the road, look over your right shoulder. There is (narrow) roadside parking beyond the high point of the road on the opposite side to the gate/stile that gives access to the path to the crag.
PLEASE PARK CONSIDERATELY and do not block any of the field access in the area. If the parking is full it is also possible to approach the left-hand end of the crag by a track which starts just west of the Back Bowden parking.

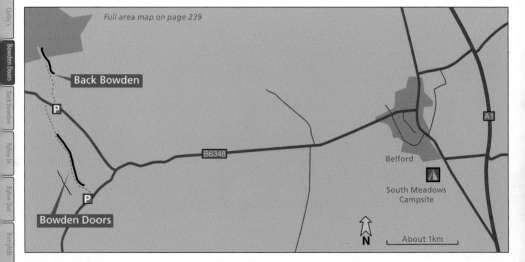

Full area map on page 239

Back Bowden

B6348

Belford

South Meadows Campsite

Bowden Doors

N

About 1km

Colin Binks inspecting the tricky last moves on *Scorpion* (VS 4c) - *page 319* - Bowden Doors. Photo: Chris Craggs

The Scoops

The Scoops

The far left-hand end of Bowden Doors sees less traffic than most of the rest of the cliff, though it is popular as a bouldering venue. Some of the more significant and independent problems are described but many more exist, and the initial moves of most of the routes also often give quality problems though repeated use is damaging some.

1 Evening Wall . . . . S 4b
7m. The groove bounding the right-hand side of the slab.

2 Scoop 3 . . . . E1 5b
7m. Climb the right-trending flake and the short wall above.
FA. Steve Blake c1978

3 Scoop 2 . . . . E1 5b
8m. Follow the pale flakes then finish direct, or just to the right.
FA. Allan Austin 1968

4 Toffs V5 (6b)
Gain holds under the bulge direct (reachy) or from the left (fingery). Jump off or continue by undercuts and a flake - **E3**.
FA. Bob Smith 1982

5 Working Class V10
Undercut and stretch to the break. A sit-start is **V12**.
FA. Ben Moon 1990s

6 Poverty V8
Use tiny undercuts and pockets to eventually match on a flake. Jump off. The full route to the top is worth **E5**. Variations abound.
FA. Bob Smith 1984

7 His Eminence E4 6a
8m. A direct line up the dark wall just to the left of the groove of Scoop 1. The start is a hard **V6** and the finish is just hard.
FA. Bob Smith 1980

8 Scoop 1 . . . . E1 5b
8m. The first set of flakes left of the deep corner give a good and pumpy pitch at the grade.
FA. Steve Blake 1978

The steep wall left of the deep corner/groove has a trio of excellent routes, all being steep and pumpy exercises.

9 The Judge E4 6a
10m. Climb the right-hand edge of the left-hand black streak to the top break then move out left for a finish. Low in the grade.
FA. Tommy Smith 1978

10 The Trial E3 6a
10m. The centre of the wall gives a classic pitch, sustained climbing on generally good holds leads to the highest break, then move left and sprint up the flake to the top.
FA. Bob Hutchinson 1972

11 The Jury E3 5c
10m. The right-hand side of the wall is also worth the effort. Start up the flake and climb to a decent hold below the bulges. Step right and finish direct.
FA. Tommy Smith 1978

12 Bloody Crack . . . . VS 5a
9m. The wide leaning crack in the angle is well named for many.

13 Bloody Nose . . . . . . HS 5a
9m. Flakes in the right-hand side of the arete to the right of the corner show the way.

14 The Shiner V1 (5b)
A short lived battle with the bulges. Continue to the top at **VS**.

15 The Skate V2 (5c)
Undercut leftwards then stretch up and right to a break and poor jams. Finish direct more easily.
FA. Bob Smith 1978

16 Flying Fish V3 (6a)
Use the undercut to reach crusty flakes then move left to a sloper. Finish more easily above. The fingery wall just to the right of the undercuts is **Flying Stag, V8 (6c)**.
FA. Tommy Smith 1978. FA. (Flying Stag) Malcolm Smith c2003

17 The Sting E3 6a
10m. Follow the trio of finger-flakes up the wall by tricky climbing then tackle the bulges on rounded holds with difficulty.
FA. Bob Hutchinson 1975

18 Honeycomb Wall . . V10
10m. The bubbly wall is climbed to the break where an escape into The Sting is possible.
FA. Malcolm Smith 2003

19 The Manta E3 6a
10m. The superb and elegant curving flake looks easy enough until you get on it, at which point it proves to be both strenuous and precarious at the same time. From the end of the flake, finish direct.
Variation Starts - Left-hand - **V7**, Direct - **V5**, Right-hand - **V5**.
FA. Jeff Lamb c1976

The Manta

⑳ **Vienna** . . . . 🚫 [   ] ?
The famous dyno has become very worn through over-use.
FA. Pete Kirton 1980s

㉑ **Rising Damp** . . . . 🔝 [   ] **E4 6b**
20m. The traverse is a taxing stamina problem with sustained difficulties as far as the sandy hollows, then an easier finish.
FA. Bob Smith 1979. The crag's first undisputed 6b.

㉒ **Inner Space** . . . 🔝 [   ] **E5 6b**
12m. Start through the right-hand end of a diagonal overlap and continue up the wall to reach the break. Move right a metre or so then exit through the bulges with difficulty.
FA. Hugh Harris 1991

㉓ **The Wave** . . . . 🔝 [   ] **E5 6a**
14m. A classic, the second route to breach the Wave. Climb the white flakes to their top, then make difficult moves up to reach the break. Move right a couple of metres then climb though the Wave, trending right to a tricky finish.
FA. Bob Hutchinson 1978

㉔ **High Tide** . . . . 🔝 [   ] **E5 6a**
16m. Climb *The Wave* to the break then head strenuously leftwards until above the sandy hollows on *Rising Damp*. Finish directly through the bulge.
FA. Bob Smith 1979

㉕ **Captain Haddock** . . . 🔝 [   ] **V5 (6b)**
Thin moves up the wall right of the white flake.

㉖ **Rough Passage** 🔝 [   ] **E6 6b**
14m. The tough wall leads past two old bolts to the break. Swing left for three metres to exit via a scoop, with difficulty.
FA. Bob Smith 1988

㉗ **Poseidon Adventure** [Top 50] [   ] **E4 6a**
12m. A fine climb, the first to breach the Wave's defences. A right-trending line leads to a worrying stretch for the break. Shuffle right and pull over the centre of the huge thread.
Photo on page 237.
FA. Steve Blake 1976

㉘ **The Bends** . . . . 🔝 [   ] **E4 6b**
12m. Climb the wall, trending slightly leftwards past a diagonal undercut, to reach a shallow scoop with difficulty. Exit via *Poseidon Adventure* which is directly above. A right-hand exit is *Narcosis*, **E6 6b.** The direct start is **Growlers, V11.**
FA. Bob Smith 1983. FA. (Narcosis) Hugh Harris 1991
FA. (Growlers) Andrew Earl 2000s

㉙ **Green Crack** . . . . 🔝 [   ] **HVS 5b**
11m. The crack in the corner is an adventure. It sees fewer ascents than most of the E5s hereabouts.

㉚ **Rip the Lip** . . . . 🔝 [   ] **E6 6a**
24m. It had to be done - the pumpfest, linking the top of *Green Crack* with the finish of *The Wave*. The difficulties are sustained rather then technical, but it keeps heaping on the pressure.
FA. Ian Cummings 1990

The Wave
A magnificent feature, a wide wall of impeccable rock topped off by a rolling wave of rippled sandstone. All the routes that climb to and through the feature known as the Wave are well worth doing. The area is not very popular; though this is more to do with grades than quality.

The Wave

Barbarian

The Wave

Bouldering cave

Barbarian
A couple of lesser buttresses towards the left-hand end of the cliff, though with a smattering of worth-while routes and a spot of pumpy bouldering that sees a fair bit of action. *Barbarian* is the one to do here - if you are up to it.

1 Staggered V8
Up the blunt rib to join *Barbarian*. Descend it or jump onto your mat. The sit-down start is **V10**.
FA. Richie Patterson 1990s. FA. (SS) Malcolm Smith 2003

2 Barbarian E5 6b
10m. The superb curving flake (a *Manta* look-a-like) leads left-wards with hard moves on sketchy footholds to pass the gap in the flake. All that remains is a tussle to gain the flutings (awkward to place runner) and a wild exit. High in the grade.
FA. Bob Smith 1978. Whilst trying the route in the 1970s Jeff Lamb imported two single bed mattresses to pad the boulders - obviously a visionary.

The cave area left of Giant's Ear is an excellent bouldering spot with many problems and eliminates.

3 Giant's Ear .... VS 5a
10m. The hanging flake is approached from the left, struggle up the wide awkward crack behind it.

4 Bull's Lug E2 6a
8m. The short hanging wall is taxing.

5 Robber's Rib .... VS 5b
7m. The crack in the south-facing rib to a leftward exit.

6 Arrow Crack .... VDiff
10m. The widening crack in the left-hand end of the next wall.

7 Billy Liar E2 5c
8m. The rounded arete right of *Arrow Crack* on its right side.
FA. Bob Smith c1978

8 Crunchie E2 5c
10m. Head up the centre of the wall.
FA. Steve Blake c1978

9 Temptation V6 (6c)
The right-hand side of the wall has a stopper move to reach (or not) the break. Jump off.
FA. John Welford 1988

10 Blind Wall .... S 4a
10m. Climb the right-slanting flake to its end then pull out left and climb the wall on good flake holds.

11 Hanging Crack E1 5b
10m. Start up *Blind Wall*, but at the bulges head up and right-wards to enter the wide and wrigglesome crack.
FA. Hugh Banner 1972. Alan Austin had just failed on the line.

The next wall is crossed by a black overhang for most of its length. There are several routes here, only the best one is listed.

12 Boomer E4 5c
10m. Climb the black flake to the roof then pass this leftwards before trending back right to finish.
FA. John Earl 1978

Hanging Crack

Banana Wall and Tiger's Wall

These two adjacent faces have a great set of routes that have climbing that is a bit slabbier than much of the cliff. The Orange Spot trio of *The Runnel*, *Banana Wall* and *Tiger's Wall* are especially worthwhile.

1 Wall End . . . . **VDiff**
7m. The left-most line on the wall, trending right.

2 Wall End Direct . . . . **HS 4c**
8m. The right-trending flakes give a pleasant pitch. Finish out left.

3 Yellow Peril **E2 5c**
10m. A bit of an eliminate, though with good moves.
FA. Tommy Smith c1979

4 The Runnel . . . . **VS 5a**
10m. Lovely climbing and a little bold up the beckoning half-pipe that runs up the wall.
FA. John Earl 1972

5 Banana Wall . . . . **VS 4c**
10m. Not in the slightest bit slippery. Climb to a ledge (choice of ways) then follow the left-trending flake line to a nice finish up the fossilised forest crowning the crag. Only 4b after the start, but bold.

6 Abanana **E1 5c**
10m. The centre of the right side of the wall gives a precarious pitch on rounded holds and with little in the way of gear.
FA. Bob Hutchinson 1974

7 Banana Groove . . . . **HVS 5a**
10m. Start up the crack but move out left and follow the diagonal scoops to the top.

8 Black Crack . . . . **VDiff**
10m. Up the crack to the jutting snout and scoot right to jugs.

9 Red Crack . . . . **HS 4c**
10m. The right-hand crack has a steep central section that requires a bit of steady jamming.

10 Leo **E2 5b**
10m. Climb the left arete of the face then move right across the face and follow the finger-flakes to the top. More direct versions feel a little contrived as the holds lead you rightwards.
FA. Bob Smith 1978

11 Tiger's Wall . . . . **HVS 5a**
11m. A vaunted classic and with good reason. Low in the grade (for Northumberland). Climb the tricky wall to below the bulge - awkward protection - then pull through on good but spaced holds and romp up the crack-line.

12 The Cheetah **E2 5c**
10m. A bit squeezed in but its upper part has good climbing. Climb the open scoop and overhang, the short wall and the final flakes, in that order.
FA. Bob Smith 1980

13 The Rajah **E5 6b**
12m. Fine and arduous; the only way up the impressive wall to the right. Climb the wall powerfully to the roof (poor cams) then move right to locate a good hold over the lip. Stand up with difficulty (poor cam) and continue with trepidation to the top.
FA. Bob Smith 1978

14 Antihydrol **V11**
The blank wall gives this fierce problem.
FA. Andy Earl

15 Slab Crack **E1 5b**
10m. The crack bounding the wall is a battle from start to finish.

Lorraine

Lorraine and Castle Crack

A couple of fine buttresses with a selection of worthwhile climbs and a couple of real Bowden classics on which queuing might be expected at busy times.

5 Crescent Wall . . . . S 4b
8m. The left side of the buttress is climbed left then right. Pleasant.

6 Pitcher Wall . . . . . . HVS 5a
10m. Jugtastic climbing but the rock is still a bit snappy. Some weaving is required to make use of the best of the pitchers. More direct versions to the right (**E1**) and the left (**E2**) feel inferior.
FA. Allan Austin 1967

7 The Belford Pie Shop . . E3 6a
10m. The smooth wall has some taxing moves at half-height.
FA. Ian Kyle 1984

8 Castle Crack . . . . . . HVD
10m. A cracker at the grade, steep and quite pushy feeling. Pull up and right into the crack and follow it on excellent holds. A little tricky to protect because of the width of the main crack.

9 Bella E2 5c
8m. Pull over the low roof left and climb to the niche. Finish up the fluted wall.

10 Sue . . . . S 4c
9m. Follow the slanting cracks into the middle of the face then move back right and climb flakes just short of the arete.

11 Sue Direct . . . . HVS 5b
9m. Follow *Sue* to the middle of the face then finish directly and delicately up the wall.

12 Flake Wall . . . . Diff
8m. The left arete of the deep chimney on generous holds.

13 Flake Chimney . . . . Diff
8m. The deep rift on the right.

1 Don't Let Go E2 5c
10m. The left arete is started on the right (useful flake out right) then swing left to tackle the crack through the left-hand side of bulge. There are holds above, honest!
FA. Steve Blake 1977

2 Lorraine . . . . VS 5a
12m. A little beauty and doubtless harder than you will be expecting. A fingery layback and long stretch gains the break. Pump left along this quickly and delicately climb the wall right of the arete.
FA. Malcolm Rowe 1968

3 Little Red Rooster E1 5c
10m. The thin flaky wall leads to the bulges. Pull through (runners to the left) then finish using the solitary left-hand fluting.

4 Runt . . . . VS 5a
8m. The stunted flakes on the right. Short lived.

From mid morning | 5 min | Windy

Lorraine

Castle Crack

Castle Wall and Scorpion

The small bulbous buttress under the wall and the wider face to the right has some interesting climbing up flakes and cracks plus some fingery test-pieces up the intervening 'blank' walls. Apart from *Scorpion* and *Crab Wall*, the area is not especially popular.

1 Castle Wall .... S 4b
8m. Climb the face rightwards and finish up the deep flutings.

2 Wall Crack .... VS 4c
8m. A tricky start up the leaning crack leads to easy ground.

3 Triple Cracks .... HS 4c
6m. The trio of offset cracks give a good and awkward little pitch.

4 Short Crack .... VDiff
4m. A couple of jamming moves that are over too soon.

5 Creepy Crawly V3 (6a)
The left-hand side of the wall has this technical tinker.
FA. Bob Smith 1979

6 The Harvest Bug V3 (6a)
Trend left up the line of poor holds that cross the drainage streak. Another technical piece of climbing.
FA. Steve Blake c1979

7 Woolman's Wall ... VS 5a
10m. Start up thin flakes then head left to a thinner creaking one and a worrying finish.
FA. Allan Austin 1967. Named after Austin's Yorkshire based trade.

8 Listen to the Rain E4 5c
10m. A direct finish to *Woolman's Wall*. A couple of flakes point the way to the harrowing final couple of moves.
FA. Lewis Grundy 1991

9 The Lobster E2 5c
10m. Climb to the arch, pull over, then climb the taxing wall to a finish up a short flake-crack.
FA. Bob Smith 1978

10 Crab Wall .... HS 4b
8m. Climb steeply then follow the large rounded flakes to the top with hardly a sideways move in sight.

11 Scorpion .... VS 4c
8m. Access the slanting groove and climb this to its top and a tricky exit. The scoured state of the footholds points to plenty of pondering having gone on over the last couple of moves.
Photo on page 313.

12 Nutcracker .... HVS 5b
8m. The broken flake is followed to its end then trend right up the wall to the arete. A direct finish is **5c**.

13 Brutally Handsome E2 5c
7m. Do battle with the hanging nose. Climb left up the lower section until a hold on the right allows the snout to be accessed, then scale it with difficulty.
FA. Paul Stewart 1979

14 Nose Chimney .... Diff
7m. The deep rift is often used as a descent route.

Leaning Grooves   **Canada Crack**

Leaning Grooves and Canada Crack

The central section of the cliff has many fine climbs up interesting features and on good rock. All of those listed here are well worth the effort.

1 Blocked Chimney Corner . . . . . [ ] **HS 4c**
7m. The groove that bounds the wall is obvious from its name.

2 Second Leaning Groove [ ] **VS 5a**
8m. The left-hand of the two right-slanting grooves gives steady climbing to a leftward exit and a sprint up the flutings.

3 First Leaning Groove . . . [ ] **HVS 5a**
10m. Climb the right-hand groove - the flake out right is used by most - then make bold moves to better holds and a steep finish.
FA. Malcolm Rowe 1969

4 Street Runner . . . . . [ ] **E4 5c**
10m. The wall direct gives a bold pitch. Access the flake on First Leaning Groove from the right then move right across the wall to reach respite at the horizontal break. Finish direct.
FA. Bob Smith 1979

5 The Big Splash . . . . [ ] **E2 5c**
10m. The two horizontals in the right-hand side of the wall are linked by an extended reach and usually a bit of pedalling.
FA. Steve Blake 1976

6 Long John . . . . [ ] **S 4c**
10m. Climb into and up the hanging chimney. Awkward.

7 Transformer . . . . [ ] **V3 (6a)**
The sharp arete is accessed from the right and gives a couple of taxing moves until Jackdaw Crack just to the right can be reached. Finishing straight up the arete is worth **E3**.
FA. Steve Blake 1977

8 Jackdaw Crack . . . . . . [ ] **HVS 5b**
10m. Do battle with the disjointed cracks in the left wall of the long groove. The move between the cracks is tricky, as is the exit.

9 Long Crack . . . . [ ] **HVS 5a**
11m. The long widening crack in the groove gives a good tussle.

10 First Century . . . . . [ ] **E4 6a**
10m. The wall just right of Long Crack is bold and hard. There is a decent hold at about half-height where a tough undercut move gives access to the final wall.
FA. Bob Smith 1980

11 Klondyke Wall . . . . [ ] **E2 5c**
10m. Climb round the curving overlap and continue up the wall until forced right to use the edge of Canada Crack to exit.
FA. Steve Blake c1979

12 Canada Crack . . . . [ ] **HVS 5a**
10m. A great climb, strenuous but in a nice honest way. Layback the right-hand side of the flake then hand traverse its top (pumped yet?) and make one more strenuous move up into the continuation crack. Finish up this on good holds. It is also possible to start from Klondyke Wall, the grade is about the same as the regular start, but it is (even) more strenuous.
FA. Eric Rayson 1967. Just before he emigrated!

13 Quatra Twinkley . . . . . . [ ] **E3 6a**
8m. The arete is climbed on its left-hand side to a rounded exit.
FA. Steve Nagy 1996

14 Dog Eat Dog . . . . . . [ ] **V5 (6b)**
A popular highball up the bulging wall just right of the arete.

Leaning Grooves
Canada Crack
The Overhanging Crack
Main Wall

The Overhanging Crack

From mid morning | 5 min | Windy

❶ Death Knell . . . . 🔟 🖐 ☐ **E6 6b**
10m. The steep wall left of *Overhanging Crack* gives a serious and sustained piece of climbing
FA. Mark Liprot 1988

❷ The Overhanging Crack . 🔟 🖐 ☐ **E2 5c**
10m. A classic test-piece, the wide awkward exit stops many attempts dead in their tracks.
FA. John Earl 1971. Climbed sometime earlier with a chockstone for aid by John Hiron.

❸ Russet Groove . . . . ┌Top┐└50┘ 🖐 ☐ **VDiff**
10m. A lovely little route on bounteous holds. Climb the groove rightwards to ledges out near the arete then traverse left for a steep and well positioned finish.

❹ Red Nose . . . . ☐ **VS 4c**
8m. Climb the black groove then the juggy rib. Artificial but nice.

The Overhanging Crack

The section of rock to the left of the Main Wall is less extensive and less impressive. Despite this, *Russet Groove* is an excellent and popular VDiff whereas the imposing fissure of *The Overhanging Crack* sees fewer attempts and even fewer successes.

❺ Exhibition Crack . . . . . . 🔟 🖐 ☐ **HS 4c**
8m. Gaining the crack which doesn't quite reach the ground proves to be tricky.
FA. Tommy Smith 1975

❻ Guard's Exit . . . . ☐ **VDiff**
7m. Follow the crack into the hanging recess, then select a way out of it, the right-hand crack is the most often used.

❼ The Corner . . . . 🖐 ☐ **HVS 5a**
7m. The blank angle, short lived but quite taxing.

Causey Quarry · Crag Lough · Peel Crag · Callerhues · Great Wanney · E. Woodburn · Sandy Crag · Ravensheugh · Simonside · Drake Stone · Corby's · Bowden Doors · Back Bowden · Kyloe In · Kyloe Out · Berryhill

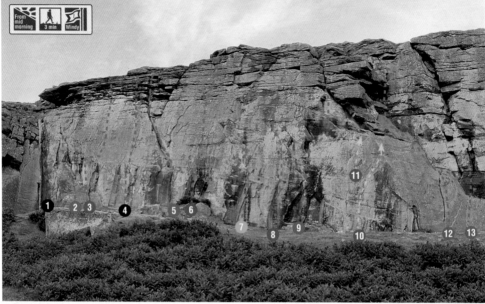

Main Wall

The first section of the crag reached from the road consists of a couple of steep walls that appeared to have been quarried long ago. There is an excellent set of climbs here across the grade spectrum.

❶ Crater Maker . . . . 🧗🪢 ⬜ **E4 6a**
10m. A hard climb up the wall just right of the corner.
FA. Bob Smith 1979

❷ Flake Crack . . . . 🔄 ⬜ **S 4b**
12m. The slab and flake lead to a steep finish rightwards.

❸ Goose Step . . . . . . 🔄🪢🧗 ⬜ **E3 6a**
12m. From a squat pedestal, climb up and left to a block in the crack then move out right to a couple of finger-slots in the slab. Continue direct from these with difficulty.
FA. Bob Hutchinson 1978

❹ Kaiser Bill . . . . 🔄🧗 ⬜ **E4 6b**
12m. Climb via two short square grooves to reach the thin flake-crack in the right-hand side of the face, up this, trending leftwards. The difficulties gradually ease.
FA. Bob Smith 1980

❺ Grovel Groove . . . . 🔄 ⬜ **S 4a**
12m. Better climbing than the name suggests, if you stay outside the groove. Up the left-slanting trough to a steep juggy finish.

❻ The Gauleiter . . . . 🔄🧗 ⬜ **E3 6a**
12m. Starting from an embedded block, the centre of the russet wall has hard moves at half-height.
FA. John Earl 1978. The name is a high ranking Nazi official (and nick-name of the leader) if you are interested.

❼ The Scoop . . . . 🔄🧗 ⬜ **VS 4c**
12m. A tricky start (especially for the short) gains the scoop which has more holds and runners than it appears from the ground. It is steep enough to ensure that the interest is well maintained. *Photo opposite.*

❽ Black and Tan Direct . . . 🧗🚪 ⬜ **E2 6a**
12m. Start up a blank groove and climb the face above by fingery and reachy moves.
FA. Bob Smith c1983

❾ Black and Tan . . . . 🔄🧗 ⬜ **S 4c**
14m. Start up the black flakes (hard) then move out right steeply to access the easier, left-slanting cracks to finish.

❿ Y Front . . . . 🔄 ⬜ **V3 (6a)**
6m. The right-hand side of the face just left of the arete.

⓫ Jock Strap . . . . 🧗 ⬜ **V5 (6b)**
6m. Start up *Y Front* but trend left. Also recorded as *Y Front Direct* and *Left-hand Finish*. There are several variations here.

⓬ Second Staircase . . . . 🔄 ⬜ **Diff**
12m. The slabby ramp and steeper juggy finish is a worthwhile beginners' climb.

⓭ Deception Crack . . . . 🔄 ⬜ **VDiff**
12m. The steep widening crack in the left-hand section of the wall is approached via a short slab and followed pleasantly.

⓮ Stretcher Wall . . . . 🔄🚪 ⬜ **E1 5c**
14m. Good (and reachy) climbing up the left-hand side of the face. Start up the black right-facing flake then climb more or less directly up the wall. Easier for the tall.
FA. John Earl 1972

⓯ The Viper .... 🗼 📖 ☐ **E1 6a**
16m. Start just right of the black rock and climb to the break. Traverse right until below the beckoning thin crack, and gains this with difficulty (good gear). Climb to join *Main Wall* then move out right for a pleasant finale.

⓰ Hissing Sid .... 📖 📷 ☐ **E1 5c**
14m. A bit of an eliminate crossing the traverse of *The Viper* then heading straight up the wall above.
FA. Bob Smith 1980

⓱ Main Wall .... 🗼 🪝 ☐ **HVS 5b**
16m. A classic, devious but with excellent moves. Climb the left-hand of the two blackened grooves to its top, pull right then climb the wall until it is possible to move left into the left-slanting crack. Finish up this.
FA. Malcolm Rowe 1969

⓲ Main Wall Eliminate ... 🗼 📷 ☐ **HVS 5b**
16m. The right-hand blackened flake leads to the break, the short wall above gives some precarious moves. Continue steeply just left of the upper arete.
FA. Paul Stewart c1979

⓳ Handrail Eliminate .... 📷 📷 ☐ **HVS 5c**
10m. The thin flake and wall above are, as expected, an eliminate.

⓴ Handrail .... 📷 ☐ **VS 4c**
10m. The flakes a short distance left of the arete give a few interesting moves.

㉑ Introductory Staircase ..... 🗼 ☐ **Mod**
12m. The line of big steps is the first, last and easiest route on the cliff. The crack up and right is **Banister Crack**, VDiff which offers a harder finish for those who want it.

Chris Craggs enjoying *The Scoop* (VS 4c) - *opposite* - Bowden Doors. Photo: Sherri Davy

	No star			
Mod to S	2	5	1	-
HS to HVS	1	-	2	-
E1 to E3	2	12	5	4
E4 and up	1	9	5	9

A lovely crag tucked away in a sheltered wooded valley to the west of Belford. Unlike the continuous edge of the nearby Bowden Doors, Back Bowden consists of a series of separate buttresses spread along the valley side, tailing off into some woods. The sheltered nature of the place means it can get a bit hot and fly-blown in humid conditions but it also makes a top venue on cold clear days. Many of the routes here range from hard to very hard though there are enough easier offerings scattered around the cliff to make a visit worthwhile by most folks, whatever their aspirations.

Conditions
The crag faces south west and catches the sun from mid morning, though the left-hand end is tucked in behind the trees and does get very green and mossy in the wetter months. The left-hand section is also so steep that it is shaded in the summer.

Approach   See map on page 312
There is limited parking on the verge by the side of the narrow road that branches north off the B6349 Belford to Wooler road. This parking is just beyond the high point of the road and is by the gate that gives access to the path to the crag. There have been problems here in the past with people blocking access to the gate which, under-standably, has annoyed the landowner. His solution is simple, you block his gate and he will move your car - see the sign.
To avoid future access problems - PLEASE PARK CONSIDERATELY.

CARS PARKED IN THIS GATEWAY WILL BE REMOVED WITHOUT CONSULTATION.

PLEASE VACATE THE ROCKS BY 6.30 p.m.

Merlin · The Witch · On the Verge · The Tube · Roof Route · Big Aerial Dynamite

Graham Parkes inspecting the finishing moves on *Tube* (E4 5c) - *page 330* - one of the best routes at Back Bowden. Photo: Chris Craggs

Not much sun / 5 min

Merlin

The leaning mass of the Merlin Wall is one of the most impressive bits of rock in Northumberland - a place for displays of technical wizardry and super stamina. From the first chink in its armour - *Merlin* (1981) - the wall has seen a steady trickle of impressive and significant routes with *The Dark Side* (2003) being the current state of the art. The wall doesn't see much sun because of the encroaching trees and its angle. It can be dry in the rain if there has been a decent dry spell. Unsurprisingly the routes see little attention and so are usually dirty. Prospective on-sighters might want someone to clean the finishing holds before they set off into the unknown. The grades and stars given here are for routes that are in tip-top condition.

On the far left is a quarried bay with half a dozen unpopular routes. The first route described is just right of this.

1 Twisting Crack . . . . **HS 4c**
8m. A steep start leads to pleasant jamming above the bulge.

2 County Ethics **E7 7a**
10m. The leaning wall and shallow scoop above the lip gives the line. Despite being relatively safe it still doesn't see much action and, although not really a boulder problem, it has been done above mats at around **V10**.
FA. Dave Cuthbertson 1990

3 Merlin **E5 6a**
12m. The original line here is devious but superb. Climb to the ledge, traverse right, then go direct to the top. There are cams available in the high break and a thread runner in the final wall.
FA. Bob Smith1981

4 The Pixies **E6 6b**
12m. A counter diagonal to *Merlin* with poor gear and hard moves.
FA. Dave Pegg 1991

5 Morgan **E5 6a**
14m. Climb leftwards to the right end of the *Merlin* ledge, then climb the wall before moving right and heading through the bulges strenuously.
FA. Bob Smith 1986

6 I Bet He Drinks Carling Black Label
. . . . **E8 6c**
20m. A traverse of the high break from *Morgan* to *Mordreth* is a wild and pumpy trip. Probably not the best route in the World!
FA. Steve Roberts 1994

7 The Dark Side . **E9 7b**
12m. How hard do you want it to be? The right-hand side of the pale shield and the leaning wall above lead to the break - (poor) runners - finish direct.
FA. Andy Earl 2003

8 Mordreth **E6 6b**
12m. A good line with powerful climbing and the added spice of some crusty rock. Climb to the big roof and pull over before moving right to the break then up and back left. Finish through the bulges.
FA. Bob Smith 1988

9 Macbeth **E6 6b**
12m. Climb through the roof and follow good, but spaced, holds up then right before using a mono to climb the leaning wall to the break. Move right and exit via the flutings.
FA. Bob Smith 1982. A very impressive ascent for the time.

10 The Arches **E1 5b**
16m. A fine climb and a bit more amenable. Pull onto the hanging wall and follow it right as it gets ever narrower. Sustained and awkward, especially for the tall, although good gear is available. Continue to a grand finish on the flutings.
FA. Rod Wilson 1965

11 King Lear **E6 6c**
12m. Pull onto the hanging slab as for *The Arches* then move up and left and use an undercut flake on the lip to start the wall above. Tiny holds lead to the finish of *Macbeth*.
FA. Dave Pegg 1991

12 Hard Reign **E3 5c**
14m. A fine climb up an unlikely line. Climb the hanging arete to the roofs (thread) then move out left and power through the overhangs in an impressive position.
FA. Bob Hutchinson 1978

Ali Kennedy powers through *Lost Cause* (E4 6b) - *page 330* -
to reach the super flutes of the upper wall. Photo: Jamie Moss

Descent - end of the crag

The Witch

The Witch

The attractive slab running rightwards from *Holly Tree Corner* has a good selection of climbs and, unusually, many of them are not TOO hard for their given grades. Having said that, most are either lacking in protection or have hugely undercut starts, so delicate and scary, or butch and beefy, make your choice.

① Holly Tree Corner . . . . . S 4b
14m. Struggle up the long groove with a holly at its base.

② The Witch E2 5b
12m. Follow the shallow groove to the bulges then make a tricky move to start a sustained traverse away to its right-hand end.
FA. Malcolm Rowe 1974

③ Shackletack E3 6b
12m. A direct line crossing *The Witch*.
FA. John Earl 1981

④ The Wand E3 5b
14m. Climb to a ledge above the bulge then continue directly by precarious moves.
FA. John Earl 1978

⑤ The Broomstick . . . E3 5b
14m. More precarious and poorly protected climbing.
FA. John Earl 1975

⑥ The Enchanter E3 5c
14m. ... and yet more! Start over the bulge and up the open groove to the break. Serious climbing leads to the upper break and a quick escape right to the good flutings. **V3** start.
FA. Bob Hutchinson 1975

⑦ Bottle Crack . . . . . . VS 5a
14m. The bottle-shaped crack needs some bottle (and knees) to start, then eases to give good jamming above.

⑧ The Wizard E3 5c
14m. Swing along the flake in the roof rightwards until it is possible to use a vertical flake to claw a way round onto easier angled rock. Step left and finish up the front of the broad rib. **V2** start.
FA. Bob Smith 1978

⑨ Black Magic E1 5c
14m. The direct entry into the groove across the widest part of the roof is worth doing (**V2**) the groove itself is less classy.
FA. Bob Hutchinson 1976

⑩ The Vole Direct E1 5c
14m. From a useful heel-hook, cross the roof directly to reach a choice of finishes. Originally it followed the thin diagonal flake leftwards into the bilberry groves. A **V2** start.
FA. Bob Hutchinson c1970

⑪ Sorcerer's Apprentice . . E1 5c
14m. Cross the centre of the roof, aiming for the vertical flake just above the lip. Step left to access the flutings, or traverse off for a **V2** boulder problem.
FA. Ken Wood 1968

⑫ The Sorcerer E1 5c
14m. Classy! Cross the roof steeply then pull rightwards into the base of the open groove. Finish delicately up this, or traverse off for a **V2** boulder problem. *Photo on page 18.*
FA. Allan Austin1968

⑬ The Charm E1 5c
14m. Pull through as for *The Sorcerer* then climb up leftwards by delicate moves, keeping just right of the blunt arete.
FA. A.Powell c1984

The Sorcerer

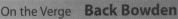

Descent

On the Verge

The attractive hanging slab bound to either side by a pair of easy groove lines. The fine set of routes on the slab are all worth doing - if you are up to the challenge, unprotected padding is pretty much the order of the day.

⑭ The Spell . . . . 🎧🔲🔲 **E1 5c**
13m. The broad rib left of *Straight Crack* is climbed with a pleasing combination of pockets and flakes. A **V2** start.
FA. Jeff Lamb 1978

⑮ Straight Crack . . . . . . 🎧🔲🔲 **HS 4b**
12m. An awkward narrowing fissure shrinks from a thin chimney to a wide crack. Once the good jams arrive, things ease.

⑯ Golden Stairs . . . . 🔲 **VDiff**
12m. Start on the right and follow the trio of steps up and left - the first one is the hardest. A **Direct Start** up the left-hand corner is a tricky **4c**.

⑰ Magic Flute . . . . . . 🎧🔲🔲🔲 **E1 5b**
12m. Start up *Golden Stairs* but move out right to gain the base of the slab awkwardly. Pad up its left-hand edge, heading for the magic fluting above. *Photo on page 236.*
FA. Malcolm Rowe 1976

⑱ Boulder Lands . . . . 🎧🔲🔲🔲 **E5 6b**
12m. Smear up the slab and shallow fluting 1m right of the arete, heading right to finish.
FA. Julian Lines 1991

⑲ Dead on Arrival . . . 🎧🔲🔲🔲 **E6 6a**
14m. Gain the base of the slab as for *Magic Flute,* then pad across it diagonally rightwards by extreme smearing to join the last couple of moves of *Peak Technique.*
FA. Tony Lickes 2003

⑳ Savage Slab . . . . . . 🎧🔲🔲🔲 **E7 6c**
14m. A dynamic leap gains holds then move right and access the foot of the slab with difficulty. Shuffle back left and, eschewing all holds, pad up the slab to glory.
FA. Mark Savage 2003

㉑ Peak Technique . . . 🎧🔲🔲🔲 **E6 6b**
12m. Climb the cracks in the left wall of the groove then move left to the ledge at the bottom right-hand corner of the slab. Indifferent gear does not instill much confidence as you pad leftwards up the line of non-holds.
FA. Tony Coutts 1987

㉒ On the Verge . . . . . 🎧🔲🔲🔲 **E4 5c**
12m. Start as for *Peak Technique* but, from the ledge, rock onto the right arete and palm a way up this - better holds soon arrive. This was a bold ascent for its day and it still is. The escape route of a leap for the ledge to the right is not recommended.
FA. John Earl 1977

㉓ Woodcutter's Crack . . . . 🎧🔲 **HVD**
12m. The groove to the right of the slab gives a steep pitch with both holds and runners.

㉔ Forester's Corner . . . . 🎧🔲 **Diff**
14m. Starting just left of the fence, climb the diagonal ramp and crack until it is possible to move left and climb the deep corner to the right of the top section of *Woodcutter's Crack.*

Tube

The impressive buttress that towers over the fence is covered in fine routes plus many variations which are only slightly less worthy. The problem is the routes are mostly hard; those that are not, are desperate.

❶ Tube . . . . `Top 50` **E4 5c**
16m. One of the easier hard classics of the crag - a great climb, devious but logical and interesting throughout. Start up the easy ramp then gain the hanging groove and climb it boldly to the break under the roof. Traverse right - plenty of gear but pumpy - to the slot in the roof and finish with a typical Northumbrian exit. A **Left-hand Exit** is a cop-out at **E3 5b** and a **Direct Finish** is a harrowing **E5 5c** but misses out the best part of the route.
Photo on page 325.
FA. Bob Hutchinson 1978

❷ Right of Reply **E5 6b**
24m. "Tube+"! Follow *Tube* to where it exits but continue the traverse until the break descends a little, thins out and then ends altogether. Hard moves up and right reach better holds leaving a quick romp up the glorious flutings.
FA. Bob Smith 1985

❸ Charlotte's Dream Direct
. . . . **E7 6b**
14m. The left-hand side of the smooth face. Follow a discontinuous series of flakes until they fizzle out at a good pocket. Continue directly up the face (small wires) on spaced holds to the break and a tough exit. The original traverse left to put runners in *Tube* misses out the main point of the challenge and is **E5 6b**.
FA. Mark Savage 2003. FA. (Original) Karl Telfer 1987

❹ On the Rocks . . `Top 50` **E7 6c**
14m. Classy climbing, technical and committing. Climb the flake to its top then, from runners (a whole bunch plus one for luck), pull left and climb the face on diminishing holds to reach *Tube* with relief. Scuttle right up *Tube* to finish (usual) or go **Direct** at a strenuous **6b**. A right-hand finish to the main section of the climb is the even harder **Off the Rocks**, **E8 6c**.
FA. (On) Bob Smith 1987. Previously top-roped by Tommy Smith.
FA. (Off) Nick Dixon 1995

❺ Duke of York **E1 5b**
14m. An easier route at last. Once a 'solid Northumbrian HVS', now upgraded. Follow the flake to its end and access the ledge on the right for a breather. Drop down off this then get pumping rightwards before you run out of steam - good gear but hard work. Finish up or down *Angle Corner*.
FA. John Earl 1977

❻ Transcendence **E8 6c**
14m. The broad edge of the buttress, front on with bold and technical climbing - a tour de force. Climb the groove then trend left to the resting ledge. Move right a short distance then attack the upper wall. The climbing eventually eases, a looooong way above the gear. Finish by taking the well deserved crown.
FA. Malcolm Smith 1994

❼ Leap of Faith **E6 6c**
14m. A hard direct start to *Lost Cause* with the big black hole being of material assistance and the name gives one possible approach method.
FA. Malcolm Smith 1994

❽ Lost Cause **E4 6b**
14m. A good route with hard but safe (if you don't mind a bit of flight time) climbing. Reverse the last section of *Duke of York* then use the flake to make tough moves to reach better holds. Finish up the flake and flutings above. *Photo on page 327.*
FA. Tommy Smith 1979

❾ Angle Corner . . . . **VDiff**
12m. The main angle is not without interest and the odd bit of shrubbery.

Cassey Quarry
Crag Lough
Peel Crag
Callerhues
Great Wanney
E. Woodburn
Sandy Crag
Ravensheugh
Simonside
Drake Stone
Corby's
Bowden Doors
Back Bowden
Kyloe In
Kyloe Out
Berryhill

Roof Route

The first crag reached from the parking has a good set of climbs; a quartet of Green Spot routes, the over-hanging crack of *Roof Route* and some tougher stuff.

1 When the Wind Blows . . E6 6b
12m. Approach the upper leaning wall via the crack and lower roof, then sort yourself out before heading up and right then back left using the snapped flake to better holds and an easier finish.
FA. Karl Telfer 1987

2 Peace At Last E5 6a
12m. The central line on the upper wall is approached by weaving though the lower overhangs. Follow the crusty lines of blisters and flakes running rightwards across the wall to finish.

3 Outward Bound E3 5c
12m. The right arete of the upper wall gives a fine pitch which is low in the grade - for the strong. Climb straight through the lower roofs to a cramped rest, then head slightly rightwards, linking mostly good holds, by powerful climbing and long reaches. There is enough gear for those who can hang on and place it.
FA. Paul Stewart 1979

4 March Line . . . . VDiff
12m. A pleasant easier outing with an impressive top pitch. Climb the short corner to belay at the left end of the long ledge. Move up under the roof then a tricky and exposed traverse leads out left. Once the overhangs are passed, head for the summit.

5 Wall and Crack . . . . S 4b
12m. Climb the crack to the ledge (possible stance) then continue up the angular corner, passing the roof out on the right arete.

6 Roof Route E1 5b
14m. The beckoning roof-crack is a beauty and high in the grade. From the ledge on *Wall and Crack*, do battle with the roof-crack - proficiency at jamming helps, a lot. From the jugs on the lip pull over then exit rightwards much more easily. A **Direct Finish, E2 5c** goes straight up to the capping overhang, then exits left.
FA. Hugh Banner 1973

7 Hazelrigg Wall Left-hand E3 6b
8m. Desperate moves up the blankest section of the wall.
FA. Bob Smith c1984

8 Hazelrigg Wall E1 5c
8m. Good climbing up the right-hand side of the green wall. Fingery and probably a bit harder then you are expecting - a high-ball **V1** or thereabouts.

9 Pinup E2 6a
8m. The leaning orange wall and left-hand side of the rib above gives a fierce little pitch. Crank on those pimples. Highball **V3**.
FA. Steve Blake c1978

10 Original Route . . . . VDiff
14m. Climb the groove to the ledge then pull over the left-hand side of the big roof on thankfully substantial holds (VDiff!) and finish up the juggy wall.

11 Highland Fling E1 5c
14m. The crack in the lower wall leads to the ledge and roof. A mighty heave is needed to get established on the easier upper wall.

12 Final Wall . . . . VDiff
12m. The pleasant wall and the corner behind the holly bush.

The final buttress described is up and right of the Roof Route Buttress. It has two technical desperates.

13 Big Aerial Dynamite . . . E5 7a
8m. Desperate moves through the roof and up the wall.
FA. Dave Pegg 1991

14 Dwarfs' Nightmare E2 6b
8m. Access the niche with considerable difficulty.
FA. Tommy Smith 1979

	No star	⚀	⚁	⚂
Mod to S	6	4	2	-
HS to HVS	7	10	3	2
E1 to E3	4	11	6	4
E4 and up	-	3	2	6

An accurate name for a lovely little crag hidden away in a huge and silent forest - it makes you wonder how it was ever discovered and what else lurks in the dark Northumbrian forests? On first sight the crag is a bit disappointing, green and dwarfed by the trees, though on closer inspection, two things become obvious, firstly, that the rock is of superb quality and, secondly, the crag might not be very tall, but it is certainly steep, especially in its lower section. The place has been popular for many years with boulderers and a few of the more significant problems, plus the routes that are normally done as boulder problems, are listed here. If you are doing the routes that go to the top of the crag, be aware that the exits can be covered in pine needles - a novel objective danger.

Conditions

The crag faces south west and gets some sun although the closeness and size of the trees means that much of the rock sees little full on sunshine for extended periods. The crag is very sheltered from the wind and several areas are steep enough to be considered as ever-dry although it will stay damp in the winter months. The sheltered nature means that it can get rather hot and airless on summer days, when the flies can be an unpleasant distraction from the job in hand.

Approach

Kyloe in the Woods is well hidden in the pine forest to the south of the B6353 Fenwick to Lowick road. Turn west off the A1 towards Fenwick and take the first left turn after 2.3 miles. Drive past the parking for Kyloe out the Woods and park (1 mile from the junction) by a large gate across the forest track. DON'T BLOCK IT! The number of cars here will tell you how busy the crag is going to be. Follow the track into the wood for 800 metres to a Y-fork and branch to the right. Follow this for another 400m to arrive at a T-junction (it is actually an old crossroads, but the straight on branch is overgrown now). Turn right here and after another 300m the crag appears on the left. Read the warning sign, then make your way to the rocks - 15 minutes from the parking. **Note**: some maps show a path that cuts directly between the two Kyloes - I have tried to locate it on several occasions and have the scars to prove it!

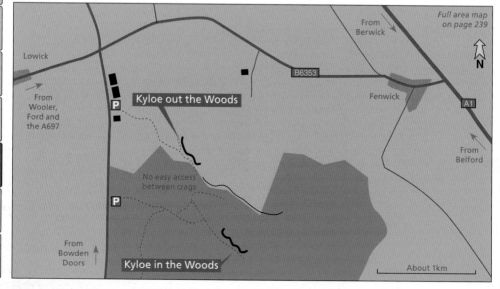

Steve Smith pushing through the move on *Badfinger* (V2) - *page 335* - at Kyloe in the Woods. Photo: Jamie Moss

The Hobbit and Swan Wall

The first rocks reached appear a bit disappointing, hardly managing to escape the greenery, though there are some pleasant short routes here. When topping out BEWARE the mossy, pine needle-ridden finishes.

1 Rivendell Crack . . . . . . ☆ 🏷️ ☐ **VS 5a**
8m. The steep crack is reached from the left.

2 Mordor Front . . . . ☐ **HVS 5a**
8m. The rounded buttress front, starting over a bulge.

3 Shelob . . . . ☐ **HVS 5b**
8m. Up the pockets in the left-hand side of the wall.

4 Evendim Corner . . . . ☐ **Diff**
8m. The wide and gloomy rift is approached up a short crack.

5 Aragorn . . . . ☐ **HS 4c**
8m. The first of a trio of cracks - steep to start.

6 Frodo . . . . ☐ **HS 4c**
8m. The central crack passing a bulge.

7 Legolas . . . . ☐ **VS 4c**
8m. ... and the right-hand crack.

8 The Hobbit . . . .[👤]☐ **VDiff**
8m. The wide left-slanting fissure is awkward.

9 Bilbo . . . . ☐ **S 4b**
8m. Skip up the rib and crack in the front of the buttress.

To the right is a deeply incised rift which offers the easiest descent at this end of the cliff. It can be slippery.

10 Swan Wall Arete . . . . 🤚☐ **V3 (5c)**
The undercut arete right of the descent gully. Highball.
FA. Paul Stewart 1980s

11 Swan Wall Direct . . . . ☆ ☐ **V2 (5c)**
The undercut technical wall leads to easy ground.
FA. Steve Blake 1970s

12 Swan Wall . . . . ☆ 🏷️ ☐ **VS 4c**
8m. The left-hand crack is followed to its termination, then head out to the arete to finish.

13 Ostrich Crack . . . . ☆ ☐ **VDiff**
8m. The right-hand parallel crack leads to the roof where an exit to the right is the best option.

14 White Wine . . . . ☐ **V1 (5b)**
Climb the wall to gain the flutings.

15 Marmoset . . . . ☆ ☐ **VB (4c)**
Hop onto the left-facing flake and climb it to the flutings.

16 Pink Gin . . . . ☆ 👤☐ **V4 (6b)**
A direct line to the flake on *Red Rum*.
FA. Bill Wayman, Paul Stewart 1970s

17 Red Rum . . . . ☆☆ 👤☐ **V4 (6a)**
The right-facing flake is followed to the end where reachy moves access a shorter flake - then the flutings, or aim down.
FA. Bob Hutchinson 1977

Monty Python's

Monty Python's

The undercut bulging walls and striking crack-lines are especially popular with boulderers, the ever-dry nature of the walls means that it is almost always possible to get something done here. The down-side is the unsightly chalk build-up as it never washes off. If you intend to top out BEWARE the mossy, pine needle-ridden finishes.

1 The Elf Direct V2 (5c)
Head up the blunt rib to the left-hand end of the capping overhang where the regular route is joined for an exit.
FA. Steve Blake 1970s

2 The Elf . . . . VS 5a
12m. Climb the centre of the left wall of the recess then move left and up to the roof before escaping out left.

3 Bad News E3 6a
10m. The left-hand corner of the recess leads to the roof where a mildly wild hand-traverse leads out right to a grovelly exit.
FA. John Earl 1981

4 Right-hand Recess Crack . . . . . VDiff
10m. Obvious from the name, exiting rightwards at the top.

5 The Twitch . . . . HS 4c
9m. The undercut right wall of the recess, near the arete.

6 Badfinger V2 (5c)
The wall just right of the arete. It is **E2** if you top-out.
Photo on page 333.
FA. Bob Hutchinson 1976

7 Bad Company V2 (5c)
The leaning wall right again. **E2** if you go all the way.
FA. Paul Stewart 1977

8 Catapult V11
A flying leap from a sloper and a mono to the distant break.

9 Monk Life V14
Levitate up the blankest section of the wall.
FA. Malcolm Smith 2003

10 Monty Python's Flying Circus V5 (6b)
The perplexing crack gained from the niche. Originally given VS! The direct start is actually slightly easier **V4 (6a)**.
FA. Dave Cuthbertson 1977

11 Crouching Tiger, Hidden Dragon
. . . . V8
The wall left of the *Crack of Gloom*, finishing at the break.

12 Crack of Gloom . . . . . . VS 4c
10m. The corner-crack is tricky to get established on.
FA. Allan Austin 1969

13 The Pearler V2 (5c)
The crack which runs halfway up the wall is climbed to its end. For the full **E3** tick, continue up the leaning wall and head left to the arete. There are several hard variation starts.
FA. John Earl

14 Jocks and Geordies V5 (6b)
The two diagonal cracks splitting the overlaps show the way. Finish at the big sloper, or press on at **E3**.
FA. Dave Cuthbertson, Murray Hamilton, Bob Smith, John Earl, Ian Kyle 1985

15 The Yorkshireman . . V8
The solitary diagonal crack is very tough.

16 Thin Hand Special E1 5c
10m. The thin crack is a real gem, get it done whatever size your hands are. **V2 (5c)** as a problem.
FA. Hugh Banner

17 Hitchhiker's Guide to the Galaxy
. . . . V7 (6c)
The flake in the middle of the wall reached from the block to the right. Without the block, it is a grade harder. *Photo on page 339.*
FA. Colin Binks, Willie Jeffrey, Chris Craggs 1974. The big fella' formed the base of a human pyramid to reach the first decent hold!
FFA. Steve Blake 1978

18 The Rack Direct . . . V9
The steep wall left of two diagonal cracks to a ledge. Start from sitting at this grade.

19 Leviathan . V14
A Northumbrian expedition and a true test of climbing stamina. Start on the arete left of *Bad Finger* and traverse all the way rightwards to finish up *The Rack Direct*. There are rules though - no resting on jams and no low foot ledges. The easier version is **Lothlorian, V13** which finishes up *The Yorkshireman*.
FA. Malcolm Smith 2003

The Flutings   Descent

The Nadser

The Flutings

Further into the woods is this lovely selection of climbs, based around the open corner of *Piccolo*. The rock is good and holds are often generous, if a bit fingery. All the routes are worth doing. If you intend to top out BEWARE the mossy, pine needle-ridden finishes.

① Greensleaves .... **S 4b**
10m. The jamming crack on the left leads to a floral exit. A good one to practice the dark art on.

② The Missing Link .... **HVS 5b**
9m. The disjointed crack systems give another worthwhile gem.
FA. Hugh Banner 1960s

③ Stirring up Trouble **E3 5c**
9m. The left arete of the bay has a steep start, until the holds lead round to the left to reach a balancy finish.
FA. Steve Blake 1970s

④ Trouble Shooter **E3 6a**
10m. The face midway between the arete and *The Flutings* gives a good technical and fingery pitch. Finish up the solitary fluting.
FA. Paul Stewart 1977

⑤ The Flutings Direct .... **VS 4c**
11m. A fine climb up the twin runnels in the centre of the left-hand wall of the recess. The lower section is the hard, thereafter the holds improve dramatically.

⑥ Piccolo .... **S 4a**
11m. The main angle gives a good bridging pitch - straightforward but nice and steep at the grade.

⑦ Verticality **E1 5a**
12m. Climb the smooth-looking wall right of the corner direct to the break. Pull through the bulges and finish (carefully) into the mulch above.

⑧ Zed Climb .... **VS 4c**
12m. A zig-zagging line up the right-slanting crack, then back left under the roof and finally back out right to finish.
FA. Frank Montgomery 1966

⑨ The Harp .... **VS 5a**
10m. A good route, and quite pumpy despite its brevity. Start up the fingery wall to reach the left-hand end of the handrail that runs out right under the roof. Commit to this, then pull from its end to reach easier angled ground.

⑩ Orpheus. **E3 5c**
10m. A counter diagonal to *The Harp*. Climb the crinkly wall to *The Harp's* hand-traverse, then pull through to reach the flake in the roof. Follow this strenuously leftwards until a stretch gains the finishing holds.

⑪ The Nadser ...... **V6 (6c)**
The side wall of the buttress around to the right is climbed on tiny holds by some quality moves. Fontesque.

The Nadser

Green Man Wall

Green Man

Bobby Dazzler Wall

The next long wall is set back at a slightly higher level.

1 The Hulk E1 5c
8m. The wall to a reachy finish.

2 Green Man . . . . VS 4c
8m. The right side of the wall is like climbing a big Swiss cheese.
FA. Bob Smith

3 Evergreen Wall . . . . V0+ (5b)
The bumpy wall left of *Primitive Crack* is testing at the grade.

4 Primitive Crack . . . . S 4a
8m. The jamming crack is good, if a bit short lived. Often used as a descent by the competent.

5 Dingly Dell V2 (5c)
The wall right of *Primitive Crack* usually feels hard for the grade. Climb up then trend right to the break and an easy finish.
FA. Bob Hutchinson

Bobby Dazzler

This slabby little wall increases in size as it runs right-wards. Near the left-hand side is the prominent jamming crack of *Primitive Crack* and the right-hand side is marked by the awkward *Fluted Crack*. The bouldering here mostly ends at the ramp of *Piano*.

6 Bobby Dazzler V2 (5c)
Climb the left-hand side of the first flute. The start feels (mighty) tough for the grade.
FA. Bob Hutchinson

7 Autowind V3 (6a)
The right-hand fluting and wall to its right give a few hard moves before the ramp on the right can be reached.
FA. Paul Stewart 1979

8 Twinkle Toes V5 (6b)
The line of non-holds up the steep slab.

9 Robber's Dog V2 (5c)
Head up the wall just to the left of the *Fluted Crack's* arete to easy ground. The arete should be avoided, unless you can't. The arete itself is **Robber's Dog Arete, V3 (6a)**.

10 Piano . . . . S 4c
16m. A nice pitch. Start up the crack then use the flake on the left to access the ramp. Balance up this until the flutings arrive.

11 Fluted Crack . . . . S 4b
12m. The wide crack has an 'udgy' start.
FA. Allan Austin 1969

12 Penny Whistle E2 5c
12m. The fingery wall just to the right of the crack eases with height, as they all do hereabouts.
FA. Bob Smith 1978

Bobby Dazzler

Change in viewing angle

High T and The Crucifix

Two features mark out the next areas. The T crack is on the right of a steep and rather unattractive looking wall - oddly it is home to some excellent routes. Past the crag's last great challenge is a large cross-shaped crack high on the wall. Most folks just call in to do the classic crack of *The Crucifix* and the pleasant arete of *The Gauntlet*. The two other striking lines of *The Prow* and *Hourglass Chimney* see less attention.

1 The Entertainer

.... E3 5c

14m. Pull onto the wall and climb direct, then right to reach better holds and some runners. Move back to the left and stretch for the top.
FA. Bob Hutchinson 1977

2 Feanor E6 6b

15m. Start as for *The Entertainer,* move a little to the right and follow the line of most resistance. The better holds and runners of *The Entertainer* arrive, then finish up and right.
FA. Darren Stevenson early 2000s

3 Upper Crust E5 6b

20m. A girdle of the wall with a lot of good climbing. Start up *The Entertainer,* but head right across the horizontal break on *High T.* Move up to access the right-trending ramp then follow this and the horizontal break to its right to a finish close to the edge of the wall.
FA. Bob Smith 1986

4 High Society .. E6 6b

15m. An eliminate based around the 'T'. Climb straight through the bulges to the 'T', sort some gear, then head rightwards along the lower edge of the wall, eventually joining the *Upper Crust* exit.
FA. Tim Gallagher 1986

5 High T E3 5c

15m. The pick of the bunch, high quality. Climb a crack to the roof then head out left and climb to a rest in the 'T'. Continue up and left to good holds and an awkward exit
FA. Bob Hutchinson 1978

15m to the right is a prominent cross in the wall.

6 The Crucifix

.... HVS 5a

12m. Classy climbing up a stunning line. The crimpy wall leads to the base of the soaring crack-line, which succumbs to a forceful approach.
FA. Hugh Banner 1970s

7 Crucifixion

.... E3 5c

20m. A long right-hand exit is a good pitch but may well need a once-over before an ascent. From the right-hand arm of *The Crucifix,* head right along the break-line linking pockets and slopers to a finish up the distant flutings.

8 The Prow E9 7a

12m. The soaring arete is climbed on small spaced holds to a finish up the right-hand side of the arete.
FA. Andrew Earl early 2000s

9 Hourglass Chimney ...... S 4b

11m. The wet overhanging and narrowing chimney is included because it is a great line. The whole affair is grim and the grade is traditional - you have been warned.

10 The Gauntlet E1 5b

10m. The cracked rib has a tricky, fingery start leading to easier ground. The start can be done as a **V0** boulder problem.
FA. Rod Valentine 1970s

11 The Iron Fist E1 5c

10m. The fingery wall just to the right leads to a fluttery mantelshelf - **V2** . Finish up or down *The Gauntlet.*

Beyond The Gauntlet are another half a dozen routes of no great note and the bouldering based around the usually dry rock under the big overhang of The Arch.

Steve Smith trying hard on *Hitchhiker's Guide to the Galaxy* (V7) - *page 335* - Kyloe in the Woods. Photo: Jamie Moss

	No star	✶	✶✶	✶✶✶
Mod to S	9	5	-	1
HS to HVS	6	12	7	2
E1 to E3	4	5	-	1
E4 and up	-	4	1	2

A small but varied set of buttresses tucked away in a sheltered valley, often simply called Kyloe (its proper name is Collar Heugh) - the 'out the Woods' tag has been added to reduce confusion. Despite its name, much of the right-hand section of the cliff is well in the trees, which means it can be green, midgy and slow to dry.

The accessibility of the crag and the good selection of easier routes means that the place is quite popular with groups; the erosion of the cliff base around *Flake Crack* and *Slab and Wall* are clear pointers to the damage that overuse can cause.

Conditions

The crag faces just west of south and so gets the sun for much of the day. The sunny aspect and sheltered setting means it can get hot here, though also it can be a great winter venue. In summer, neck high bracken smothers the hillside making access to some parts of the cliff tricky and unpleasant - best check yourself for ticks after a day here.

Approach

See map on page 332

Turn west off the A1, 4.5 miles north of Belford, drive through Fenwick and take the first left turn after 2.3 miles. On the left, just beyond the farm buildings, is limited parking by the gate that gives access to the track leading across the fields to the cliff. Follow the track straight up the field (ignore one going right into the next field) until level with the valley that runs under the cliff and bear right into it.

Note: some maps show a path that cuts directly between the two Kyloes - I have tried to locate it on several occasions and it has proved elusive.

Colin Binks on the well positioned *Cloister Wall* (HS 4b) - *page 344* - Kyloe out the Woods. Photo: Chris Craggs

Casey Quarry | Crag Lough | Peel Crag | Callerhues | Great Wanney | E. Woodburn | Sandy Crag | Ravensheugh | Simonside | Drake Stone | Corby's | Bowden Doors | Back Bowden | Kyloe In | Kyloe Out | Berryhill

The Quarry
The left-hand section of the crag consists of a couple of bays that were quarried in antiquity, doubtless providing stone for the grander farmhouses in the area.
Approach - From Saint's Wall, follow a path left over a bump and a stile then round into the quarry.

Original Sin

❶ **Fence Post Corner** . . . . [ ] **VDiff**
12m. The main angle to an ugly and prickly exit.

❷ **The Seventh Day. . .** [ ] **E5 6c**
14m. Climb the wall to the break, then continue with great difficulty to a wobbly (in more ways than one) finish.
FA. Hugh Harris 1991

❸ **The Sabbath.** . . . . [ ] **E4 6a**
20m. Devious, but worthwhile. Climb the wall to the break, move right to do the hard move on *Original Sin*, then continue right along the upper break to reach the arete.
FA. Bob Smith 1980

❹ **Original Sin** . . . . [ ] **E4 6a**
14m. A fine route - varied and technical. Climb to a standing position on the flake, then continue left and right by a tricky mantelshelf. Reachy moves gain easy ground.
FA. Steve Blake 1978. Named because of the 1st recorded use of chalk in the County by a local.

❺ **Baptism.** . . . . [ ] **E2 5c**
40m. For those looking for something a little longer. Pump along the break from the arete to the far away corner.
FA. Bob Smith 1980

❻ **Active Service** . . . . [ ] **HS 5b**
14m. A technical start up the blunt arete leads to easy ground.

❼ **Incisor.** . . . . [ ] **S 4a**
12m. A short steep wall leads to easy ground.

❽ **Canine Wall.** . . . . [ ] **Diff**
14m. Follow the slab out to the left to some gentle mantels.

❾ **Bird's Nest Corner.** . . . . [ ] **VDiff**
10m. The angle to a prickly and blocky exit.

❿ **Devil's Edge.** . . . . [ ] **HVS 5a**
12m. Excellent. Climb the right side of the arete to good holds then use a jug on the right to reach the next break which allows a swing round the arete to a rest. Finish up the wall.
FA. Geoff Oliver 1957

⓫ **Back to the Egg** . . . [ ] **E2 5c**
12m. Start up *Devil's Edge* but move right and make extended reaches up and right to a poor bridged rest and a steep finish.

⓬ **Learning to Fly.** . . . [ ] **V11**
A huge dyno up the diagonal overlap.

Devil's Edge

Belays at the top of the cliff are awkward, the stoutest gorse stumps are adequate, or run a rope to the distant tree.

Saint's Wall
The wide wall above the path is split by a narrow chimney. It has a good selection of lower grade climbs and a couple of harder ones. This buttress is always popular.

The Quarry - 100m

① Parity . . . . HS 4b
12m. Start up the groove and move left at the bulges to the crack system. Follow this left then back right to a rounded exit.
FA. Dave Ladkin 1960s

② Trinity . . . . VS 4c
12m. Continue up the crack system (small wires) to a ledge with a useful gorse bush. Finish up the awkward groove.
FA. Eric Clarke 1950s

③ Waverly Wafer E2 5c
14m. Climb the crack in the side wall of the face to the top ledge then finish up the rounded arete on the right with difficulty.

④ Waverly Variation . . . . VS 4c
14m. Follow *Waverly Wafer* to the last bulge then sneak off right into the chimney.

⑤ Temptation. . . . . Mod
12m. The wide and straightforward chimney.

⑥ Threadbare . . . . HVS 5a
12m. The slab right of the chimney has a tricky lower section and a rounded exit.

⑦ Pink Socks on Top. E1 5b
12m. From the cave/hole, climb to the upper break, mantel through the heather and finish up the wall.

⑧ Saint's Progress . . . . . . S 4b
16m. Devious but logical. From the cave/hole traverse the break right to a shallow groove and follow this to the break. Traverse back left to a finish up the forked-lightning crack.

⑨ Holy Mother of Inspiration (don't fail me now)
. . . . E3 6a
12m. Climb the face (hard and serious even with distant side-runners) to the ledges. Finish up the wall.

⑩ St. Ivel . . . . VS 4c
12m. A great little route. Trend right to the shallow green groove, and climb this on its right-hand side to the ledges. Finish up the wall on small holds.

⑪ Litany . . . . VS 5a
12m. Pull rightwards though the overhangs to a ledge, finish up the crack though the upper bulges.

⑫ Saint's Arete . . . . HVS 5b
12m. Power through the bulges to access the right arete, then finish up the groove above.

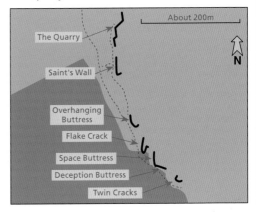

About 200m

The Quarry

Saint's Wall

Overhanging Buttress

Flake Crack

Space Buttress

Deception Buttress

Twin Cracks

N

Overhanging Buttress

A fine buttress, the tallest on the whole crag, towering above the arrival point of the main path. Generally the routes are steep and strenuous, though the mid-height ledge can be used as a breather, or a place to call up the second and suggest it is their turn for a bit of leading.

❶ Easy Traverse. . . . . ☐ **Diff**
12m. An easy line to nowhere. Follow the flakes rightwards from the left arete. Belay on the ledge then escape right.

❷ Cloister Wall . . . . ☐ **HS 4b**
22m. Quite high in the grade. An indifferent start leads to a grand finale. Climb rightwards to the ledge then move back left to access the upper wall. Climb this steeply, trending left then right, with superb positions throughout. *Photo on page 340.*

❸ Lost Property . . . . . ☐ **HVS 5a**
20m. Pull over the bulge and climb to the ledge (possible stance). Then continue through the upper bulges (loose block) and up the wall above.
FA. Tommy Smith 1980s

❹ Hot Spring . . . . ☐ **E3 6a**
20m. Pull through the roof to reach the flutings then climb these with difficulty to the ledge - possible stance. Follow the rounded rib to a good break then pull rightwards and through the bulges.
FA. John Earl, Bob Smith (alts) early 1980s

❺ Birdlime Crack . . . . ☐ **HVD 4a**
8m. The juggy crack (good gear) to the ledge. Escape right.

❻ The Elevator. . . . . ☐ **HVS 5a**
10m. A fine exposed pitch on the upper tier. Climb a ladder of good holds to the break and scoot left to a good rest before finishing up the shallow groove above.
FA. Dave Ladkin 1971

❼ Coldstream Corner . . . . ☐ **HVS 5a**
18m. A strenuous classic that is usually split into two pitches. Trend right to climb the short crack to the ledge. Climb the crack into the groove then bridge and jam this to the top. Short lived but quality pumping.
FA. Allan Austin 1970

❽ Penitent's Walk . . . . . . ☐ **HVS 5a**
18m. Climb the crack then trend right and climb to the ledge (**4c**). The upper wall is climbed to the roof where a good jug allows access to the upper slab. Finish easily.
FA. Allan Austin 1970

❾ Albatross . . . . ☐ **E6 6c**
18m. The big roof above the half-height ledge is well named.

To the right the path gets squeezed between the rock and some massive trees. There are several routes here though their gloomy setting ensures that they don't see much attention. After 100m the path emerges in front of a fine wall with a severely undercut right-hand rib.

Flake Crack

Flake Crack

This lozenge-shaped wall is riven by myriad flakes of all sizes. The routes here are generally excellent though the gloomy setting means it is slow to dry after rain.

1 The Pincer . . . . **HVS 5b**
8m. Trend right up the wall to the undercuts then head direct.
FA. Johh Earl 1970s

2 Flake Crack . . . . **S 4b**
12m. The left-trending crack splitting the centre of the wall gives a classic piece of climbing - follow the crack.

3 Wasted Time **E1 5b**
12m. The wall between the two cracks gives a good pitch.
FA. Bob Smith 1979

4 Tacitation . . . . **VS 5a**
12m. Pull through the roof (hard) to gain the crack and then follow it a lot more pleasantly. A start from the left is technically no easier but manages to feel like a cop-out.
FA. Nev Hannaby 1957

5 Prime Time . . . **E4 6b**
12m. The leaning side wall is climbed with great difficulty to access the scary and precarious face above.
FA. Steve Blake mid 1980s

6 Australia Crack **E3 6b**
12m. The leaning crack/groove gives a desperate piece of upside-down work to eventually reach the easy rib above.
FA. Bob Hutchinson early 1970s. Northumberland's first 6b.

7 Oversight . . . . **HS 4b**
10m. A gloomy groove on the right gives a short struggle.

Australia Crack

Space Buttress

Descent

Descent Deception Buttress

Across gully

Afternoon 10 min Sheltered

Evening 10 min Sheltered

❶ Christmas Tree Arete . . . . . . ☆1 [ ] VDiff
14m. A good easier climb. Follow the crack towards the overhang. Step left into a groove which leads pleasantly to the pine.

❷ Direct Finish . . . . [ ] VS 4c
14m. Jam the short lived leaning crack.

❸ Gargarin's Groove . . ☆2 [ ] HVS 5a
14m. Steep and exhilarating. Move right from the crack to access the hanging groove which is followed with interest.
FA. John Earl 1975

❹ Elder Brother . . ☆1 [ ] E4 6b
14m. An arduous outing round the left-hand side of the Space roofs. Climb into and up the hanging corner and a bridged rest. Pull rightwards over the final roof with difficulty - good wires, awkward to place - then sprint up the juggy final wall.
FA. Tommy Smith 1980s

❺ First Born . . . . ☆2 [ ] E4 6b
14m. Fine and exciting climbing through the big roofs. Approach from the right and cross the first overhang to the second one. Undercut past this to reach jugs, then step left and finish up the flutings. A big cam in a pocket above the roof helps - a lot.
FA. Bob Smith 1980. Originally given 7a.

❻ Spacewalk . . . . ☆1 [ ] E2 5c
12m. The hanging left arete of the Space is gained from the face on the right. Climb a groove to a big spike runner, step down and balance out to the arete. Swap sides and finish more easily.
FA. Bob Hutchison 1970s

To the right is an easy descent gully then a striated wall split centrally by a deep groove.

Space Buttress and Deception Buttress
A pair of contrasting buttresses: Space is home to one easy classic and some high and wild offerings that tackle the tiered overhangs above the trees. The adjacent Deception with its easier climbs on both of its facets is much the more popular venue as witnessed by the erosion at the base of the routes.

❼ West Wall Groove . . . . [ ] VS 5a
8m. The short groove in the upper section of the wall.

❽ Deception Wall . . . . . . ☆1 [ ] HS 4c
10m. Pull onto the wall left of the overhangs and climb direct, generally on good holds, though it is quite sustained and pumpy.

❾ Deceiver . . . . [ ] HVS 5b
10m. The wall left of the arete is sustained and one or two of the holds feel a bit snappy.

❿ Deception Crack . . . . . . ☆1 [ ] HS 4b
10m. The groove gives an awkward but well protected central section. Exit right on jugs.
FA. Eric Clarke 1950s

⓫ Wilfred Prickles . . . . . . ☆1 [ ] HVS 5a
10m. The centre of the fluted face is sustained, with tricky moves to the break. Finish steeply on huge holds. Low in the grade.
FA. John Earl 1970s. Named after an extinct gorse bush.

⓬ Fakir's Crack . . . . [ ] VDiff
10m. The flake-crack on the right-hand side of the wall.

⓭ Fakir's Groove . . . . [ ] VDiff
10m. Around the arete is a deep groove.

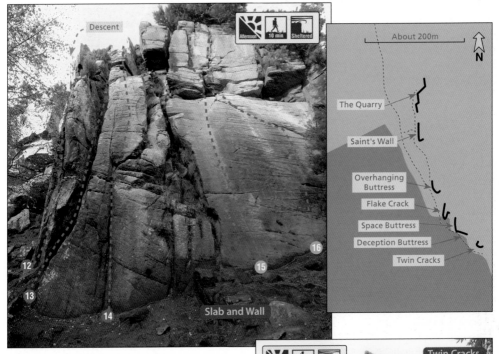

Descent

The Quarry

Saint's Wall

Overhanging Buttress

Flake Crack

Space Buttress

Deception Buttress

Twin Cracks

About 200m

N

Slab and Wall

The right-hand face of Deception Buttress has a slabbier and sunnier aspect than that just round to the left. These two factors, plus a bunch of green zone routes, help explain its popularity.

⑭ **Fakir's Slab** . . . . ⟨1⟩ [　　] **HVD**
10m. Climb the short groove and the flat slabby rib above.

⑮ **Slab and Groove** . . . ⟨1⟩ 🔲 🔲 [　　] **VS 5a**
12m. The left-hand side of the slab is precarious and balancy. The shallow upper groove is steep and awkward - crimp or layback.

⑯ **Slab and Wall** . . . . ⟨1⟩ [　　] **VS 4c**
12m. Balance up the right-hand side of the slab then follow curving crack to access the right-hand crack in the upper wall.

Twin Cracks
After a break in the crag there is one final buttress.

⑰ **John's Wall** . . . . [　　] **S 4b**
12m. Use the block to access the side wall and climb this to an exit left or right.

⑱ **Chris's Arete** . . . . ⟨1⟩ [　　] **HS 4b**
12m. Climb the arete in two parts to a finish on the left.
Photo on page 341.
FA. Chris Craggs mid 1970s. He has to wait 30 years and write his own guide to get due recognition.

⑲ **Twin Cracks** . . . . [　　] **S 4b**
12m. Any combination of the steep cracks in the front face.

Twin Cracks

Descent

	No star	🛈	🛈	🛈
Mod to S	2	6	2	-
HS to HVS	4	4	1	1
E1 to E3	2	1	-	-
E4 and up	3	-	-	-

A charming little cliff, the most northerly in the book, tucked away in a shallow valley and facing south-ish so it gets the sun all day long. Much of the rock is soft and/or brittle, so despite the number of lower grade routes it is not an ideal venue for beginners. The soft nature of the rock also makes it an UNSUITABLE destination for large groups intent on abseiling or top-roping as this will rapidly damage the rock.

Conditions

The crag faces just a little west of south so makes a good afternoon venue, it is sheltered enough to be a fair bet on cold clear days and not so high as to be affected by wild weather.

Approach and Access

The crag lies just west of the B6354, just north of Etal, which is a few miles north of Wooler. Berryhill Farm is to the east of the road and it is possible to park by the track running up to the farm. **PERMISSION TO CLIMB MUST BE SOUGHT BEFORE HEADING TO THE CLIFF.** The crag can be reached by following the track left of the buildings, heading through a gate on the right then crossing the hillside to the edge of the cliff. Alternatively, follow the path through the farm buildings and around into the valley that runs under the cliff. Either approach takes about five minutes.

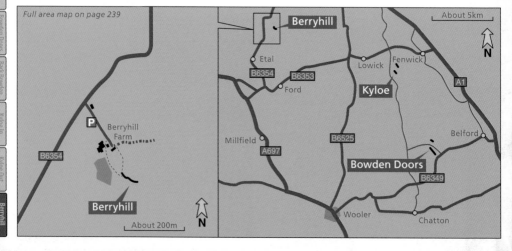

Full area map on page 239

Overhanging Crack

Western Walls
The left-hand side of the crag consists of some rambling walls, mostly made of rather soft rock. There are a few interesting routes here, though nothing outstanding.

1 No 'O' Levels Required .   **E3 5c**
8m. From the high grass ledge, climb the severely overhang arete on rock that isn't above suspicion. Scary.
FA. Bob Smith 1984

2 Overhanging Crack ....   **VS 4c**
8m. The steep crack is a worthwhile pitch to a rightward exit.

3 Much Ado About Nothing ...   **E1 5b**
6m. The short wall is steep and soft.
FA. Bob Smith 1990

4 Legal Separation **E4 6a**
6m. The blank leaning groove leads to an exposed escape right.
FA. Bob Smith 1982

5 Western Arete ....   **VS 4c**
12m. The jutting left-hand arete of the crag gives a good pitch with superb positions. Climb the crack on the left then move out right and monkey onto the nose and finish up the easier arete.

6 Cheat ....   **VDiff**
14m. Wander up the lower tier - all a bit soft - then pull over the roof and climb the groove and slabby rock above.

7 Kinmont Willie ....   **VDiff**
14m. The wide crack in the upper wall is approached via the lower slab and some scruffy ledges. The crack itself is better.

8 Jock o' the Syde ....   **VDiff**
14m. The groove that bounds the right-hand side of the upper face is approached by some pedestrian rambling, then accessed directly or, easier, by the slab to the right.

9 Wall and Fluted Slab........   **S 4a**
14m. Climb the short right-facing wall via a thin crack to ledges, then head left up easier rock with flutings galore.

10 Reiver's Way ....   **Diff**
16m. Climb the steep cracks to a large cave two thirds of the way up the cliff (not visible on topo) then access the left-slanting crack from further to the left, via an awkward high step.

Behind the tree in the gully to the right, and reached by a short scramble, is a steep undercut wall with a prominent line of flutings in its centre.

11 Steep Fluted Wall ..   **HVS 4c**
10m. Climb through the bulges - soft - and up the flutings.

12 A Pocket Full of Lichenight .   **HVS 5a**
10m. The line of pockets up the right-hand side of the wall.
FA. Tim Catterall 1994

Western Arete   Reiver's Way

Descent

The Boulder

Eastern Arete

Marcher Lord

Eastern Walls

The right-hand side of the crag has two tall impressive buttresses with an interesting set of climbs including the classic of *Marcher Lord* - the best route here.

① Slab Crack . . . . **Diff**
14m. A groove and slab lead to the mid-height ledges. From these follow the left-trending crack to a groove and the top.

② The Flutings . . . . **VDiff**
14m. The right-hand side of the slab leads to a good ledge. Move left to access the upper slab then climb the fine set of flutings all the way to the crest of the wall.

③ Hi Diddle Diddle . . . . **VS 4b**
14m. The crack in the right-hand side of the front face of the buttress leads steeply to ledges. Continue up the face above to reach the multiple flutings right of the arete and zip up these.

④ Marcher Lord . . . . **VS 5a**
14m. A fine climb, well worth calling in for. A short awkward groove leads to the base of the crack proper which gives steep juggy climbing then some more awkward moves to a rest out right. From here an escape route is apparent, but instead launch leftwards across the overhangs on massive holds. Superb!
Photo on page 349.
FA. Ken MacDonald c1970

⑤ This Pedestrian . . . **E3 5c**
14m. The stacked overhangs and pocketed orange wall to the right of *Marcher Lord* give a strenuous outing. Finish up the black and orange streaked prow.
FA. Karl Telfer 1991

⑥ Potters Way . . . . **VS 5a**
14m. Follow the slanting crack, continuation groove and overhang to a rest below the final roof. Traverse left and pull through the roof leftwards as for *Marcher Lord*.
FA. John Earl 1982

Footsloggers Trip, **VS 4c** *is devious but worthwhile, linking the start of Potters Way with the finish of Hi Diddle Diddle by a nice bit of traversing.*

⑦ Slanting Crack . . . . **HVD 4a**
12m. Nice easy climbing up the slabby face to the foot of the slanting crack, up this to finish.

⑧ Eastern Arete . . . . **S 4a**
12m. Start just left of the arete and climb up and right spiralling above the bulges to an exposed finish around to the right above the big overhangs. A bit bold. *Photo on page 1.*

⑨ Do or Die **E4 6a**
12m. The left-hand side of the roof leads to the hanging wall, head up and left to join *Eastern Arete*. A direct finish over the second roof is the harder and bolder **Faye of Flying, E5 6a**.
FA. Bob Smith 1984. FA. (Faye of Flying) Karl Telfer 1992

⑩ Death Or Glory **E4 5c**
12m. The right-hand side of the roof on large and suspect holds.
FA. Bob Smith 1982

⑪ Border Ballad . . . . **HVS 5b**
12m. Follow the overhanging crack out right until forced to have a breather on *Thrutch*. Move back left for an excellent finish.

⑫ Thrutch . . . . **S 4a**
8m. The short grovelly crack to the right of the overhangs.

⑬ Boulder Direct . . . . . . **HVS 5a**
6m. Follow the left arete then trend left up the bulging wall.

⑭ Boulder Right-hand . . . . **VS 5a**
6m. The middle of the slab then the roof to the right.

The short wall up and behind the Boulder has four tiny routes; the easy chimney on the left - **Route 1**, **Mod**; *the fingery wall to the right -* **Route 2**, **HVS 5b**; *the thin slanting crack -* **Route 3**, **VS 5a**; *and the easier crack on the right -* **Route 4**, **Mod**.

Cassey Quarry · Crag Lough · Peel Crag · Coffenhaus · Great Wanney · E. Woodburn · Sandy Crag · Ravenscleugh · Simonside · Drake Stone · Corby's · Bowden Doors · Back Bowden · Kyloe In · Kyloe Out · Berryhill

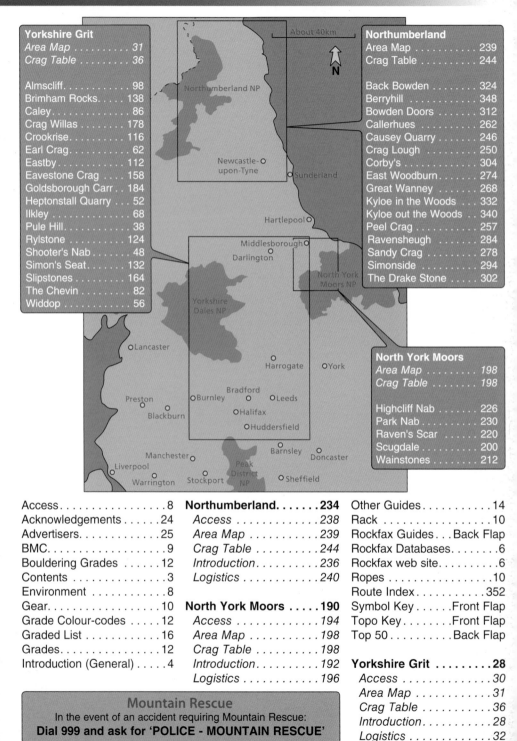

Mountain Rescue
In the event of an accident requiring Mountain Rescue:
Dial 999 and ask for 'POLICE - MOUNTAIN RESCUE'